The Political Economy
of International Relations

The Political Economy
of International Relations

Robert Gilpin

WITH THE ASSISTANCE
OF Jean M. Gilpin

PRINCETON UNIVERSITY PRESS

PRINCETON, NEW JERSEY

Published by Princeton University Press, 41 William Street,
Princeton, New Jersey 08540
In the United Kingdom: Princeton University Press, Guildford, Surrey

All Rights Reserved

Library of Congress Cataloging in Publication Data will be found
on the last printed page of this book

ISBN 0-691-07732-0   ISBN 0-691-02262-3 (pbk.)

This book has been composed in Linotron Sabon

Clothbound editions of Princeton University Press books are printed
on acid-free paper, and binding materials are chosen for strength
and durability. Paperbacks, although satisfactory for personal
collections, are not usually suitable for library rebinding

Printed in the United States of America by Princeton University Press,
Princeton, New Jersey

In memory of John Robert

Contents

Figures and Tables

Preface

THIS BOOK is both a personal statement and a synthesis of certain recurrent and prevalent themes in the field of international political economy. Although I have endeavored to keep the personal and synthetic elements distinct from one another, I have presented my own views on selected questions of international political economy and have also incorporated those ideas and theories of others that are most relevant to the theses being developed. No single volume could do justice to all the important writings on these subjects, but I have tried to integrate those contributions that, in themselves or as representatives of larger bodies of work, help to illuminate critical and theoretical issues and our understanding of the reality of the contemporary international political economy itself.

My own interest in these themes first emerged as I prepared for a seminar at the Center of International Affairs at Harvard University in June 1970. The occasion was the initial presentation of the papers that eventually became *Transnational Relations and World Politics* (1972), conceived and edited by Robert Keohane and Joseph Nye. That seminal volume transformed the American discipline of international relations and most certainly my own research agenda.

The underlying motif of the seminar and the Keohane-Nye book was that transnational actors and processes were integrating the globe and displacing the state-centric view of international relations then dominant. Transnational actors (for example, multinational corporations and political movements), welfare and other domestic objectives, and nonmilitary sources of influence were believed to be of increasing importance in the determination of world affairs. A new paradigm for the discipline was said to be necessary.

As I prepared my contribution, a chapter on the role of multinational corporations in creating this new international environment, I kept turning over in my mind the experience of having lived in France at the time of President Charles de Gaulle's assault on the U.S. corporations that were then rapidly penetrating the newly formed European Common Market. De Gaulle and other nationalists in Western Europe, Canada, and the Third World regarded these giant corporations as agents of an expanding American imperialism rather than as politically neutral transnational actors; yet de Gaulle's concerted effort to drive them out of the Common Market was effectively thwarted by West Germany's refusal to support him. I realized that the American corporations and the transnational phenomenon they represented would have been destroyed had the West Germans followed de Gaulle's nationalistic leadership.

Gradually, I came to several general conclusions: that multinational corporations were indeed expressions of an American economic expansionism and therefore could not be separated from the larger foreign policy objectives of the United States, that the security ties of the United States and Western Europe greatly facilitated this overseas expansion of American corporations, and that the Pax Americana provided the political framework within which these economic and other transnational activities were taking place. My thinking on these matters was strongly influenced by E. H. Carr's (1951) analysis of the role of British power in the spread of economic liberalism and free trade under the Pax Britannica. The parallel between the British experience in the nineteenth century and the American in the twentieth seemed pertinent. Although I did not fully appreciate it at the time, I had returned to a realist conception of the relationship of economics and politics that had disappeared from postwar American writings, then almost completely devoted to more narrowly conceived security concerns.

My explicit linkage of economics and politics and the resulting analysis of the implicit tradeoff of the American military defense of West Germany for the German political defense of American foreign direct investment in the Common Market, as well as a similar tradeoff with Japan, brought forth sharp rejoinders from some members of the seminar. The United States in 1970 was in the throes of the Vietnam War, and anyone who linked U.S. foreign policy to overseas economic expansion was considered almost by definition to be Marxist. I was certain that I was not a Marxist, but I did believe firmly that a connection between economics and politics existed. Some alternative formulation was obviously called for. From that point on I sought to clarify my own analysis of the relations of international politics and international economics.

When I began, I knew little about international trade, monetary relations, and the like. With the assistance of such able tutors as Benjamin J. Cohen and William Branson, I began to read widely in economics. I also turned to earlier writers on political economy, such as Friedrich List, Jacob Viner, and J. B. Condliffe, and studied the more contemporary writings of Albert Hirschman, Charles Kindleberger, Raymond Vernon and others. The Woodrow Wilson School, with its emphasis on economic analysis, was ideal for this effort to pull myself up by my bootstraps. Although I found myself disagreeing with many of their political and social assumptions, I appreciated deeply my economist colleagues' generosity with their time and their toleration of my lack of technical sophistication.

My book U.S. *Power and the Multinational Corporation* (1975) was the first product of this endeavor to clarify my own intellectual position and to contribute to what was becoming the field of international political economy. There I expanded the argument of my earlier paper while also contrasting major perspectives on political economy: liberalism, Marxism, and realism. I argued that the overseas expansion of U.S. multinationals could only be understood in the context of the global political system established after the Second World War. I expressed a deep concern with the problem of American decline, a concern resulting from my association with Harold Sprout, who did pioneering work on the problem of British decline.

My increasing interest in the rise and decline of great or hegemonic powers and the significance of this seemingly cyclical phenomenon for the dynamics of international relations led to my volume *War and Change in World Politics* (1981). In addition to older issues, that book gave attention to the Marxist (or, rather, quasi-Marxist) theory of dependency, a new theme that had entered American academic life in the late 1960s and 1970s, largely in response to the Vietnam War, and to the growing concern over the problems of the less developed countries. Although I accepted the view of dependency theorists that the structure of the world is hierarchical and dominated by the great powers, I argued (following the classical Marxist formulation) that this relationship causes the diffusion of the sources of power, the undermining of the hegemonic state, and the eventual creation of a new hegemonic system. Thus, although it acknowledged contemporary Marxist theories of the international system, the book's purpose was to extend the realist perspective of the nature and the dynamics of international relations.

This volume incorporates these earlier interests and themes and attempts to develop them in a more systematic way. It sets forth in greater detail the three ideologies of political economy and discusses their strengths and limitations. Though it stresses the liberal emphasis on the importance of market efficiency, this book also takes seriously the Marxist critique of a world market or capitalist economy. Throughout, however, the realist or economic nationalist perspective on trade, monetary, and investment relations is emphasized and contrasted with rival interpretations of the international political economy. Earlier themes of economic hegemony, the dynamics of the world economy, and the tendency of economic activity over the long term to transform the structure of the international political system are explored from new perspectives.

My prior preoccupation with the relative decline of American power, the role of political factors in determining international economic relations, and the dynamic nature of economic forces in altering global political relations appear again below. Other elements, however, appear for the first time. I emphasize the meteoric rise of Japan and its challenge to the liberal international economic order. The remarkable shift in the locus of the center of the world economy from the Atlantic to the Pacific in the closing decades of the twentieth century is given special attention. And the significance of both the changing position of Western Europe in the world economy and its steady retreat from liberal principles is evaluated. The possible implications of these historic developments for the international political economy provide major themes. This book foresees a very different world economy from the one created by the hegemonic United States at the end of the Second World War.

Perhaps I should say a word about what this book does *not* do. It does not attempt to advance novel theories or interpretations of international political economy. Nor does it pretend to incorporate all the important themes and writings of scholars in the burgeoning field of international political economy. It does elaborate on and synthesize certain established themes and interpretations that I consider to be of central importance. I am especially interested in assessing our accumulated knowledge of how international politics and international economics interact and affect one another. This approach, which stresses the international system, obviously limits the book in that it gives inadequate attention to important domestic determinants of state behavior, but no single book can do everything.

I have given little attention to East-West economic relations, to international migration, or to the use of economic weapons for political ends. This is because I believe that the minuscule ties (trade, investment, and money) between East and West have little effect on the international political economy, that the international movement of people has declined in its economic significance, and that economic sanctions and other acts of economic warfare have been thoroughly examined in a number of recent studies.[1] This work, which is already long enough,

[1] See Chapter Three, note 14.

focuses on "normal" economic activities, that is, monetary relations, international trade, and foreign investment.

IN THE preparation of this book I have been fortunate to have had the assistance of a number of institutions, and now is the time to convey my appreciation. I would like to thank the Center of International Studies and the Woodrow Wilson School of Public and International Affairs of Princeton University for their generous support. The University's liberal leave policy gave me time free from teaching and other responsibilities to devote to my scholarship. During the fall of 1984, I taught at the International University of Japan at Niigata and had a wonderful opportunity to learn about that fascinating country. I would like to express my appreciation to Professors Chihiro Hosoya and Seigen Miyasato as well to other colleagues and students at that interesting and pioneering institution. Upon returning from Japan I was able to continue my research with the financial support of the Japan–United States Educational Commission (Fulbright Program) and the Sumitomo Bank. The completion of this seemingly endless project would have been much more difficult without their help.

President William Bowen of Princeton University is fond of quoting his mentor Jacob Viner's defense of the openness of the university and the value of scholarly criticism: "There is no limit to the nonsense one may propound if he thinks too long alone." I would like to invoke this sage characterization of the dangers of intellectual solitude in thanking all those who have read and criticized the various drafts of this book or given me other assistance. Kent Calder, Michael Doyle, Joanne Gowa, Robert Keohane, Atul Kohli, Helen Milner, M. J. Peterson, David Spiro, and Mira Wilkins read part or all of the manuscript and gave me invaluable suggestions for revision, and John Ikenberry arranged to have sections of the manuscript discussed at his colloquium on political economy. My research assistants, Elizabeth Doherty and Michael Alcamo, were very helpful and saved me from innumerable errors. Elizabeth Pizzarello typed the bibliography; Sally Coyle typed the index. My secretaries during the course of the work's composition, Lenore Dubchek, Dorothy Gronet, and Heidi Schmitt, also have my deep gratitude. I would like to thank Elizabeth Gretz for her excellent and conscientious editing of the manuscript.

For three summers in a row I promised my wife, Jean, a relaxing respite from her own teaching career and took her to one of the most beautiful lakes in Vermont. Once there she was chained from early morning until late evening to the manuscript of this book. Her editorial and substantive contribution was extraordinary and she deserves more than the usual thanks that authors extend to their spouses. Without her great assistance this book would never have been written. To her goes my love and deep appreciation for sharing my scholarship and my life.

November 1, 1986

The Political Economy
of International Relations

Introduction

A SIGNIFICANT transformation of the postwar international economic order has occurred. The Bretton Woods system of trade liberalization, stable currencies, and expanding global economic interdependence no longer exists, and the liberal conception of international
economic relations has been undermined since the mid-1970s. The
spread of protectionism, upheavals in monetary and financial markets,
and the evolution of divergent national economic policies among the
dominant economies have eroded the foundations of the international
system. Yet inertia, that powerful force in human affairs, has carried
the norms and institutions of a decreasingly relevant liberal order into
the 1980s. What has happened to the system? What are the implications of the failure of the system for the future? This book formulates
an explanation.

At a more general and theoretical level, this work is part of an expanding body of scholarship on the political economy of international
relations; it assumes that an understanding of the issues of trade, monetary affairs, and economic development requires the integration of the
theoretical insights of the disciplines of economics and political science.
Too often policy issues are analyzed as if the realms of economics and
politics can be isolated from one another. Events in the final years of the
twentieth century are forcing students of international relations to focus their attention on the inevitable tensions and continuing interactions between economics and politics; this study is intended to help
narrow the gap between the two.

There is a pressing need to integrate the study of *international* economics with the study of *international* politics to deepen our comprehension of the forces at work in the world. Many important issues and
questions cross the intellectual division between the two disciplines.
Transformations in the real world have made economics and politics
more relevant to one another than in the past and have forced the recognition that our theoretical understanding of their interactions has always been inadequate, oversimplified, and arbitrarily limited by disci-
plinary boundaries.

Economic factors have played an important role in international relations throughout history. Economic objectives, resources, and instru-

ments of foreign policy have always been significant elements in the struggles among political groups. It is unlikely that, in Homeric times, Helen's face—contributing factor though it may well have been—was the primary reason for launching a thousand ships and causing King Agamemnon to lay siege to Troy. More likely, the Greeks' crucial motive was their desire to seize control of the lucrative trade route that passed through the Dardanelles. Centuries later, the Persian Empire used its great hoard of gold to influence the foreign policies of lesser states. In the fifth century B.C. the Athenian closure of ports of the Delian League to an ally of its Spartan rival provides one of the earliest recorded cases of economic warfare. History is replete with similar examples of the role of economic factors in the affairs of nations; in this sense, the political economy of international relations has always existed.

Although economic and political factors have had a reciprocal influence on one another throughout history, in the modern world this interaction has been transformed in fundamental ways. Over the past several centuries, the interdependence of national economies has increased due to greatly enhanced flows of trade, finance, and technology. Public awareness of the economic content of political issues has also expanded, and people can (or at least think that they can) more easily trace the causes of economic discontent or bounty to the specific actions of specific groups at home and abroad (Hauser, 1937, pp. 10-12). And the spread of this economic consciousness and of political democracy has led to the nearly universal realization that the state can be used to effect economic outcomes and in particular to redistribute wealth in one's favor (Bonn, 1939, p. 33). Thus, the distribution of wealth, the scourge of unemployment, and rampant inflation are now viewed as the results of human actions rather than as the consequences of some immutable economic laws. This has meant the inevitable politicization of economic affairs.

Profound changes underlie these developments. Since the sixteenth century, the primacy of the nation-state has been the organizing principle of the international political order. The nation-state has largely displaced such premodern forms of political organization as city-states, tribes, and empires, while simultaneously the market has become the primary means for organizing economic relations, displacing other means of exchange: reciprocity, redistribution, and imperial command economies. These two opposed forms of social organization, the modern state and the market, have evolved together through recent centuries, and their mutual interactions have become increasingly crucial to the character and dynamics of international relations in our world.

These changes in social organization and human consciousness have elevated economic issues to the highest level of international relations. The economic well-being of peoples and the fate of nations have become intimately joined to the functioning and consequences of the market. The direction of financial flows, the inevitable shifts in comparative advantage, and the international distribution of productive activities are preoccupations of modern statecraft. As the distinguished political geographer, Halford Mackinder, prophesied early in this century, statesmen's growing awareness of these changes has concentrated their attention on "the struggle for relative efficiency" (Mackinder, 1962 [1904], p. 242).

Despite these changes, the disciplines of political science and economics continue to study contemporary developments in ways that keep separate and distinct the spheres of the state and the market. The reasons for this academic specialization are appropriate and understandable: social reality, like physical reality, must be broken down into manageable pieces if it is to be studied and theory is to progress. Yet efforts are also necessary to bring the individual pieces together into a larger and integrated theoretical framework of political economy in order to understand the totality of political and economic reality.

This study, then, proceeds on two levels. At one level, it is a practical inquiry into the reality of the contemporary international political economy and how the interaction of state and market is transforming international relations in the closing decades of the twentieth century. It asks what the consequences are likely to be as the locus of "relative efficiency" shifts from Western Europe and the United States to Japan and other rising economic powers in Asia and the developing world. At another level, this book is theoretical; it attempts to integrate the principal ways in which scholars have conceived of international political economy in general and in such specific areas as trade, monetary affairs, and foreign investment. This dual approach is premised on the assumption that the study of contemporary developments and of theoretical questions should be pursued together, and an attempt will be made, throughout the discussion that follows, to draw out implications for the emergent international economic and political order.

The evolution of the international political economy over the next several decades will be profoundly influenced by three major developments. The first is the relative decline of American economic leadership of the postwar liberal international economy; with decreased American power the forces of global economic interdependence have been thrown on the defensive.[1] The second is the ongoing shift in the locus

---

[1] Kenneth Waltz (1979) analyzes the role of the international political system as a significant factor in the development of economic interdependence.

of the core of the world economy from the Atlantic to the Pacific; in the 1970s the flow of commerce across the Pacific exceeded that of the Atlantic. The third is the increasing integration of the American and Japanese economies, which have become linked to a degree that is unprecedented for sovereign nations.

The increasing integration of the American and Japanese economies has become one of the dominant features of the contemporary world economy. In trade, production, and finance these two economies are increasingly interdependent. Driven by the economic policies of the Reagan Administration and the descent of the United States into debtor status, the creation of what can be called the *Nichibei* economy has proceeded with amazing rapidity.[2] Accounting for 30 percent of world output, this trans-Pacific relationship has eclipsed the former primacy in the world economy of the American–West European relationship.[3] The massive trade flows between the two economies, the evolving alliances among their multinational cooperations, and the pivotal role of Japanese capital in the American economy have transformed the relations of these two countries from one of superior and subordinate to a more equal partnership. The nature, dynamics, and stability of this key relationship will largely determine global economic relations.

The centrality of the American-Japanese relationship for international relations resides in the fact that the dollar is the keystone of the U.S. world position. Along with the extension of America's nuclear deterrent over its Japanese and European allies, the role of the dollar as the key currency in the international monetary system has cemented its system of global alliances and has been the foundation of American hegemony. With the dollar providing the base of the monetary system, the United States has been able to fight foreign wars, to maintain troops abroad, and to finance its hegemonic position without placing substan-

[2] According to *The Economist* (December 7, 1985, Survey Japan, p. 17), "this joint economy is called *Nichibei* in Japanese: a blend of the Japanese characters for Japan (*Nihon*) and America (*Beikoku*, or rice country)." I have not been able to verify that the Japanese do in fact use this term to refer to the increasing integration of the American and Japanese economies. Nevertheless, as it does appear to be quite appropriate, the expression will be used in this book.

[3] It is indicative of the profound change that has taken place in the 1970s and 1980s that Richard Cooper's influential book, *The Economics of Interdependence: Economic Policy in the Atlantic Community* (1968), published under the auspices of the Council on Foreign Relations, was devoted almost exclusively to trans-Atlantic relations. Cooper's argument regarding the clash between state autonomy and market interdependence has become relevant for American-Japanese relations. As I shall argue, the fundamental problem set forth by Cooper two decades ago is of increasing significance and a solution has yet to be found.

6

tial economic costs on the American taxpayer and thereby lowering the American standard of living. This crucial role of the dollar and the "extravagant privileges," to use the term of Charles de Gaulle, that it has conferred on the United States has required a foreign partner to help support the dollar. In the contemporary era, this task has fallen to the Japanese and their immense capital outflows to the United States. U.S. financial dependence on Japan and the growing interdependence of the Nichibei economy is a major theme of this book.

The organization below reflects these practical and theoretical purposes. The first three chapters set forth the intellectual perspective and theoretical issues to be explored. Chapter One defines the nature of international political economy as the interaction of state and market and analyzes the significance of this relationship. In Chapter Two, the three prevailing views (or ideologies) of the character of this interaction are evaluated. Chapter Three then analyzes the dynamics of the international political economy.

The next chapters turn to substantive issues of the contemporary international political economy. The international monetary system constitutes the necessary nexus of an efficiently functioning international economy, and it is the subject of Chapter Four. Chapters Five and Six discuss the increasingly interrelated topics of international trade and the multinational corporation. In Chapter Seven the controversy over the impact of the international economy on the economic development and well-being of the less developed countries is evaluated. Chapter Eight analyzes the crucial importance of the international financial system in linking together national economies, its central role in sustaining global economic development, and the threat that its increasing vulnerability poses to global economic stability. These chapters thus begin with money and end with finance. The former facilitates the functioning and integration of the world market; the latter underlies the dynamics of the world economy but also constitutes its weakest link.

The concluding chapters assess the issues and problems of the international political economy in the late 1980s. Chapter Nine analyzes the political, economic, and technological changes that have transformed the world economy over the past several decades. The significance of these changes for international economic relations is the subject of Chapter Ten, which evaluates the increasing importance of mercantilism, regionalism, and sectoral protectionism.

The Nature of Political Economy

THE PARALLEL existence and mutual interaction of "state" and "market" in the modern world create "political economy"; without both state and market there could be no political economy. In the absence of the state, the price mechanism and market forces would determine the outcome of economic activities; this would be the pure world of the economist. In the absence of the market, the state or its equivalent would allocate economic resources; this would be the pure world of the political scientist. Although neither world can ever exist in a pure form, the relative influence of the state or the market changes over time and in different circumstances. Therefore, the conceptions of "state" and "market" in the following analysis are what Max Weber has called ideal types.

The very term "political economy" is fraught with ambiguity. Adam Smith and classical economists used it to mean what today is called the science of economics. More recently, a number of scholars, such as Gary Becker, Anthony Downs, and Bruno Frey, have defined political economy as the application of the *methodology* of formal economics, that is, the so-called rational actor model, to all types of human behavior. Others who use the term political economy mean employment of a specific economic *theory* to explain social behavior; game, collective action, and Marxist theories are three examples. The public choice approach to political economy draws upon both the methodology and theory of economics to explain behavior. Still other scholars use political economy to refer to a set of *questions* generated by the interaction of economic and political activities, questions that are to be explored with whatever theoretical and methodological means are readily available (Tooze, 1984).

Although the approaches to political economy based on the application of the method and theory of economic science are very helpful, they are as yet inadequate to provide a comprehensive and satisfactory framework for scholarly inquiry. Concepts, variables, and causal relations have not yet been systematically developed; political and other noneconomic factors are frequently slighted. In fact, a unified methodology or theory of political economy would require a general comprehension of the process of social change, including the ways in which the social, economic, and political aspects of society interact. Therefore, I use the term "political economy" simply to indicate a set of questions to be examined by means of an eclectic mixture of analytic methods and theoretical perspectives.

These questions are generated by the interaction of the state and the market as the embodiment of politics and economics in the modern world. They ask how the state and its associated political processes affect the production and distribution of wealth and, in particular, how political decisions and interests influence the location of economic activities and the distribution of the costs and benefits of these activities. Conversely, these questions also inquire about the effect of markets and economic forces on the distribution of power and welfare among states and other political actors, and particularly about how these economic forces alter the international distribution of political and military power. Neither state nor market is primary; the causal relationships are interactive and indeed cyclical. Thus, the questions to be explored here focus on the mutual interactions of very different means for ordering and organizing human activities: the state and the market.

This formulation is certainly not an original one; it is at least as old as Georg Hegel's critical distinction in *Philosophy of Right* (1945 [1821]) between state and society (economy). Similar definitions have been offered by other scholars. Charles Lindblom (1977), for example, proposes "exchange" and "authority" as the central concepts of political economy. Peter Blau (1964) uses "exchange" and "coercion"; Charles Kindleberger (1970) and David Baldwin (1971) prefer "power" and "money"; and Klaus Knorr (1973) employs "power" and "wealth." Whereas Oliver Williamson (1975) contrasts "markets" and "hierarchies," Richard Rosecrance (1986) contrasts "market" and "territoriality"; both of these conceptualizations are close to the one chosen here. Each of these views of political economy has its respective merits.

Charles Kindleberger has noted (1970, p. 5) that both the state's budget and the market are mechanisms of product and resource allocation. In a purely political world in which the market did not exist, the state would allocate available resources on the basis of its social and political objectives; such state allocative decisions would take the form of the state's budget. In a purely "market" world in which state intervention did not occur, the market would allocate and operate on the basis of relative prices for goods and services; decisions would take the form of the individual pursuit of self-interest. Students of international political economy, therefore, must attempt to understand how these

9

contrasting modes of organizing human activities and of decision making affect one another and thereby determine social outcomes.

Although the state as the embodiment of politics and the market as the embodiment of economics are distinctive features of the modern world, they obviously cannot be totally separated; indeed, their interrelationship is a theme of this book. The state profoundly influences the outcome of market activities by determining the nature and distribution of property rights as well as the rules governing economic behavior (Gerth and Mills, 1946, pp. 181-82). People's growing realization that the state can and does influence market forces and thereby significantly determines their fate is a major factor in the emergence of political economy. The market itself is a source of power that influences political outcomes. Economic dependence establishes a power relationship that is a fundamental feature of the contemporary world economy. In brief, although it is possible to regard politics and economics as distinct forces creating the modern era, they do not operate independently of one another.

The state and the market have tended to displace other forms of political and economic organization in the modern world because of their efficiency in the production of power and/or wealth. Originating in early modern Europe, state and market have subsequently spread from that relatively small corner of the globe to embrace a substantial fraction of mankind. Very few peoples today are excluded from statehood; those who are regard the achievement of statehood as one of their highest goals, as is witnessed in the struggle of Jews, Palestinians, and others to acquire homelands. Following an ebb and flow pattern, the market form of economic exchange has also spread, gradually bringing more and more societies into the web of economic interdependence.[1]

The relationship of state and market, and especially the differences between these two organizing principles of social life, is a recurrent theme in scholarly discourse. On the one hand, the state is based on the concepts of territoriality, loyalty, and exclusivity, and it possesses a monopoly of the legitimate use of force. Although no state can long survive unless it assures the interests and gains the consent of the most powerful groups in society, states enjoy varying degrees of autonomy with respect to the societies of which they are a part. On the other hand, the market is based on the concepts of functional integration, contrac-

[1] The historical relationship of state and market is a matter of intense scholarly controversy. Whether each developed autonomously, the market gave rise to the state, or the state to the market are important historical issues whose resolution is not really relevant to the argument of this book. State and market, whatever their respective origins, have independent existences, have logics of their own, and interact with one another.

tual relationships, and expanding interdependence of buyers and sellers. It is a universe composed mainly of prices and quantities; the autonomous economic agent responding to price signals provides the basis of decision. For the state, territorial boundaries are a necessary basis of national autonomy and political unity. For the market, the elimination of all political and other obstacles to the operation of the price mechanism is imperative. The tension between these two fundamentally different ways of ordering human relationships has profoundly shaped the course of modern history and constitutes the crucial problem in the study of political economy.[2]

This conception of political economy differs in a subtle way from the definition employed in my earlier book on the subject, which defined political economy as "the reciprocal and dynamic interaction . . . of the pursuit of wealth and the pursuit of power" (Gilpin, 1975, p. 43). Although both are concerned with the effects of the relationship of "economics" and "politics," the formulation here stresses the organization of these activities in the modern era; the earlier work stressed the objective of the activity. Obviously, these conceptions cut across one another. As noted above, markets certainly constitute a means to achieve and exercise power, and the state can be and is used to obtain wealth. State and market interact to influence the distribution of power and wealth in international relations.

THE ISSUES OF POLITICAL ECONOMY

The conflict between the evolving economic and technical interdependence of the globe and the continuing compartmentalization of the world political system composed of sovereign states is a dominant motif of contemporary writings on international political economy.[3] Whereas powerful market forces in the form of trade, money, and foreign investment tend to jump national boundaries, to escape political control, and to integrate societies, the tendency of government is to restrict, to channel, and to make economic activities serve the perceived interests of the state and of powerful groups within it. The logic of the market is to locate economic activities where they are most productive and profitable; the logic of the state is to capture and control the process of economic growth and capital accumulation (Heilbroner, 1985, pp. 94-95).

[2] The concepts of state and market used in this book are derived primarily from Max Weber (1978, vol. 1, pp. 56, 82, and passim).
[3] Perhaps the first writer to address this theme systematically was Eugene Staley (1939).

Debate has raged for several centuries over the nature and consequences of the clash of the fundamentally opposed logic of the market and that of the state. From early modern writers such as David Hume, Adam Smith, and Alexander Hamilton to nineteenth-century luminaries such as David Ricardo, John Stuart Mill, and Karl Marx to contemporary scholars, opinion has been deeply divided over the interaction of economics and politics. The conflicting interpretations represent three fundamentally different ideologies of political economy, which the next chapter will discuss.

The inevitable clash gives rise to three general and interrelated issues that pervade the historic controversies in the field of international political economy. Each is related to the impact of the rise of a world market economy on the nature and dynamics of international relations.[4] Each is found in the treatises of eighteenth-century mercantilists, in the theories of classical and neoclassical economists over the past two centuries, and in the tomes of nineteenth-century Marxists and contemporary radical critics of capitalism and the world market economy. This long tradition of theorizing and speculation is crucial to an understanding of contemporary problems in trade, finance, and monetary relations.

The first issue is concerned with the economic and political causes and effects of the rise of a market economy. Under what conditions does a highly interdependent world economy emerge? Does it promote harmony or cause conflict among nation-states? Is a hegemonic power required if cooperative relations among capitalist states are to be ensured, or can cooperation arise spontaneously from mutual interest? On this issue theorists of different schools of thought have profoundly conflicting views.

Economic liberals believe that the benefits of an international division of labor based on the principle of comparative advantage cause markets to arise spontaneously and foster harmony among states; they also believe that expanding webs of economic interdependence create a basis for peace and cooperation in the competitive and anarchical state

---

[4] Obviously, the choice of these three issues as the central ones will not meet with the approval of everyone in the field of international political economy. Many would quite rightly come up with another set. These issues exclude, for example, such topics as the making and substance of foreign economic policy. Although this subject is important, the principal focus of this book is on the structure, functioning, and interaction of the international economic and political systems. A parallel and not invidious distinction can be and usually is made between the study of the foreign policies of particular states and the study of the theory of international relations. Although these subjects are closely related, they ask different questions and are based on different assumptions. Gaddis (1982) and Waltz (1979) are respectively excellent examples of each approach.

system. Economic nationalists, on the other hand, stress the role of power in the rise of a market and the conflictual nature of international economic relations; they argue that economic interdependence must have a political foundation and that it creates yet another arena of interstate conflict, increases national vulnerability, and constitutes a mechanism that one society can employ to dominate another. Although all Marxists emphasize the role of capitalist imperialism in the creation of a world market economy, they divide between the followers of V. I. Lenin, who argue that relations among market economies are by nature conflictual, and those of Lenin's chief protagonist, Karl Kautsky, who believe that market economies (at least the dominant ones) cooperate in the joint exploitation of the weaker economies of the globe. The alleged responsibility of the market system for peace or war, order or disorder, imperialism or self-determination, is embedded in this important issue, as is the crucial question of whether the existence of a liberal international economy requires a hegemonic economy to govern the system. The challenge to the United States and Western Europe from Japan and other rising economic powers at the end of this century dramatically highlights the importance of these matters.

The second issue pervading the subject of international political economy is the relationship between economic change and political change. What are the effects on international political relations and what problems are associated with structural changes in the global locus of economic activities, leading economic sectors, and cyclical rates of economic growth? And, vice versa, how do political factors affect the nature and consequences of structural changes in economic affairs? For example, one may question whether or not major economic fluctuations (business cycles) and their political effects are endogenous (internal) to the operation of the market economy, or whether economic cycles are themselves due to the impact on the economic system of exogenous (external) factors such as major wars or other political developments. It is also necessary to ask whether or not economic instabilities are the cause of profound political upheavals such as imperialist expansion, political revolution, and the great wars of the past several centuries.

This book is thus concerned in part with the effects of economic changes on international political relations. These economic changes undermine the international status quo and raise profound political problems: What will be the new basis of economic order and political leadership? Can or will adjustment to the changed economic realities, for example, new trading and monetary relations, take place? How will the inevitable clash between the desire of states for domestic autonomy and the need for international rules to govern change be reconciled? These issues of transition between historical epochs have again arisen with the global diffusion of economic activities and the profound shifts in the leading economic sectors taking place in the late twentieth century. It is important to probe the relationship between these structural changes and the crisis of the international political economy.

The third issue with which this book will deal is the significance of a world market economy for domestic economies. What are its consequences for the economic development, economic decline, and economic welfare of individual societies? How does the world market economy affect the economic development of the less developed countries and the economic decline of advanced economies? What is its effect on domestic welfare? How does it affect the distribution of wealth and power among national societies? Does the functioning of the world economy tend to concentrate wealth and power, or does it tend to diffuse it?

Liberals and traditional Marxists alike consider the integration of a society into the world economy to be a positive factor in economic development and domestic welfare. Trade, most liberals argue, constitutes an "engine of growth"; although the domestic sources of growth are more important, the growth process is greatly assisted by international flows of trade, capital, and productive technology. Traditional Marxists believe that these external forces promote economic development by breaking the bonds of conservative social structures. On the other hand, economic nationalists in both advanced and less developed countries believe that the world market economy operates to the disadvantage of the economy and domestic welfare. Trade, in their view, is an engine of exploitation, of underdevelopment, and, for more advanced economies, of economic decline. This controversy over the role of the world market in the global distribution of wealth, power, and welfare constitutes one of the most intensely debated and divisive questions in political economy.

These three issues, then—the causes and effects of the world market economy, the relationship between economic and political change, and the significance of the world economy for domestic economies—constitute the major theoretical interests of this book. Not all aspects of these issues can be examined here in detail, of course. I shall be concerned with those specific matters that illuminate the problems of the contemporary world economy.

In the rest of this chapter the nature of the market, its economic, social and political consequences, and the political responses to these effects will be discussed. In subsequent chapters, the role of the state in shaping and attempting to control market forces will be emphasized. However, prior to a consideration of the theoretical issues that arise out of this interaction and their relevance for understanding such areas as trade, money, and foreign investment, a question should be asked regarding this focus on the market. Why stress it as the crucial feature of modern economic life rather than, say, the rise of capitalism, the advent of industrialism, or the impact of scientific technology?

The Importance of the Market

This study of political economy focuses on the market and its relationship to the state because the world market economy is critical to international relations in the modern era; even in socialist societies the key issue in economic debates is the appropriate role for internal and external market forces. As Karl Polanyi said in his classic study of the transformation of modern society:

the fount and matrix of the [modern economic and political] system was the self-regulating market. It was this innovation which gave rise to a specific civilization. The gold standard was merely an attempt to extend the domestic market system to the international field; the balance-of-power system was a superstructure erected upon and, partly, worked through the gold standard; the liberal state was itself a creation of the self-regulating market. The key to the institutional system of the nineteenth century [as well as our own] lay in the laws governing market economy (Polanyi, 1957, p. 3).

Karl Marx, on the other hand, stressed capitalism or the capitalist mode of production as the creator and unique feature of the modern world. The defining characteristics of capitalism, as defined by Marx and his collaborator, Friedrich Engels, and which I accept, are the private ownership of the means of production, the existence of free or wage labor, the profit motive, and the drive to amass capital. These features provide capitalism with its dynamism; the dynamic character of the capitalist system has in turn transformed all aspects of modern society. As Gordon Craig has pointed out, the revolutionary nature of capitalism lay in the fact that, for the first time, the instinct to accumulate wealth became incorporated in the productive process; it was this combination of the desire for wealth with the economic system that changed the face of the earth (Craig, 1982, pp. 105-106).

This characterization of the dynamic nature and impact of capitalism is certainly accurate; the aggressive spirit of acquisitive capitalism does animate the market system (Heilbroner, 1985). But it was the market that first released these forces of capitalism and that subsequently also channeled them. Capitalism works its profound effects on social relations and the political system through the market mechanism. The market and exchange certainly tie the economic world together, yet one cannot really speak of an international mode of capitalist production. Despite the emergence of the multinational corporation and international finance, production and finance are still nationally based and, despite the increase in economic interdependence, few economies are tightly integrated into the world economy. Moreover, the socialist or nonmarket bloc is increasing its participation in the world market economy in the final decades of the century. The world market is far larger than but not identical with the capitalist system itself.

The dynamism of the capitalist system is due precisely to the fact that the capitalist, driven by the profit motive, must compete and survive in a competitive market economy. Competition weeds out the inefficient while rewarding efficiency and innovation; it encourages rationality. In the absence of a market, capitalism loses its creativity and essential vigor (McNeill, 1982). The distinctive features of the capitalistic mode of production, as defined by Marxists, would not have led to economic progress without the spur of market competition. In the presence of a market, however, even socialist or nationalized firms must strive to become profitable and competitive. The advent of socialism may not necessarily alter the underlying dynamics, provided that market competition or its functional equivalent survives. There is, as John Rawls reminds us, "no essential tie between the use of free markets and private ownership of the instruments of production" (Rawls, 1971, p. 271). Capitalism and the market exchange system are not necessarily connected.

The concept of "market" is thus broader than that of "capitalism." The essence of a market, defined in greater detail below, is the central role of relative prices in allocative decisions. The essence of capitalism, as noted above, is the private ownership of the means of production and the existence of free labor. Theoretically, a market system could be composed of public actors and unfree labor as envisioned in the concept of market socialism. The increasing role of the state and public actors in the market has recently led to a mixed economy of public and private enterprise. In practice, however, the market system has tended to be associated with international capitalism.

In summary, although the connection between the market exchange system and the capitalist mode of production is close, these terms are not the same—even though they will sometimes be used interchangeably in this book. Capitalism is too ambiguous a label to be used as an analytical category. There are in fact many varieties of capitalism that function differently. Is France truly capitalist, with 90 percent of its financial sector and much of its heavy industry nationalized and in state hands? How is one to categorize Japanese capitalism, with the central role of its state in guiding the economy? The contemporary world is composed largely of mixed economies that at the international level are forced to compete with one another.

Other scholars have identified industrialism, industrial society, and/ or the development of scientific technology as the defining characteristics of modern economic life.[5] The development of both industrial technology and modern science are obviously important for the prosperity and character of the modern world. One cannot account for the Industrial Revolution and the advent of modern science simply as a response to market forces; without science-based technology the modern market economy could not have progressed very far.

The scientific breakthroughs of the seventeenth and eighteenth centuries that laid the foundations for modern industry and technology are not reducible to the operation of economic motives. Science is an intellectual creation resulting from human curiosity and the search for understanding of the universe. Yet without market demand for greater efficiencies and new products, the incentive to exploit science and develop innovations in technology would be greatly reduced. Although the advance of science increases the potential supply of new industries and technology, the market creates the demand necessary to bring the technologies into existence. Thus the crucial role of the market in propelling and organizing economic life is the reason for our focus here on the market and the implications of economic interdependence for international relations.

The concept of market or economic interdependence is a highly ambiguous term, and many different definitions exist.[6] In this book the *Oxford English Dictionary* definition of economic interdependence favored by Richard Cooper will be used; it defines interdependence as "the fact or condition of depending each upon the other; mutual dependence" (Cooper, 1985, p. 1196). In addition, as Robert Keohane and Joseph Nye (1977) have noted, economic interdependence can refer to a power relationship, that is, to what Albert Hirschman (1945) calls vulnerability interdependence. Economic interdependence can also mean sensitivity interdependence, that is, changes in prices and quantities in different national markets respond readily to one another.

[5] Goldthorpe (1984, ch. 13), Giddens (1985), and Rostow (1975) are representative of these positions.

[6] An excellent analysis of these various meanings is Cooper (1985, pp. 1196-1200).

Although these different meanings of the term can in theory be easily distinguished from one another, this is not always the case in reality. Unless otherwise noted, I use "interdependence" to mean "mutual albeit not equal dependence." I thus accept economic interdependence as a "fact" or "condition," but do not accept many of its alleged economic and political consequences.

If by increasing economic interdependence one means the operation of the "law of one price," that is, that identical goods will tend to have the same price, then global interdependence has reached an unprecedented level. The conclusions to be drawn from this fact, however, are not readily obvious. Although this book will discuss the integration of national markets into an expanding interdependent global economy, it will also question a number of the effects that this growing interdependence is alleged to have upon international relations. Interdependence is a phenomenon to be studied, not a ready-made set of conclusions regarding the nature and dynamics of international relations.

The Economic Consequences of a Market

Although a market is an abstract concept, a market economy can be defined as one in which goods and services are exchanged on the basis of relative prices; it is where transactions are negotiated and prices are determined. Its essence, as one economist has put it, is "the making of a price by higgling between buyers and sellers" (Condliffe, 1950, p. 301). Phrased in more formal terms, a market is "the whole of any region in which buyers and sellers are in such free intercourse with one another that the prices of the same goods tend to equality easily and quickly" (Cournot, quoted in Cooper, 1985, p. 1199). Its specific characteristics are dependent upon its degree of openness and the intensity of the competition among producers and sellers. Markets differ with respect to the freedom of participants to enter the market and also the extent to which individual buyers or sellers can influence the terms of the exchange. Thus, a perfect or self-regulating market is one that is open to all potential buyers or sellers and one in which no buyer or seller can determine the terms of the exchange. Although such a perfect market has never existed, it is the model of the world implicit in the development of economic theory.

A market economy is a significant departure from the three more traditional types of economic exchange. Although none of these forms of exchange has ever existed to the exclusion of the others, one type or another has tended to predominate. The most prevalent economic system throughout history, one that is still characteristic of many less developed economies, is localized exchange, which is highly restricted in terms of available goods and geographic scope. The second type of exchange is that of command economies, such as those of the great historic empires of Assyria and, to much lesser extent, Rome, or of the socialist bloc today; in these planned economies, the production, distribution, and prices of commodities tend to be controlled by the state bureaucracy. Third, there is, or rather there was, long-distance trade in high-value goods. The caravan routes of Asia and Africa were the principal loci of this trade. Although this trade was geographically extensive, it involved only a narrow range of goods (spices, silks, slaves, precious metals, etc.). For a number of reasons, markets tend to displace more traditional forms of economic exchange.

One reason for the primacy of the market in shaping the modern world is that it forces a reorganization of society in order to make the market work properly. When a market comes into existence, as Marx fully appreciated, it becomes a potent force driving social change. As one authority has put it, "once economic power is redistributed to those who embrace the productive ideal, their leverage as buyers, investors, and employers is seen as moving the rest of society. The critical step in establishing a market momentum is the alienation of land and labor. When these fundamental components of social existence come under the influence of the price mechanism, social direction itself passes to economic determinants" (Appleby, 1978, pp. 14-15).

In the absence of social, physical, and other constraints, a market economy has an expansive and dynamic quality. It tends to cause economic growth, to expand territorially, and to bring all segments of society into its embrace. Groups and states seek to restrain the operation of a market because it has the potential to exert a considerable force on society; efforts to control markets give rise to the political economy of international relations.

Three characteristics of a market economy are responsible for its dynamic nature: (1) the critical role of relative prices in the exchange of goods and services, (2) the centrality of competition as a determinant of individual and institutional behavior, and (3) the importance of efficiency in determining the survivability of economic actors. From these flow the profound consequences of a market for economic, social, and political life.

A market economy encourages growth for both static and dynamic reasons. A market increases the efficient allocation of existing resources. Economic growth occurs because the market fosters a reallocation of land, labor, and capital to those activities in which they are most productive. Also, since market competition forces the producer (if it is to prosper or even merely survive) to innovate and move the economy to higher levels of productive efficiency and technology, the market dynamically promotes technological and other types of innovation, thus increasing the power and capabilities of an economy. Although both the static and dynamic aspects of markets have encouraged economic growth throughout history, the dynamic factor has become of decisive importance since the advent of modern science as the basis of productive technology.

A market economy tends to expand geographically, spilling over political boundaries and encompassing an ever-increasing fraction of the human race (Kuznets, 1953, p. 308). The demand for less expensive labor and resources causes economic development to spread (H. Johnson, 1965b, pp. 11-12). Over time, more and more of the nonmarket economic periphery is brought within the orbit of the market mechanism. The reasons for this expansionist tendency include efficiencies of scale, improvements in transportation, and growth of demand. Adam Smith had this in mind when he stated that both the division of labor and economic growth are dependent on the scale of the market (Smith, 1937 [1776], p. 17). In order to take advantage of increased efficiencies and to reduce costs, economic actors try to expand the extent and scale of the market.

Yet another characteristic of a market economy is a tendency to incorporate every aspect of society into the nexus of market relations. Through such "commercialization," the market generally brings all facets of traditional society into the orbit of the price mechanism. Land, labor, and other so-called factors of production become commodities to be exchanged; they are subject to the interplay of market forces (Heilbroner, 1985, p. 117). Stated more crudely, everything has its price and, as an economist friend is fond of saying, "its value *is* its price." As a consequence, markets have a profound and destabilizing impact on a society because they dissolve traditional structures and social relations (Goldthorpe, 1978, p. 194).

At both the domestic and international levels a market system also tends to create a hierarchical division of labor among producers, a division based principally on specialization and what economists call the law of comparative advantage (or costs). As a consequence of market forces, society (domestic or international) becomes reordered into a dynamic core and a dependent periphery. The core is characterized principally by its more advanced levels of technology and economic development; the periphery is, at least initially, dependent on the core as a market for its commodity exports and as a source of productive techniques. In the short term, as the core of a market economy grows, it incorporates into its orbit a larger and larger periphery; in the long term, however, due to the diffusion of productive technology and the growth process, new cores tend to form in the periphery and then to become growth centers in their own right. These tendencies for the core to expand and stimulate the rise of new cores have profound consequences for economic and political affairs (Friedmann, 1972).

The market economy also tends to redistribute wealth and economic activities within and among societies. Although everyone benefits in absolute terms as each gains wealth from participation in a market economy, some do gain more than others. The tendency is for markets, at least initially, to concentrate wealth in particular groups, classes, or regions. The reasons for this tendency are numerous: the achievement of economies of scale, the existence of monopoly rents, the effects of positive externalities (spillovers from one economic activity to another) and feedbacks, the benefits of learning and experience, and a host of other efficiencies that produce a cycle of "they who have get." Subsequently, however, markets tend to diffuse wealth throughout the system due to technology transfer, changes in comparative advantage, and other factors. It may also produce in certain societies a vicious cycle of decline, depending on their flexibility and capacity to adapt to changes. A diffusion of wealth and growth, however, does not take place evenly throughout the system; it tends to concentrate in those new cores or centers of growth where conditions are most favorable. As a consequence, a market economy tends to result in a process of uneven development in both domestic and international systems.

A market economy, if left to its own devices, has profound effects on the nature and organization of societies as well as on the political relations among them. Although many of these consequences may be beneficial and much desired by a society, others are detrimental to the desires and interests of powerful groups and states. The resulting tendency, therefore, is for states to intervene in economic activities in order to advance the effects of markets beneficial to themselves and to counter those that are detrimental.

MARKET EFFECTS AND POLITICAL RESPONSES

In the abstract world of economists, the economy and other aspects of society exist in separate and distinct spheres. Economists hypothesize a theoretical universe composed of autonomous, homogeneous, and maximizing individuals who are free and able to respond to market forces in terms of their perceived self-interest. They assume that economic structures are flexible and behaviors change automatically and predictably in response to price signals (Little, 1982, ch. 2). Social classes, ethnic loyalties, and national boundaries are assumed not to exist. When once asked what was missing from his classic textbook, Nobel laureate Paul Samuelson is reported to have responded, "the class struggle." This puts the point well, although he could have added, without undue exaggeration or violation of the spirit of the text, "races, nation-states, and all the other social and political divisions."

The essence of economics and its implications for social and political organization, as viewed by economists, are contained in what Samuelson has called "the most beautiful idea" in economic theory, namely, David Ricardo's law of comparative advantage. The implication of this simple concept is that domestic and international society should be organized in terms of relative efficiencies. It implies a universal division of labor based on specialization, in which each participant benefits absolutely in accordance with his or her contribution to the whole. It is a world in which the most humble person and the most resource-poor nation can find a niche and eventually prosper. A fundamental harmony of interest among individuals, groups, and states is assumed to underlie the growth and expansion of the market and of economic interdependence.

In the real world, divided among many different and frequently conflicting groups and states, markets have an impact vastly different from that envisaged by economic theory, and they give rise to powerful political reactions. Economic activities affect the political, social, and economic well-being of various groups and states differentially. The real world is a universe of exclusive and frequently conflicting loyalties and political boundaries in which the division of labor and the distribution of its benefits are determined as much by power and good fortune as they are by the laws of the market and the operation of the price mechanism. The assumption of a fundamental harmony of interest is most frequently invalid, and the growth and expansion of markets in a socially and politically fragmented globe have profound consequences for the nature and functioning of international politics. What then are these consequences that give rise to political responses?

One consequence of a market economy for domestic and international politics is that it has highly disruptive effects on a society; the introduction of market forces and the price mechanism into a society tends to overwhelm and even dissolve traditional social relations and institutions. The competition of the efficient drives out the inefficient and forces all to adapt to new ways. As noted earlier, markets have an inherent tendency to expand and bring everything into their orbit. New demands are constantly stimulated and new sources of supply sought.

Further, markets are subject to cyclical fluctuations and disturbances over which the society may have little control; specialization and its resulting dependencies increase vulnerabilities to untoward events. In short, markets constitute a powerful source of sociopolitical change and produce equally powerful responses as societies attempt to protect themselves against market forces (Polanyi, 1957). Therefore, no state, however liberal its predilections, permits the full and unregulated development of market forces.

Another consequence of a market economy is that it significantly affects the distribution of wealth and power within and among societies. In theory, all can take advantage of market opportunities to better themselves. In practice, however, individuals, groups, or states are differently endowed and situated to take advantage of these opportunities and therefore the growth of wealth and the spread of economic activities in a market system tends to be uneven, favoring one state or another. Thus, states attempt to guide market forces to benefit their own citizens, resulting, at least in the short run, in the unequal distribution of wealth and power among the participants in the market and the stratification of societies in the international political economy (Hawtrey, 1952).

Another important consequence of a market economy for states is due to the fact that economic interdependence establishes a power relationship among groups and societies. A market is not politically neutral; its existence creates economic power which one actor can use against another. Economic interdependence creates vulnerabilities that can be exploited and manipulated. In the words of Albert Hirschman, "the power to interrupt commercial or financial relations with any country . . . is the root cause of the influence or power position which a country acquires in other countries" through its market relations (Hirschman, 1945, p. 16). In varying degrees, then, economic interdependence establishes hierarchical, dependency, and power relations among groups and national societies. In response to this situation, states attempt to enhance their own independence and to increase the dependence of other states.

A market economy confers both benefits and costs on groups and societies. On the one hand, economic specialization and a division of labor foster economic growth and an increase in the wealth of market participants. Although gains are unevenly distributed, in general everyone benefits in absolute terms. Therefore few societies choose to absent themselves from participation in the world economic system. Yet, on the other hand, a market economy also imposes economic, social, and political costs on particular groups and societies, so that in relative

23

terms, some benefit more than others. Thus, states seek to protect themselves and limit the costs to themselves and their citizens. The struggle among groups and states over the distribution of benefits and costs has become a major feature of international relations in the modern world.

CONCLUSION

The central concerns of this book, then, are the impact of the world market economy on the relations of states and the ways in which states seek to influence market forces for their own advantage. Embedded in this relationship of state and market are three closely related issues of importance to the student of politics. The first is the way in which market interdependence affects and is affected by international politics and in particular by the presence or absence of political leadership. The second is the interaction of economic and political change that gives rise to an intense competition among states over the global location of economic activities, especially the so-called commanding heights of modern industry. The third is the effect of the world market on economic development and the consequent effort of states to control or at least to be in a position to influence the rules or regimes governing trade, foreign investment, and the international monetary system as well as other aspects of the international political economy.

Behind seemingly technical issues of trade or international money lurk significant political issues that profoundly influence the power, independence, and well-being of individual states. Thus, although trade may well be of mutual benefit, every state wants its own gains to be disproportionately to its advantage; it wants to move up the technological ladder to reap the highest value-added return from its own contribution to the international division of labor. Similarly, every state wants to have its say in decision making about the rules of the international monetary system. In every area of international economic affairs, economic and political issues are deeply entwined.

Scholars and other individuals differ, however, on the nature of the relationship between economic and political affairs. Although many positions can be identified, almost everyone tends to fall into one of three contrasting perspectives, ideologies, or schools of thought. They are liberalism, nationalism, and Marxism, and the next chapter will evaluate their strengths and limitations. In particular, the fundamental challenge raised by nationalism and especially Marxism with respect to the prospects for the continuation of the postwar liberal international economy will be considered.

CHAPTER TWO

Three Ideologies of Political Economy

O VER THE PAST century and a half, the ideologies of liberalism, nationalism, and Marxism have divided humanity. This book uses
"ideology" to refer to "systems of thought and belief by which [indi-
viduals and groups] explain . . . how their social system operates and
what principles it exemplifies" (Heilbroner, 1985, p. 107). The conflict
among these three moral and intellectual positions has revolved around
the role and significance of the market in the organization of society
and economic affairs.

Through an evaluation of the strengths and weaknesses of these
three ideologies it is possible to illuminate the study of the field of international political economy. The strengths of each perspective set
forth here will be applied to subsequent discussions of specific issues,
such as those of trade, investment, and development. Although my values are those of liberalism, the world in which we live is one best described by the ideas of economic nationalism and occasionally by those
of Marxism as well. Eclecticism may not be the route to theoretical precision, but sometimes it is the only route available.

The three ideologies differ on a broad range of questions such as:
What is the significance of the market for economic growth and the distribution of wealth among groups and societies? What ought to be the
role of markets in the organization of domestic and international society? What is the effect of the market system on issues of war or peace?
These and similar questions are central to discussions of international
political economy.

These three ideologies are fundamentally different in their conceptions of the relationships among society, state, and market, and it may
not be an exaggeration to say that every controversy in the field of international political economy is ultimately reducible to differing conceptions of these relationships. The intellectual clash is not merely of
historical interest. Economic liberalism, Marxism, and economic nationalism are all very much alive at the end of the twentieth century;
they define the conflicting perspectives that individuals have with regard to the implications of the market system for domestic and international society. Many of the issues that were controversial in the

eighteenth and nineteenth centuries are once again being intensely debated.

It is important to understand the nature and content of these contrasting "ideologies" of political economy. The term "ideology" is used rather than "theory" because each position entails a total belief system concerning the nature of human beings and society and is thus akin to what Thomas Kuhn has called a paradigm (Kuhn, 1962). As Kuhn demonstrates, intellectual commitments are held tenaciously and can seldom be dislodged by logic or by contrary evidence. This is due to the fact that these commitments or ideologies allege to provide scientific descriptions of how the world *does* work while they also constitute normative positions regarding how the world *should* work.

Although scholars have produced a number of "theories" to explain the relationship of economics and politics, these three stand out and have had a profound influence on scholarship and political affairs. In highly oversimplified terms, economic nationalism (or, as it was originally called, mercantilism), which developed from the practice of statesmen in the early modern period, assumes and advocates the primacy of politics over economics. It is essentially a doctrine of state-building and asserts that the market should be subordinate to the pursuit of state interests. It argues that political factors do, or at least should, determine economic relations. Liberalism, which emerged from the Enlightenment in the writings of Adam Smith and others, was a reaction to mercantilism and has become embodied in orthodox economics. It assumes that politics and economics exist, at least ideally, in separate spheres; it argues that markets—in the interest of efficiency, growth, and consumer choice—should be free from political interference. Marxism, which appeared in the mid-nineteenth century as a reaction against liberalism and classical economics, holds that economics drives politics. Political conflict arises from struggle among classes over the distribution of wealth. Hence, political conflict will cease with the elimination of the market and of a society of classes. Since both nationalism and Marxism in the modern era have developed largely in reaction to the tenets of liberal economics, my discussion and evaluation of these ideologies will begin with economic liberalism.

THE LIBERAL PERSPECTIVE

Some scholars assert that there is no such thing as a liberal theory of political economy because liberalism separates economics and politics from one another and assumes that each sphere operates according to particular rules and a logic of its own.[1] This view is itself, however, an ideological position and liberal theorists do in fact concern themselves with both political and economic affairs. Whether it is made explicit in their writings or is merely implicit, one can speak of a liberal theory of political economy.

There is a set of values from which liberal theories of economics and of politics arise; in the modern world these political and economic values have tended to appear together (Lindblom, 1977). Liberal economic theory is committed to free markets and minimal state intervention, although, as will be pointed out below, the relative emphasis on one or the other may differ. Liberal political theory is committed to individual equality and liberty, although again the emphasis may differ. We are primarily concerned here with the economic component of liberal theory.

The liberal perspective on political economy is embodied in the discipline of economics as it has developed in Great Britain, the United States, and Western Europe. From Adam Smith to its contemporary proponents, liberal thinkers have shared a coherent set of assumptions and beliefs about the nature of human beings, society, and economic activities. Liberalism has assumed many forms—classical, neo-classical, Keynesian, monetarist, Austrian, rational expectation, etc. These variants range from those giving priority to equality and tending toward social democracy and state interventionism to achieve this objective, to those stressing liberty and noninterventionism at the expense of social equality. All forms of economic liberalism, however, are committed to the market and the price mechanism as the most efficacious means for organizing domestic and international economic relations. Liberalism may, in fact, be defined as a doctrine and set of principles for organizing and managing a market economy in order to achieve maximum efficiency, economic growth, and individual welfare.

Economic liberalism assumes that a market arises spontaneously in order to satisfy human needs and that, once it is in operation, it functions in accordance with its own internal logic. Human beings are by nature economic animals, and therefore markets evolve naturally without central direction. As Adam Smith put it, it is inherent in mankind to "truck, barter and exchange." To facilitate exchange and improve

---

[1] The term "liberal" is used in this book in its European connotation, that is, a commitment to individualism, free market, and private property. This is the dominant perspective of most American economists and of economics as taught in American universities. Thus, both Paul Samuelson and Milton Friedman, despite important differences between their political and theoretical views, are regarded here as representatives of the American liberal tradition.

their well-being, people create markets, money, and economic institutions. Thus, in his "The Economic Organization of a P.o.W. Camp," R. A. Radford (1945) shows how a complex and sophisticated market arose spontaneously in order to satisfy human wants, but his tale also demonstrates how a form of government was necessary to police and maintain this primitive market system.[2]

The rationale for a market system is that it increases economic efficiency, maximizes economic growth, and thereby improves human welfare. Although liberals believe that economic activity also enhances the power and security of the state, they argue that the primary objective of economic activity is to benefit individual consumers. Their ultimate defense of free trade and open markets is that they increase the range of goods and services available to the consumer.

The fundamental premise of liberalism is that the individual consumer, firm, or household is the basis of society. Individuals behave rationally and attempt to maximize or satisfy certain values at the lowest possible cost to themselves. Rationality applies only to endeavor, not to outcome. Thus, failure to achieve an objective due to ignorance or some other cause does not, according to liberals, invalidate their premise that individuals act on the basis of a cost/benefit or means/ends calculus. Finally, liberalism argues that an individual will seek to acquire an objective until a market equilibrium is reached, that is, until the costs associated with achieving the objective are equal to the benefits. Liberal economists attempt to explain economic and, in some cases, all human behavior on the basis of these individualistic and rationalistic assumptions (Rogowski, 1978).

Liberalism also assumes that a market exists in which individuals have complete information and are thus enabled to select the most beneficial course of action. Individual producers and consumers will be highly responsive to price signals, and this will create a flexible economy in which any change in relative prices will elicit a corresponding change in patterns of production, consumption, and economic institutions; the latter are conceived ultimately to be the product rather than the cause of economic behavior (Davis and North, 1971). Further, in a truly competitive market, the terms of exchange are determined solely by considerations of supply and demand rather than by the exercise of power and coercion. If exchange is voluntary, both parties benefit. In colloquial terms, a "free exchange is no robbery."

Economics, or rather the economics taught in most American universities (what Marxists call orthodox or bourgeois economics), is as-

---

[2] I would like to thank Michael Doyle for bringing this interesting article to my attention.

sumed to be an empirical science of maximizing behavior. Behavior is believed to be governed by a set of economic "laws" that are impersonal and politically neutral; therefore, economics and politics should and can be separated into distinct spheres. Governments should not intervene in the market except where a "market failure" exists (Baumol, 1965) or in order to provide a so-called public or collective good (Olson, 1965).

A market economy is governed principally by the law of demand (Becker, 1976, p. 6). This "law" (or, if one prefers, assumption) holds that people will buy more of a good if the relative price falls and less if it rises; people will also tend to buy more of a good as their relative income rises and less as it falls. Any development that changes the relative price of a good or the relative income of an actor will create an incentive or disincentive to acquire (or produce) more or less of the good; this law in turn has profound ramifications throughout the society. Although certain exceptions to this simple concept exist, it is fundamental to the operation and success of a market system of economic exchange.

On the supply side of the economy, liberal economics assumes that individuals pursue their interests in a world of scarcity and resource constraints. This is a fundamental and inescapable condition of human existence. Every decision involves an opportunity cost, a tradeoff among alternative uses of available resources (Samuelson, 1980, p. 27). The basic lesson of liberal economics is that "there is no such thing as a free lunch"; to get something one must be willing to give up something else.

Liberalism also assumes that a market economy exhibits a powerful tendency toward equilibrium and inherent stability, at least over the long term. This "concept of a self-operating and self-correcting equilibrium achieved by a balance of forces in a rational universe" is a crucial one for the economists' belief in the operation of markets and the laws that are believed to govern them (Condliffe, 1950, p. 112). If a market is thrown into a state of disequilibrium due to some external (exogenous) factor such as a change in consumer tastes or productive technology, the operation of the price mechanism will eventually return it to a new state of equilibrium. Prices and quantities will once again balance one another. Thus, a change in either the supply or the demand for a good will elicit corresponding changes in the price of the good. The principal technique of modern economic analysis, comparative statics, is based on this assumption of a tendency toward systemic equilibrium.[3]

---

[3] The method of comparative statics was invented by David Ricardo. It consists of a model of a market in a state of equilibrium, the introduction of an exogenous variable

An additional liberal assumption is that a basic long-term harmony of interests underlies the market competition of producers and consumers, a harmony that will supercede any temporary conflict of interest. Individual pursuit of self-interest in the market increases social well-being because it leads to the maximization of efficiency, and the resulting economic growth eventually benefits all. Consequently, everyone will gain in accordance with his or her contribution to the whole, but, it should be added, not everyone will gain equally because individual productivities differ. Under free exchange, society as a whole will be more wealthy, but individuals will be rewarded in terms of their marginal productivity and relative contribution to the overall social product.

Finally, most present-day liberal economists believe in progress, defined most frequently as an increase in wealth per capita. They assert that the growth of a properly functioning economy is linear, gradual, and continuous (Meier and Baldwin, 1963, p. 70). It proceeds along what an economist colleague has called "the MIT standard equilibrium growth curve." Although political or other events—wars, revolution, or natural disasters—can dramatically disrupt this growth path, the economy will return eventually to a stable pattern of growth that is determined principally by increases in population, resources, and productivity. Moreover, liberals see no necessary connection between the process of economic growth and political developments such as war and imperialism; these political evils affect and may be affected by economic activities, but they are essentially caused by political and not by economic factors. For example, liberals do not believe that any causal relationship existed between the advance of capitalism in the late nineteenth century and the upheavals of imperialism after 1870 and the outbreak of the First World War. Liberals believe economics is progressive and politics is retrogressive. Thus they conceive of progress as divorced from politics and based on the evolution of the market.

On the basis of these assumptions and commitments, modern economists have constructed the empirical science of economics. Over the past two centuries, they have deduced the "laws" of maximizing behavior, such as those of the theory of comparative advantage, the theory of marginal utility, and the quantity theory of money. As Arthur Lewis has commented to me, economists discover new laws at the rate of about one per quarter century. These "laws" are both contingent and

into the system, and a calculation of the new equilibrium state. Because this mode of analysis is generally unconcerned with the origins of the exogenous variable itself, it is limited as a means of examining the problem of economic change.

normative. They assume the existence of economic man—a rational, maximizing creature—a variant of the species homo sapiens that has been relatively rare in human history and has existed only during peculiar periods of favorable conditions. Further, these laws are normative in that they prescribe how a society must organize itself and how people must behave if they are to maximize the growth of wealth. Both individuals and societies may violate these laws, but they do so at the cost of productive efficiency. Today, the conditions necessary for the operation of a market economy exist, and the normative commitment to the market has spread from its birthplace in Western civilization to embrace an increasingly large portion of the globe. Despite setbacks, the modern world has moved in the direction of the market economy and of increasing global economic interdependence precisely because markets *are* more efficient than other forms of economic organization (Hicks, 1969).

In essence, liberals believe that trade and economic intercourse are a source of peaceful relations among nations because the mutual benefits of trade and expanding interdependence among national economies will tend to foster cooperative relations. Whereas politics tends to divide, economics tends to unite peoples. A liberal international economy will have a moderating influence on international politics as it creates bonds of mutual interests and a commitment to the status quo. However, it is important to emphasize again that although everyone will, or at least can, be better off in "absolute" terms under free exchange, the "relative" gains will differ. It is precisely this issue of relative gains and the distribution of the wealth generated by the market system that has given rise to economic nationalism and Marxism as rival doctrines.

THE NATIONALIST PERSPECTIVE

Economic nationalism, like economic liberalism, has undergone several metamorphoses over the past several centuries. Its labels have also changed: mercantilism, statism, protectionism, the German Historical School, and, recently, New Protectionism. Throughout all these manifestations, however, runs a set of themes or attitudes rather than a coherent and systematic body of economic or political theory. Its central idea is that economic activities are and should be subordinate to the goal of state building and the interests of the state. All nationalists ascribe to the primacy of the state, of national security, and of military power in the organization and functioning of the international system. Within this general commitment two basic positions can be discerned. Some nationalists consider the safeguarding of national economic interests as the minimum essential to the security and survival of the state. For lack of a better term, this generally defensive position may be called "benign" mercantilism.[4] On the other hand, there are those nationalists who regard the international economy as an arena for imperialist expansion and national aggrandizement. This aggressive form may be termed "malevolent" mercantilism. The economic policies of Nazi economic minister Hjalmar Schacht toward eastern Europe in the 1930s were of this type (Hirschman, 1969).

Although economic nationalism should be viewed as a general commitment to state building, the precise objectives pursued and the policies advocated have differed in different times and in different places. Yet, as Jacob Viner has cogently argued in an often-quoted passage, economic nationalist (or what he calls mercantilist) writers share convictions concerning the relationship of wealth and power:

I believe that practically all mercantilists, whatever the period, country, or status of the particular individual, would have subscribed to all of the following propositions: (1) wealth is an absolutely essential means to power, whether for security or for aggression; (2) power is essential or valuable as a means to the acquisition or retention of wealth; (3) wealth and power are each proper ultimate ends of national policy; (4) there is long-run harmony between these ends, although in particular circumstances it may be necessary for a time to make economic sacrifices in the interest of military security and therefore also of long-run prosperity (Viner, 1958, p. 286).

Whereas liberal writers generally view the pursuit of power and wealth, that is, the choice between "guns and butter," as involving a tradeoff, nationalists tend to regard the two goals as being complementary (Knorr, 1944, p. 10).

Economic nationalists stress the role of economic factors in international relations and view the struggle among states—capitalist, socialist, or whatever—for economic resources as pervasive and indeed inherent in the nature of the international system itself. As one writer has put it, since economic resources are necessary for national power, every conflict is at once both economic and political (Hawtrey, 1952). States, at least over the long run, simultaneously pursue wealth and national power.

As it evolved in the early modern era, economic nationalism responded to and reflected the political, economic, and military developments of the sixteenth, seventeenth, and eighteenth centuries: the

---

[4] One can identify Friedrich List with the benign mercantilist position. List believed that true cosmopolitanism could only be possible when all states had been developed. For a discussion of benign and malevolent mercantilism, see Gilpin 1975, pp. 234-37 and Chapter Ten below.

emergence of strong national states in constant competition, the rise of a middle class devoted at first to commerce and increasingly to manufacturing, and the quickening pace of economic activities due to changes within Europe and the discovery of the New World and its resources. The evolution of a monetarized market economy and the wide range of changes in the nature of warfare that have been characterized as the "Military Revolution" were also critically important (Roberts, 1956). Nationalists (or "mercantilists," as they were then called) had good cause to identify a favorable balance of trade with national security.

For several reasons, the foremost objective of nationalists is industrialization (Sen, 1984). In the first place, nationalists believe that industry has spillover effects (externalities) throughout the economy and leads to its overall development. Second, they associate the possession of industry with economic self-sufficiency and political autonomy. Third, and most important, industry is prized because it is the basis of military power and central to national security in the modern world. In almost every society, including liberal ones, governments pursue policies favorable to industrial development. As the mercantilist theorist of American economic development, Alexander Hamilton, wrote: "not only the wealth but the independence and security of a country appear to be materially connected to the prosperity of manufactures" (quoted in Rostow, 1971, p. 189); no contemporary dependency theorist has put it better. This nationalist objective of industrialization, as will be argued in Chapter Three, is itself a major source of economic conflict.

Economic nationalism, both in the early modern era and today, arises in part from the tendency of markets to concentrate wealth and to establish dependency or power relations between the strong and the weak economies. In its more benign or defensive form it attempts to protect the economy against untoward external economic and political forces. Defensive economic nationalism frequently exists in less developed economies or in those advanced economies that have begun to decline; such governments pursue protectionist and related policies to protect their nascent or declining industries and to safeguard domestic interests. In its more malevolent form, economic nationalism is the conduct of economic warfare. This type is most prevalent in expanding powers. The classic example is Nazi Germany.

In a world of competing states, the nationalist considers relative gain to be more important than mutual gain. Thus nations continually try to change the rules or regimes governing international economic relations in order to benefit themselves disproportionately with respect to other economic powers. As Adam Smith shrewdly pointed out, everyone wants to be a monopolist and will attempt to be one unless prevented by competitors. Therefore, a liberal international economy cannot develop unless it is supported by the dominant economic states whose own interests are consistent with its preservation.

Whereas liberals stress the mutual benefits of international commerce, nationalists as well as Marxists regard these relations as basically conflictual. Although this does not rule out international economic cooperation and the pursuit of liberal policies, economic interdependence is never symmetrical; indeed, it constitutes a source of continuous conflict and insecurity. Nationalist writers from Alexander Hamilton to contemporary dependency theorists thus emphasize national self-sufficiency rather than economic interdependence.

Economic nationalism has taken several different forms in the modern world. Responding to the Commercial Revolution and the expansion of international trade throughout the early period, classical or financial mercantilism emphasized the promotion of trade and a balance of payments surplus. Following the Industrial Revolution, industrial mercantilists like Hamilton and List stressed the supremacy of industry and manufacturing over agriculture. Following the First and Second World Wars these earlier concerns have been joined by a powerful commitment to the primacy of domestic welfare and the welfare state. In the last decades of this century, the increasing importance of advanced technology, the desire for national control over the "commanding heights" of the modern economy, and the advent of what might best be called "policy competitiveness" have become the distinctive features of contemporary mercantilism. In all ages, however, the desire for power and independence have been the overriding concern of economic nationalists.

Whatever its relative strengths and weaknesses as an ideology or theory of international political economy, the nationalist emphasis on the geographic location and the distribution of economic activities provide it with powerful appeal. Throughout modern history, states have pursued policies promoting the development of industry, advanced technology, and those economic activities with the highest profitability and generation of employment within their own borders. As far as they can, states try to create an international division of labor favorable to their political and economic interests. Indeed, economic nationalism is likely to be a significant influence in international relations as long as the state system exists.

THE MARXIST PERSPECTIVE

Like liberalism and nationalism, Marxism has evolved in significant ways since its basic ideas were set forth by Karl Marx and Friedrich Engels in the middle of the nineteenth century.[5] Marx's own thinking changed during his lifetime, and his theories have always been subject to conflicting interpretations. Although Marx viewed capitalism as a global economy, he did not develop a systematic set of ideas on international relations; this responsibility fell upon the succeeding generation of Marxist writers. The Soviet Union and China, furthermore, having adopted Marxism as their official ideology, have reshaped it when necessary to serve their own national interests.

As in liberalism and nationalism, two basic strands can be discerned in modern Marxism. The first is the evolutionary Marxism of social democracy associated with Eduard Bernstein and Karl Kautsky; in the contemporary world it has tapered off and is hardly distinguishable from the egalitarian form of liberalism. At the other extreme is the revolutionary Marxism of Lenin and, in theory at least, of the Soviet Union. Because of its triumph as the ruling ideology in one of the world's two superpowers, this variation is the more important and will be stressed here.

As Robert Heilbroner (1980) has argued, despite the existence of these different Marxisms, four essential elements can be found in the overall corpus of Marxist writings. The first element is the dialectical approach to knowledge and society that defines the nature of reality as dynamic and conflictual; social disequilibria and consequent change are due to the class struggle and the working out of contradictions inherent in social and political phenomena. There is, according to Marxists, no inherent social harmony or return to equilibrium as liberals believe. The second element is a materialist approach to history; the development of productive forces and economic activities is central to historical change and operates through the class struggle over distribution of the social product. The third is a general view of capitalist development; the capitalist mode of production and its destiny are governed by a set of "economic laws of motion of modern society." The fourth is a normative commitment to socialism; all Marxists believe that a socialist society is both the necessary and desirable end of historical development (Heilbroner, 1980, pp. 20-21). It is only the third of these beliefs that is of interest here.

Marxism characterizes capitalism as the private ownership of the means of production and the existence of wage labor. It believes that capitalism is driven by capitalists striving for profits and capital accumulation in a competitive market economy. Labor has been dispos-

---

[5] Although there were important differences between the views of Engels and Marx, I shall refer to Marx throughout this discussion as standing for the combined contribution of both men.

sessed and has become a commodity that is subject to the price mechanism. In Marx's view these two key characteristics of capitalism are responsible for its dynamic nature and make it the most productive economic mechanism yet. Although its historic mission is to develop and unify the globe, the very success of capitalism will hasten its passing. The origin, evolution, and eventual demise of the capitalist mode of production are, according to Marx, governed by three inevitable economic laws.

The first law, the law of disproportionality, entails a denial of Say's law, which (in oversimplified terms) holds that supply creates its own demand so that supply and demand will always be, except for brief moments, in balance (see Sowell, 1972). Say's law maintains that an equilibrating process makes overproduction impossible in a capitalist or market economy. Marx, like John Maynard Keynes, denied that this tendency toward equilibrium existed and argued that capitalist economies tend to overproduce particular types of goods. There is, Marx argued, an inherent contradiction in capitalism between its capacity to produce goods and the capacity of consumers (wage earners) to purchase those goods, so that the constantly recurring disproportionality between production and consumption due to the "anarchy" of the market causes periodic depressions and economic fluctuations. He predicted that these recurring economic crises would become increasingly severe and in time would impel the suffering proletariat to rebel against the system.

The second law propelling the development of a capitalist system, according to Marxism, is the law of the concentration (or accumulation) of capital. The motive force of capitalism is the drive for profits and the consequent necessity for the individual capitalist to accumulate and invest. Competition forces the capitalists to increase their efficiency and capital investment or risk extinction. As a result, the evolution of capitalism is toward increasing concentrations of wealth in the hands of the efficient few and the growing impoverishment of the many. With the petite bourgeoisie being pushed down into the swelling ranks of the impoverished proletariat, the reserve army of the unemployed increases, labor's wages decline, and the capitalist society becomes ripe for social revolution.

The third law of capitalism is that of the falling rate of profit. As capital accumulates and becomes more abundant, the rate of return declines, thereby decreasing the incentive to invest. Although classical liberal economists had recognized this possibility, they believed that a solution could be found through such countervailing devices as the export of capital and manufactured goods and the import of cheap food

(Mill, 1970 [1848], pp. 97-104). Marx, on the other hand, believed that the tendency for profits to decline was inescapable. As the pressure of competition forces capitalists to increase efficiency and productivity through investment in new labor-saving and more productive technology, the level of unemployment will increase and the rate of profit or surplus value will decrease. Capitalists will thereby lose their incentive to invest in productive ventures and to create employment. This will result in economic stagnation, increasing unemployment, and the "immiserization" of the proletariat. In time, the ever-increasing intensity and depth of the business cycle will cause the workers to rebel and destroy the capitalist economic system.

The core of the Marxist critique of capitalism is that although the individual capitalist is rational (as liberals assume), the capitalist system itself is irrational. The competitive market necessitates that the individual capitalist must save, invest, and accumulate. If the desire for profits is the fuel of capitalism, then investment is the motor and accumulation is the result. In the aggregate, however, this accumulating capital of individual capitalists leads to the periodic overproduction of goods, surplus capital, and the disappearance of investment incentives. In time, the increasing severity of the downturns in the business cycle and the long-term trend toward economic stagnation will cause the proletariat to overthrow the system through revolutionary violence. Thus, the inherent contradiction of capitalism is that, with capital accumulation, capitalism sows the seeds of its own destruction and is replaced by the socialist economic system.[6]

Marx believed that in the mid-nineteenth century, the maturing of capitalism in Europe and the drawing of the global periphery into the market economy had set the stage for the proletarian revolution and the end of the capitalist economy. When this did not happen, Marx's followers, such as Rudolf Hilferding and Rosa Luxemburg, became concerned over the continuing vitality of capitalism and its refusal to disappear. The strength of nationalism, the economic successes of capitalism, and the advent of imperialism led to a metamorphosis of Marxist thought that culminated in Lenin's *Imperialism* (1939), first published in 1917. Written against the backdrop of the First World War and drawing heavily upon the writings of other Marxists, *Imperialism* was both a polemic against his ideological enemies and a synthesis of

---

[6] In effect, the Marxists are accusing the defenders of capitalism with employing the fallacy of composition. This is "a fallacy in which what is true of a part is, on that account alone, alleged to be also *necessarily* true of the whole" (Samuelson, 1980, p. 11). Similarly, Keynes argued that although individual saving is a virtue, if everyone saved it would be a calamity.

Marxist critiques of a capitalist world economy. In staking out his own position, Lenin in effect converted Marxism from essentially a theory of domestic economy to a theory of international political relations among capitalist states.

Lenin set himself the task of accounting for the fact that nationalism had triumphed over proletarian internationalism at the outbreak of the First World War and thereby sought to provide the intellectual foundations for a reunification of the international communist movement under his leadership. He wanted to show why the socialist parties of the several European powers, especially the German Social Democrats under Karl Kautsky, had supported their respective bourgeoisies. He also tried to explain why the impoverishment of the proletariat had not taken place as Marx had predicted, and instead wages were rising and workers were becoming trade unionists.

In the years between Marx and Lenin, capitalism had experienced a profound transformation. Marx had written about a capitalism largely confined to western Europe, a closed economy in which the growth impulse would one day cease as it collided with various constraints. Between 1870 and 1914, however, capitalism had become a vibrant, technological, and increasingly global and open system. In Marx's day, the primary nexus of the slowly developing world economy was trade. After 1870, however, the massive export of capital by Great Britain and subsequently by other developed economies had significantly changed the world economy; foreign investment and international finance had profoundly altered the economic and political relations among societies. Furthermore, Marx's capitalism had been composed mainly of small, competitive, industrial firms. By the time of Lenin, however, capitalist economies were dominated by immense industrial combines that in turn, according to Lenin, were controlled by the great banking houses *(haut finance)*. For Lenin, the control of capital by capital, that is, of industrial capital by financial capital, represented the pristine and highest stage of capitalist development.

Capitalism, he argued, had escaped its three laws of motion through overseas imperialism. The acquisition of colonies had enabled the capitalist economies to dispose of their unconsumed goods, to acquire cheap resources, and to vent their surplus capital. The exploitation of these colonies further provided an economic surplus with which the capitalists could buy off the leadership ("labor aristocracy") of their own proletariat. Colonial imperialism, he argued, had become a necessary feature of advanced capitalism. As its productive forces developed and matured, a capitalist economy had to expand abroad, capture colonies, or else suffer economic stagnation and internal revolution.

Lenin identified this necessary expansion as the cause of the eventual destruction of the international capitalist system.

The essence of Lenin's argument is that a capitalist international economy does develop the world, but does not develop it evenly. Individual capitalist economies grow at different rates and this differential growth of national power is ultimately responsible for imperialism, war, and international political change. Responding to Kautsky's argument that capitalists were too rational to fight over colonies and would ally themselves in the joint exploitation of colonial peoples (the doctrine of "ultra-imperialism"), Lenin stated that this was impossible because of what has become known as the "law of uneven development":

This question [of the possibility of capitalist alliances to be more than temporary and free from conflict] need only be stated clearly enough to make it impossible for any other reply to be given than that in the negative; for there can be *no* other conceivable basis under capitalism for the division of spheres of influence . . . than a calculation of the *strength* of the participants in the division, their general economic, financial, military strength, etc. And the strength of these participants in the division does not change to an equal degree, for under capitalism the development of different undertakings, trusts, branches of industry, or countries cannot be *even*. Half a century ago, Germany was a miserable, insignificant country, as far as its capitalist strength was concerned, compared with the strength of England at that time. Japan was similarly insignificant compared with Russia. Is it "conceivable" that in ten or twenty years' time the relative strength of the imperialist powers will have remained *un*changed? Absolutely inconceivable (Lenin, 1939 [1917], p. 119).

In effect, in this passage and in his overall attempt to prove that an international capitalist system was inherently unstable, Lenin added a fourth law to the original three Marxist laws of capitalism. The law is that, as capitalist economies mature, as capital accumulates, and as profit rates fall, the capitalist economies are compelled to seize colonies and create dependencies to serve as markets, investment outlets, and sources of food and raw materials. In competition with one another, they divide up the colonial world in accordance with their relative strengths. Thus, the most advanced capitalist economy, namely Great Britain, had appropriated the largest share of colonies. As other capitalist economies advanced, however, they sought a redivision of colonies. This imperialist conflict inevitably led to armed conflict among the rising and declining imperial powers. The First World War, according to this analysis, was a war of territorial redivision between a declining Great Britain and other rising capitalist powers. Such wars of colonial division and redivision would continue, he argued, until the industrial-

39

izing colonies and the proletariat of the capitalist countries revolted against the system.

In more general terms, Lenin reasoned that because capitalist economies grow and accumulate capital at differential rates, a capitalist international system can never be stable for longer than very short periods of time. In opposition to Kautsky's doctrine of ultra-imperialism, Lenin argued that all capitalist alliances were temporary and reflected momentary balances of power among the capitalist states that would inevitably be undermined by the process of uneven development. As this occurred, it would lead to intracapitalist conflicts over colonial territories.

The law of uneven development, with its fateful consequences, had become operative in his own age because the world had suddenly become finite; the globe itself had become a closed system. For decades the European capitalist powers had expanded, gobbling up overseas territory, but the imperialist powers increasingly came into contact and therefore into conflict with one another as the lands suitable for colonization diminished. He believed that the final drama would be the imperial division of China and that, with the closing of the global undeveloped frontier, imperialist clashes would intensify. In time, conflicts among the imperialist powers would produce revolts among their own colonies and weaken Western capitalism's hold on the colonialized races of the globe.

Lenin's internationalization of Marxist theory represented a subtle but significant reformulation. In Marx's critique of capitalism, the causes of its downfall were economic; capitalism would fail for economic reasons as the proletariat revolted against its impoverishment. Furthermore, Marx had defined the actors in this drama as social classes. Lenin, however, substituted a political critique of capitalism in which the principal actors in effect became competing mercantilistic nation-states driven by economic necessity. Although international capitalism was economically successful, Lenin argued that it was politically unstable and constituted a war-system. The workers or the labor aristocracy in the developed capitalist countries temporarily shared in the exploitation of colonial peoples but ultimately would pay for these economic gains on the battlefield. Lenin believed that the inherent contradiction of capitalism resided in the consequent struggle of nations rather than in the class struggle. Capitalism would end due to a revolt against its inherent bellicosity and political consequences.

In summary, Lenin argued that the inherent contradiction of capitalism is that it develops the world and plants the political seeds of its own destruction as it diffuses technology, industry, and military power. It creates foreign competitors with lower wages and standards of living who can outcompete the previously dominant economy on the battle-field of world markets. Intensification of economic and political competition between declining and rising capitalist powers leads to economic conflicts, imperial rivalries, and eventually war. He asserted that this had been the fate of the British-centered liberal world economy of the nineteenth century. Today he would undoubtedly argue that, as the U.S. economy declines, a similar fate threatens the twentieth-century liberal world economy, centered in the United States.

With the triumph of Bolshevism in the Soviet Union, Lenin's theory of capitalist imperialism became the orthodox Marxist theory of international political economy; yet other heirs of the Marxist tradition have continued to challenge this orthodoxy. It has also been modified by subsequent changes in the nature of capitalism and other historical developments. Welfare-state capitalism has carried out many of the reforms that Lenin believed to be impossible, the political control of colonies is no longer regarded by Marxists as a necessary feature of imperialism, the finance capitalist of Lenin's era has been partially displaced by the multinational corporation of our own, the view that capitalist imperialism develops the less developed countries has been changed to the argument that it underdevelops them, and some Marxists have been so bold as to apply Marxist theory to Lenin's own political creation, the Soviet Union. Thus modified, at the end of the twentieth century Marxism in its various manifestations continues to exercise a powerful influence as one of the three dominant perspectives on political economy.

A CRITIQUE OF THE PERSPECTIVES

As we have seen, liberalism, nationalism, and Marxism make different assumptions and reach conflicting conclusions regarding the nature and consequences of a world market economy or (as Marxists prefer) a world capitalist economy. The position of this book is that these contrasting ideologies or perspectives constitute intellectual commitments or acts of faith. Although particular ideas or theories associated with one position or another may be shown to be false or questionable, these perspectives can be neither proved nor disproved through logical argument or the presentation of contrary empirical evidence. There are several reasons for the persistence of these perspectives and their resistance to scientific testing.

In the first place, they are based on assumptions about people or society that cannot be subjected to empirical tests. For example, the liberal concept of rational individuals cannot be verified or falsified; individuals who appear to be acting in conflict with their own interest may actually be acting on incorrect information or be seeking to maximize a goal unknown to the observer and thus be fulfilling the basic assumption of liberalism. Moreover, liberals would argue that although a particular individual in a particular case might be shown to have behaved irrationally, in the aggregate the assumption of rationality is a valid one.

Second, predictive failure of a perspective can always be argued away through the introduction into the analysis of ad hoc hypotheses.[7] Marxism is replete with attempts to explain the predictive failures of Marxist theory. Lenin, for example, developed the concept of "false consciousness" to account for the fact that workers became trade unionists rather than members of a revolutionary proletariat. Lenin's theory of capitalist imperialism may also be viewed as an effort to explain the failure of Marx's predictions regarding the collapse of capitalism. More recently, as will be discussed below, Marxists have been compelled to formulate elaborate theories of the state to explain the emergence of the welfare state and its acceptance by capitalists, a development that Lenin said was impossible.

Third, and most important, the three perspectives have different purposes and to some extent exist at different levels of analysis. Both nationalists and Marxists, for example, can accept most of liberal economics as a tool of analysis while rejecting many of its assumptions and normative foundations. Thus Marx used classical economics with great skill, but his purpose was to embody it in a grand theory of the origins, dynamics, and end of capitalism. The fundamental difference, in fact, between liberalism and Marxism involves the questions asked and their sociological assumptions rather than the economic methodology that they employ (Blaug, 1978, pp. 276-77).

As reformulated by Lenin, Marxism has become nearly indistinguishable from the doctrine of political realism (Keohane, 1984a, pp. 41-46). Political realism, like economic nationalism, stresses the primacy of the state and national security. Although the two are very close, realism is essentially a political position whereas economic nationalism is an economic one. Or, put another way, economic nationalism is based on the realist doctrine of international relations.

Both in Lenin's theory and in political realism, states struggle for wealth and power, and the differential growth of power is the key to

---

[7] See Blaug (1978, p. 717) on the use of ad hoc hypotheses to explain away predictive failures.

international conflict and political change (Gilpin, 1981). However, the assumptions of the two theories regarding the basis of human motivation, the theory of the state, and the nature of the international system are fundamentally different. Marxists regard human nature as malleable and as easily corrupted by capitalism and correctable by socialism; realists believe that political conflict results from an unchanging human nature.

Whereas Marxists believe that the state is ultimately the servant of the dominant economic class, realists see the state as a relatively autonomous entity pursuing national interests that cannot be reduced to the particularistic interests of any class. For Marxists, the international system and foreign policy are determined by the structure of the domestic economy; for realists, the nature of the international system is the fundamental determinant of foreign policy. In short, Marxists regard war, imperialism, and the state as evil manifestations of a capitalism that will disappear with the communist revolution; realists hold them to be inevitable features of an anarchical international political system.

The difference between the two perspectives, therefore, is considerable. For the Marxist, though the state and the struggles among states are a consequence of the capitalist mode of production, the future will bring a realm of true harmony and peace following the inevitable revolution that the evil capitalist mode of production will spawn. The realist, on the other hand, believes there will be no such nirvana because of the inherently self-centered nature of human beings and the anarchy of the international system itself. The struggle among groups and states is virtually ceaseless, although there is occasionally a temporary respite. It seems unlikely that either prediction will ever receive scientific verification.

Each of the three perspectives has strengths and weaknesses, to be further explored below. Although no perspective provides a complete and satisfactory understanding of the nature and dynamism of the international political economy, together they provide useful insights. They also raise important issues that will be explored in succeeding chapters.

Critique of Economic Liberalism

Liberalism embodies a set of analytical tools and policy prescriptions that enable a society to maximize its return from scarce resources; its commitment to efficiency and the maximization of total wealth provides much of its strength. The market constitutes the most effective means for organizing economic relations, and the price mechanism operates to ensure that mutual gain and hence aggregate social benefit tend to result from economic exchange. In effect, liberal economics says to a society, whether domestic or international, "if you wish to be wealthy, this is what you must do."

From Adam Smith to the present, liberals have tried to discover the laws governing the wealth of nations. Although most liberals consider the laws of economics to be inviolable laws of nature, these laws may best be viewed as prescriptive guides for decision makers. If the laws are violated, there will be costs; the pursuit of objectives other than efficiency will necessarily involve an opportunity cost in terms of lost efficiency. Liberalism emphasizes the fact that such tradeoffs always exist in national policy. An emphasis on equity and redistribution, for example, is doomed to failure in the long run if it neglects considerations of efficiency. For a society to be efficient, as socialist economies have discovered, it cannot totally disregard the pertinent economic "laws."

The foremost defense of liberalism is perhaps a negative one. Although it may be true, as Marxists and some nationalists argue, that the alternative to a liberal system could be one in which all gain equally, it is also possible that the alternative could be one in which all *lose* in absolute terms. Much can be said for the liberal harmony of interest doctrine; yet, as E. H. Carr has pointed out, evidence to support this doctrine has generally been drawn from historical periods in which there was "unparalleled expansion of production, population and prosperity" (Carr, 1951 [1939], p. 44). When sustaining conditions break down (as happened in the 1930s and threatens to occur again in the closing decades of the century), disharmony displaces harmony and, I shall argue, the consequent breakdown of liberal regimes tends to lead to economic conflict wherein everyone loses.

The major criticism leveled against economic liberalism is that its basic assumptions, such as the existence of rational economic actors, a competitive market, and the like, are unrealistic. In part, this attack is unfair in that liberals knowingly make these simplifying assumptions in order to facilitate scientific research; no science is possible without them. What is more important, as defenders correctly point out, is that they should be judged by their results and ability to predict rather than by their alleged reality (Posner, 1977, ch. 1). From this perspective and within its own sphere, economics has proven to be a powerful analytical tool.

By the same token, however, liberal economics can be criticized in several important respects. As a means to understand society and especially its dynamics, economics is limited; it cannot serve as a comprehensive approach to political economy. Yet liberal economists have tended to forget this inherent limitation, to regard economics as the master social science, and to permit economics to become imperialistic. When this occurs, the nature and basic assumptions of the discipline can lead the economist astray and limit its utility as a theory of political economy.

The first of these limitations is that economics artificially separates the economy from other aspects of society and accepts the existing sociopolitical framework as a given, including the distribution of power and property rights; the resource and other endowments of individuals, groups, and national societies; and the framework of social, political, and cultural institutions. The liberal world is viewed as one of homogeneous, rational, and equal individuals living in a world free from political boundaries and social constraints. Its "laws" prescribe a set of maximizing rules for economic actors regardless of where and with what they start; yet in real life, one's starting point most frequently determines where one finishes (Dahrendorf, 1979).

Another limitation of liberal economics as a theory is a tendency to disregard the justice or equity of the outcome of economic activities. Despite heroic efforts to fashion an "objective" welfare economics, the distribution of wealth within and among societies lies outside the primary concern of liberal economics. There is some truth in the Marxist criticism that liberal economics is a tool kit for managing a capitalist or market economy. Bourgeois economics is, in the Marxist view, a discipline of engineering rather than a holistic science of society. It tells one how to achieve particular objectives at the least cost under a given set of constraints; it does not purport to answer questions regarding the future and destiny of man, questions dear to the hearts of Marxists and economic nationalists.

Liberalism is also limited by its assumption that exchange is always free and occurs in a competitive market between equals who possess full information and are thus enabled to gain mutually if they choose to exchange one value for another. Unfortunately, as Charles Lindblom has argued, exchange is seldom free and equal (Lindblom, 1977, pp. 40-50). Instead, the terms of an exchange can be profoundly affected by coercion, differences in bargaining power (monopoly or monopsony), and other essentially political factors. In effect, because it neglects both the effects of noneconomic factors on exchange and the effects of exchange on politics, liberalism lacks a true "political economy."

A further limitation of liberal economics is that its analysis tends to be static. At least in the short run, the array of consumer demands, the institutional framework, and the technological environment are accepted as constants. They are regarded as a set of constraints and opportunities within which economic decisions and tradeoffs are made. Questions about the origins of, or the directions taken by, economic institutions and the technological apparatus are, for the liberal, a secondary matter. Liberal economists are incrementalists who believe that social structures tend to change slowly in response to price signals. Although liberal economists have attempted to develop theories of economic and technological change, the crucial social, political, and technological variables affecting change are considered to be exogenous and beyond the realm of economic analysis. As Marxists charge, liberalism lacks a theory of the dynamics of international political economy and tends to assume the stability and the virtues of the economic status quo.

Liberal economics, with its laws for maximizing behavior, is based on a set of highly restrictive assumptions. No society has ever or could ever be composed of the true "economic man" of liberal theory. A functioning society requires affective ties and the subordination of individual self-interest to larger social values; if this were not the case the society would fly apart (Polanyi, 1957). Yet Western society has gone far in harnessing for social and economic betterment a basic tendency in human beings toward self-aggrandizement (Baechler, 1971). Through release of the market mechanism from social and political constraints, Western civilization has reached a level of unprecedented affluence and has set an example that other civilizations wish to emulate. It has done so, however, at the cost of other values. As liberal economics teaches, nothing is ever achieved without a cost.

Critique of Economic Nationalism

The foremost strength of economic nationalism is its focus on the state as the predominant actor in international relations and as an instrument of economic development. Although many have argued that modern economic and technological developments have made the nation-state an anachronism, at the end of the twentieth century the system of nation-states is actually expanding; societies throughout the world are seeking to create strong states capable of organizing and managing national economies, and the number of states in the world is increasing. Even in older states, the spirit of nationalist sentiments can easily be inflamed, as happened in the Falkland War of 1982. Although other actors such as transnational and international organizations do exist and do influence international relations, the economic and military efficiency of the state makes it preeminent over all these other actors.

The second strength of nationalism is its stress on the importance of security and political interests in the organization and conduct of international economic relations. One need not accept the nationalist emphasis on the primacy of security considerations to appreciate that the security of the state is a necessary precondition for its economic and political well-being in an anarchic and competitive state system. A state that fails to provide for its own security ceases to be independent. Whatever the objectives of the society, the effects of economic activities upon political independence and domestic welfare always rank high among its concerns (Strange, 1985c, p. 234).

The third strength of nationalism is its emphasis on the political framework of economic activities, its recognition that markets must function in a world of competitive groups and states. The political relations among these political actors affect the operation of markets just as markets affect the political relations. In fact, the international political system constitutes one of the most important constraints on and determinant of markets. Since states seek to influence markets to their own individual advantage, the role of power is crucial in the creation and sustaining of market relations; even Ricardo's classic example of the exchange of British woolens for Portuguese wine was not free from the exercise of state power (Choucri, 1980, p. 111). Indeed, as Carr has argued, every economic system must rest on a secure political base (Carr, 1951 [1939]).

One weakness of nationalism is its tendency to believe that international economic relations constitute solely and at all times a zero-sum game, that is, that one state's gain must of necessity be another's loss. Trade, investment, and all other economic relations are viewed by the nationalist primarily in conflictual and distributive terms. Yet, if cooperation occurs, markets *can* bring mutual (albeit not necessarily equal) gain, as the liberal insists. The possibility of benefit for all is the basis of the international market economy. Another weakness of nationalism is due to the fact that the pursuit of power and the pursuit of wealth usually do conflict, at least in the short run. The amassing and exercising of military and other forms of power entail costs to the society, costs that can undercut its economic efficiency. Thus, as Adam Smith argued, the mercantilist policies of eighteenth-century states that identified money with wealth were detrimental to the growth of the real wealth created by productivity increases; he demonstrated that the wealth of nations would have been better served by policies of free trade. Similarly, the tendency today to identify industry with power can weaken the economy of a state. Development of industries without regard to market considerations or comparative advantage can weaken a society economically. Although states in a situation of conflict must on occasion pursue mercantilistic goals and policies, over the long term, pursuit of these policies can be self-defeating.

In addition, nationalism lacks a satisfactory theory of domestic society, the state, and foreign policy. It tends to assume that society and state form a unitary entity and that foreign policy is determined by an objective national interest. Yet, as liberals correctly stress, society is pluralistic and consists of individuals and groups (coalitions of individuals) that try to capture the apparatus of the state and make it serve their own political and economic interests. Although states possess varying degrees of social autonomy and independence in the making of policy, foreign policy (including foreign economic policy) is in large measure the outcome of the conflicts among dominant groups within each society. Trade protectionism and most other nationalist policies result from attempts by one factor of production or another (capital, labor, or land) to acquire a monopoly position and thereby to increase its share of the economic rents. Nationalist policies are most frequently designed to redistribute income from consumers and society as a whole to producer interests.[8]

Nationalism can thus be interpreted as either a theory of state building or a cloak for the interests of particular producer groups that are in a position to influence national policy. In their failure to appreciate fully or distinguish between the two possible meanings of economic nationalism, nationalists can be faulted for not applying, both to the domestic level and to the determination of foreign policy, their assumption that the political framework influences economic outcomes. They fail to take sufficient account of the fact that domestic political groups frequently use a nationalist rationale, especially that of national security, to promote their own interests.

Whereas in the past, land and capital were the primary carriers of nationalist sentiments, in advanced economies labor has become the most nationalistic and protectionist of the three factors of production. In a world of highly mobile capital and resources, labor seeks to use the state to advance its threatened interests. The increased power of labor in the contemporary welfare state, as I shall argue below, has become a major force for economic nationalism.

The validity of nationalists' emphasis on protectionism and industrialization is more difficult to ascertain. It is true that all great industrial powers have had strong states that protected and promoted their

---

[8] The literature on the political economy of tariffs and other forms of trade protectionism as rent-seeking is extensive. As noted earlier, the subject of economic policy making falls outside the scope of this book. Frey (1984b) is an excellent discussion of this approach to tariff policy and related topics.

industries in the early stages of industrialization and that without such protectionism, the "infant" industries of developing economies probably would not have survived the competition of powerful firms in more advanced economies. Yet it is also the case that high levels of protectionism in many countries have led to the establishment of inefficient industries and even retarded economic development (Kindleberger, 1978b, pp. 19-38). In the final quarter of the twentieth century, economies like those of Taiwan and South Korea, which have limited protectionism while favoring competitive export industries, have performed better than those less developed countries that have attempted to industrialize behind high tariff walls while pursuing a strategy of import substitution.

The nationalist's bias toward industry over agriculture also must get a mixed review. It is true that industry can have certain advantages over agriculture and that the introduction of industrial technology into a society has spillover effects that tend to transform and modernize all aspects of the economy as it upgrades the quality of the labor force and increases the profitability of capital.[9] Yet one must remember that few societies have developed without a prior agricultural revolution and a high level of agricultural productivity (Lewis, 1978a). In fact, certain of the most prosperous economies of the world, for example, Denmark, the American farm belt, and western Canada, are based on efficient agriculture (Viner, 1952). In all these societies, moreover, the state has promoted agricultural development.

One may conclude that the nationalists are essentially correct in their belief that the state must play an important role in economic development. A strong state is required to promote and, in some cases, to protect industry as well as to foster an efficient agriculture. Yet this active role of the state, though a necessary condition, is not a sufficient condition. A strong and interventionist state does not guarantee economic development; indeed, it might retard it. The sufficient condition for economic development is an efficient economic organization of agriculture and industry, and in most cases this is achieved through the operation of the market. Both of these political and economic conditions have characterized the developed economies and the rapidly industrializing countries of the contemporary international system.

It is important to realize that, whatever its relative merits or deficiencies, economic nationalism has a persistent appeal. Throughout modern history, the international location of economic activities has been a

---

[9] Cornwall (1977) provides a representative argument of the benefits of industry over agriculture in economic development.

leading concern of states. From the seventeenth century on states have pursued conscious policies of industrial and technological development. Both to achieve stable military power and in the belief that industry provides a higher "value added" (see Chapter Three, note 26) than agriculture, the modern nation-state has had as one of its major objectives the establishment and protection of industrial power. As long as a conflictual international system exists, economic nationalism will retain its strong attraction.

Critique of Marxist Theory

Marxism correctly places the economic problem—the production and distribution of material wealth—where it belongs, at or near the center of political life. Whereas liberals tend to ignore the issue of distribution and nationalists are concerned primarily with the *international* distribution of wealth, Marxists focus on both the domestic and the international effects of a market economy on the distribution of wealth. They call attention to the ways in which the rules or regimes governing trade, investment, and other international economic relations affect the distribution of wealth among groups and states (Cohen, 1977, p. 49).[10] However, it is not necessary to subscribe to the materialist interpretation of history or the primacy of class struggle in order to appreciate that the ways in which individuals earn their living and distribute wealth are a critical determinant of social structure and political behavior.

Another contribution of Marxism is its emphasis on the nature and structure of the division of labor at both the domestic and international levels. As Marx and Engels correctly pointed out in *The German Ideology*, every division of labor implies dependence and therefore a political relationship (Marx and Engels, 1947 [1846]). In a market economy the economic nexus among groups and states becomes of critical importance in determining their welfare and their political relations. The Marxist analysis, however, is too limited, because economic interdependence is not the only or even the most important set of interstate relations. The political and strategic relations among political actors are of equal or greater significance and cannot be reduced to merely economic considerations, at least not as Marxists define economics.

The Marxist theory of international political economy is also valuable in its focus on international political change. Whereas neither liberalism nor nationalism has a comprehensive theory of social change,

----

[10] The volume edited by Krasner (1982c) contains a wide-ranging discussion of the concept of international regimes.

Marxism emphasizes the role of economic and technological developments in explaining the dynamics of the international system. As embodied in Lenin's law of uneven development, the differential growth of power among states constitutes an underlying cause of international political change. Lenin was at least partially correct in attributing the First World War to the uneven economic growth of power among industrial states and to conflict over the division of territory. There can be little doubt that the uneven growth of the several European powers and the consequent effects on the balance of power contributed to their collective insecurity. Competition for markets and empires did aggravate interstate relations. Furthermore, the average person's growing awareness of the effects on personal welfare and security of the vicissitudes of the world market and the economic behavior of other states also became a significant element in the arousal of nationalistic antagonisms. For nations and citizens alike, the growth of economic interdependence brought with it a new sense of insecurity, vulnerability, and resentment against foreign political and economic rivals.

Marxists are no doubt also correct in attributing to capitalist economies, at least as we have known them historically, a powerful impulse to expand through trade and especially through the export of capital. The classical liberal economists themselves observed that economic growth and the accumulation of capital create a tendency for the rate of return (profit) on capital to decline. These economists, however, also noted that the decline could be arrested through international trade, foreign investment, and other means. Whereas trade absorbs surplus capital in the manufacture of exports, foreign investment siphons off capital. Thus, classical liberals join Marxists in asserting that capitalist economies have an inherent tendency to export goods and surplus capital.

This tendency has led to the conclusion that the nature of capitalism is international and that its internal dynamics encourage outward expansionism. In a closed capitalist economy and in the absence of technological advance, underconsumption, surplus capital, and the resulting decline in the rate of profit would eventually lead to what John Stuart Mill called "the stationary state" (Mill, 1970 [1848], p. 111). Yet, in an open world economy characterized by expanding capitalism, population growth, and continuing improvement in productivity through technological advance, there is no inherent economic reason for economic stagnation to take place.

On the other hand, a communist or socialist economy has no inherent *economic* tendency to expand internationally. In a communist economy, investment and consumption are primarily determined by the national plan and, moreover, the state has a monopoly of all foreign exchange.[11] A communist economy may of course have a political or strategic motive for exporting capital, or it may need to invest abroad in order to obtain vital sources of raw materials. A Marxist regime may also find it profitable to invest abroad or to engage in other commercial transactions. Certainly the Soviet Union has been rightly credited on occasion with being a shrewd trader, and Ralph Hawtrey's point that the advent of a communist or socialist government does not eliminate the profit motive but merely transfers it to the state has some merit (Hawtrey, 1952). Nevertheless, the incentive structure of a communist society with its stress on prestige, power, and ideology is unlikely to encourage the economy's expansion abroad. The tendency is rather for economics to be subordinated to politics and the nationalistic goals of the state (Viner, 1951).

Marxists are certainly correct that capitalism needs an open world economy. Capitalists desire access to foreign economies for export of goods and capital; exports have a Keynesian demand effect in stimulating economic activity in capitalist economies, and capital exports serve to raise the overall rate of profit. Closure of foreign markets and capital outlets would be detrimental to capitalism, and a closed capitalist economy would probably result in a dramatic decline in economic growth. There is reason to believe that the capitalist system (certainly as we have known it) could not survive in the absence of an open world economy. The essential character of capitalism, as Marx pointed out, is cosmopolitan; the capitalist's ideology is international. Capitalism in just one state would undoubtedly be an impossibility.

In the nineteenth and twentieth centuries the dominant capitalist states, Great Britain and the United States, employed their power to promote and maintain an open world economy. They used their influence to remove the barriers to the free flow of goods and capital. Where necessary, in the words of Simon Kuznets, "the greater power of the developed nations imposed upon the reluctant partners the opportunities of international trade and division of labor" (Kuznets, 1966, p. 335). In pursuit of their own interests, they created international law to protect the property rights of private traders and investors (Lipson, 1985). And when the great trading nations became unable or unwilling to enforce the rules of free trade, the liberal system began its steady retreat. Up to this point, therefore, the Marxists are correct in their identification of capitalism and modern imperialism.

[11] Wiles (1968) presents a valuable analysis of the contrasting behavior of capitalist and communist economies.

The principal weakness of Marxism as a theory of international political economy results from its failure to appreciate the role of political and strategic factors in international relations. Although one can appreciate the insights of Marxism, it is not necessary to accept the Marxist theory that the dynamic of modern international relations is caused by the needs of capitalist economies to export goods and surplus capital. For example, to the extent that the uneven growth of national economies leads to war, this is due to national rivalries, which can occur regardless of the nature of domestic economies—witness the conflict between China and the Soviet Union. Although competition for markets and for capital outlets can certainly be a cause of tension and one factor causing imperialism and war, this does not provide an adequate explanation for the foreign policy behavior of capitalist states.

The historical evidence, for example, does not support Lenin's attribution of the First World War to the logic of capitalism and the market system. The most important territorial disputes among the European powers, which precipitated the war, were not those about overseas colonies, as Lenin argued, but lay within Europe itself. The principal conflict leading to the war involved redistribution of the Balkan territories of the decaying Ottoman Empire. And insofar as the source of this conflict was economic, it lay in the desire of the Russian state for access to the Mediterranean (Hawtrey, 1952, pp. 117-18). Marxism cannot explain the fact that the three major imperial rivals—Great Britain, France, and Russia—were in fact on the same side in the ensuing conflict and that they fought against a Germany that had few foreign policy interests outside Europe itself.

In addition, Lenin was wrong in tracing the basic motive force of imperialism to the internal workings of the capitalist system. As Benjamin J. Cohen has pointed out in his analysis of the Marxist theory of imperialism, the political and strategic conflicts of the European powers were more important; it was at least in part the stalemate on the Continent among the Great Powers that forced their interstate competition into the colonial world (Cohen, 1973). Every one of these colonial conflicts (if one excludes the Boer War) was in fact settled through diplomatic means. And, finally, the overseas colonies of the European powers were simply of little economic consequence. As Lenin's own data show, almost all European overseas investment was directed to the "lands of recent settlement" (the United States, Canada, Australia, South Africa, Argentina, etc.) rather than to the dependent colonies in what today we call the Third World (Lenin, 1939 [1917], p. 64). In fact, contrary to Lenin's view that politics follows investment, international finance during this period was largely a servant of foreign policy, as was also the case with French loans to Czarist Russia.[12] Thus, despite its proper focus on political change, Marxism is seriously flawed as a theory of political economy.

THREE CHALLENGES TO A WORLD MARKET ECONOMY

Despite its serious limitations as a theory of the market or the capitalist world economy, Marxism does raise three issues that cannot be easily dismissed and that are crucial to understanding the dynamics of international relations in the contemporary era. The first is the economic and political implications of the process of uneven growth. The second is the relationship of a market economy and foreign policy. The third is the capacity of a market economy to reform and moderate its less desirable features.

The Process of Uneven Growth

There are two fundamentally opposed explanations for the fact that uneven economic growth tends to lead to political conflict. Marxism, especially Lenin's law of uneven development, locates the sources of the conflict in the advanced capitalist economies' need to export surplus goods and capital and to engage in imperialistic conquest. Political realism holds that conflict among states over economic resources and political superiority is endemic in a system of international anarchy. From the realist perspective, the process of uneven growth generates conflict between rising and declining states as they seek to improve or maintain their relative position in the international political hierarchy.

As already argued, there appears to be no reliable method to resolve this controversy and choose one theory over the other. Both Marxism and political realism can account for the tendency of uneven growth to cause political conflict among states. Awkward facts and contrary evidence can easily be "explained away" by the use of ad hoc hypotheses. As neither of these theories appears capable of meeting the test of falsifiability, scholars of international political economy are forced to identify with one or another depending on their assumptions about the relationship of international economics and international politics.

My position on this issue is that of political realism; the process of uneven growth stimulates political conflict because it undermines the international political status quo. Shifts in the location of economic activities change the distribution of wealth and power among the states

[12] Herbert Feis (1964 [1930]) and Eugene Staley (1935) have effectively made this argument.

in the system. This redistribution of power and its effect on the standing and welfare of individual states accentuate the conflict between rising and declining states. If this conflict is not resolved it can lead to what I have elsewhere called a "hegemonic war" whose ultimate result is to determine which state or states will be dominant in the new international hierarchy (Gilpin, 1981). A realist interpretation, I believe, is far superior to that of Marxism in explaining the relationship of uneven growth and political conflict.

Thus, in contrast to Lenin's use of the "law of uneven development" to explain the First World War, one can counterpose Simon Kuznets' essentially realist explanation. In his *Modern Economic Growth*, Kuznets interrupts his detailed analysis of economic growth to inquire whether a connection existed between the phenomenon of economic growth and the first great war of this century (Kuznets, 1966).

Kuznets first emphasizes the great growth in power that preceded the outbreak of the war. "The growing productive power of developed nations, derived from the science-oriented technology that played an increasing role in modern economic growth, has meant also greater power in armed conflict and greater capacity for protracted struggle" (Kuznets, 1966, p. 344). Together, continuing capital accumulation and modern technology had enabled nations to conduct wars of unprecedented magnitude.

Second, Kuznets regards such great wars as the "ultimate tests of changes in relative power among nations, tests to resolve disagreements as to whether such shifts have indeed occurred and whether the political adjustments pressed for are really warranted" (Kuznets, 1966, p. 345). In other words, the role of war is to test whether the redistribution of power in the system wrought by economic growth has operated to change the fundamental balance of power in the system, and if the balance has shifted, then consequent political and territorial adjustments reflecting the new distribution are to be expected. In an age of rapid and continuous economic growth there will be frequent and significant shifts of relative economic, and hence of military, power. "If wars are needed to confirm or deny such shifts, the rapidity and frequency with which shifts occur may be the reason for the frequent conflicts that serve as tests" (ibid.). Thus a great war is caused by the uneven growth of state power.

And, finally, Kuznets argues that "major wars are associated with the emergence in the course of modern economic growth of several large and developed nations" (Kuznets, 1966, p. 345). A century of uneasy peace had been possible because, during much of the period, there was only one large advanced country generating economic growth. The

55

emergence of other industrialized and growing societies, especially Germany after 1870, eventually led to hegemonic war. The emergence of several large economically developed countries is the necessary, if not sufficient, condition for the occurrence of world wars. "In this sense it was a century of Pax Britannica that ended when the leading country could no longer lead and impose its peace on such a large part of the world" (ibid.). It seems impossible to say more than this about the connection between economic growth and military conflict.

Market Economies and Foreign Policy

Another Marxist criticism of a market or capital society is that it tends to pursue an aggressive foreign policy. Liberals, of course, take the opposite position that capitalist economies are fundamentally pacific. For example, Joseph Schumpeter in his essay on imperialism argued that capitalists are antibellicose and modern wars are due to the holdover of precapitalist "vestigial" social structures (Schumpeter, 1951). In a truly capitalist society, he maintained, the foreign policy would be pacifist.[13] Marxists, liberals, and nationalists have long debated the issue of whether economic interdependence is a source of peaceful relations or a source of conflict among nation-states. Liberals believe that the mutual benefits of trade and the expanding web of interdependence among national economies tend to foster cooperative relations. They believe, as Norman Angell tried to demonstrate in his famous *The Great Illusion* (1910), written four years prior to the First World War, that war has become unthinkable because it is antithetical to modern industrial society and does not pay. But for nationalists, trade is merely another arena for international competition, because economic interdependence increases the insecurity of states and their vulnerability to external economic and political forces.

From Montesquieu's statement that "peace is the natural effect of trade," through the writings of John Bight and Richard Cobden in the nineteenth century, to contemporary theorists of functionalism and economic interdependence, liberals have viewed international economics as separable from politics and as a force for peace. Whereas politics tends to divide, economics tends to unite peoples. Trade and economic interdependence create bonds of mutual interest and a vested interest in international peace and thus have a moderating influence on international relations.

The basic assumption of Marxists and economic nationalists, on the

[13] Michael Doyle (1983) has argued in an excellent two-part article that liberal economies, which he—in contrast to Schumpeter—distinguishes from capitalist ones, do in fact have a low propensity to war in comparison with other liberal societies.

other hand, is that international interdependence is not only a cause of conflict and insecurity, but it creates dependency relations among states. Because interdependence is never symmetrical, trade becomes a source for increasing the political power of the strong over the weak. Therefore Marxists and economic nationalists advocate policies of economic autarky.

The historical record does not lend much support to either position; the patterns of economic and political relations are highly contradictory. Political antagonists may be major trading partners, as was the case with Great Britain and Germany in the First World War; or, as was the case with the United States and the Soviet Union after the Second World War, they may have negligible economic intercourse. What the evidence suggests is that whether trade aggravates or moderates conflicts is dependent upon the political circumstances. Attention, therefore, should be given to interrelated factors that appear to influence the ways in which trade affects international political relations.

The first factor affecting the political consequences of trade is the existence or absence of a dominant or hegemonic liberal power that can establish and manage the international trading system. The great eras of economic interdependence have been identified with the unchallenged supremacy of hegemonic trading power such as Great Britain in the nineteenth century and the United States after the Second World War. When the domination of these powers waned and they were challenged by rising powers, trade conflicts increased.

The second factor determining the political effects of trade is the rate of economic growth in the system. Although it is true that the decline of protectionism and the enlargement of world markets stimulates economic growth, the corollary is also true; a rapid rate of economic growth leads to increasing trade and economic interdependence. By the same token, a slowdown in the rate of economic growth makes adjustment difficult, intensifies international trade competition, and exacerbates international political relations.

The third factor affecting the political results of trading relations is the degree of homogeneity or heterogeneity of industrial structure, which in turn determines the composition of imports and exports (Akamatsu, 1961). Although it is true that industrial nations trade more with one another than with nonindustrial countries, when nations have highly homogeneous or even similar industrial structures and exports, competitive trading relations and commercial conflict frequently result in periods of economic stagnation (Hicks, 1969, pp. 56-57). By the same token, heterogeneity of industrial structure tends to produce complementary trading relations. Thus, the heterogeneity of the industrial structures of Great Britain and other nations in the early and mid-nineteenth century resulted in generally harmonious trading relations. As other nations industrialized by the end of the century, commercial conflict became intense. The same phenomenon may be observed in the contemporary era, as rising industrial powers such as Japan and the newly industrializing countries (NICs) overtake and surpass the United States.

The major point to be made in these matters is that trade and other economic relations are not in themselves critical to the establishment of either cooperative or conflictual international relations. No generalizations on the relationship of economic interdependence and political behavior appear possible. At times economic intercourse can moderate and at others aggravate these relations. What can be said with some justification is that trade is not a guarantor of peace. On the other hand, the collapse of trade has frequently led to the outbreak of international conflict (Condliffe, 1950, p. 527). In general, the character of international relations and the question of peace or war are determined primarily by the larger configurations of power and strategic interest among both the great and small powers in the system.

The Significance of Welfare Capitalism

The third problem raised by the the Marxist critique of a market or capitalist economy is its capacity to reform itself. At the heart of the debate between Lenin and Kautsky on the future of capitalism was the possibility that capitalism could eliminate its worst features. For Kautsky and the social democrats, the peaceful transition of capitalism into socialism was possible as a result of the growth of workers' strength in the Western democracies. To Lenin this seemed impossible and in fact absurd because of the very nature of a capitalist economy:

It goes without saying that if capitalism could develop agriculture, which today lags far behind industry everywhere, if it could raise the standard of living of the masses, who are everywhere still poverty-stricken and underfed, in spite of the amazing advance in technical knowledge, there could be no talk of a super-abundance of capital. This "argument" the petty-bourgeois critics of capitalism [read Kautsky] advance on every occasion. But if capitalism did these things it would not be capitalism; for uneven development and wretched conditions of the masses are fundamental and inevitable conditions and premises of this mode of production (Lenin, 1939 [1917], pp. 62-63).

Leaving aside the tautological nature of Lenin's argument, what he described as an impossibility under capitalism now exists in the welfare states of the mid-twentieth century. Even if one admits that the welfare state was forced on the capitalist class by the working class, the crucial point is that it has largely addressed all three of the Marxist laws of cap-

TABLE I. Nullification of Marxist Laws by Welfare States

Marxist Law	Welfare State
(1) Law of Disproportionality	Demand management through fiscal and monetary policy
(2) Law of Accumulation	Income redistribution through progressive income tax and transfer payments Support for trade unions Regional and small business policies
(3) Law of the Falling Rate of Profit	Government support of education and research to increase the efficiency of all factors of production

italism and has satisfied most of Lenin's requirements for a reformed capitalism, that is, a capitalism that guarantees full employment and the economic welfare of the masses. The productivity of agriculture has been vastly increased through government support of research programs, the progressive income tax and other programs involving transfer payments have significantly redistributed income, and the advent of Keynesian economics and demand management through fiscal and monetary policy have moderated the operation of the "law of disproportionality" and dampened cyclical fluctuations through the stimulation of consumer demand.

In addition, government regulations and antitrust policies decrease the concentration of capital while government support of mass education and industrial research and development increases the efficiency and profitability of both labor and capital. As Joseph Schumpeter has written, capitalism is the first economic system to benefit the lower rungs of society (Schumpeter, 1950). Indeed, one can argue that capitalism has done all those things that Lenin predicted it could not do and has done so even though the reforms of capitalism embodied in the welfare state were initially strongly resisted by the capitalist class.[14] (See Table I.) In fact, the expansion of capitalism following the Second World War produced the greatest era of general economic prosperity in the history of the world.

[14] Contemporary Marxists themselves have attempted to explain this anomaly in Marxist theory by arguing that the capitalist state is semiautonomous and can take actions that, though contrary to the interests of individual capitalists, are in the interest of the preservation of capitalism as a system. Such arguments among Marxists over the theory of the state have become highly scholastic (Carnoy, 1984). These theories are not convincing and, like Lenin's theory of imperialism, are best regarded as ad hoc hypotheses that seek to explain away the predictive failures of Marxist theory rather than as extensions of the theory.

However, the Marxist critique of a capitalist or global market economy still cannot be easily dismissed; it raises an important question regarding the future of the market system. Although capitalism by itself cannot be held accountable for imperialism and war and although it has survived numerous crises and has proved that it could be highly flexible and reform itself, its continued existence is still problematic. Therefore let us turn directly to the question of the capacity of welfare capitalism to survive in the rapidly changing world of nation-states in the final years of this century.

Welfare Capitalism in a Non-Welfare Internationalist Capitalist World

Despite capitalism's successes and domestic reforms, one can reasonably argue that Lenin's fourth law of uneven development remains in force, and that this will eventually doom capitalism and the liberal market economy. It is possible that, with the advent of the welfare state, the inherent contradictions of capitalism have simply been transferred from the domestic level of the nation-state to the international level. At this level there is no welfare state; there is no world government to apply Keynesian policies of demand management, to coordinate conflicting national policies, or to counter tendencies toward economic disequilibrium. In contrast to domestic society, there is no state to compensate the losers, as is exemplified in the dismissal by wealthy countries of the demands of the less developed countries for a New International Economic Order (NIEO); nor is there an effective international government response to cheating and market failures.

In the anarchy of international relations, the law of uneven development and the possibility of intracapitalist clashes still applies. One could even argue that the advent of national welfare states has accentuated the economic conflicts among capitalist societies (Krauss, 1978). The new commitment of the capitalist welfare state to full employment and domestic economic well-being causes it to substitute interventionist policies for the free play of market forces and thereby brings it into conflict with the policies of other states pursuing a similar set of economic goals.

Welfare states are potentially highly nationalistic because governments have become accountable to their citizenry for the elimination of economic suffering; sometimes the best way to achieve this goal is to pass on economic difficulties to other societies. In times of economic crisis public pressures encourage national governments to shift the burdens of unemployment and economic adjustment to other societies;

thus, economic and interstate competition through the market mechanism subtly shifts to interstate conflict for economic and political advantage. This nationalistic struggle to gain economic advantage and to shift the costs of economic distress to others again threatens the future of international capitalism.

The issue of the future of capitalist society in the era of the welfare state is central to the question of the applicability of the core of Marx's general theory of historical development to the world of the late twentieth century. One proposition of Marx's theory was that "no social order ever perishes before all the productive forces for which there is room in it have developed; and new, higher relations of production never appear before the material conditions of their existence have matured in the womb of the old society itself" (Marx, 1977 [1859], p. 390), that is, one mode of production is not transcended by the next until it has exhausted its inherent productive potential. Each phase of human experience, according to Marxism, has its own historical mission to fulfill in elevating human productive capacities and thereby setting the stage for the phase to follow. Each mode advances until further progress is no longer possible; then historical necessity dictates that the fetters holding back society are removed by the class chosen to carry it to the next level of material achievement and human liberation.

The implications of this formulation are intriguing for the future of capitalism envisioned by Marxist theory. According to Marx, the historical function of capitalism was to develop the world and its productive potential and then to bequeath to its heir, socialism, a fully developed and industrialized world economy. Although Marx provided no timetable for this cataclysmic event to take place, he lived out his life in the expectation that the revolution was imminent.

As Albert Hirschman has shown, Marx failed to recognize (or more likely suppressed) the significance of these ideas for his analysis of the eventual demise of capitalism, that is, if no mode of production comes to an end until it plays out its historical role and if the assigned task of capitalism is to develop the world, then the capitalist mode of production has many decades, perhaps centuries or even millennia, yet to run (Hirschman, 1981, ch. 7). If one further discounts, as Marxists do, the "limits to growth" argument, capitalism's assigned task of the economic development of the planet, including its oceans and nearby space, will require a very long time indeed.

Hirschman suggests that this must have been an uncomfortable thought for Marx, who until his dying day was so frequently disappointed in his longing to see the coming of the revolution. In Hirschman's view, this explains why Marx focused on European capitalism as a closed rather than an open economy and why he failed to develop a theory of imperialism even though one would have expected this of him as an assiduous student of Hegel. As Hirschman points out, Hegel anticipated all subsequent theories of capitalist imperialism.

Hirschman concludes that Marx, in his own writings, suppressed Hegel's theory of capitalist imperialism because of its disturbing implications for Marx's predictions concerning the survivability of capitalism. If no social system is displaced by another until it exhausts the productive potential inherent in it, then an imperialistic capitalism as it expands beyond Europe into Asia, Africa, and elsewhere will add new life to the capitalist mode of production. Through the mechanisms of overseas trade and foreign investment, the inevitable collapse of capitalism may thus be postponed for centuries. Indeed, if such a collapse must await the elevation of the developing world to the economic and technological levels of the most advanced economy, then in a world of continuing technological advance, the requisite full development of the productive capacities of capitalism may never be reached.

Rosa Luxemburg appears to have been the first major Marxist theorist to appreciate the historic significance of this reasoning; she argued that as long as capitalism remains an open system and there are underdeveloped lands into which the capitalist mode of production can expand, Marx's prediction of economic stagnation and political revolution will remain unfulfilled.[15] In response to this troubling (at least for Marxists) prospect, Lenin's *Imperialism*, as noted earlier, transformed the Marxist critique of international capitalism. He argued that although capitalism does develop the world and is an economic success, the closing-in of political space through capitalist imperialism and the territorial division of the globe among rising and declining capitalist powers leads to international conflict. Thus, Lenin argued that the masses would revolt against capitalism as a war-prone political system rather than as a failed economic system.

Whether or not one accepts these several formulations and reformulations of Marxist thought, they do raise a fundamental issue. As Marx himself pointed out, the logic of the dynamics of a market or capitalist economy is expansive and international. The forces of the market reach out and bring the whole world within their confines, and they are destructive of traditional ways. The basic anarchy of the market mechanism produces instabilities in the lives of individuals and whole societies.

The modern welfare state and protectionism have developed to cush-

---

[15] Rousseas (1979) is an excellent discussion of her views.

ion these deleterious effects, and herein lies the most serious problem for the capitalist system and its survival. As Keynes appreciated, the logic of the welfare state is to close the economy, because the government must be able to isolate the economy from external restraints and disturbances in order to control and manage it. The international flow of trade, money, and finance undermines the Keynesian management of an economy by decreasing domestic policy autonomy. Goods, Keynes wrote at the height of the Great Depression, should be "homespun" (Keynes, 1933), and capital should stay at home where it can benefit the nation and the nation's working class.

Thus, the logic of the market economy as an inherently expanding global system collides with the logic of the modern welfare state. While solving the problem of a closed economy, the welfare state has only transferred the fundamental problem of the market economy and its survivability to the international level. The problem of reconciling welfare capitalism at the domestic level with the nature of the international capitalist system has become of increasing importance.

The resolution of this basic dilemma between domestic autonomy and international norms is essential to the future viability of the market or capitalist economy. How can one reconcile these two opposed means of organizing economic affairs? Which will prevail—national economic interventionism or the rules of the international market economy? What are the conditions that promote peace and cooperation among market economies? Is a dominant or hegemonic power required to resolve the conflict? A look at the past successes and failures of international capitalism reveals that temporary resolutions of this dilemma or failures to resolve it have been crucial in recent history. In the 1980s the future of the world market economy and the continuing survival of the capitalist mode of production are dependent upon solutions developed or not developed by the United States and its major economic partners.

In another guise this was the problem posed by Richard Cooper in his influential book, *The Economics of Interdependence* (1968). An increasingly interdependent world economy requires either an international agreement to formulate and enforce the rules of an open world market economy and to facilitate the adjustment of differences or a high degree of policy coordination among capitalist states. Without one or the other, a market economy will tend to disintegrate into intense nationalist conflicts over trade, monetary arrangements, and domestic policies. With the relative decline of American power and its ability or willingness to manage the world economy, this issue has become preeminent in the world economy. If there is no increase in policy coordination or decrease in economic interdependence among the leading capitalist economies, the system could indeed break into warring states, just as Lenin predicted.

The long-term survivability of a capitalist or international market system, at least as we have known it since the end of the Second World War, continues to be problematic. Although the welfare state "solved" the problem of domestic capitalism identified by Marx, continuing conflicts among capitalist societies over trade, foreign investment, and international monetary affairs in the contemporary world remind us that the debate between Lenin and Kautsky over the international nature of capitalism is still relevant. As American power and leadership decline due to the operation of the "law of uneven development," will confrontation mount and the system collapse as one nation after another pursues "beggar-my-neighbor" policies, as Lenin would expect? Or, will Kautsky prove to be correct that capitalists are too rational to permit this type of internecine economic slaughter to take place?

Conclusion

The foregoing analysis of economic ideologies leads to three general propositions. The first is that the global or territorial distribution of economic activities, especially of industry and technology, is a central concern of modern statecraft; behind the technical discussions of trade, foreign investment, and monetary affairs are conflicting national ambitions and the fundamental question of "who is to produce what and where." The second point is that the international division of labor is a product of both national policies and relative efficiency; although states can and do ignore the market as they seek to influence the location of economic activities, this entails economic costs; the price mechanism operates to transform national efficiencies and international economic relations over the long run. And third, due to these changes and the uneven growth of national economies, the inherent stability of the international market or capitalist system is highly problematic; it is the nature of the dynamics of this system that it erodes the political foundations upon which it must ultimately rest and thereby raises the crucial question of finding a new political leadership to ensure the survival of a liberal international economic order.

The Dynamics of the International Political Economy

THE MARKET system has become a major factor in shaping modern society; market competition and the responsiveness of economic actors to relative price changes propel society in the direction of increased specialization, greater efficiency, and (if liberal and Marxist predictions ultimately prove correct) the eventual economic unification of the globe. Marx observed that the market, or capitalist system, was a revolutionary departure in world history and also argued that traditional cultures and political boundaries would crumble in its path as it moved inexorably toward the full development and integration of the planet's productive capacities.[1]

Although the market system is driven largely by its own internal dynamics, the pace and direction of its forward movement are profoundly affected by external factors. The interaction of the market and environmental conditions account for much of the economic and political history of the modern world. Among the so-called exogenous variables that affect the operation of markets are the structure of society, the political framework at the domestic and the international levels, and the existing state of scientific theory and technological development, all of which constitute constraints and/or opportunities affecting the functioning of economic actors. However, the market itself affects and transforms external factors in important ways; it dissolves social structures, alters political relations, and stimulates both scientific and technological advance. An understanding of the ways in which market forces and external factors affect one another is essential to comprehension of the dynamics of the international political economy.

CONTEMPORARY THEORIES OF THE INTERNATIONAL POLITICAL ECONOMY

Three contemporary theories accounting for the emergence, expansion, and functioning of the international political economy have

---

[1] The *Communist Manifesto* is a paean to the productive and unifying power of international capitalism.

gained influence in recent years. The first, derived principally from economic liberalism, will be called the theory of the "dual" economy; it regards the evolution of the market as a response to the universal desire for increased efficiency and the maximization of wealth. The second, strongly influenced by Marxism, is best identified as the theory of the Modern World System (MWS); the world market is essentially a mechanism for the economic exploitation of the less developed countries by the advanced capitalist economies. The third, closely but not entirely associated with political realism, has become known as the theory of hegemonic stability; it interprets the rise and operation of the modern international economy in terms of successive liberal dominant powers.[2] Although these theories contradict one another in a number of particulars, they can also be considered complementary in other ways, and together they provide important insights into the reasons for the dynamics and functioning of the international political economy.

The Theory of the Dual Economy

The theory of the dual economy[3] (dualism) asserts that every economy, domestic and international, must be analyzed in terms of two relatively independent sectors: a modern, progressive sector characterized by a high level of productive efficiency and economic integration, and a traditional sector characterized by a backward mode of production and local self-sufficiency. The theory argues that the process of economic development involves the incorporation and transformation of the traditional sector into a modern sector through the modernization of economic, social, and political structures. Global integration of markets and institutions is the consequence of an inexorable movement of economic forces toward higher levels of economic efficiency and global interdependence. Individualism, economic rationality, and maximizing behavior drive out age-old values and social mores.

In this view, the rise of a market economy is the natural result of the unleashing of market forces. Human beings, in their natural tendency "to truck and barter," will expand their economic activity as external constraints are removed and opportunities unfold. Advances in communications and transportation, the development of efficient economic institutions, and the reduction of transactions costs (the costs of doing

---

[2] The expression, "the theory of hegemonic stability," was coined by Robert Keohane (1980). "Hegemony" comes from the Greek word for political leadership. In the opinion of some writers, however, it has a pejorative ring and they prefer the term *leadership* itself.

[3] Although the concept of the dual economy is as old as Adam Smith, Hicks (1969) is an excellent recent statement of the argument.

business) have led to the continuous displacement of traditional economies by modern ones. Dualism views the modern world economy as having evolved through the global expansion of the market mode of production and the incorporation of new areas into the international economy, rather than as having suddenly come into existence in the sixteenth century through an act of force by European capitalist states. The modern sector has displaced the backward sector gradually as more and more societies have adapted to the market mode of economic organization.

The primary forces at work in this process have been economic, organizational, and technological; they include innovation of new products and productive techniques, opening of new markets and sources of supply, and new means of organizing and managing economic activities (Schumpeter, 1950). The monetarization of economic life, the rise of cities, and advances in communications and transportation such as the telephone and the railroad have been particularly important; these developments have reduced the costs of economic transactions and thereby facilitated the expansion of individual markets and their integration into an evolving global economic interdependence. The process of economic evolution is driven by market competition and the price mechanism toward ever higher levels of productive efficiency and wealth maximization. Inefficient actors are forced to adjust their behavior and to innovate or else face economic extinction. The resulting expansion of markets, accumulation of capital and other factors of production, and innovation of new technologies and organizational forms have set the world on a course of continuous economic growth and global interdependence. Although this process of economic modernization may be affected in the short run by social and political developments, in the long run it is largely independent of these external influences; fundamentally, the creation of the modern world is a consequence of factors internal to the market.

The Theory of the Modern World System

The basic thesis of the Modern World System (MWS) position is that the history and operation of the international political economy can only be understood in terms of the "Modern World System," defined by one proponent as "a unit with a single division of labor and multiple cultural systems" (Wallerstein, 1974b, p. 390).[4] Each of the terms embedded in the name of this theory expresses a crucial aspect of this

---

[4] Paul Baran (1967), Emmanual Wallerstein (1974a), and Andre Gunder Frank (1969) are three of the most prominent theorists of the Modern World System.

conception of international history. "Modern" economic and political relations are believed to be fundamentally different from premodern antecedents. The "world" is a structural whole (although the term obviously does not include the entire globe) and is the appropriate unit and level of analysis. And the modern world must be understood as a "system" in which all the various parts of the structure are functionally and necessarily related, a system that operates in accordance with a set of economic laws. Proponents of the Modern World System position assert that the primary task for political economists is the analysis of the origins, structure, and functioning of this system.[5]

Although the advocates of this position are not necessarily Marxists and indeed some adherents deviate from classical Marxism in a number of important respects, the MWS theory is grounded in the Marxist conception of social reality (Michalet, 1982). First, the theory accepts the primacy of the economic sphere and the class struggle over political and group conflict as a determinant of human behavior. However, traditional Marxism focuses on the domestic class structure and struggle, and the Modern World System theory speaks of an international hierarchy and struggle of states and economic classes. Second, the analysis centers on capitalism as a global phenomenon; however, whereas traditional Marxism regards the international economy as producing development, albeit unevenly, and evolving toward global unity, the MWS theory assumes an already unified world economic system composed of a hierarchy of class-dominated states held together by economic forces and producing underdevelopment throughout the dependent periphery. Finally, this modern world economy is believed to be characterized by inherent contradictions and functions according to deterministic laws that govern its historical development, inevitable crises, and eventual demise. Traditional Marxism asserts that capitalism has a historic mission to develop the world, but MWS theorists argue that the world capitalist system underdevelops the less developed countries.

The Modern World System position is based upon the classic Marxist thesis that both the nation-state of the nationalists and the market of the liberals are derivative from underlying and more fundamental social and economic forces. Rather than being independent actors or variables, they are the consequences of a peculiar juncture of ideas, institutions, and material capabilities (Cox, 1981). State and market are the products of a particular historical epoch and are firmly embedded in a larger social matrix. The task of understanding the international

[5] Brewer (1980) is an excellent critique of this thinking.

political economy, therefore, is one of comprehending the nature and dynamics of this more basic reality of the Modern World System.

Although proponents differ with one another and the theory itself is rife with inconsistencies, the central argument is that the world economy contains a dominant core and a dependent periphery that interact and function as an integrated whole. Whereas dualism considers the advanced core and the traditional periphery to be loosely joined, if at all, in a beneficial relationship, the Modern World System theory views them as an integrated whole so that the same mechanisms that produce capital accumulation and development in the core produce economic and political underdevelopment in the periphery.[6]

In contrast to the emphasis of dualism on the tendency toward separation of core and periphery and especially on the economic isolation of large parts of the periphery, MWS theorists see core and periphery as closely connected. Modern and traditional sectors are functionally related; the latter is held back by its connections to the former. The theory of dualism is thus considered to be a myth designed to hide from the Third World the real source of its backwardness. In the words of Andre Gunder Frank, the integrated commercial networks of advanced and backward sectors necessarily lead to the "development of underdevelopment." The periphery is the source of the wealth of the core; the latter exploits and siphons off the resources of the former. According to Frank, economic development and economic underdevelopment are merely the opposite sides of the same coin:

Thus the metropolis expropriates economic surplus from its satellites and appropriates it for its own economic development. The satellites remain underdeveloped for lack of access to their own surplus and as a consequence of the same polarization and exploitative contradictions which the metropolis introduces and maintains in the satellite's domestic economic structure (Frank, 1969, p. 9).

According to this position, the international economy functions to distort the economies of the Third World. The international division of labor imposes class and state structures on the periphery and dependent economies that prevent their economic development. External relations of the society rather than internal factors are believed responsible for economic underdevelopment and the creation of weak states.

---

[6] The core/periphery formulation goes back at least to the early nineteenth century in the writings of Johann Heinrich von Thünen (Giersch, 1984, p. 107) and remains the central idea in regional economics. It is ironic that although in its original formulation the core develops the periphery, this idea has been corrupted by contemporary radical thinkers. According to most of these writings, the core underdevelops the periphery.

Contrary to the dual economy model, the more that the world economy progresses, the more difficult it is for the periphery to develop and the greater is the revolutionary effort required to escape global market forces.

Different adherents of the MWS theory emphasize different aspects, explanations, and organizing principles. Undoubtedly the most systematic and influential statement of the position is that of Immanuel Wallerstein (1974a). According to his formulation, the pluralistic balance-of-power system of western Europe was the necessary prerequisite for the emergence of the Modern World System. Until the advent of the nation-state political system in early modern Europe, the international system was characterized by successive "world empires." Capital accumulation and productive investments in these premodern imperial systems and command economies were thwarted by the absorption of the economic surplus by parasitic bureaucracies. As the market was never able to escape political control, commerce and capitalism could not reach their full potential for producing wealth and transforming society. The substitution of the nation-state system for these premodern imperial economic and political systems permitted market forces to escape from political control. The market was thus freed to develop and transform the world economy according to its own internal logic.

Although this theory of the Modern World System asserts that a pluralistic state system was the primary prerequisite for the creation of the world economy, it considers the interaction of international trade and investment to be the fundamental mechanism for the perpetuation of its structural features. This structure, according to Wallerstein, is defined by a single capitalist world division of labor. The efficient global organization of production is characterized by an expanding regional specialization based on different methods of labor control. The world economy is an international structure of unequal states that maintains the international division of labor and is responsible for the accumulation of capital in the advanced capitalist states and for the cycle of backwardness and underdevelopment in the rest.

The major components in this international division of labor are three hierarchically ordered tiers of states, differentiated by the position they have been able to wrest for themselves in the market pecking order: the core, the semiperiphery, and the periphery. The core states tend to specialize in manufacturing, the periphery is relegated to the production of raw materials, and the semiperiphery is somewhere in between. These structural features of modern capitalism, it is argued, have remained essentially unchanged over centuries. In stating his agreement with Paul Baran (1967), one of the first exponents of the position, Andre Gunder Frank sums up the essence of the position: "It is capitalism, both world and national, which produced underdevelopment in the past and which still generates underdevelopment in the present" (quoted in Brewer, 1980, p. 158).

The most important feature said to characterize this Modern World System is that, functioning as an integrated whole, it extracts economic surplus and transfers wealth from the dependent periphery to imperial centers. The components of the system, their relations to one another, and their internal social and other characteristics are determined by the overall system. There can be "no such thing as 'national development' " independent of the function of the world system (Wallerstein, 1974b, p. 390). As Theda Skocpol has observed, "the only definite dynamics of Wallerstein's world capitalist system are market processes: commercial growth, worldwide recessions, and the spread of trade in necessities to new regions of the globe" (Skocpol, 1977, p. 1078).

The following statement captures the wholistic and functional nature of the system:

The capitalist world system is divided into three tiers of states, those of the *core*, the *semi-periphery* and the *periphery*. The essential difference between these is in the strength of the state machine in different areas, and this, in turn, leads to transfers of surplus from the periphery to the core, which further strengthen the core states. State power is the central mechanism since "actors in the market" attempt to "avoid the normal operation of the market whenever it does not maximize their profit" by turning to the nation state to alter the terms of trade (Brewer, 1980, p. 165).

The original placement of a state in this inexorable international division of labor determines whether a state is "hard" or "soft." Whereas the former is able to resist external market forces, channel them to its own advantage, and can effectively manage its own economy, the latter is pliable, at the mercy of external market forces, and cannot control its own economic affairs. Thus, "soft" states and dependent economies are caught in a web of market forces from which escape is very difficult.[7]

In summary, according to Wallerstein, the modern system put into place by Western capitalism in the sixteenth and seventeenth centuries has not been altered in its essentials over the centuries. It is a system that tends to reproduce itself as the rich get richer and the poor get

[7] The concept of "hard" and "soft" or "strong" and "weak" states is a highly ambiguous one and deserves more analysis than it has so far received. I believe that the distinction can be misleading. Krasner (1978, ch. 3), Zolberg (1981), and Ikenberry (1986b) provide contrasting treatments of the subject.

poorer. Over the long term, however, it cannot escape the inevitable laws of the demise of the capitalist mode of production set forth by Marxist theory (Skocpol, 1977, p. 1078). As will be shown, this conception of the world economy has profoundly influenced many less developed countries and their demands for a New International Economic Order.

The Theory of Hegemonic Stability

According to the theory of hegemonic stability as set forth initially by Charles Kindleberger (although he preferred the term "leadership" or "responsibility"), an open and liberal world economy requires the existence of a hegemonic or dominant power. In the words of Robert Keohane, the theory "holds that hegemonic structures of power, dominated by a single country, are most conducive to the development of strong international regimes whose rules are relatively precise and well obeyed. . . . the decline of hegemonic structures of power can be expected to presage a decline in the strength of corresponding international economic regimes" (Keohane, 1980, p. 132). The hegemonic power is both able and willing to establish and maintain the norms and rules of a liberal economic order, and with its decline the liberal economic order is greatly weakened.

The key word in the preceding paragraph is "liberal," that is, the theory relates to the existence of an international economy based on the precepts of the free market such as openness and nondiscrimination. The theory does not argue that an international economy would be unable to exist and function in the absence of hegemony. International economies obviously have always existed in one form or another. Rather, it argues that a particular type of international economic order, a liberal one, could not flourish and reach its full development other than in the presence of such a hegemonic power.

The mere existence of a hegemonic power, however, is not sufficient to ensure the development of a liberal international economy. In addition, the hegemon itself must be committed to the values of liberalism or, to use John Ruggie's language, its social purpose and domestic distribution of power must be favorably disposed toward a liberal international order (Ruggie, 1982, p. 382). The domestic economic structures of the hegemon and of other societies are obviously important determinants of the disposition of states toward a liberal international economy (Katzenstein, 1976). Hegemony without a liberal commitment to the market economy is more likely to lead to imperial systems and the imposition of political and economic restrictions on lesser powers, for example, the Soviet bloc today. And, finally, "a congruence of social purpose" in support of a liberal system must exist among the major economic powers (Ruggie, 1982, p. 384). Other powerful states must also have an interest in the growth of market relations; the hegemon can encourage but cannot compel other powerful states to follow the rules of an open world economy. Thus, three prerequisites—hegemony, liberal ideology, and common interests—must exist for the emergence and expansion of the liberal market system. (These conditions are treated in greater detail in Gilpin, 1981, ch. 3.)

Hegemony or leadership is based on a general belief in its legitimacy at the same time that it is constrained by the need to maintain it; other states accept the rule of the hegemon because of its prestige and status in the international political system (Frohlich, Oppenheimer, and Young, 1971). A considerable degree of ideological consensus, or what Marxists following Antonio Gramsci would call "ideological hegemony," is required if the hegemon is to have the necessary support of other powerful states (Keohane, 1984a, pp. 44-45). If other states begin to regard the actions of the hegemon as self-serving and contrary to their own political and economic interests, the hegemonic system will be greatly weakened. It will also deteriorate if the citizenry of the hegemonic power believes that other states are cheating, or if the costs of leadership begin to exceed the perceived benefits. In such situations, powerful groups become less and less willing to subordinate their interests to the continuation of the systems.

Historically, the conjuncture of circumstances favorable to hegemonic leadership and the emergence of a liberal world economy has occurred only twice. The first was the era of the Pax Britannica that extended from the end of the Napoleonic Wars to the outbreak of the First World War. With the political triumph of the middle class, committed to the ideology of liberalism, Great Britain used its influence to usher in the age of free trade. The example of British economic success, the general acceptance of liberal ideals among the major economic powers, and the recognized benefits of trade encouraged states to negotiate tariff reductions and to open their borders to the world market (Kindleberger, 1978b, ch. 3). Similarly, the United States took the lead in promoting a liberal international economic order following the Second World War. The General Agreement on Tariffs and Trade (GATT) and the International Monetary Fund (IMF), embodying liberal principles, were established by the United States and its allies. American leadership was exercised subsequently in the reduction of trade barriers. During these eras of British and American preeminence the international market and global economic interdependence expanded.[8]

---

[8] A number of writers identify Holland in the seventeenth century as a hegemonic power, but the case is not a convincing one. Although Holland certainly was the leading

As formulated originally by Kindleberger and subsequently extended and modified by others, including this writer, the theory of hegemonic stability argues that an open market economy constitutes a collective or public good (Olson, 1965). Such a good "is one the consumption of which by an individual, household, or firm does not reduce the amount available for other potential consumers" (Kindleberger, 1981, p. 243). A road or a sidewalk is a prime example. However, because an individual can "consume" the good without paying for it, collective goods tend to be underprovided unless the interests of some actor cause it to assume a disportionate share of the costs or some agency (e.g., government) exists that can force consumers to pay for the good.

In the realm of international relations, a number of collective goods are said to exist. An open and liberal trading regime based on the Most-Favored Nation (MFN) principle of nondiscrimination and unconditional reciprocity—that is, a tariff concession made to one country must be extended to others—is an example of such a collective good.[9] Another frequently cited example is a stable international currency, because it facilitates commerce from which everyone can benefit. A third, and more debatable, collective good is the provision of international security (Jervis, 1982). Individual states, the argument runs, can enjoy these collective goods whether or not they contribute to the maintenance of the good.

According to the theory, the hegemon or leader has the responsibility to guarantee provision of the collective goods of an open trading system and stable currency. The theory assumes that a liberal economic system cannot be self-sustaining but must be maintained over the long term through the actions of the dominant economy. An open world economy is particularly threatened by the "free rider" problem, wherein cheaters benefit from the collective goods but refuse to pay their "fair" share toward providing it (Frey, 1984b, ch. 7). Also, particular states attempt to advance their interests at the expense of others, for example, by exploiting a monopolistic position. According to the theory of hegemonic stability, these temptations to cheat and exploit others too frequently overwhelm the liberal argument that a hegemon is unnecessary because trade is by definition of mutual benefit.

---

economy, it did not exercise influence over the international system comparable to Great Britain in the nineteenth and the United States in the twentieth century. The seventeenth century, it should be recalled, was the height of the first mercantilist era.

[9] The term "unconditional reciprocity" means that concessions made to one member of the GATT are automatically available to all other members. Thus, it is very close to the Most-Favored Nation principle. "Conditional reciprocity," on the other hand, means that concessions are made only to those other parties who specifically reciprocate.

The hegemonic economy, according to the theory of hegemonic stability, performs several roles crucial to the operation of the world economy. It uses its influence to create international regimes defined simply as "principles, norms, rules, and decision-making procedures around which actor expectations converge in a given issue-area" (Krasner, 1982a, p. 185). The regime prescribes legitimate and proscribes illegitimate behavior in order to limit conflict, ensure equity, or facilitate agreement (Keohane, 1982a, p. 354). The hegemonic power must prevent cheating and free riding, enforce the rules of a liberal economy, and encourage others to share the costs of maintaining the system. The gold standard of the nineteenth century and the postwar Bretton Woods system are notable examples of an economic regime in which the hegemon establishes and enforces the rules of a liberal market regime and suppresses the ever-present tendencies toward economic nationalism.

As Kindleberger has argued, "for the world economy to be stable, it needs a stabilizer, some country that would undertake to provide a market for distress goods, a steady if not countercyclical flow of capital, and a rediscount mechanism for providing liquidity when the monetary system is frozen in panic" (Kindleberger, 1981, p. 247). The hegemon must also prevent states with monopoly power from exploiting others. It must also encourage states that at least initially would lose from free trade to remove their trade barriers (H. Johnson, 1976, pp. 17, 20).

Furthermore, in a world of flexible exchange rates and integrated capital markets, the hegemon "must also manage, in some degree, the structure of foreign-exchange rates and provide a degree of coordination of domestic monetary policies" (Kindleberger, 1981, p. 247). If there were no hegemonic power to create and manage international regimes, this theory suggests, the international economy would become unstable as liberalism and free trade gave way to the forces of economic nationalism.[10]

In addition, the growth and dynamism of the hegemonic power serve as an example of the benefits of the market system and perform as an engine of growth for the rest of the system; its imports stimulate the growth of other economies and its investments provide developing countries with the financing needed for growth. Through the process of technology transfer and knowledge diffusion, it also supplies developing economies with the technology and technical expertise required for

[10] Keohane (1984a) provides a critique of the reasoning that a hegemonic power is necessary for the creation and preservation of a liberal international economy.

their industrialization and economic development. This role of the hegemon in the global process of economic growth is a cement that helps hold the system together; when this growth declines, centrifugal forces increasingly manifest themselves.[11]

Although the two hegemons in the modern world have in turn been the dominant military state in the international system, they have radiated their influence largely through the exercise of economic power. The hegemon, in the words of Robert Keohane, "must have control over raw materials, control over sources of capital, control over markets, and competitive advantages in the production of highly valued goods" (Keohane, 1984a, p. 32). The hegemon is provided with the means of leadership over other economies through control of financial capital, particular technologies, and natural resources.

Thus, although hegemonic leadership benefits those economies able to take advantage of liberalized exchange, an interdependent world economy also creates external vulnerabilites and a nexus of power relations. As Hirschman (1945, p. 16) has written, the essence of economic power, or at least one form of it, is the capacity to interrupt commercial intercourse. The actual or threatened cutoff of trade, finance, or technology can be a potent means of leverage over other states. The ability of the hegemon to exercise its power through the mechanisms of economic interdependence contributes to its governance and management of the international market economy, but, as will be pointed out below, it also enables the hegemon to exploit its dominant position.[12]

The relatively large size of the hegemon's market is a source of considerable power and enables it to create an economic sphere of influence.[13] The hegemon can gain influence over other states by opening its market to "friendly" states or denying access to "unfriendly ones." Although the utility of economic sanctions tends to be greatly exaggerated, they are the foremost example of this power.[14] As will be discussed later, the United States has also extended its hegemonic power

[11] I am indebted to Robert Walker for this observation.

[12] The relationship of interdependence and power is a complex one. In part this is the case because "interdependence" has so many meanings. Cooper (1985, pp. 1196-1200) explores numerous aspects of this subject.

[13] The concept of an economic sphere of influence is an interesting but undeveloped one. It is found, for example, in the writings of Alfred Marshall. See Choucri (1980, p. 110) for a brief discussion of the subject.

[14] In recent years much has been written on economic sanctions and related topics. My own view that economic sanctions are of little utility is discussed in Gilpin (1984). David Baldwin (1985) and Hufbauer and Schott (1985) are the best and most extensive recent examinations of the subject.

considerably through the overseas expansion of its powerful multinational corporations.

The central role of the hegemon's currency in the international monetary system provides it with financial and monetary power. Both Great Britain in the nineteenth century and, to a much greater extent, the United States in the twentieth have used to their own advantage the right of seigniorage "which is the profit that comes to the seigneur, or sovereign power, from the issuance of money" (Kindleberger, 1981, p. 248). The United States has also employed its financial power to reward friends with access to capital markets and to punish enemies through the denial of access. Also, in the case of the United States, the financial perquisites of the hegemon have been crucial to its ability to maintain its dominant position and domestic prosperity into the 1980s.

The ultimate basis of the economic strength of the hegemon is the flexibility and mobility of its economy (Hawtrey, 1952). In the long term, economic power is neither the possession of particular monopolies and/or technologies nor economic self-sufficiency, but rather the capacity of the economy to transform itself and to respond to changes in the global economic environment, such as shifts in comparative advantage or price changes. The inflexibility of the British economy in the late nineteenth century in response to the rise of new industrial powers was an important cause of its decline (Lewis, 1978b, p. 133). Similarly, the difficulties experienced by the United States during the closing decades of the twentieth century in adjusting to profound shifts in the global location of industry and the revolution in the price of energy have undermined its power and international position.[15]

Although a favorable political environment is required for the release and development of market forces, the international market tends to operate according to a logic of its own. As noted above, economic competition and the price mechanism drive the market economy toward ever higher levels of productive efficiency, economic growth, and the integration of national markets. In time, the market produces profound shifts in the location of economic activities and affects the international redistribution of economic and industrial power. The unleashing of market forces transforms the political framework itself, undermines the hegemonic power, and creates a new political environment to which the world must eventually adjust. With the inevitable shift in the international distribution of economic and military power from the core to rising nations in the periphery and elsewhere, the capacity of the

---

[15] Kindleberger (1962, ch. 7) analyzes the problem of economic transformation and its importance for adjustment to economic change.

hegemon to maintain the system decreases. Capitalism and the market system thus tend to destroy the political foundations on which they must ultimately depend.

Although both Great Britain and the United States accelerated their relative decline through their own actions, the hegemonic system is ultimately unstable (Kindleberger, 1981, p. 251). For internal and external reasons, the hegemonic power loses its will and its ability to manage the system. Domestic consumption (both public and private) and the costs of defending the system militarily rise relative to national savings and productive investment, as seen in the case of the United States (Oye et al., 1983, ch. 1). The hegemon grows weary and frustrated with the free riders and the fact that its economic partners are gaining more from liberalized trade than it is. More efficient, dynamic, and competitive economies rise that undercut the hegemon's international position and the economic surplus that had financed the costs of global hegemony (Gilpin, 1981). In time, the hegemon becomes less able and willing to manage and stabilize the economic system. Thus, an inherent contradiction exists in a liberal world economy: the operation of the market system transforms the economic structure and diffuses power, thereby undermining the political foundations of that structure.

The important and interesting question of how hegemonic decline can be inevitable, given the alleged overwhelming power of the hegemon, lies beyond the scope of this book. Suffice it to say that although all dominant powers must one day decline, they display great differences in their longevity. Venice may be said to have been the hegemonic economic power of the western Mediterranean for a millennium; British hegemony lasted over a century; and American hegemony was in decline after a brief three decades. (Some speculations on these matters are presented in Gilpin, 1981, ch. 4.)

As Kindleberger suggests (in part echoing Cooper's views discussed earlier), renewed economic stability requires either a new hegemon, an agreed-upon set of rules binding all (including the weakened hegemon), or continuous policy coordination among the reigning economic powers (Kindleberger, 1981, pp. 251-52). The declining hegemon may also seek, as did the Reagan Administration, to reassert its dominant economic and political position. If none of these options materializes, the liberal system begins to break down. Although no particular outcome is inevitable, the theory suggests that the world economy will be increasingly characterized by economic conflicts.

The extent of these conflicts depends upon the capacity of the hegemon to adjust to its decline. As the locus of economic growth and the leading sectors shift in new directions, can the hegemon develop new competitive industries? Is it able to bring its political commitments and economic power back into balance? Can the hegemon and the rising economic powers cooperate to solve the problems that inevitably attend major economic transformations? The answers to these and other questions determine whether a liberal economic order can survive hegemonic decline.

Although the liberal international regimes associated with the declining hegemon may erode, other factors such as the force of inertia, the absence of an alternative, and the residue of common interests or social purposes among the dominant powers operate to maintain the system (Krasner, 1976, pp. 342-43). As Keohane (1984a) cogently argues, the norms of the regimes themselves inhibit proscribed behavior. Regimes are more easily maintained than created, as states learn their benefits (Haas, 1980). In Kindleberger's words, "regimes are more readily maintained than established since marginal costs are below average costs; as hegemonic periods come to an end with the waning of the leading country's economic vitality, new regimes needed to meet new problems are difficult to create. . . . it took [eighty years] to create and get functioning the World Health Organization despite the clear benefits to all countries from controlling the spread of disease. And it takes work to maintain regimes; in the absence of infusions of attention and money, they tend in the long run to decay" (Kindleberger, 1986, p. 8). And just as it is more costly to create than to maintain a regime, considerable costs must be incurred to bring down a regime. Thus, as has been pointed out, the nineteenth century trading and monetary regimes continued to survive long after British hegemony began its decline with the emergence of rival powers.

With the relative decline of the hegemon in international competitiveness and other measures of economic capabilities, however, the possibility increases that a financial crisis or some other calamity will occur that will cause a dramatic collapse of the system, particularly if a divergence of interests among the major powers takes place. For example, the financial panic of 1929 and the subsequent conflictual policies of the Great Powers utterly destroyed the economic regimes that had been revived after the First World War. Although a similar eventuality is highly unlikely in the contemporary world, one should not assume that the regimes created by American hegemonic leadership are somehow invulnerable.

The crucial role of the hegemon, Kindleberger points out, is that of crisis management and not simply the routine one of regime maintenance. If a liberal world economy is to survive, the hegemon must be able and willing to respond quickly to threats to the system. For example, as Kindleberger has argued, the ability of Great Britain to be the "lender of last resort" substantially moderated the financial crises of 1825, 1836, 1847, 1866, and 1907; in contrast, its inability to play this crisis management role in 1929 and the unwillingness of the United States to take over this task of "lender of last resort" in the face of pyramiding bank failures was a major cause of the collapse of the international financial system and of the Great Depression (Kindleberger, 1986, pp. 8-9). In the final decades of the twentieth century the international economy confronts the dangers accompanying the relative decline of American hegemony. The international debt problem, the increase in trade protectionism, and other issues could trigger a crisis over which the United States and its economic partners could easily lose control. Such a failure of crisis management could once again bring down the liberal international economic order.

THE POLITICAL ECONOMY OF STRUCTURAL CHANGE

Each of these three theories provides important insights into the dynamics of the international political economy. First, it is obvious that the historical context emphasized by the MWS position is crucial in the determination of economic and political change. As already noted, the market system and the nation-state are both products of modern society and of profound changes in human consciousness, productive technology, and social forces. It is equally obvious, however, that human beings have always organized themselves into what Ralf Dahrendorf (1959) has called "conflict groups," such as tribes, empires, and city-states. In the modern epoch, as the theory of hegemonic stability stresses, nation-states and the conflicts among them are the foremost manifestation of man's nature as a "political animal." Far from being mere creatures of economic and historical forces, states are independent actors in economic and political affairs.

It should also be equally obvious that the market and "economic man" have achieved an independent reality. Once having come into existence the modern market cannot be reduced to sociological forces. Although it is correct, as Karl Polanyi has written, that the important role of the market and economic laws in the modern world is the outcome of a peculiar set of historic circumstances, the market, like the modern state, has come to exercise a powerful influence over historical developments (Polanyi, 1957). The dynamics of the international political economy must be understood in terms of the interaction of state and market within their larger historical setting.

At some future date modern social science may unlock the secrets of history and explain scientifically the interactions among social forces, political actors, and economic activities. Perhaps, as Marxists and proponents of the Modern World System theory both argue, state and market as well as other aspects of social life can be explained through the workings of historical laws. But our understanding of our own behavior is primitive indeed; rather than validated laws and theories we have conflicting perspectives and partial insights into these matters. With only a single historical example of a world dual economy or Modern World System, depending upon one's point of view, and two hegemonic systems, it is obviously impossible to prove or disprove any of these theories.

With this caveat in mind, the strengths and weaknesses of these three "theories" as means to explain and understand structural change will be discussed. My understanding of structural change and of the dynamics of the international political economy is derived from my evaluation of these theories.

By "structure," I mean simply "the parts of an economic whole which, over a period of time, appear relatively stable alongside the others" (Marchal, quoted in Hartwell, 1982, p. 102). These structures provide constraints and opportunities within which actors attempt to achieve their objectives. A major goal of states and powerful organizations is to change the structures themselves. These structures include social institutions, the distribution of property rights, the division of labor and location of economic activities, the organization of particular markets, and the norms or regimes governing economic affairs. The term "structural change" is defined as the alteration of these institutions and fundamental relationships. What, then, are the contributions of the three theories of the international political economy to our understanding of the nature of structures and structural change?

The liberal theory of the dual economy correctly stresses the important role of self-interest and the seemingly universal desire to maximize gains as driving forces in the evolution of the world economy. Whatever the underlying motive, be it greed or, as Adam Smith speculated, emulation, when constraints are removed and opportunities present themselves, human beings seek to engage in economic intercourse. The consequence of this drive to "truck and barter" is the steady erosion of traditional ways and the eventual creation of modernized economies.

In addition, relative prices and price changes play a powerful role in the dynamics of the international political economy. In the economist's universe of prices and quantities, any changes on the supply or the demand side of the economy or the innovation of new products and productive processes will cause responses throughout the system (Nelson and Winter, 1982). For example, the profound impact of the increased cost of world energy on international economic and political affairs in the 1970s was an excellent example of the potency of a price change. The market does matter in determining the structure and dynamics of the international political economy.

Another strength of this theory is the central role that it gives to technological advances in the evolution of the international political economy. Improvements in communications and transportation that reduce the costs of conducting business have encouraged the integration of once isolated markets into an expanding global interdependence. From the innovation of oceangoing sailing ships to contemporary information-processing systems, technological advances have been an almost inexorable force for uniting the world economy.

The economist's method of comparative statics, however, is very limited as a tool for understanding structural change. It lacks any means of predicting and explaining the shifts in supply or demand that cause changes in relative prices. Economists also lack an explanation of technological change. Nor can they analyze in a systematic fashion the longer-term effects of such changes and innovations on economic, political, and social affairs. Economic theory treats as exogenous and tends to ignore the institutional, political, and historical framework (e.g., the distribution of power and property rights, reigning ideologies, and technological factors) within which the price mechanism works its effects. Thus, the dual economy theory tends to neglect the political and social environment that influences and channels the evolution of the market.

The basic problem is that economists lack a theory of economic change. In the words of Walter Rostow, "the most vital and fully articulated bodies of modern economic thought have been developed within Marshallian short-period assumptions; that is, the social and political framework for the economy, the state of the arts, and the levels of fixed capacity are assumed to given and, usually, fixed" (quoted in R. Cameron, 1982, p. 29). The basic assumption of their studies is the existence of equilibrium and, as one writer has put it, history is never about "equilibrium" (Hartwell, 1982, p. 92). Economists are not generally interested in structural change nor do they have the analytical apparatus to explore it in any depth.[16]

The emphasis of the theory of the Modern World System on "the historical structure of the world political economy" also makes a valuable

---

[16] North (1981) and Northrop (1947) provide contrasting evaluations of the possibility of developing an economic theory of structural change.

contribution to our understanding of the dynamics of the international political economy (Tooze, 1984, p. 13). The setting of ideas, technology, and social forces within which state and market operate creates opportunities and constraints on political and economic behavior. The state could not exist, in fact, without the supporting ideology of nationalism; nor could the market survive without liberalism. This theory, however, is flawed by its economic determinism and its static conception of the international political economy.

According to this theory, the international political economy must be viewed as an integrated structure of core and periphery. The primary nexus of this system is the hierarchical international division of labor, which determines the place of a society in the system. The structure of the world economy is responsible both for the external relations and the internal characteristics of individual societies. The essential structure of the Modern World System, this theory argues, was put into place in the sixteenth century and has not been substantially altered over the succeeding three centuries.

The argument that the pluralist European state system was a necessary condition for the rise of a market economy is an important insight.[17] Every state has a powerful disposition to attempt to gain control over economic activities and to make them serve its ends. The sufficient conditions for the rise of a world market economy, however, were the economic, institutional, and technological developments stressed by the dual economy theorists. One cannot, for example, reduce the development and subsequent evolution of science, which has so profoundly transformed the modern world, to the propositions advanced by supporters of the MWS theory. Nor can one account for the dynamics of the international system, as this position tends to do, solely in terms of the evolution of market forces.

Although the argument of the MWS theory that the world economy should be understood in hierarchical and structural terms is a necessary corrective to the emphasis of the dual economy theorists on an egalitarian and disaggregated market, it errs in several important particulars. First, although the economic structure does significantly influence the policies of powerful states, it is equally influenced by them. Second, the nexus among states is primarily political and strategic rather than

---

[17] The first writer to argue that a pluralistic state system was necessary for the rise of a global market economy appears to have been Jean Baechler (1971) and not Wallerstein (1974a). Whereas the latter employed this idea in a radical critique of capitalism, the approach of the former is a strong defense of capitalism. As noted elsewhere in this book, writers in political economy frequently employ the same basic ideas to justify very different intellectual and political positions.

economic, and political relations provide the framework for economic activities. Third, whether a state is "soft" or "hard" (for example, Argentina and Japan, respectively) is basically a function of internal social and political factors. Fourth, as the Japanese today and the Germans before them have proven, more than anything else it is the nature of the society and its policies that determine its position in the international division of labor. Fifth, the structure of the international market has changed dramatically over the past several centuries due to the evolution of the international division of labor and the changing position of economies in the system.

The argument that the structure of the world economy has been static is patently wrong. The market economy, as Marx pointed out, develops the world. It is an evolutionary system that over time has incorporated more and more of the world. The colonial empires of the early modern period integrated a very small fraction of Asia, Africa, and the New World into the so-called Modern World System; the largest segment of the world's periphery of traditional economies, as proponents of the dual economy thesis rightly point out, lay outside the system. Until the end of the nineteenth century, in fact, Europe remained relatively self-sufficient in food and raw materials. It could feed itself and possessed most of its required industrial raw materials, especially coal and iron (Dillard, 1967). Only with the second phase of the Industrial Revolution and the huge growth of population late in the century did the European core require commodity imports; these came, however, mainly from the "lands of recent settlement" in the temperate zones and a few tropical entrants into the system (Lewis, 1978a). What the MWS theorists call the periphery remained marginal until quite recently.

In truth, the modern world system in its present form did not really come into existence until the decades immediately preceding the First World War, when the dominant industrial economies emerged. The same countries that were important prior to the First World War were still the core economies in the post-1945 period. Most of the lands that Wallerstein and others would later assign to the periphery have been largely ignored by traders and investors until relatively recently (except for slaves and precious metals). The contemporary international division of labor between the industrialized Northern core and the nonindustrialized Southern periphery actually took shape in the closing decades of the last century. As Arthur Lewis (1978a) has shown, the modern world system is less than a hundred years old.

Contrary to the views of the MWS theorists, the modern world system was a consequence of the development of the North rather than the cause of its development. It has been the rapid development of the core and its need for food and raw materials that has led to the integration of the periphery into the system and the subsequent growth of those peripheral economies that could take advantage of this fact. As one Marxist economist has argued, modern capitalist economies have not been dependent upon exploitation of the periphery for their development, and the growth of the capitalist economies was due to the achievement of internal efficiency (Brewer, 1980, pp. 170-71). The Northern core has served as an engine of growth for the South throughout this history. The world economy diffuses rather than concentrates wealth.

Although it is appropriate to view the world economy as a hierarchical structure or system composed of core and periphery, it should be noted that the geographic locus of the core and the global distribution of economic activities have shifted continuously over the past three centuries, from the Mediterranean to the North Atlantic and, in our own age, toward the Pacific. The emergence of new industrial powers in Asia and Latin America is transforming the international division of labor and has resulted in profound changes in the leadership and nature of the international political economy.[18] Providing a better understanding of the causes and consequences of this dynamic process is a major challenge.

One strength of the theory of hegemonic stability is its focus on the role of the nation-state system and that of international political relations in the organization and management of the world economy. Although the MWS theory is obviously correct that the modern nation-state is ultimately the product of historical forces, the nation-state and its actions cannot simply be reduced to economic forces. Once the nation-state exists, it behaves in accordance with the logic of the competitive state system.

The theory of hegemonic stability begins with recognition of the intensely competitive nature of international relations. The modern nation-state is first and foremost a war-making machine that is the product of the exigencies of group survival in the condition of international anarchy. The security and political interests of states are primary and determine the international context within which economic forces must operate. The expansion and success of the market in integrating modern economic life could not have occurred without the favorable political environment provided by the liberal hegemonic power.

---

[18] Braudel (1979) develops this important theme of the shifting locus of the core of the international political economy.

Since its original formulation by Kindleberger, the theory of hegemonic stability has been subjected to intense criticism, some of which has been warranted, revealing its limitations. Others, however, have grossly misinterpreted the theory. There is confusion about its nature, about its actual content, and especially about the significance of hegemonic decline for the continuation of a liberal international regime. My position follows.

The phrase, "the theory of hegemonic stability," was formulated originally by Robert Keohane to refer to the ideas of a rather diverse group of scholars regarding the relationship of a dominant economy and a liberal international system (Keohane, 1980). Unfortunately, this expression implied a much more unified, systematic, and deterministic "theory" than was intended by its proponents; thereby, many of its subsequent opponents were easily misled. (It is noteworthy that Keohane himself, a critic of the theory, is frequently identified as one of its major proponents.)

The theory of hegemonic stability in its simplest form argues that the existence of a hegemonic or dominant liberal power is a necessary (albeit not a sufficient) condition for the full development of a world market economy. Contrary to the overly simplistic characterization of the theory by some critics as deterministic, the theory holds that the hegemonic political structure is permissive, but does not determine either the nature of commercial policy or the content of economic transactions (Gilpin, 1981, pp. 129-30). Commercial policy is determined primarily by domestic coalitions and interests, or what Ruggie has called "social purpose" (1982, pp. 382, 404), and economic transactions mainly by economic variables. Thus, although a pluralist and nonhegemonic system like that of the seventeenth and eighteenth centuries obviously does facilitate the growth of the world market, in the absence of a hegemon, mercantilistic competition and nationalistic policies tended to predominate. It was only after the Napoleonic Wars and the emergence of Great Britain as a liberal hegemonic power that the world entered the liberal era of free trade.

There are several versions of the theory of hegemonic stability that differ importantly from one another. My own views have changed in response to criticism by other scholars and my own reflections on the subject. Although it is not possible to examine all the issues raised by the theory itself and by its critics here, several points important to the argument of this book need to be examined.

One issue is whether it is possible to refer to "international collective goods," or whether they are merely private goods masked as public ones. Some argue that the trade and monetary regimes are not true collective goods because the number of beneficiaries is so small. The definition of a "public good" requires "indivisibility" and "nonappropriability." Some critics assert that international collective goods cannot meet these two requirements (i.e., "indivisibility"—in which the consumption of the good by one does not preclude consumption by another, or "nonappropriability"—in which no one can be denied access to the good). These same critics note that the requirements could be easily violated if, for example, the consumption of the good by one actor precludes its consumption by another, and if particular actors can be denied access to the good. Further, some point out that international actors can and do provide the goods for themselves through bargaining, mutual cooperation, and the punishment of cheaters. Therefore, some writers assert that the appropriate model for the international economy is that of a Prisoner's Dilemma or collective action problem in which individual nations cooperate and bargain to achieve their economic objectives (Conybeare, 1985).

These criticisms have merit and do weaken the collective goods argument supporting the need for a hegemon. The number of beneficiaries is sufficiently small (at least among the major economies) to facilitate cooperation and enable them to provide for themselves; it should be noted, however, that as the number of states has expanded and power has shifted toward Japan and the less developed countries in recent decades, trade and monetary cooperation have become more difficult to maintain and the free-rider problem has worsened. Also, it is true that very few *pure* collective goods actually exist in the international realm. Almost every so-called international collective good exists only with respect to a particular constituency. But this criticism can be applied to virtually every collective good. An individual may consider almost any good to be a private good; a sidewalk, which is the classic example of a collective good, is after all accessible only to those individuals actually admitted to the country. The rich may benefit the most from the police, but the poor can benefit as well. Similarly, the General Agreement on Tariffs and Trade (GATT) and the International Monetary Fund (IMF) are public goods only for their members, but a trade war or unstable monetary system would harm everyone. Even the Soviet Union can and does take advantage of a stable international monetary system.

Other critics maintain that the hegemon can exploit its position, and the theory of hegemonic stability itself is said to have a normative content. It can be used to defend the role of the hegemon as not only necessary but also beneficial (Snidal, 1985, p. 582). That is, these critics assert that the theory can be used and in fact is used to support and rationalize American imperialism and domination of other countries. Proponents of the theory of hegemonic stability, however, are fully aware that the hegemon can exploit its position for its own nationalistic ends. Kindleberger himself has been one of the most severe critics of American economic behavior in recent years, and I second these criticisms.[19]

My position is that a hegemon is necessary to the existence of a liberal international economy. Whether such an economy is conceived as a collective good or a private good shared by a particular group of states, historical experience suggests that, in the absence of a dominant liberal power, international economic cooperation has been extremely difficult to attain or sustain and conflict has been the norm. As John Condliffe (1950, p. 219) has written, referring to the liberal system of the nineteenth century, "leadership in establishing the rule of law lay . . . as it always lies, in the hands of the great trading nations." British power and interest tried to maintain an open and integrated world economy throughout much of the century, but as British power waned, so did the fortunes of the liberal world economy. With the outbreak of the First World War, the liberal world economy collapsed. Following the war, efforts to revive the liberal system broke down as economic nationalism, "beggar-my-neighbor" policies, and imperialistic rivalries spread. Protectionism and economic nationalism are once again threatening the liberal international economic order with the relative decline of American power.

It is valid to probe the motivations that the hegemon may have to create and sustain a liberal international economy. Proponents of the theory posit motives ranging from cosmopolitan to enlightened self-interest (Krasner, 1982a, pp. 198-99). For example, whereas Kindleberger tends to view the hegemon as motivated by cosmopolitan economic goals, I believe that the United States has been motivated more by enlightened self-interest and security objectives. The United States has assumed leadership responsibilities because it has been in its economic, political, and even ideological interest to do so, or at least it has believed this to be the case. To secure these long-term interests the United States has been willing to pay the short-term and additional costs of supporting the international economic and political system.

[19] Americans tend to argue that the United States made economic concessions to achieve political goals; West Europeans more frequently take the opposite view. Many believe, for example, that the United States exploited its postwar technological monopolies. Although there is some basis for the European position, the United States certainly has been constrained by its allies from taking even greater advantage than it has of its dominant economic position.

However, because of the free-rider problem, the hegemon does tend to pay far more than its share of the costs of maintaining the public good over the long run (Olson and Zeckhauser, 1966). In addition, economic benefits to other states may be disproportionately favorable because of the larger size of the hegemon's market. The hegemonic country as a whole (in contrast to particularistic interests) can lose economically through the opening of its market (Conybeare, 1985, p. 74). Indeed, during much of the postwar era the United States has created and maintained an international economy advantageous, perhaps disproportionately so, to other countries.

The hegemon, however, can and may exploit its position so that it "exerts power to produce a result more favorable to it than if that power had not been exerted" (Kindleberger, 1981, p. 245). It can become coercive and attempt to improve its own position through the use of optimum tariffs, currency manipulation, or other interferences in economic relations (Young, 1982). As John Conybeare has argued, "the first best policy for the hegemon is to apply optimal trade restrictions" and thereby improve its terms of trade (Conybeare, 1985, p. 74). This argument assumes that the maximization of economic gain is the highest priority of the hegemon. The possibilities of retaliation and of negative effects on relations with friendly states and political allies and the ideological commitment to liberalism inhibit the hegemon's use of this strategy. Yet the hegemon is increasingly tempted to take advantage of its position as its power declines, as has occurred with the United States in the 1980s.

Throughout most of the nineteenth century, the British followed the path of self-restraint and frequently even took actions contrary to their own economic interests. Indeed, one might even argue that the British were excessively bound by their liberal ideology and consequently suffered economically. They could have taken a number of interventionist measures to arrest or at least slow their economic decline (Stein, 1984). It was only in the 1930s and in response to the Great Depression that they began to subordinate their liberal internationalism to more narrowly nationalistic goals.

When the United States launched the Bretton Woods system of fixed exchange rates, implemented the Marshall Plan, and took the lead in the GATT negotiations on trade liberalization, it acted in enlightened self-interest. The United States as well as other countries gained through the lowering of trade and other economic barriers. At least into the mid-1960s and following the implementation of the Kennedy Round of tariff reductions, the United States undoubtedly gained substantially from liberalization because of its technological monopolies and strong competitive position in world markets. At the same time, it should be recalled, in the interest of alliance solidarity, the United States for most of tbe postwar period tolerated European and Japanese discrimination against its exports.

The United States had ideological, political, and strategic motives to seek a liberal world economy; it desired to promote its values abroad, to create a secure international order, and to strengthen political ties with its allies. For two decades following the Second World War, the United States, largely for political and security reasons, subordinated many of its parochial economic interests to the economic well-being of its alliance partners. With certain notable exceptions, such as the economic containment of the Soviet bloc or demanding national treatment for American multinational corporations, in the early postwar years the United States eschewed the temptation to exercise its political and economic power for nationalistic ends. Indeed, the United States created an international economy of which others could take full advantage.

In the late 1960s, however, the United States began to pursue economic policies that were more self-centered and were increasingly denounced by foreign critics (Strange, 1985c, p. 256). Beginning with the escalation of the war in Vietnam and continuing in the Reagan Administration, with its massive budget deficit, the United States exploited its hegemonic position in ways that released inflationary forces and contributed to global economic instability. Although other countries can certainly be faulted for equally self-serving behavior, the American hegemon undermined its own legitimacy and the acceptance of its rule when it failed to fulfill what others considered to be its leadership responsibilities. By the 1980s, the United States was pursuing protectionist, macroeconomic, and other policies that could be identified as appropriate to what Conybeare has called "a predatory hegemon" (Conybeare, 1985, p. 406). With its relative decline, the United States began to shift from a benevolent to a predatory hegemon, a change that will be discussed in Chapter Ten.

Although the hegemonic system does provide some collective goods for some states, it also contains characteristics of the classic Prisoner's Dilemma, that is, states may have an incentive to cooperate, but they also have an incentive to cheat and thereby increase their relative gain (Conybeare, 1984). As the hegemon declines, these latent conflictual elements come increasingly to the fore; as they do, the Prisoner's Dilemma model, rather than the collective goods model, becomes an applicable description of the system. Controversies arise over the fact that a nation may have access to foreign markets without reciprocation or that it may pursue macroeconomic policies that put other countries at a disadvantage. Bilateralism, discriminatory policies, and economic nationalism begin to supplant liberalism.

Perhaps the most misunderstood and controversial aspect of the theory of hegemonic stability is the significance of the decline of the hegemon for the continued openness of the international economy. The theory is not, as critics charge, deterministic. What it says about openness and closure is that "a hegemonic distribution of potential economic power is likely to result in an open trading structure" (Krasner, 1976, p. 318), and "the tendency toward breakdown or fragmentation of the system greatly increases with the relative decline of the [hegemon]" (Gilpin, 1975, p. 73). This obviously does not preclude continued international cooperation in a period "after hegemony" (to use Keohane's phrase [1984a]), *provided* that the interests and social purposes of the major economic powers are congruent (Ruggie, 1982, p. 384). The theory does not say that international cooperation is impossible in the absence of hegemony. To quote Kindleberger, the author of the theory, some countries might "take on the task of providing leadership together, thus adding to legitimacy, sharing the burdens, and reducing the danger that leadership is regarded cynically as a cloak for domination and exploitation" (1981, p. 252). What the theory does say is that this scenario is unlikely and that, with the decline of the hegemon, the preservation of a liberal international regime (with emphasis on the term *liberal*) will be much more difficult.

The theory of hegemonic stability (at least in its more crude forms) has tended to overemphasize the role of the state and of political factors in the existence and operation of the international market economy. It has underemphasized the importance of motivating ideologies and domestic factors, of social forces and technological developments, and of the market itself in determining outcomes.[20] Whether its proponents ever intended it to be or not, critics have assessed and criticized it as a general theory of international political economy (Lake, 1984). They have correctly noted its limited scope, its inability to demonstrate a close asssociation between power and outcome, and its failure to predict when and how the hegemon will act in particular instances (Keohane, 1984a, ch. 3).

I consider the theory to be a necessary corrective to the complete focus on economic factors of the dual economy and Modern World System theories. The hegemonic stability theory sets forth the political

[20] I am endebted to Joanne Gowa for first making me aware of this significant limitation of the theory of hegemonic stability.

conditions for the existence of a liberal international economic order and the idea that the rise and decline of the hegemon is an important determinant of structural change. It thus contributes one element to an understanding of the dynamics of the international political economy.

THE MECHANISMS OF STRUCTURAL CHANGE

Religious passions, social institutions, and material conditions (resources and technology) motivate people and create the constraints and opportunities for human action, as Max Weber, Karl Polanyi, and others have taught us. In the modern West, the ideologies of secularism, liberalism, and nationalism, the spread of democratic societies, and the continuing industrial revolution have led to the emergence of the market and the nation-state as the primary means of organizing economic and political life. Yet, as Marxists and other critics of capitalism properly remind us, these social forms are the product of particular historical forces that may one day pass from the scene. The spread of socialist ideas, the growing importance of non-Western and nonliberal societies, and technological developments could undermine either or both of these institutions. Nevertheless, market and state are well entrenched in the present period and will continue to be the most dynamic factors in contemporary society into the foreseeable future.

Within the historical setting of constraints and opportunities, state and market interact to create the structure of the international political economy, that is, those relatively enduring aspects of the world economy that include the international division of labor, the network of trade, and the international monetary and financial system as well as rules or regimes governing these economic activities. These structures tend to reflect both the power of actors and the operation of market forces.

Throughout history these structures have been created following the great or hegemonic wars, which have determined the international hierarchy. As Wallerstein, Braudel, and others have noted, prior to the era of the nation-state, imperial structures or "world empires" tended to characterize international economic and political relations. In the modern world, the structures of the international political economy have been the consequence primarily of the actions of successive hegemonic nation-states. These core economies—Great Britain in the nineteenth century and the United States in the twentieth—have used their military and economic power to establish liberal international market economies (Gilpin, 1981).

Although reflecting the interests of dominant economies, these successive economic and political structures have also provided opportunities for the growth and expansion of other economies. As time passes, changes in the social environment, in the distribution of economic and military power, and in the interests of economic actors undermine the foundations of the structure; actors who would benefit from changes attempt to reform the old structure or create a new one by altering the trading, monetary, and other aspects of the international economy and of its governing rules. The economic actors who would lose from changes, including the declining hegemon, resist such demands or attempt to alter the structure to benefit themselves. This inevitable conflict between rising and declining powers is eventually resolved either through a resort to force or through peaceful adjustments that result in a new or reformed structure that reflects the changed array of national interests and the distribution of military and economic power.

Underlying the mechanism of structural change is the fact that although the market system does promote the economic and political development of the world, it does not do so evenly. Indeed, the process of economic growth is uneven in several respects. The growth rate varies considerably from one region of the globe to another, and the primary locus of growth shifts from one country and region to another. Various sectors of an economy also grow at different rates, and the high-growth sector shifts, in time, from less to more technically advanced industries; leading, trailing, and declining economic sectors exist in every economy. Furthermore, the rate of economic growth is uneven over time; it fluctuates from periods of slow to rapid growth. These three fundamental tendencies in any growing economy undermine the existing structure of the international political economy and create challenges that must be met if the economy is to remain stable.

Uneven Growth among National Economies

Every economy is a hierarchical structure composed of a dominant core (or cores) and a dependent periphery.[21] Whether it is a city, region, or country, the core is the growth pole of the economy, drawing resources (food, raw materials, and labor) from the periphery and supplying goods, services, and markets to the periphery. The core expands and incorporates an ever-greater periphery into the economic system as industry and other economic activities grow. Although there are wide-ranging variations of this expanding interdependent relationship, the division of labor between dynamic core and dependent periphery is a universal characteristic of every economy (Friedmann, 1972).

[21] The following paragraphs have been adapted from Gilpin (1975).

93

This process of growth has two opposed consequences for the distribution of wealth, power, and economic activities within the economy. On the one hand, what Gunnar Myrdal has called the "backwash" and Albert Hirschman the "polarization" effect takes place: capital, industry, and economic activity tend to concentrate in the core. On the other hand, in opposition to this agglomeration effect, there is a tendency for a "spread" (Myrdal) or "trickling-down" (Hirschman) effect to take place; that is, wealth and economic activities diffuse from the center or growth pole to the periphery and distribute themselves at new nodal points in the system.[22] As David Hume was undoubtedly the first to note and as later economists have stressed, a powerful tendency exists for industry to migrate toward cheaper pools of labor and natural resources.[23]

The opposing tendencies of concentration and spread are of little consequence in the liberal model of political economy. Furthermore, due to the absence of political or other boundaries within domestic societies, these opposed tendencies are not of crucial significance within domestic societies. Despite the possibility of temporary dislocations, the movement of labor and capital between core and periphery within a domestic society tends to produce an economic and political equilibrium as labor moves freely from the periphery to the core and capital from the core to the periphery, thereby equalizing wages and rates of return. In the international realm, however, where political boundaries divide core and periphery and restrict the free movement of labor and capital, the process of concentration and spread has profound political implications. It releases powerful forces of economic nationalism, first in the periphery and perhaps subsequently in the core.

The initial advantage of the core over the periphery is its technical and organizational superiority, and this advantage underlies the division of labor between the advanced industries of the core and the low-technology and raw material producers of the periphery. Because of its lead in innovation and its industrial superiority, the center tends to enjoy favorable terms of trade with its economic partners. The greater efficiency and consequently higher rates of profit and capital accumulation are the most important reasons for the rapid economic growth and the concentration of wealth and power in the core. In the short term, therefore, and in the absence of political resistance by peripheral states,

[22] This discussion is derived from the writings of Hirschman (1958) and Myrdal (1971) on the spatial aspects of economic growth.

[23] On the historic tendency of industry to spread geographically, see H. Johnson (1968). The reference to Hume comes from an essay by Lewis (1957, p. 582). Those observations are directly counter, of course, to the views of dependency theory.

the polarization effects at the core tend to predominate over spread effects to the periphery.

Over the longer term, however, the rate of growth in the core tends to slow and the location of economic activities tends to diffuse to new growth centers in the periphery. For a variety of reasons, such as the increasing cost of labor and declining marginal returns on investment, the core begins to lose its dynamism and competitive advantage. Simultaneously industry spreads from the core to the periphery through the mechanisms of trade, investment, and the transfer of technology. In this process of diffusion, the periphery enjoys the "advantages of backwardness": lower labor costs, the most modernized plants, and expanding investment opportunities (Gerschenkron, 1962). As a consequence, newly industrializing cores in the former periphery eventually displace the old core as the growth poles of the system.

As a number of writers have observed, the growth and evolution of the market system is to a considerable extent a frontier phenomenon.[24] Economic growth is promoted through the discovery of new sources of food and raw materials and the development of new markets at the frontier or periphery of the system. In previously untapped regions, profits and monopoly rents tend to be higher than in already developed regions. Furthermore, technological advance and other forms of innovation frequently function, for example, with novel modes of transportation or communications, to open up the economic frontier through the reduction of transaction costs. As traditional Marxists in particular have appreciated, this continual expansion into peripheral frontiers gives new vigor to capitalism at the same time that it develops the frontiers and creates new economic competitors.

The diffusion of economic activities and the growth process, however, does not take place evenly throughout all of the periphery. The distribution of raw materials, the existence of entrepreneurial skills, and the networks of communications as well as the policies of governments and other factors favor one area over another. Nations commence their development at different times and grow at different rates, and spread takes place unevenly in the form of new concentrations of economic power and wealth (Hawtrey, 1952, p. 70). In time, what was an undifferentiated part of the periphery becomes a growth pole in its own right and may even become a center for the further diffusion of economic growth.

[24] Economic growth as a frontier phenomenon is a frequent theme in historical writings and is closely related to the expansionist tendency of a market system. See, for example, the many writings of William McNeill on historical patterns. Di Tella (1982) presents a systematic analysis of this subject.

95

This process of uneven growth among national economies in a liberal world economy results in an increasing economic and political differentiation of states and creates an international hierarchy of wealth, power, and dependency relations among emergent core economies and periphery economies dependent upon the former for the major sources of their growth. Powerful nationalistic reactions are stimulated as new centers of economic growth arise and other economies decline. Individual states and economic interests attempt to counter and channel the operation of economic forces.

In effect, economic nationalism arises in the periphery as a protective measure against those market forces that first concentrate wealth and then divide the international economy into advanced core and dependent periphery. Economic nationalism reflects the desire of the periphery to possess and control an independent industrial core in which wealth, attractive careers, and power are located. Its objective is to transform the international division of labor through industrialization and to transform the peripheral nation into a relatively independent industrial core. As industrialism spreads to the periphery and creates new sources of competition, the core may become protectionist in an attempt to slow or arrest its industrial decline.

Because of the initial industrial superiority and competitive advantages of the core, the later the industrialization of the periphery the greater the effort necessary to develop viable industries and to break into world markets. There is a corresponding need for a strong national authority or "hard state" to offset the market forces that tend to concentrate wealth, economic activity, and power in the core. Although the spread of growth, as well as the concentration of wealth, can be explained in large part by market forces, the existence of some centralized political authority or strong state that can counteract the economic power of existing centers and the centralizing tendency of market forces is a necessary condition for spread to take place at the rate desired by the periphery.

Once set upon the course of industrialization, however, the late industrializers enjoy the "advantages of backwardness" mentioned earlier, which eventually enable them to surpass the rate of growth of the industrial leader. Utilizing the most advanced and efficient techniques and lessons learned by the more advanced economies, the late starters catch up with and may, in fact, overtake the industrial leaders, in time shifting the center of world industrial power and, of course, the international balance of military power.

As world industry and economic activities spread to rising centers of economic power in the periphery, the original core (or cores) comes under increasing competitive pressures. With relatively high wage rates and increasingly inefficient industries, its exports are displaced in world markets by those of lower-cost foreign producers. Decreasingly competitive industries begin to lose the domestic market, thereby unleashing within the declining core economy itself powerful forces of economic protectionism to defend threatened industries and the economy's position within the system. Liberalism gives way to nationalistic policies, and protectionism spreads throughout the international system. As a consequence the liberal world economy threatens to fragment into competing economic nations or regional blocs.

The process of uneven growth described here may be characterized as follows: During the early phase of an interdependent world economy, polarization effects predominate over spread effects. Over time, however, due to the growth of efficiency in the periphery and to increasing diseconomies in the core, spread overtakes polarization. Certain peripheral economies grow and industrialize at a more rapid rate than the core. As this happens, the competition between rising peripheral economies and declining core economies intensifies, thereby threatening the stability of the liberal economic system.

The Rise and Decline of Leading Sectors

Another characteristic of economic growth is that various sectors of the economy grow at different rates; the process of economic growth is an unbalanced one. In every economy, whether regional, national, or international, there are leading or rapidly expanding sectors that pace and drive the rest of the economy, relatively stagnant sectors that exist in a state of overall equilibrium, and declining sectors, former growth sectors that have become brakes on the rest of the economy. A market economy evolves through successive structural changes produced by what Joseph Schumpeter called a process of "creative destruction" (Schumpeter, 1950).

Underlying this phenomenon of uneven sectoral growth in the modern world is the law of industrial growth and retardation or what will subsequently be called the "product cycle."[25] First described by Simon Kuznets (1930), the pattern of development of significant industrial innovation follows an S or logistics curve. The initial period is one of rapid economic growth characterized by quantitative increases in output and qualitative improvements in the basic technology; secondary

---

[25] On the law of industrial growth or retardation, see Kuznets (1930, ch. 1). This idea is basic to the concept of product cycle. Much of the argument in this section centers on this concept.

and tertiary industries are spun off and radiate growth throughout the economy. In time, however, the growth impulse of the innovation flags and the industry recedes as a generator of high rates of profit, wages, and employment. Eventually, the industry declines and is displaced by rapidly expanding industries beginning their ascent of the curve. Rising and declining industrial technologies characterize the dynamic economy and significantly affect its politics (Kurth, 1979).

Since the Industrial Revolution, the major cause of economic growth has been a series of technological innovations that have provided new opportunities for investment and economic expansion. A new product, a more efficient industrial process, or a novel mode of transportation constitutes a powerful stimulus to a particular sector of the economy. In time, however, the expansion of these "epochal" innovations, to use Kuznets's term, begins to dwindle, causing a decline in the marginal return on investment and its displacement by other new and expanding sectors (Kuznets, 1966, p. 5).

The history of the world economy over the last two hundred years is one of successive leading economic sectors. These rising and declining areas of economic activity have been responsible for the process of economic growth; they define the various phases of the continuing industrial revolution and they reshape the political landscape as well. Technical breakthroughs in steam power, iron metallurgy, and textiles propelled economic growth and resulted in the industrial preeminence of Great Britain. Subsequently, the development of the railroad and the opening of new lands in America and elsewhere in the "lands of recent settlement" provided the great stimulus to investment and growth. In the latter part of the nineteenth and into the twentieth century, new methods of industrial organization and the science-based technologies of steel, electricity, and chemicals led the process of growth, especially in the two emergent industrial powers, Germany and the United States. In the middle of the twentieth century and during the era of American hegemony, consumer durables, the automobile, and petroleum-based industries paced the world economy. In the last decades of this century, the new technologies of electronics, computers, and communications and the so-called service sectors are bringing important changes in the structure of the international economic and political system.

In the liberal model of an economy, this process of uneven sectoral growth and structural change takes place relatively smoothly. In such an economy, sectors on the steep part of the curve grow at a rapid rate and absorb the productive resources (labor, capital, and land) that are released from the declining sectors of the economy. Others are at the top of the curve, ceasing to be sources of continued growth. Still other

98

sectors are on the downward slope of the curve, declining and releasing resources that can feed the expanding sectors of the economy. Although disaggregate growth among various sectors is uneven, in the aggregate the economy continues to grow and thus ensures a steady rate of employment, profits, and economic welfare.

In the real world, however, this process of uneven sectoral growth and structural change is far from smooth. Intense conflict over resources and markets usually exists between expanding and declining sectors. Labor and capital in declining sectors resist being displaced by labor and capital in expanding sectors and become proponents of protectionism and nationalist policies. Political conflict ensues between declining and rising sectors over the control of economic policy. This political tension is especially acute when the expanding sector is located in one nation and the declining sector is located in another. In a world of nation-states and political boundaries, capital and especially labor cannot migrate easily from declining to rising sectors to find new employment. As a consequence, interstate conflicts arise as individual states seek either to promote their expanding industries or to protect their declining ones.

A major objective of states in the modern world is to be the locus of the growing sectors of the international economy. States aspire to be the source of technological innovation and to acquire industrial superiority over other societies. The possession of a technological monopoly in the expanding sectors of the world economy enables a state to extract "technological rents" from other economies in the system. In the language of contemporary economics, every state, rightly or wrongly, wants to be as close as possible to the innovative end of "the product cycle" where, it is believed, the highest "value added" is located.[26]

As Schumpeter argued in *The Theory of Economic Development*, profits and high rates of return on investment are due to the existence of monopoly (Schumpeter, 1961). In a system of perfect competition, profit would not exist. Monopoly profits tend to be highest in the expanding sectors of the economy before an initial technological advantage diffuses to economic competitors. Smith's observation that every businessman aspires to be a monopolist and enjoy monopoly profits or rents can also be applied to states. For this reason, interstate competition for growth and high value-added sectors is a major aspect of the

[26] Dixit (1985, pp. 22-23) is a good discussion of the concept of "value added" or super-profit and its utility.

dynamics of the international political economy. One of its fundamental issues is the global location of these activities.

Although these tendencies have always existed, they have become more intense and significant due to an increased rate of technological diffusion and resulting changes in comparative advantage. In this more dynamic world, leading economic sectors are destroyed with increasing rapidity, forcing painful adjustment costs on capital and labor. When this process of economic change and adjustment takes place across national boundaries, as has happened with the remarkable rise of Japanese competition in the late twentieth century, the phasing out of declining industries and creating of new growth sectors have powerful political effects.

Long-Term Variations of Economic Growth

Economic growth has been truly remarkable throughout the long-term history of the world economy in the modern age. A prolonged and massive increase in aggregate wealth per capita has taken place over several centuries. As liberals point out, the world economy has followed an upward linear growth path. This process, however, has been uneven over time just as it has been uneven with respect to regions of the world and economic sectors. This phenomenon of cyclical economic growth also has significant political effects.

The fact of uneven rates of economic growth is not a matter of serious dispute among economists. Business cycle theorists have identified a number of cyclical patterns, such as the Kitchin (about three years), the Juglar (nine or so), and (more debatable) the Kuznets (approximately twenty years).[27] Economists differ regarding the causes and dynamics of these cyclical phenomena, for example, the types of shocks that cause the economic system to depart from its equilibrium growth path and the factors that account for subsequent failure to adjust quickly and thereby to return to a state of equilibrium growth. Economists also disagree about the susceptibility of business cycles to control through fiscal or monetary policy.

A more controversial and significant problem for the world economy is the alleged existence of long cycles of economic expansion and contraction. First given international prominence by the Soviet economist N. D. Kondratieff in the 1920s and subsequently incorporated into the business cycle theories of Joseph Schumpeter and others, these "long waves" or "Kondratieff" cycles are said to be of approximately fifty years' duration. Relegated to the intellectual scrapheap by liberal econ-

[27] Lewis (1978b, p. 19) summarizes the different types of economic cycles.

omists and an embarrassment to most Marxists, the theory of long waves of economic growth and stagnation refuses to go away.[28]

According to the long-wave hypothesis, these upward and downward swings are an inherent feature of the operation of the world economy. The theory argues that the world has experienced several Kondratieff cycles since the Industrial Revolution of the late eighteenth century. From 1788 to 1815, there was an expansionary phase of economic growth and rising prices, which was followed by contraction and falling prices from 1815 to 1843. The period from 1843 to 1873 was one of expansion but, following the major depression of 1873, slower yet substantial growth and falling prices characterized the world economy until 1897. Another expansionary phase then began; it continued until the economic collapse of the Great Depression. The recovery that commenced in the late 1930s and 1940s led to the unprecedented expansion of the late 1950s and 1960s. Since 1973, economic contraction and, until the 1980s, rising prices have characterized the world economy. Kondratieff cycle theorists view the history of the world economy as one of periodic crests and troughs with the separation between one crest and the next lasting approximately fifty years.

Although Kondratieff himself associated the outbreak of major wars with economic upswings, a number of contemporary social theorists have gone further and posited a determinant and systematic linkage between such long-term economic cycles and what they identify as cycles of great wars and world political leadership.[29] Although this is an intriguing idea, the causal relationship has not been adequately demonstrated. At least, however, as the theory of hegemonic stability suggests, the existence of a "liberal" world political leader does facilitate the stability and growth of the world economy and, furthermore, the economic health of the hegemon and of the world economy more generally are no doubt closely related. (See discussion below.) For the moment, however, with the existence of "long waves" themselves in dispute, these still bolder theories connecting economic and political cycles should be regarded with some reserve.[30]

Although few economists would deny that the world economy has experienced alternating long periods of rapid growth and of relatively

[28] The revival of this theory in the 1970s led to a number of writings by Marxist and other scholars. Van Duijn (1983) provides an extensive discussion of the theory. By the mid-1980s, with economic recovery, the theory had once again receded into the background.

[29] Modelski (1978) is a systemic discussion of the relationship of long waves and political development.

[30] See Levy (1985) and Gilpin (1986) for an evaluation of this theory.

slow (or no) growth, most would dispute the interpretation that these ups and downs represent a regularized and cyclical phenomenon (Maddison, 1982, p. 72). Skeptics point out that there are too few occurrences of major upswings and downswings to establish the existence of a cycle; or, to put it another way, there are insufficient points on the curve to support any generalizations. More important, in the absence of an identifiable mechanism to explain successive periods of expansion and contraction, one must assume that they are due to random events; that is to say, what appears to be a wavelike characteristic inherent in or endogenous to the process of economic growth is really due to a variety of exogenous political and other developments. Finally, insofar as any pattern can be said to exist, it is primarily a price phenomenon in which the upswings and downswings represent rising and falling prices that may or may not affect the level of real phenomena, for example, levels of employment or aggregate output.

Yet even the skeptics believe that certain conclusions may be valid regarding these alleged long waves. They agree that the world economy has experienced a series of alternating periods of rising and of falling prices for reasons that are not well understood. They also acknowledge that periods of rising prices tend to be associated with rapid economic expansion and those of falling prices, with economic contraction. They note, however, that even during the latter times, the general trend has been continuing, although reduced, growth. Thus, although the evidence does not confirm the hypothesis of a fifty-year Kondratieff cycle, it does support the existence of alternating periods of rising and falling prices and of changing rates of economic growth.

Even though long waves may be merely price phenomena, which are unrelated to "real" phenomena, rising and falling price levels can and do have a profound impact on both domestic and international society. Prolonged periods of inflation and deflation redistribute income among social classes and can trigger social and political discontent. Changes in relative prices also alter the terms of trade between industrial and agricultural products. For example, the falling prices from 1873 to 1897 that brought hard times to many farmers, workers, and particular industries stimulated economic nationalism and a global retreat from free trade. Due to the high level of global economic interdependence and the vulnerability of domestic economies to change in the world economy, such vicissitudes transmit shocks throughout the system and cause profound economic and political dislocations.

Further, several of the economic troughs have in fact represented a profound slowing, at least momentarily, of the engine of economic growth. Although it is perhaps only a coincidence that these alternating crests and troughs have occurred approximately fifty years apart, it is important to recognize that in the three major recessions over the past century—post-1873, the Great Depression of the 1930s, and again beginning in 1973—there have been significant consequences for international relations. The recession of 1873 undoubtedly was a factor in the subsequent rapid spread of economic nationalism, commercial rivalries, and imperialistic conflict. The Great Depression with its spawning of Hitler and other dictators, was a major factor leading to the Second World War. And the slowing of economic growth in the late twentieth century has again strained global political relations. In short, the transmission of these recessions as well as other untoward economic dislocations throughout the interdependent world economy has caused individual countries to retreat into economic isolation in order to protect themselves and has also stimulated nationalistic antagonisms.

The periodization of these long swings in economic activity is a disputable enterprise at best, given the paucity of reliable data. One of the most noteworthy and helpful charting efforts is that of Arthur Lewis. Lewis has calculated that over the past century and a half, the world economy has experienced several alternating periods of extraordinary growth, good growth, and terrible growth (Lewis, 1984, p. 15). (See Fig. 1.) There have been two periods of extraordinary growth (1853-1873 and 1951-1973); two periods of good growth (1873-1913 and

FIGURE 1
Economic Growth and Political Hegemony

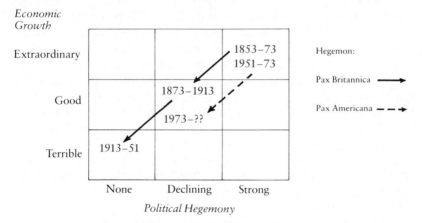

SOURCE: Adapted from W. Arthur Lewis, *The Rate of Growth of the World Economy* (Taipei: The Institute of Economics, Academia Sinica, 1984), p. 15.

1973-present); and one period of terrible growth (1913-1951), in an era that included two world wars and a severe depression. These periods are very interesting from the perspective of the theory of hegemonic stability. (See McKeown, 1983, for another view.)

Although the causal connections are unclear and debatable, it is worth noting that the periods of extraordinary growth coincided with the eras of British and American economic and political hegemony and that the periods of slower but still good growth paralleled the decline of these hegemonies. The period of terrible growth was the interregnum between these two eras of hegemonic leadership. Whatever the causal relationships, a strong association certainly exists between relative rates of global economic growth and the global political structure.

As Lewis points out, the periods of extraordinary growth have three important characteristics. First, these are catching-up periods in which other countries adopt those technological innovations within the leading sectors of economic growth that have been pioneered by the more advanced countries. For example, during the 1853-1873 period of rapid growth, continental Europe, the United States, and Japan adopted the technologies that Britain had innovated during the first phase of the Industrial Revolution: textiles, iron smelting, railroads, and the steamship. In the next rapid-growth period, Europe and Japan led the world in economic growth by adopting technologies developed by the United States during the interwar period: automobiles, electricity, consumer durables, synthetic fibers, telephones, and aircraft. Indeed, the "Americanization" of Europe and Japan and their conversion to mass consumer societies were major factors in the postwar period of rapid growth.

A second aspect of this phenomenon of alternating periods of slow and rapid growth is that the catching-up periods are preceded by slack periods and the accumulation of a scientific and technological backlog. In the words of A. C. Pigou, "there is evidence that in slack periods technical devices and improvements accumulate in the sphere of knowledge, but are not exploited till times improve" (quoted in G. Clark, 1937, p. 39). The initial period of extraordinary growth followed an era of famine, social unrest, and revolution in the 1840s, an era that depressed investment. The next period followed a series of disasters; two devastating world wars and a great depression were responsible for both a pent-up demand and a large supply of unexploited technologies and investment opportunities that led to postwar economic growth throughout the world.

A third feature of these periods of extraordinary growth is that they are characterized by a movement toward free trade under the leadership of the hegemonic economy. Preceding the surges of world trade have been periods of rapid industrialization. The repeal of the Corn Laws in 1846 witnessed British launching of an era of free trade that lasted until the revival of economic nationalism in the 1870s. Due largely to American policy initiatives, international trade expanded even more rapidly than domestic economies during the 1950s and 1960s. The two periods of growing interdependence among national economies appear to have been triggered by increasing prosperity. Economic growth undoubtedly encourages the expansion of interdependence as much or more than interdependence fosters economic growth, but the relationship between growth and interdependence is obviously cyclical.

Eventually, the completion of the catching-up process and the slowing of the global rate of economic growth stimulate forces of economic nationalism, so that economic interdependence is then challenged by increasing trade protectionism. Although particular individual countries will continue to enjoy rapid rates of economic growth, as did Germany and the United States in the latter part of the nineteenth century and as do Japan and certain other economies in the 1980s, the global rate of growth declines until new sources of economic growth and a new economic leader emerge. The era of extraordinary economic growth that ended with the decline of British hegemony in the latter part of the nineteenth century was not renewed until new sources of growth emerged at the time of American hegemony in the 1950s.

In summary, although a regularized, systemic, and cyclical pattern of expansion and contraction may not exist, the modern world economy has in fact undergone a traumatic experience approximately every fifty years and has experienced alternating periods of rapid and slow growth. These massive swings up and down have affected mainly the price level; in some cases, however, they have entailed significant changes in economic output and in the rate of unemployment. Moreover, these erratic economic shifts have been global phenomena. Originating in the core economies, their effects have been transmitted through the market mechanism and the nexus of economic interdependence to the extremities of the planet, shattering individual economies and setting one economy against another as each nation has tried to protect itself against destructive economic forces. The periods of expansion and contraction have also been associated with profound shifts in the structure of the international economic and political system.

Several prominent and contending theories have been set forth to explain these alternating periods of rapid and slow growth.[31] Each can be supported with certain facts, but none of them is flawless. However,

[31] Hansen (1964) is a thorough discussion of these theories.

since they do illuminate the dynamics of the international market system, some will be evaluated in the following paragraphs. (Because the Marxist theory of capitalist crisis has been evaluated earlier, it will not be discussed here.)[32]

One theory of economic swings is that they are closely associated with major wars. Although a number of versions of this theory exist, one of the most important is that long waves are caused by the preparation for and the aftermath of great wars. According to this view, the long periods of rising prices and economic expansion are caused by large governmental expenditures associated with preparation for war. Then, following the war, the curtailment of war expenditures and the difficult adjustments to the reduced Keynesian stimulus of the war brings on a period of economic contraction. Thus, "long waves" are intimately related to the fiscal stimulus associated with the great or hegemonic wars of modern history.

Evidence for this theory is inconclusive and contradictory. The first "long wave" of economic expansion (1788-1815) and the subsequent contraction (1815-1843) were undoubtedly a consequence of the Napoleonic Wars; war expenditures and peacetime adjustments were key to the economic fortunes of these periods. War expenditures particularly stimulated development of those technological innovations associated with the Industrial Revolution, and overexpansion of industry during the wars followed by the postwar decrease in stimulus brought on the recession phase of the cycle. However, during most of the nineteenth century and the first part of this century, the connection between war expenditures and economic activities was less strong. War preparations once again were a stimulus after 1936. The period of expansion immediately following the Second World War was unrelated to military expenditures. The Korean War provided some stimulus, as did the Vietnam War, which was followed by contraction and high inflation. On balance, one can conclude that preparations for war can exert a Keynesian or demand stimulus, provided that growth and investment opportunities exist in exploitable technological innovations or newly available resources; further, long wars usually do cause serious economic problems in their aftermath. It is very difficult, however, to establish the existence of any necessary and systemic connections between war and economic activity.

A second theory of long waves (applicable primarily to the nineteenth century) associates the waves with changes in the effective supply of the monetary gold stock and the increasing volume of trade. For-

[32] Joshua Goldstein (1985) reviews the major theories of capitalist crisis.

tuitous discoveries of gold such as the California strikes of the 1840s gave a monetary stimulus to the economy, and the increase in the gold supply from the mid-nineteenth century to 1913 is said to have led to a rise in the price level and an era of economic expansionism. This line of reasoning, however, is very difficult to support; at best, gold served as an economic stimulant because of favorable "real" factors such as existing investment opportunities and favorable terms of trade for developed economies. From this perspective expansionary American monetary policy in the postwar era has been a major factor in the high rate of economic growth.

A third theory argues that the movement of agricultural and commodity prices is primarily responsible for long waves. Food shortages, for example, increase inflationary pressures whereas food surpluses are deflationary.[33] The period from 1873 to 1896 was one of agricultural depression; this was followed by an era of agricultural prosperity (1896-1920) and subsequently by further difficulties in the 1920s and the 1930s. The stagflation of the 1970s was certainly triggered and aggravated by the rapid rise in food and energy prices. Surpluses and shortages in supply do dramatically affect the terms of trade between commodity and industrial sectors. As will be argued below, supply constraints greatly limited growth in the 1970s. On the other hand, in the mid-1980s the drop in oil prices and overcapacity in most commodities were associated with global recession.

From the perspective of this book the most interesting theories focus on capital investment and technological innovation. One theory argues that long cycles arise from massive overinvestment in and depreciation of capital goods such as railroads and factories, and another attributes them to the clustering of major innovations in particular sectors at particular times (Joshua Goldstein, 1985). Although these theories are very closely related in that innovations stimulate investment, the second will be emphasized here.

According to a theory formulated by Knut Wicksell, Joseph Schumpeter, and others, economic cycles are caused by the relative abundance or scarcity of investment opportunities. Periods of economic expansion are due to development of technological and other innovations as well as discovery of new resources that provide the basis for the growth of real investment. During such expansive periods the pace of technological advance and the diffusion of innovations to developing economies is greater than usual. Thus periods of expansionism are caused by an

[33] Rostow (1978) discusses the relationship of commodity prices and economic swings.

explosion of revolutionary new technologies and investment opportunities that sweep through and transform the entire world economy.

When investment possibilities resulting from revolutionary technological breakthroughs or discoveries of new resources are exhausted, the rate of real investment and economic growth slows, thereby ushering in an era of reduced growth. Although economic growth slows, real income usually continues to rise due to the higher levels of productivity reached in the buoyant period and to continuing marginal technological improvements. During this less active period, investment declines but general economic advance continues, although at a slower pace. The post-1973 period is characteristic of this phenomenon.

Underlying this theory is the assumption that major technological innovations tend to cluster in time as well as in space. Although technological advance in general is incremental and continuous over time, this theory holds that the revolutionary innovations that accelerate the pace of economic growth and propel the economy in novel directions are clustered. For example, the innovation of the automobile and the consequent need to build highways spurred investments in steel, petroleum, cement, and other areas. The shape of cities, the industrial base of the economy, and the landscape itself were transformed. It is such a clustering tendency of revolutionary technologies and their secondary effects throughout the economy that are said to produce the great upswings of the world economy and the successive restructuring of economic activities.

According to this theory, therefore, the first period of economic expansion (1788-1815) was the result of the Industrial Revolution and its revolutionary technologies in textiles, coal, and iron. The subsequent era of hard times (1815-1843) was one of readjustment while these technologies were incorporated into the economic system. The second period of expansionism (1843-1873) was alleged to be based on what Schumpeter called the "railroadization of the world" and the opening of new lands, especially in North America.[34] This was followed by the sharp decline of the last part of the century (1873-1897). Then a new clustering of innovations in the electrical, chemical, and automobile industries ushered in the good times of the years prior to the First World War (1897-1913). The electrification and motorization of the Western world resumed in the 1920s, only to be stopped short by the Great Depression. Following the Second World War, the electrical, chemical, and automobile industries were joined by electronics, aviation, and others to feed the investment boom of the 1950s and 1960s. The ex-

[34] This discussion is based in part on Schumpeter's writings.

haustion of growth possibilities in these technologies and the increased cost of energy are believed to be partially responsible for the drop in the growth rate in the 1970s.

In addition to the fact that technological innovations tend to cluster during particular periods, they tend to occur within particular economies. The innovative technologies of the Industrial Revolution and the first upswing—textile, steam, and iron—were located principally in Great Britain. The railroad and the mechanization of production that fed the second upswing were developed primarily in Great Britain, France, and Germany. By the time of the third upswing the front runners in the technologies of electricity, chemicals, and automobiles were Germany and the United States. In the upswing following the Second World War, the United States has been joined by Japan. If this pattern of rising and declining national leadership in technological innovation continues, Japan should be the next locus of revolutionary technological breakthrough.

The clustering of technological innovation in time and space helps explain both the uneven growth among nations and the rise and decline of hegemonic powers. The innovative hegemon becomes the core of the international economy and, as the most efficient and competitive economy, has a powerful incentive to encourage and maintain the rules of a liberal open world economy. As it loses its inventiveness, the declining hegemon is unable to maintain an open world and may even retreat into trade protectionism. For a time, the declining center (or centers) of growth is unable to sustain the momentum of the world economy and the rising center is unable or reluctant to assume this responsibility. Periods of slowing rates of growth appear to be associated with the shift from one set of leading industrial sectors and centers of economic growth to another and with the transition from one hegemonic leader to the next.

This technological theory of business cycles has a certain plausibility and may indeed explain much about changing price levels and uneven growth. However, as Nathan Rosenberg and Claudio R. Frischtak (1983) have argued, this theory presents several serious problems. In the first place, proponents of the theory do not have a satisfactory explanation of why revolutionary technologies appear to cluster, especially every fifty years or so. Second, the theory does not adequately connect the process of technological innovation, diffusion, and investment to the "long wave" phenomenon. Third, even if major technological breakthroughs do tend to cluster, it has not yet been demonstrated that these innovations do in fact exercise a measurable impact on the total economy. For Rosenberg and most economists, therefore, the apparent clustering of major innovations and the phenomenon of uneven growth constitute historical accidents determined by random events, accidents that in themselves cannot explain the experience of economic growth.

The absence of a satisfactory explanation of the phenomenon of technological innovation and its importance for uneven growth, however, does not lessen its significance. Whatever the cause may be, the growth of the world economy has proceeded as if long waves of rapid and slow growth do in fact exist. There have been alternating periods of rising and falling prices as well as eras of extraordinary growth and deep recessions during recent centuries. Economic dislocations have been global in character and have been followed by profound economic, social, and political disturbances. So, although little is known about the nature and causes of technological and other types of innovation, it is known that a strong tendency for innovations to cluster in space and time does exist. The major innovations that stimulate the growth of the dominant economy and subsequently carry the world economy into an expansionary phase tend to take place in particular national economies and at particular times. This clustering phenomenon helps account for the rise of the dominant economy and its crucial role as an engine of growth in the larger world economy. In time, however, the impetus provided by this burst of innovation recedes and the rate of world economic growth slows. The revival of economic growth appears to require a novel cluster of innovations and, it would appear, a new dominant economy to lead the world economy.

In a truly liberal world economy, the inevitable shifts in the locus of innovation underlying the process of uneven growth would proceed with little difficulty. Centers of innovation would rise and decline depending solely upon considerations of relative efficiency and comparative advantage. As old centers declined, they would release their underutilized resources of capital and labor to the rising centers of economic growth. The rising centers would in turn be receptive to absorbing such surplus capital and labor. Investment capital and unemployed workers would be free to migrate from declining to rising national centers of innovation and economic growth.

In the real world of nation-states and political boundaries, the transition from one center of innovation and growth to another is anything but smooth. It is highly conflictual as declining states and economic sectors resist the forces of technological change, and rising states and economic sectors try to break down trade and other barriers. Since capital and especially labor are unable to move freely throughout the system, structural rigidities prevent easy adjustment to emergent economic reality. Inefficiencies, bottlenecks, and restrictions slow the rate of adjustment and economic growth.

Instead of an easy transition from one industrial leader to another and a phasing out of dying industries, periods of structural change tend to be characterized by intense nationalistic competition. The newly industrializing countries, following in the footsteps of their predecessors, adopt the latest technologies and eventually challenge previous leaders in world markets; the old try to maintain their position and preserve their threatened industries. Consequently, the resistance to adjustment in the declining industrial sectors gives rise to intense trade protectionism. In the rising industries, potential technological leaders scramble for dominant positions, and trade rivalries become fierce. As Michael Beenstock has pointed out, these phenomena are symptomatic of the transition from one structure of global economic relations to its successor (Beenstock, 1983). In the late nineteenth century, in the 1920s, and again in the 1980s, transitions from one global industrial structure to another have been characterized by intensive commercial conflict. Structural crises of this type appear to be an inherent feature of the modern world political economy.

Over the past two centuries, technological innovation, population growth, and the development of new territories and associated resources have propelled the growth of the market economies. They have provided investment opportunities that have led to continuing capital accumulation. This growth of the Western economies has, on balance, stimulated growth in the less developed economies. The socialist economies have benefited through trade and adapting Western innovated technologies to their own development needs; few novel technologies have in fact originated in the Soviet Union and its bloc. When such factors as technological innovations, demographic growth, and discovery of new resources have coincided, the world has experienced the growth spurts of the mid-nineteenth and twentieth centuries. When one factor or another has been deficient, the engine of growth has slowed in the Western economies and subsequently throughout the entire globe. This process of uneven growth has provided much of the dynamics of modern history.

Structural Change and Economic Conflict

The process of uneven growth and structural change is accompanied by intermittent periods of economic cooperation and conflict. The history of the world economy has been one of vibrant eras of liberalism, openness, and free trade followed by eras of stagnation, protectionism, and nationalist conflicts. Although the theories associated with the political economy of trade and protection are helpful, those theories that stress interest groups and other domestic factors are only partial explanations.[35] In addition, it is necessary to consider structural change at the international level. A recent formulation, originally set forth by Gautam Sen and extended here, may provide insight into the process by which structural change causes economic conflict (Sen, 1984).

According to this theory, all states want to possess modern industries because of the linkages among industry and overall economic development, the goal of economic self-sufficiency and political autonomy, and the fact that industrialism is the basis of military power and hence of national independence. This nationalist desire for industrial power leads states to promote industrialization based on the importation of foreign technologies. The less developed economy attempts to acquire the most advanced technology from the hegemonic power and from other highly developed economies. As Marx noted, "the country that is more developed industrially only shows, to the less developed, the image of its own future" (quoted in Sen, 1984, p. 15). The follower has the great advantage, moreover, of being able to skip economic stages and to overtake the industrial leader.

The political consequences of this diffusion of comparative advantages and of the rise of new industrial powers are powerfully affected by the speed at which the changes take place and how long is required for the rising challenger to take a significant share of world markets. The shorter the period, the greater will be the adjustment problem imposed on other states and the greater the resistance of domestic interests. Rapid shifts in comparative advantage give rise to intense economic conflicts between rising and declining economies.

In the modern world, four nations have captured substantial shares of international trade in manufacturing in relatively brief periods. The first was Great Britain after the Napoleonic Wars and continuing late into the nineteenth century. The second was Germany between 1890 and 1913, and the third was the United States, also beginning in 1890 and greatly accelerating in the twentieth century. The contemporary era is witnessing the spectacular rise of Japan as a trading power (Lewis, 1957, p. 579). The resultant impact of the export drives and the dislocations caused to other economies have generated strong resistance and deep resentment.

As Lewis points out, the process of diffusion was well understood by David Hume in the mid-eighteenth century: "Manufactures gradually

[35] See R. Baldwin (1984b, ch. 12) for a good summary of this literature.

shift their places, leaving those countries and provinces which they have already enriched, and flying to others, whither they are allured by the cheapness of provisions and labour" (quoted in Lewis, 1957, p. 582). Then technological imitation and the creation of similar industrial structures lead to a global overcapacity in particular sectors and trade conflict.[36]

Although advanced countries trade with one another more than with nonindustrialized countries, the creation of highly homogeneous industrial structures can cause commercial conflict in a number of manufacturing sectors. This is a recurrent feature of the world economy.[37] In Sen's words, "the reproduction of similar structures of production introduces a secular tendency towards the creation of surplus capacity in substantial areas of manufacturing since internal and external economies of scale compel a level of production which most countries cannot sustain through domestic consumption alone" (Sen, 1984, p. 158).

Initially, the less developed economy pursues nationalist policies in order to protect its infant industries and overcome the advantages possessed by the earlier industrializers. Eventually, it must attempt to break into world markets to achieve efficient economies of scale and to obtain foreign currency to finance imports of required resources and capital goods (Sen, 1984, pp. 157-58). To the extent that this industrialization is successful, the developing economy, with its lower wage structure, undercuts the industrial position of the more advanced economies. The resulting generation of surplus industrial capacity in the world economy is intimately related to the process of the relative industrial decline of the hegemon, intensified trade competition, and the possible onset of a global economic crisis.[38]

The problem posed for the hegemon by the spread of industrialization was recognized by the early nineteenth-century British critics of free trade who argued that other nations, as they industrialized, would close their markets to British goods and become Britain's competitors in world markets. Since the spread of industrialism would mean the inevitable decline of British industry and power, these critics said that the diffusion of British technology should be prevented (Gilpin, 1975, pp. 74-75). This argument, which can be labeled the Torrens thesis after

[36] Beenstock (1983) presents an interesting theory of these recurrent global economic crises.

[37] Akamatsu (1961), Hicks (1969), and Lewis (1957), among others, make this argument.

[38] Contrary to the view of Peter Cowhey and Edward Long (1983) that the theory of hegemonic stability and the theory of surplus capacity are alternative interpretations of economic crisis, they are really complementary explanations.

Robert Torrens, its foremost proponent, held that "as the several nations of the world advance in wealth and population, the commercial intercourse between them must gradually become less important and beneficial" (Torrens, 1821, p. 288). This idea has been revived in more recent times as the "law of diminishing trade."[39]

The weakness of the Torrens thesis is that it takes into account only the negative consequences for trade of the spread of industry. It neglects the fact that the diffusion of industry from advanced to developing economies has opposed effects (Hirschman, 1952, pp. 270-71). On the one hand, the spread is market-destroying as the newly industrializing countries become able to meet their own needs and eventually appear as competitors in world markets. On the other hand, the spread on industry is market-creating as the newly industrializing countries import capital goods from the advanced countries and, with increasing wealth, their total demand increases for both domestic and imported products. The overall growth in global wealth and volume of trade will thus be generally beneficial for all countries (League of Nations, 1945).

Whether the trade-destroying or trade-creating effects of the spread of industrialism will predominate in a particular situation depends upon a number of specific factors: the flexibility of the older industrial centers and their capacity to adjust to more advanced industries and exports, the nature and extent of protectionism, and the rates of economic growth in developed and less developed economies. These factors determine whether the hegemon and other advanced countries will try to protect their threatened industries or will transform their economies to the new international economic realities.

The paradox of this situation is that the hegemon, and other advanced economies for that matter, must run faster and faster to maintain their economic position. They must continually adjust their economic structures and shift resources out of declining sectors into new ones. For a society this poses what one author has called the "clash between progress and security" (Fisher, 1935). A powerful temptation exists to elect the latter. In the 1930s, this refusal to adjust was a major cause of the severity and longevity of the Great Depression.

The response of the threatened hegemonic power and other declining economies to shifts in the location of industry is therefore a crucial factor in determining whether economic conflict or adjustment takes place

---

[39] The "law of diminishing trade" is a recurring theme in the literature. Actually the opposite is the case, provided that political circumstances are favorable to the expansion of trading relations. Technological advances, especially in transportation and communication, have in fact made more types of goods and services tradeable and have thereby increased international economic interdependence.

(Ikenberry, 1985). One possibility is for the hegemon to protect itself and shift the costs of adjustment to other economies, as President Nixon did when he devalued the dollar in August 1971 (Gowa, 1983). Another possibility is to adjust to the structural changes and shift resources to more efficient and competitive industries. The third, of course, is to do nothing or very little; this was essentially the choice taken by Great Britain when its hegemony was threatened in the latter decades of the nineteenth century. In *Growth and Fluctuations, 1870-1913*, Arthur Lewis demonstrates how "Britain was caught in a set of ideological traps. All the strategies available to her were blocked off in one way or another" (1978b, p. 133). As a result of this inaction, the British failed to arrest their economic decline.[40]

Economic theory suggests that a powerful incentive exists for the hegemon to pursue a protectionist strategy. In traditional trade theory, for example, the economic monopolies enjoyed by a reigning hegemon mean that all factors of production benefit from free trade. This tends to create a national consensus in favor of economic liberalism. According to the Stolper-Samuelson theorem, however, once that monopoly is broken, the scarce factor loses; within the hegemonic power, labor is the scarce factor and it therefore becomes highly protectionist (Helpman, 1984, p. 362). Yet in the case of Great Britain, labor was never powerful enough to impose its will on trade policies. Moreover, British capital continued to benefit through foreign investment and used its powerful influence against economic protectionism. In the case of the declining American hegemon, the crucial choices have not been made as of late 1986.

The process of uneven growth poses the problem of economic adjustment, or what Kindleberger (1962, ch. 7) calls "the capacity to transform." The preferred strategy for the hegemon and the system as a whole is to transfer resources out of declining into more efficient and competitive industries that would promote continued economic growth and thus reduce the cost of economic adjustment; in this way growth and adjustment reinforce one another in a virtuous cycle. Failure to adjust reduces the rate of economic growth and makes the cost of eventual adjustment that much higher. With low rates of economic growth and capital investment, the economy enters a vicious cycle of decline, as occurred with Great Britain in the closing decades of this century.

Although economic adjustment to global shifts in comparative ad-

---

[40] This is the theme of Mancur Olson's (1982) impressive study of the rise and decline of modern nations.

vantage is the wisest choice for an economy, the adjustment problem has become far more difficult than in the past. The increased number of economic players and more rapid shifts in comparative advantage have greatly increased the attendant costs; the astounding pace set for the rest of the world by Japan's rapid movement up the technological ladder imposes immense costs on other economies. The rise of the welfare state and government intervention in the economy have greatly increased the ability of powerful interests to resist paying the adjustment costs, and the role of the market as a facilitator of economic adjustment has been weakened by the shift in the balance of power away from the market toward the state, business, and organized labor (Olson, 1982). And the slowed rate of global economic growth itself makes adjustment more difficult; with a smaller economic pie, there are more losers. These obstacles to economic adjustment threaten the world economy with the possibility of slow growth and failure to adjust that could deteriorate into economic warfare.

CONCLUSION

The evolution of the world economy and the accompanying structural change involves three developments. The first is the shift in the locus of economic activities from one region to another. The second is the rise and decline of economic sectors. And the third is the increasing integration of national economies and the consequent impact of external forces on domestic well-being. All three, associated with the process of uneven growth, impinge significantly on the interests of states and powerful groups and suggest important questions concerning the political effects of a world market economy that were mentioned in Chapter One and will be addressed further in succeeding chapters.

The first issue raised by the process of uneven growth is that of political leadership and international cooperation. A stable and growing economy requires political leadership, yet the process of growth tends to undermine such leadership. For stability and growth to continue, some new basis of leadership or international cooperation must be found.

The second issue is the relationship of economic and political change. The process of uneven economic growth causes major structural changes in the world economy, which pose a major political problem of adjustment for individual nations; resources must be transferred from declining to expanding industries as the geographic locus of economic growth and the leading sectors shift. Economic adjustment, however, entails significant gains and losses for different individuals, groups, and nations and thus gives rise to intense political conflict. The failure, especially on the part of the hegemon, to adjust, transform its economy, and make this transition to new economic activities contributes to economic instability and the spread of economic nationalism.

The third issue raised by the growth process is its effects on the development, decline, and welfare of individual nations. A dynamic and expanding international economy leads to an increasing interdependence of national economies at the same time that states intervene in their own economies to control the process of economic growth. They may be motivated to accelerate development, arrest decline, or protect domestic welfare. Whatever the motivation, this interventionism leads to a clash between the desire for domestic autonomy and the benefits of international norms. A stable world economy requires that mechanisms exist that permit national management of the economy consistent with the norms and requirements of a liberal international economy.

The structural changes that have occurred in the postwar world economy and their implications for the liberal international economic order will be analyzed in later chapters. What are the prospects for pluralist leadership and economic cooperation? Can the United States and other powers successfully adjust to the profound shifts that are occurring in the global locus and nature of economic activities? How can the clash between domestic autonomy and international norms be resolved? Among the most important determinants of the answers to these questions will be the continued efficiency and stability of the world monetary system, which is the subject of Chapter Four.

CHAPTER FOUR
International Money Matters

ALTHOUGH analysts readily acknowledge that international trade and foreign investment have important implications for the distribution of wealth and power among nations, no similar agreement exists regarding the significance of the international monetary system.[1] Many economists believe that money and the international monetary system are, or at least can be, economically and politically neutral. However, in the modern world, the norms and conventions governing the system have important distributive effects on the power of states and on the welfare of groups within these states.

A well-functioning monetary system is the crucial nexus of the international economy. It facilitates the growth of world trade, foreign investment, and global interdependence. Establishment of a sound monetary system is a prerequisite for a prosperous world economy, and breakdown of the monetary system can be a decisive factor in a "Great Depression," as it was in the 1930s. In the present era, monetary stability has become particularly important. Money and financial flows now dwarf trade flows and have become the most crucial link among national economies. The efficiency and stability of the international monetary system, therefore, are major factors in the international political economy.

An efficient and stable international monetary system must solve three technical problems: liquidity, adjustment, and confidence (Cohen, 1977, p. 28). To assure liquidity, the system must provide an adequate (but not inflationary) supply of currency to finance trade, facilitate adjustment, and provide financial reserves. To deal with the adjustment problem, the system must specify methods to resolve national payments disequilibria; the three available methods are changes in exchange rates, contraction/expansion of domestic economic activities, and/or imposition of direct controls over international transactions.[2]

[1] This chapter draws heavily on Cohen (1977) and was inspired in part by Susan Strange's (1971) pioneering book on the subject. The title was adapted from A. James Meigs's book *Money Matters* (1972). With apologies to this monetarist, I use the title in a decidedly different way.

[2] In this book, the terminology applied to international transactions will be simple and nontechnical. It might be helpful, however, to clarify a few of the most frequently used terms. The most important ones are the following: *merchandise trade balance* = export versus imports; *current-account balance* = merchandise balance plus earnings on foreign direct investment, services, and transfers; and *basic balance* = the sum of current

The system must also prevent destabilizing shifts in the composition of national reserves. Such shifts can be caused by loss of confidence in the reserve currency or currencies. Each of these problems must be solved if an international monetary system is to operate efficiently and integrate the world economy.

Despite the belief of most economists that the monetary system is a neutral mechanism, every monetary regime imposes differential costs and benefits upon groups and states as it specifies the nature of international money, the instruments of national policy that are acceptable for balance-of-payments adjustment, and the legitimacy of different objectives of national policy. Every state therefore desires not only an efficient international monetary system but, even more important, one that does not seriously harm its own interests.

Every international monetary regime rests on a particular political order. Because the nature of the international monetary system affects the interests of states, states try to influence the nature of the system and to make it serve their own interests. As hegemonic powers rise and decline, corresponding changes take place in the monetary system. Thus, not surprisingly, the nineteenth-century monetary system primarily reflected British economic and political interests. Following the decline of British power in the early decades of this century, the monetary system collapsed in the 1930s. Similarly, it has again experienced severe strains with the relative decline of American power toward the end of the century.

Money has, of course, always been an important factor in world politics. Rulers have required money to finance their armies, support their allies, and bribe their enemies. The rise and the decline of empires and powerful states have been facilitated by the acquisition or loss of precious metals. But in the modern world the importance of money has multiplied many times and its character has changed profoundly. In fact, the enhanced role of the international monetary system in the affairs of modern states constitutes a virtual revolution in world politics. Its significance can best be appreciated through a chronological examination of the changing role of money, and economic and political implications of these changes, in the international economy.

THE ERA OF SPECIE MONEY

In the premodern period, precious metals or specie money (principally gold and silver) served as the basis of the international monetary sys-

---

account and long-term capital account. Saint Phalle (1981, ch. 1) provides a useful discussion of these relationships.

tem. Local and international currencies tended to be sharply separated from one another. Whereas local trade was dependent upon barter or locally recognized currencies, long-distance or international trade was served by the "great currencies" minted from gold or silver. These—the solidus of Constantine, the dinar of the Arabs, or the ducat of Venice— were universally accepted; they were relatively stable and sometimes held their values for centuries (Cipolla, 1956). Though the empires that issued them enjoyed the right of seigniorage, the fact that a particular currency served as international money conferred few additional special privileges on its issuer; for example, if a state decreased the precious metal content of its coins or otherwise debased its currency, it thereby undermined the attractiveness of and confidence in its currency.[3] Since such practices were self-defeating, the international monetary system based on precious metals even placed restraints on the states supplying the principal medium of exchange. In short, the supplier of the international currency gained few special privileges and the international use of a particular currency was not a source of international power.

Whether minted into the coin of the realm or left in the form of raw bullion, gold and silver constituted a neutral medium of international exchange; one state's gold or silver was as good as another's. Money could not be created by political fiat; it could only be obtained through trade, plunder, or the possession of mines. The value of international money was primarily dependent upon its supply and was largely outside the control of individual states. Local moneys, however, which were usually based on commodities or less precious metals, were very much at the mercy of governments. As their circulation was confined to the realm, they could be, and frequently were, debased to suit the interests of the ruler, at the risk, of course, of domestic inflation or some other economic disruption. The important point is that the circulation and value of these local currencies had little effect on the international position of the state.

In the premodern era, international currencies in effect enjoyed economic and political autonomy. Because their supply and value were determined by fortuitous discoveries or international trade, they were relatively free from the influence of individual governments and governments had limited ability to manipulate the currencies upon which international commerce depended. For millennia, the international monetary system was largely apolitical.

The nature and role of the system began to change in the sixteenth

[3] Seigniorage, as noted earlier, is the profit that comes to the sovereign from the issuance of the economy's money supply (Kindleberger, 1981, p. 248).

and seventeenth centuries with the discovery of gold and silver in the Americas and the expansion of international trade. The separation of local moneys from international moneys began to break down as a consequence of the great influx into Europe of New World precious metals, the growing monetarization of national economies, and increasing economic interdependence. In time, gold and silver drove out traditional local currencies. National and international currencies became increasingly intertwined through the expansion of trade and monetary flows, and governments lost even their former limited ability to manipulate local currencies; domestic economic activity and price levels were becoming subject to international changes. Under these circumstances national economies became increasingly interdependent and subordinate to the operations of the expanding international economic system.

In the early modern period the increasing integration of local and international currencies provided the occasion for the first great contribution to the science of economics and the basis for the development of liberal economics. In his price-specie flow theory, David Hume responded to the mercantilist states' obsession with amassing specie through a trade surplus and their fear that a trade deficit would cause a dangerous loss of specie. He demonstrated that if a country gained specie in payment for an excess of exports over imports, the consequent increase in its money supply would cause its domestic and then its export prices to rise. This in turn would discourage others from buying its goods. At the same time, its own citizens would be able to import more because the relative value of their currency had risen and foreign prices would have fallen due to the decreased money supply abroad. As a result, the nation's exports would decline and its imports would increase. The changed flow of trade and specie induced by price changes at home and abroad would then produce a new equilibrium. Liberal economists have elaborated modern trade and payments theory upon this simple type of equilibrium model.

Although Hume's price-specie flow mechanism continued to characterize international monetary relations into the twentieth century, the nature of the monetary system was revolutionized in the modern world due to a number of economic and political developments (Williamson, 1983, ch. 8). Stated simply, money had been transformed from a gift of nature to a creation of the state. State control over the supply and demand for money became a principal determinant of the level of national and international economic activity. This profound change in the nature of money began nearly two centuries ago, although it did not have its full impact until the Keynesian revolution in economic policy in the post–World War II period. To understand the significance of this monetary transformation, it is first necessary to comprehend what is known as the Financial Revolution and its consequences.

THE ERA OF POLITICAL MONEY

During the eighteenth and nineteenth centuries, a financial revolution occurred. Governments began to issue paper money, modern banking arose, and public and private credit instruments proliferated (Dickson, 1967). For the first time in history governments acquired extensive control over the money supply; at least in theory, they could influence the level of economic activity through the creation of money (Hicks, 1969, pp. 93-97). The full impact of this rise of political money would not be realized until the Keynesian revolution, but this financial revolution did transform the relationship of state and economy and thus had a profound impact on international economics and world politics.[4]

The Financial Revolution, while solving one major economic problem, created another. On the one hand, it solved or at least relieved the historic problem of the inadequacy of the money supply. Until the innovation of acceptable paper money and easily expandable credit, economies had frequently been hobbled and economic activity was subjected to deflationary pressures due to the inadequacy of the gold or silver supply. However, as governments gained the capacity to create money, the Financial Revolution created an inflationary bias and raised the international problem of monetary instability.

The change in the nature of money permitted development of a serious clash between domestic economic autonomy and international monetary order. Monetary stability and efficient operation of the monetary system require the subordination of domestic policies to international rules and conventions. If individual governments create too much money, the resulting inflation can destabilize international monetary relations. The conflict between domestic economic autonomy and international economic stability has become the fundamental dilemma of monetary relations. The manner in which this dilemma has or has not been resolved in large measure defines the subsequent phases in the history of the international monetary system.

Succeeding epochs (the era of British hegemony, the interwar period from 1919 to 1939, and the Bretton Woods system) will be analyzed on the basis of three characteristics of an international monetary system: the provision of an international money that solves the confidence and

---

[4] The famous early nineteenth-century controversy between the Currency and Banking Schools centered on the implications of this development (Deane, 1978, ch. 4).

liquidity problems, the establishment of a mechanism to solve the adjustment problem, and the governance of the international monetary system (Scammell, 1983, p. 207).

THE CLASSICAL GOLD STANDARD (1870-1914)

The international gold standard, which reached its zenith in the late nineteenth century, was the classic resolution of the dilemma of domestic economic autonomy versus international economic stability. In theory, this monetary system was the embodiment of the liberal, laissez-faire ideal of "an impersonal, fully automatic, and politically symmetrical international monetary order dependent simply on a combination of domestic price flexibility and natural constraints on the production of gold to ensure optimality of both the adjustment process and reserve supply" (Cohen, 1977, p. 79). Balance-of-payments disequilibria were corrected (at least in theory) and adjustment was achieved by the operation of Hume's price-specie flow mechanism.

As summarized by Benjamin J. Cohen, two key features of the system guaranteed the smooth and automatic operation of the price-specie flow mechanism: (1) the central bank of a nation on the gold standard bought and sold gold at a fixed price, and (2) private citizens could freely export and import gold (Cohen, 1977, p. 77). These two features provided a fixed exchange rate mechanism for adjusting the international balance of payments as trade and payment imbalances among nations were brought back into equilibrium through the flow of gold. In time, the resulting effects on relative prices and trade balances in time corrected any payments disequilibrium.

Comparing the decades of exchange-rate stability that this system achieved with the turmoil of the post-1973 period, many conservatives have become nostalgic about this idealized conception of the operation of the classical gold standard. They believe that return to a gold-based monetary system could eliminate the scourges of rampant inflation and monetary instability caused by the excessive creation of money (or international liquidity). However, this idealistic conceptualization ignores the political basis of the system and the central role of British leadership.

In practice, the classical gold standard operated quite differently from the liberal ideal.[5] It was not an automatic, impersonal, or politically symmetrical monetary order. On the contrary, it was a very hu-

[5] The following discussion of the gold standard is derived largely from Condliffe (1950, ch. 12).

man institution, subject to manipulation and assymetrical in the benefits that it conferred on national economies. This fact, however, does not negate the success of the gold standard; on the whole, it facilitated a then unprecedented growth of world trade, global prosperity, and international economic stability. However, its success and its economic consequences for various national economies and individual groups were due to reasons different from those assumed by many economists.

In the first place, the classical gold standard did not function automatically. The establishment of banking systems and their role in the creation of money had weakened the operation of the price-specie flow mechanism. According to theory, central banks responded to gold flows automatically, buying or selling gold to maintain the fixed exchange rate for the national currency. In practice, the banks could and did respond to gold flows in a highly discretionary manner in order to cushion the effect on domestic prices and the domestic economy. Through rather crude monetary policies, the banking system enabled a country to evade, at least for a time, the discipline of the gold standard. If the international monetary system were to work properly, some nation had to assume leadership in making it work; in the latter decades of the nineteenth century, this responsibility was assumed by Great Britain.

Second, the international monetary system under the classical gold standard did not operate impersonally. It was organized and managed by Great Britain; and the City of London, through its hegemonic position in world commodity, money, and capital markets, enforced the "rules of the system" upon the world's economies. The integration of national monetary systems with the London financial market endowed Great Britain with the ability to control to a considerable degree the world's money supply. By lowering and raising its discount rate, the Bank of England manipulated the flow of gold internationally and in effect managed world monetary policy. Nations that were errant in conducting their internal economic affairs and in adhering to the rules of the gold standard found themselves in difficulty with London money and financial managers. The monetary system under the gold standard was thus a hierarchical one, dominated by Great Britain and, to a lesser extent, by emerging financial centers in western Europe (Ruggie, 1982, p. 390).

Third, the monetary system was not politically symmetrical in its effects on various national economies. The process of balance-of-payments adjustment had very different consequences for advanced economies than for less developed ones. There were several reasons for this, but the role of international capital movements was of critical importance—a development not foreseen by Hume or other classical economists. Great Britain and other wealthy capital exporters could adjust to payments disequilibria and cushion their ill effects on economic activities through the regulation of capital flows. Capital importers, on the other hand, had no such protection. They were dependent upon decision makers in London, Paris, or Frankfurt and they tended to suffer adversely in terms of trade and with respect to the adjustments forced upon them by the operation of the system.

A principal feature of the operation of the international monetary and hence trading system was the central role of sterling in international transactions. The close integration of the London money market with the capital and commodities markets located there and with monetary centers elsewhere (Paris, Berlin, etc.) gave the system a highly centralized character. As a consequence, the lowering and raising of the bank rate by the Bank of England and its subsequent effects on the supply of credit, the flow of gold, and international prices gave Great Britain a powerful source of leverage over trade, capital movements, and national incomes. In this way the international balancing of accounts was effectively controlled by one dominant center.

In reality, as J. B. Condliffe has characterized it, the classical gold standard was "a series of credit systems based on gold and linked with each other by fixed exchange rates" (Condliffe, 1950, p. 365). Although gold was the ultimate standard of value, in every country there was a "credit superstructure" that governed the price level of the economy (ibid., p. 368). The adjustment process was essentially a matter of manipulating this credit superstructure and through it the relative level of prices (ibid., p. 366). As the creation of credit and hence the supply of money was under national control, the temptation to use credit and the money supply to maintain the price level or to reduce unemployment was great. In the late nineteenth century, the universal commitment to a system of a fixed exchange rate pegged to gold and a currency market dominated by Great Britain limited such actions. As a consequence, the world economy in effect had a uniform world currency with relatively little inflation or currency fluctuation, and the resulting stability of exchange rates was a major factor in the steady growth of trade and foreign investment.[6]

The objectives and policies pursued by the British in their hegemonic position were relatively simple. The ideology of laissez faire, along with British economic interests, dictated an emphasis on monetary stability. The goals of economic policy were modest in this prewelfare state era. Arthur Lewis has observed that Great Britain had only two economic

---

[6] Until the discovery of new sources of gold and the invention of a new process of refinement around 1900, the shortage of gold was a deflationary factor.

policies in the nineteenth century: upholding the price of gold and maintaining a balance-of-payments equilibrium. This, it should be remembered, was still an age when society's demands on government were few, and the ruling elites preferred the dangers of tight money and deflation to those of cheap money and inflation. Both the poorer nations and poorer classes within societies frequently paid the price of adjustment through higher rates of unemployment and decreased welfare. As Keynes noted, the lower orders of society resignedly accepted their lot as the natural order of things (Keynes, 1919). Judged on its own terms and neglecting its frequent negative impact on particular groups and societies, the classical gold standard was a highly successful international monetary order.

The gold standard reflected a world in which "social purposes," to use Ruggie's term, were minimal (1982, p. 382). In this era of governmental noninterventionism and before the rise of the welfare state, primacy was given to monetary stability. This was the product of British hegemony, the ideology of laissez faire, and the dominance of conservative middle classes. When these conditions changed with the First World War and the rise of the modern welfare state, the gold standard was no longer able to function. These social and political prerequisites of the stable nineteenth-century economy are too easily forgotten in the contemporary search for a reformed international monetary order (Ruggie, 1982, pp. 389-91).

During its reign, the classical gold standard provided an effective foundation for the nineteenth-century international economic and political order (Polanyi, 1957, p. 3). It solved fundamental problems of an international monetary order. The adjustment problem was solved as individual countries adjusted domestic economic activities to a level that maintained the value of their currency relative to gold; the liquidity problem was solved since the production of gold was generally sufficient to meet world demand at the prevailing price in terms of sterling; and the confidence problem was solved because people believed that Great Britain had the power and the will to maintain the prevailing sterling value of gold. These solutions subordinated domestic economic autonomy to the international goal of monetary stability.

The solution to the clash between domestic autonomy and international stability achieved under the gold standard provides an example of a dominant or hegemonic power enforcing the "rules of the game" and managing the world's monetary affairs. A hegemonic power is needed to reconcile the national policies of individual states and to establish the prerequisites of a stable international monetary order. As the world's preeminent industrial, trading, and capital-exporting nation in the late nineteenth century, Great Britain had an interest in a stable and smoothly functioning international monetary system; it performed the task of leadership because it had the power and the will to do so.

The efficiency and stability of the classical gold standard also benefited the other advanced countries. Because it worked well, the other major trading countries adopted it. Although Germany, France, and the United States resented the special benefits that world monetary leadership conferred on the British, they had neither the will nor the capacity to challenge this leadership effectively. The less developed commodity exporters, however, fared less well; the burdens of adjustment usually fell on them and the terms of trade for their commodity exports frequently suffered. Their compliance with the rules of the game was dictated by the dominant position of Great Britain and the other industrial powers.

Even though most nations probably gained in absolute terms from the well-functioning classical gold standard, relative gain is frequently more important in international relations than absolute gain. France, Germany, and other nations disliked a monetary order that benefited Great Britain most of all; less developed countries grew frustrated with paying the costs of adjustment. But as long as Britain retained economic and military primacy, London was able to resist the rising forces of economic nationalism and to maintain the international monetary order intact. For decades British leadership held off the detrimental effects of competing national policies on a highly interdependent world monetary system.

Near the end of the century, the rise of new industrial powers and the relative decline of British hegemony began to undermine the basis of British global economic leadership. Rising social discontent and a revolt against laissez faire began to shake the system. The force of economic inertia, however, continued British dominance in money and finance long after British supremacy in manufacturing had vanished. The political weakness of disadvantaged groups and classes inhibited any major change in the economic role of the state. The First World War destroyed the political foundations of this economic era and plunged the world into monetary and economic chaos for the next three decades.

THE INTERREGNUM BETWEEN BRITISH AND AMERICAN LEADERSHIP (1914-1944)

A major consequence of the First World War was a nationalization of the world monetary system. Upon the outbreak of hostilities, the belligerents acted quickly to safeguard their gold supplies and disengaged from the system of fixed exchange rates to facilitate the freeing and mobilization of their economies for war. The gold standard collapsed and its place was taken by a makeshift arrangement of floating rates. With the end of British economic leadership and the breakdown of economic interdependence, the determination of currency values once again became the responsibility of national authorities; domestic economic autonomy triumphed over international monetary order due to the exigencies of total war.

As Joseph Schumpeter observed during the depths of the war, the First World War transformed economic reality. In order to fight the war, every government had to mobilize the entire liquid wealth of its economy. Through taxation and especially through borrowing, the state acquired control over the resources of the society. Long before Keynes's *General Theory*, Schumpeter foresaw that as a consequence of this "monetarization" of the economy "monetary factors—deficits, money, credit, taxes—were going to be the determinants of economic activity and of the allocation of resources" (Drucker, 1983, p. 127). He also expected that the state, through what would later be called its "macroeconomic" (fiscal and monetary) policies, could harness the economy to its own political and social ends and thus leave behind the autonomous market of nineteenth-century laissez faire. The warfare state had paved the way for the modern welfare state. John Condliffe (1950) characterized this transformation as a "commerce of nations" displacing the nineteenth-century international economy.

The implications of the collapse of the international discipline of the gold standard and state acquisition of control over the domestic economy would one day fragment the liberal economics community. Those who would be called Keynesians focused on the opportunity that this transformation provided for the elimination of the evils of the market such as unemployment, recession, and erratic business cycles. Through manipulation of a few monetary variables—government spending, interest rates, and the money supply—public-spirited economists and their science could achieve social justice and "fine tune" the course of economic progress. Economists of a "liberal" persuasion began to believe that in a Keynesian world the "economist-king" would rule.

Schumpeter and other conservative economists, on the other hand, considered the undisciplined monetary power of the modern state to be an "invitation to political irresponsibility" because it eliminated all economic safeguards against inflation and other evils (Drucker, 1983, p. 128). They feared that the state would use its new taxing and borrowing powers to shift the distribution of national income from the producer and the saver to the nonproducer and the profligate. In a world without the restraints of the gold standard and other international norms, democratic governments seeking to court popularity and appease special interests through the expansion of costly government programs would be subjected to ever-increasing inflationary pressures; this could undermine both capitalism and democracy. In the new era of the warfare-welfare state, the generals and the politicians, rather than the economists, would govern. Several decades later, this issue appeared in the post–World War Two debates over the welfare state and Keynesian economics.

As Keynes stated in his *The Economic Consequences of the Peace* (1919), the basic task in the immediate aftermath of the First World War was reestablishment of an international economic system and the creation of a stable monetary order. A return to the gold standard was ruled out because severe inflation had eroded the purchasing power of the world's stock of gold. The Genoa Conference of 1922 created a gold-exchange standard as a solution to this problem. Nations would include gold-backed currencies, particularly British sterling, in their reserves in order to economize on the use of gold. Many believed that an international monetary order based on fixed exchange rates would again govern monetary relations among states and that international economic relations would return to the halcyon days of the classical gold standard.

However, the gold-exchange standard survived for just a few years; its collapse was a major factor in precipitating the Great Depression of the 1930s. There were many reasons for the breakdown of monetary order; some are worthy of special attention here. Many governments, using their newly gained control over monetary levers, began to value domestic welfare objectives such as economic stability and full employment more highly than a stable international monetary order. Labor and business had grown in power as a consequence of the war; they could resist the wage/price flexibility (especially in a downward direction) that had facilitated the operation of a fixed exchange rate system.

Another factor was British economic policy. When Great Britain returned to the gold standard in 1925 and reset the sterling value of gold, it did so at too high a par value; as a result, British economic growth was stunted, exports declined, and the working class experienced severe hardships. As Keynes (1925) had foreseen, the British government subordinated domestic welfare to the exigencies of maintaining the international role of sterling. The result was the General Strike of 1926, which failed in its immediate objectives but helped pave the way for the modern welfare state.

Furthermore, Great Britain no longer had the power to manage the international monetary system. Its industrial decline, the costs of the war, and the rise of new powers had resulted in a major shift in the global distribution of economic power. As Charles Kindleberger has argued in *The World in Depression, 1929-1939* (1973), the severity and duration of the Great Depression was due in part to the collapse of economic leadership. Great Britain no longer had the power to carry out the responsibilities of the hegemon in the areas of trade, money, and finance; the emergent dominant economic power, the United States, was unable or unwilling to assume the mantle of economic leadership. On the contrary, although the United States had emerged from the war as the world's foremost creditor nation, American deflation caused a shortage of global liquidity that accentuated the depression (H. Johnson, 1975, p. 272). With no one to enforce the rules and manage the system, states resorted to nationalistic "beggar-my-neighbor policies" and economic order broke down.

The social purposes and national interests of the Great Powers had changed and their economic policies had become increasingly divergent as a result of both domestic and international developments (Ruggie, 1982, pp. 390-92). Domestic welfare goals and national rivalries became more important than international norms; this made cooperation impossible (Oye, 1983). The ideologies of fascism, Nazism, and the New Deal valued domestic autonomy and national self-sufficiency more than liberal internationalism. As the fabric of international cooperation came apart and hostilities grew, the warfare state began to reassert itself. In one economy after another the state took over the reins of the economy in order to achieve its domestic welfare and foreign policy objectives. In the absence of hegemonic leadership, the triumph of illiberal ideologies and the divergence of national interests led to the collapse of the liberal world economy.

The ensuing economic chaos led to fragmentation of the international monetary system into several competing monetary blocs. At the Ottawa Conference in 1932, the British along with several of their dominions and certain trading partners established the "sterling bloc." Soon thereafter a "dollar bloc" formed around the United States and a "gold bloc" around France. Finally Germany, Italy, and Japan took advantage of the world economic crisis to launch attempts to create autarkic empires. The world economy entered an era of unprecedented economic warfare, with competitive devaluations and fluctuating currencies as each economic bloc attempted to solve its payments and employment problems at the expense of the others.

Responding to this economic anarchy, the United States began to assume the responsibilities of leadership in the mid-1930s. In 1934, the

U.S. Reciprocal Trade Act empowered the President to negotiate the reciprocal lowering of tariffs. Of little immediate consequence, this basic principle of tariff reciprocity would be embodied in the General Agreement on Tariffs and Trade (GATT) after the Second World War. In 1936, the United States, Great Britain, and France signed the Tripartite Agreement to moderate conflict among the three major currency centers (Rowland, 1976, ch. 5). Although these measures signaled a growing United States awareness of its interest in a smoothly functioning liberal world economy, an adequate reform of trade and currency matters would have to await the end of the Second World War and America's emergence as the world's unchallenged hegemonic power.

The events of the interwar period meant an end to the automatic equilibration that, on the whole, had characterized the era of the gold standard (Williamson, 1983, p. 141). The simultaneous achievement of internal and external balance through the operation of Hume's price-specie flow mechanism was decreasingly applicable to a world where central banks tried to counter its effects and prices/wages were not permitted to fall automatically in response to tight monetary policies; the era of government intervention and management of the economy had arrived.

THE BRETTON WOODS SYSTEM (1944-1976)

The Western democracies, following the trauma of the Great Depression and the sacrifices imposed on their citizenry during the Second World War, established two sets of postwar economic priorities. The first was to achieve economic growth and full employment. The Beveridge Plan in Great Britain, the French establishment of a planning commission, and the United States' passage of the Employment Act of 1946 were symbolic of this commitment to government interventionism in the economy and the establishment of the welfare state. The second priority was the creation of a stable world economic order that would prevent a return to the destructive economic nationalism of the 1930s.

The Bretton Woods Conference in 1944 was charged with the creation of such a stable world economic order. A product of American-British cooperation, the Bretton Woods system had several key features (Cooper, 1984, pp. 22-23). It envisioned a world in which governments would have considerable freedom to pursue national economic objectives, yet the monetary order would be based on fixed exchange rates in order to prevent the destructive competitive depreciations and policies of the 1930s. Another principle adopted was currency convertibility for current account transactions. Massive and destabilizing capital flows, like those that occurred in the 1930s and have also raised havoc in the 1980s, were assumed to be a thing of the past. The International Monetary Fund (IMF) was created to supervise the operation of the monetary system and provide medium-term lending to countries experiencing temporary balance-of-payments difficulties. And, finally, in the event of a "fundamental disequilibrium," the system permitted a nation to change its exchange rate with international consent; the definition of "fundamental disequilibrium," however, was left vague.

The Bretton Woods system attempted to resolve the clash between domestic autonomy and international stability, but the basic features of the system—autonomy of national policies, fixed exchange rates, and currency convertibility—conflicted with one another (Cooper, 1984, p. 22). For example, a nation cannot at the same time freely pursue macroeconomic policies and absorb foreign currencies without consequences for its exchange rate. It was assumed, however, that capital movements would be small and that conflicts of economic objectives could be reconciled by providing for international deficit financing and, if necessary, for changes in exchange rates. Indeed, this *was* possible until the late 1960s, when American monetary policy began to place severe strains on the system.

As John Ruggie has argued, the Bretton Woods system was a compromise solution to the conflict between domestic autonomy and international norms. It attempted to avoid (1) subordination of domestic economic activities to the stability of the exchange rate embodied in the classical gold standard and also (2) the sacrifice of international stability to the domestic policy autonomy characteristic of the interwar period. This so-called "compromise of embedded liberalism" was an attempt to enable governments to pursue Keynesian growth stimulation policies at home without disrupting international monetary stability. Describing this compromise, Ruggie writes that "unlike the economic nationalism of the thirties, it would be multilateral in character; unlike the liberalism of the gold standard and free trade, its multilateralism would be predicated upon domestic interventionism" (Ruggie, 1982, p. 393). The creation of institutions that limited the impact of domestic and external developments on one another was expected to solve the problem of simultaneously achieving both international liberalization and domestic stabilization.

The Bretton Woods system reflected fundamental changes in social purposes and political objectives. Whereas the nineteenth-century gold standard and the ideology of laissez faire had subordinated domestic stability to international norms and the interwar period had reversed these objectives, the postwar regime tried to achieve both. The state assumed a greater role in the economy to guarantee full employment and other goals, but its actions became subject to international rules. In this way it would be possible for domestic interventionism and international stability to co-exist. As Ruggie states, "the essence of embedded liberalism [was] to devise a form of multilateralism that is compatible with the requirements of domestic stability" (1982, p. 399).

Nations were encouraged to engage in free trade with minimal risk to domestic stability, although at some cost to allocative efficiency. If they should get involved in serious balance-of-payments difficulties, the IMF could finance deficits and supervise exchange-rate adjustments (Ruggie, 1983b, p. 434); nations would not need to restrict imports to correct a balance-of-payments disequilibrium. International cooperation would make it possible for state interventionism and the pursuit of Keynesian growth policies to occur without risking destabilization of the exchange-rate system and reversion to the competitive nationalist policies of the 1930s. Supporters of Bretton Woods believed that state and market had been successfully amalgamated.

Establishment of the Bretton Woods system did usher in an era of unprecedented growth in international trade and increasing global economic interdependence. Yet within this global Keynesianism lay an inherent flaw that in time would bring down the system. The American economy became the principal engine of world economic growth; American monetary policy became world monetary policy and the outflow of dollars provided the liquidity that greased the wheels of commerce. Following the revolution of the Organization of Petroleum Exporting Countries (OPEC) in 1973-1974, which quadrupled world energy prices, the dramatic shift of the Japanese, West Europeans, and newly industrializing countries (NICs) toward export-led growth strategies made the American role even more central to global economic growth. When America grew, the world grew; when it slowed, the world slowed.

As with the classical gold standard, a gap existed between theory and reality. The war had so weakened the economies of the industrial powers that they could not fully assume the responsibilities and obligations envisioned under the Bretton Woods system until 1958. Faced with potential chaos in the world economy, the problem of the "dollar shortage" and the onset of political conflict with the Soviet Union, the United States assumed primary reponsibility for the management of the world monetary system beginning with the Marshall Plan and partially under the guise of the IMF. The Federal Reserve became the world's banker, and the dollar became the basis of the international monetary system. The classical Bretton Woods system lasted only from 1958 to 1964, when it was replaced by what the French call the hegemony of the dollar.

Several key elements characterized what in effect became a gold-exchange standard based on the dollar. As other nations pegged their currencies to the dollar, a system of fixed exchange rates was achieved; the adjustment process involved simply taking actions that changed the par value of a currency against the dollar. Because the dollar was the principal reserve currency, international liquidity became a function of America's balance of payments, which were in frequent deficit from 1959 on. The linchpin of the system was the pledge of the United States to keep the dollar convertible into gold at $35 per ounce; as long as the United States backed this pledge and other nations had confidence in the soundness of the American economy, the system worked. The dollar was as good as gold; in fact, it was better. It became the principal medium of exchange, unit of account, and store of value for the world. For the two decades after 1959, outflows of dollars caused by the chronic American budget deficit drove the world economy. Then the crisis came and the Bretton Woods system collapsed.

THE DOLLAR AND AMERICAN HEGEMONY

American hegemony has been based on the role of the dollar in the international monetary system and on the extension of its nuclear deterrent to include its allies. Whereas the Soviet Union, situated in the heart of the Eurasian land mass, can bring its military might directly to bear on its periphery, the United States must have the foreign exchange to finance its global position, which has involved the stationing of troops overseas, the fighting of two major wars in Asia, and other costs. These economic burdens of global hegemony have been achieved in large part through taking advantage of the international position of the dollar. The price paid for America's exploitation of its role as the world's banker was the destruction of the Bretton Woods system, the transformation of the United States from a creditor into a debtor nation, and a growing dependence on Japanese capital. The latter developments will be discussed in Chapter Eight; I will consider here what economists call the Triffin Dilemma, in order to illuminate why American policy eventually destroyed the monetary system that the United States had worked so hard to create (Block, 1977).

In 1960, Robert Triffin, an economist at Yale University, published a book entitled *Gold and the Dollar Crisis* (1960), which exposed the flaw at the heart of the dollar-exchange standard. He pointed out that a fundamental contradiction existed between the mechanism of liquidity creation and international confidence in the system. The system was relying upon American balance-of-payments deficits to provide liquidity, but this chronic deficit over the long run would undermine confidence in the dollar. The growth of foreign dollar holdings that were not backed and redeemable by American-held gold at $35 per ounce would eventually destroy faith in the system, and this would lead, in turn, to financial speculation and ever-increasing monetary instability. Either America's balance-of-payments deficits had to stop (thereby decreasing the rate of liquidity creation and slowing world economic growth) or a new liquidity-creating mechanism had to be found.

For a few years, the Triffin dilemma was one of academic interest only, because America's gold reserves were adequate to cover its balance-of-payments deficit and the American inflation rate was low. After 1967, however, things began to change with the devaluation of the pound, which had been providing some protection for the dollar (Scammell, 1983, p. 179). Subsequently, the massive escalation of the Vietnam War and the consequent severe deterioration of America's balance of payments radically transformed the situation. In response to mounting world inflation (caused principally by the stepped-up war effort and President Johnson's Great Society program), increasing monetary instability, and speculative attacks on the dollar, international efforts to resolve the Triffin dilemma were accelerated.

These efforts generally involved two categories of international actions. First, there were cooperative measures taken by the leading economic powers designed to increase confidence in the dollar and to dampen monetary speculation. They included the General Arrangements to Borrow, currency swaps organized by the Bank for International Settlements, and the establishment of a "gold pool" (Kindleberger, 1977, ch. 6). Second, after intense controversy, the IMF created the Special Drawing Rights (SDR) as a reserve asset to complement the dollar as a reserve currency and thereby solve the liquidity-creation problem; this effort was only partially successful because of conflicting political interests and lack of confidence in a money created by an international institution. (For an explanation of SDR see Williamson, 1983, p. 348.) Yet, despite these severe difficulties and unresolved problems, the Bretton Woods system continued to limp along for several more years. To understand why, one must turn to the realm of international politics and the fact that American economic leadership continued, despite its failure to maintain international monetary stability.

The system of fixed rates survived for a time because it continued to rest on a firm political foundation. In essence, "an implicit bargain was struck," to use Cohen's expression, among the three dominant poles of the international economy—the United States, Western Europe, and, to a lesser extent, Japan (Cohen, 1977, p. 97). Partially for economic reasons but more for political and strategic reasons, Western Europe (primarily West Germany) and Japan agreed to finance the American balance-of-payments deficit. Commenting upon the elements of this important understanding, Cohen writes that "America's allies acquiesced in a hegemonic system that accorded the United States special privileges to act abroad unilaterally to promote U.S. interests. The United States, in turn, condoned its allies' use of the system to promote their own economic prosperity, even if this happened to come largely at the expense of the United States" (ibid.). As long as this bargain was sustained and not overly abused, the Bretton Woods system survived.

During this period the United States ran its foreign policy largely on credit by taking advantage of its role as world banker. It printed money to finance its world position, a tactic similar to the British issuance of "sterling balances" that British colonies and dependencies had once been required to hold. The willingness of Europe and Japan to loan money to the United States by holding inflated dollars in the form of interest-bearing United States government securities helped make it possible for the United States to maintain its troop commitments in Western Europe and elsewhere around the Soviet and Chinese periphery, to finance foreign aid, and, of course, to fight the Vietnam War. Lyndon Johnson did not have to compromise his cherished Great Society program or impose the costs of the program and the war on the American people through increased taxes. In return, the United States continued to tolerate not only discrimination against its exports by the European Economic Community and the Japanese but also their aggressive export expansion strategies. Each nation and the global system appeared to benefit from what can be seen in retrospect as complementary but highly self-centered and nationalistic policies.[7]

Being the supplier of the world's money had become a major source of power and independence for the United States. Initially, America's allies accepted this situation for the reasons discussed above. As time passed, however, many Europeans and Japanese began to believe that the United States was abusing the political and economic privileges conferred on it by the primacy of the dollar. As Charles de Gaulle so

[7] Whether or not the United States abused its power of seigniorage with respect to the international role of the dollar as the international currency is explored by Cooper (1975, pp. 69-73).

frequently complained, the Americans freely printed dollars to fight a colonial war in Vietnam, buy up foreign companies, and generally finance American political hegemony over Europe and the rest of the world. The solution, the French argued, was a return to the discipline of gold. Although few others accepted this Draconian measure, America's economic partners shared a growing concern over inflation, erratic currency speculation, and increasing monetary instability due to the vast overexpansion of the world's money supply. The United States was viewed as shifting the costs of its foreign and domestic policies onto other economies. The American attitude, on the other hand, was in essence that if other countries disliked what was happening, it was their responsibility to do something about it. This position became known as the doctrine of "benign neglect" and characterized U.S. policy until August 1971.

Inherent in this monetary and political arrangement were two basic asymmetries that eventually destroyed the Bretton Woods system in the 1970s. On the one hand, the role of the dollar as reserve, transaction, and intervention currency extended economic and political privileges to the United States that freed it from concern about its balance of payments in the conduct of its foreign policy or the management of its domestic economy. On the other hand, the United States, in contrast to other economies, could not devalue the dollar relative to other currencies in order to improve its trade and payments position. It was assumed that any devaluation of the dollar to improve the American competitive position would immediately have been wiped out by parallel devaluations of the pound, the mark, and other currencies.

Whereas the United States prized the first aspect of this asymmetry, it increasingly smarted under the fact that it could not devalue the dollar in order to improve America's declining trade position. Europeans and Japanese, of course, regarded this asymmetry from the opposite perspective, resenting America's export of inflation but prizing the effects of the overvalued dollar on their own exports. But as long as the American balance-of-payments deficit was moderate and the political unity of the three centers of non-Communist industrial power held firm, the issue remained largely dormant. When changing economic and political conditions accentuated the plight of the dollar and America's deteriorating trade position in the early 1970s, the asymmetries created by the international role of the dollar emerged as a basic issue in the reform of the international monetary system. Responding to these changes, the United States took decisive action to alter those aspects of the system that it disliked.

In order to understand the decisions eventually taken by the United

137

States, it must be appreciated that there is a latent political conflict in an international monetary system based on fixed rates. The basis for this conflict is the so-called N − 1 or consistency problem (Williamson, 1983, pp. 334-35). In a monetary system composed of N countries, N − 1 countries are free to change their exchange rate but one country cannot change its exchange rate, because its currency is the standard to which all other countries peg their currency values. There is a potential for conflict if everyone tries to change their exchange rate in order to improve their competitive advantage or to achieve some other objective; the conflict can be avoided only if one currency value remains fixed relative to all of the others.

For almost thirty years after the Second World War, the United States played this indifferent and stabilizing role; it was content to be passive regarding the value of the dollar. It did not care about the exchange rate of the dollar because of the overall strength of the American economy and because the foreign sector of the American economy was so small. Moreover, in the interest of cementing alliance relations with Japan and Western Europe, the United States subordinated its domestic economic interests to its larger political interests. The United States, therefore, let others change their rates or, in the case of Britain in 1949, encouraged them to change their rate primarily for the stability of the system. In short, the adjustment mechanism was essentially one of changing a currency value relative to the dollar.

This American attitude of benign neglect toward the increasingly overvalued dollar and declining trade balance began to change in the late 1960s and early 1970s. With the acceleration of the Vietnam War and the simultaneous expansion of the Great Society program by the Johnson Administration, American dollars flooded world financial markets. As other economies were forced to accept these dollars in order to maintain the fixed rates of exchange, U.S. inflation was transmitted to its economic partners via the monetary system. Subsequently, the Nixon Administration, in anticipation of the 1972 presidential election, provided yet another massive stimulus to the American economy, unleashing new inflationary forces and further undermining the value of the dollar. A number of other governments standing for reelection also stimulated their economies at the same time. The cumulative effects of this synchronization of the political-business cycle further accelerated world inflation and put increased strains on the system of fixed rates.[8] To appreciate these developments, it is necessary to return to a discussion of economic theory.

[8] See Tufte (1978) on the theory of the political business cycle.

In the 1960s, "the theory of economic policy" was developed to accommodate this more complex Keynesian world; it recognized that governments required separate policy instruments to achieve the internal objective of noninflationary growth with full employment and at the same time an external balance of international payments. The proper application of the theory would reconcile increased government intervention and international stability. As Harry Johnson wrote, "the post–World War II development of the theory of economic policy for an open economy by Meade, Tinbergen and others restored the concept of an automatic system, on the basis of the assumption that once the theory had been clearly laid out governments could be relied on to apply it intelligently, and deflate and revalue or reflate and revalue in the appropriate combinations as circumstances required" (H. Johnson, 1972, p. 409). These economists expected that nations would replace the automaticity of the gold standard with the choice of correct policy instruments at the *national* level, and for some years they believed that the Bretton Woods system had achieved these goals. But, as Johnson cautioned, "[the] major defect of [this policy prescription] is its assumption that governments have both the understanding and the power to follow its precepts, and that they will do so instead of using the understanding and the power to play international politics against their neighbors" (ibid.). This hope and admonition were not to be realized.

As the rise and ultimate decline of the Bretton Woods system illustrate, advances in economic theory per se did not solve the fundamental problem of the international monetary system, the potential conflict between national objectives and international order. Intelligent international leadership was the necessary condition for its resolution and, in the postwar era, as long as the United States was willing and able to supply such leadership, a liberal order triumphed over the forces of economic nationalism. When U.S. leadership faltered in response to the exigencies of the Vietnam War and the relative decline of U.S. power, technical economics could find no solution. The subsequent crisis of the international monetary system was less a problem of inadequate economic theory and more a political problem of inadequate economic and political leadership.

The persistent growth of global inflation from the late 1950s to the early 1970s, which would lead to American actions disruptive to the Bretton Woods system, presented itself as a new phenomenon (Williamson, 1983, pp. 386-87). In the past, inflation had been thought of as basically a national problem resulting from overambitious full employment policies. With the expansion of economic interdependence by the late 1960s, it became clear that inflation was an international macroeconomic problem. Due to excessive monetary creation by the United States, inflationary forces were spilling over from one country to another throughout the entire world economy via the channel of price levels in integrated commodity and product markets as well as via capital flows. This novel "age of inflation" distorted currency values and undermined economic stability at both the domestic and global levels.

By mid-1971, the dollar had become seriously out of line with other major currencies and the differential rates of inflation between the United States and other market economies had produced a fundamental disequilibrium in exchange rates. Confidence in the dollar was rapidly eroding and causing havoc in foreign exchange markets. The American government was under pressure to convert tens of billions of dollars into gold, and the international monetary system was threatening to break down. Richard Nixon, faced with this rapidly deteriorating situation, announced on August 15, 1971, what would become, in effect, a new U.S. foreign economic policy. Responding to the first American trade deficit since 1893, rising pressures for protectionism, a massive outflow of gold, accelerating attacks on the dollar, and fears of a financial collapse, he took a series of forceful and unilateral actions designed to stem the outflow of gold and reverse America's rapidly declining economic fortunes (see Gowa, 1983).

First, the President suspended the convertibility of the dollar into gold and thus placed the world monetary system on a pure dollar standard. Second, he imposed a surcharge on U.S. imports in order to force the Europeans and the Japanese to revalue their currencies against the dollar. And third, he instituted wage and price controls as a means of arresting the accelerating rate of American inflation. The most significant outcome of these actions was a substantial devaluation of the dollar in December 1971 (the Smithsonian Agreement). Though successful in achieving its purpose, Nixon's blunt tactics of monetary reform proved disruptive to the relations among the dominant economic powers. He destroyed a central pillar of the Bretton Woods system by unilaterally delinking gold and the dollar.

In brief, as Joanne Gowa (1983) has argued, the American hegemon smashed the Bretton Woods system in order to increase its own freedom of economic and political action. The growing power of Western Europe and Japan was threatening to place restraints on American autonomy, because the vast holdings of dollars by Europeans and Japanese meant that if the dollar were to hold its value and the dollar-exchange system were to be preserved, American policy would have to conform to their wishes. Rather than see its autonomy curbed, the

United States chose to abandon the system. As a former American official put it, "the growing economic and political strength of Europe and Japan made the Bretton Woods system obsolete" (quoted in Keohane, 1985, p. 97).

In 1973, the Bretton Woods system came to an end. In March, the decision was taken to let exchange rates float. Then, the quadrupling of world energy prices in the OPEC revolution dealt another severe blow to the system (Williamson, 1983, p. 392). Its impact on international balances of payment and on financial markets confronted the dominant economic powers once again with the task of realigning their currencies. In contrast to the Smithsonian Agreement, however, in which the currency realignments had been forced upon other countries by the United States and then negotiated multilaterally, the key actor this time was West Germany, which refused to continue to support the dollar. In effect, the United States and its economic partners decided to abandon the postwar system of fixed exchange rates in favor of one based on flexible rates. The refusal of an important ally to follow American economic leadership led to the abandonment of a key component of the Bretton Woods system.

The de facto end of fixed exchange rates and the Bretton Woods system was made de jure in 1976, at a meeting of the leading IMF members held in Kingston, Jamaica. The Jamaica Conference decided as follows: (1) floating exchange rates were legalized, (2) the reserve role of gold was reduced, (3) IMF quotas were increased, especially those of OPEC countries, (4) funding for the less developed countries was increased, and, most important, (5) the determination of the par value of a currency became the responsibility of the country itself. Domestic autonomy had triumphed over international rules; nations disengaged from the requirements of a fixed-exchange system in order to pursue one or another national objectives such as expanding exports, stimulating economic activities, or preventing the importation of inflationary pressures.

The Jamaican meeting confirmed the end of one monetary regime but it did not signal the birth of its successor. It failed to establish the essential characteristics of a stable monetary order: an international money, an adjustment mechanism, and monetary leadership. Although other currencies such as the yen and the mark increased in importance, the dollar could no longer be exchanged for gold; the world was left in essence with a pure (but inherently unstable) dollar standard. Efforts to solve the liquidity problem, such as absorbing excess dollars through the creation of a substitution account or strengthening the role of the SDR, were abandoned. Erratic American monetary policy remained free to pour too much or too little liquidity into the system and thus to cause unstable exchange rates and cyclical economic fluctuations. Nor was the issue of the international distribution of liquidity and its effects on the less developed countries addressed. The confidence problem and the danger it posed to international monetary stability was not resolved. The adjustment problem was assumed to have been eliminated by the shift to flexible rates that would enable the operation of the price mechanism to realign currencies automatically. Regrettably, it was not to be this simple, as the 1980s would demonstrate.

To summarize, Jamaica was silent on such critical aspects of a stable international monetary order as adjustment and liquidity. In effect, each nation was free to determine monetary matters for itself rather than subordinate to international rules. As Peter Kenen has described it, what took place in Jamaica in 1976 was a move toward renationalization of the world monetary system; individual nations were given greater responsibility for the determination of their own currency values (Kenen, 1976, p. 9). The dilemma of national autonomy vs. international norms appeared to have been resolved in favor of the former.

The abandonment of Bretton Woods and the system of fixed exchange rates meant the loss of international financial discipline. The door had been opened for the vast expansion of private, national, and international debt that occurred in the late 1970s and early 1980s. Without fixed exchange rates, there were no longer external restraints on national behavior. As a result the world monetary and financial system became increasingly unstable, and the threat of a collapse of this system became a major concern for the international political economy. The danger of global inflation became inherent in the system.

By its actions in the 1960s and 1970s, the United States had forfeited its role of monetary leadership. With its adoption of inflationary policies and its stance of "benign neglect," the United States had in fact become part of the problem rather than the leader in the search for a solution. In the mid-1980s, the relative decline of American power and America's unwillingness to manage the international monetary system stimulated proposals for collective leadership, especially in the form of policy coordination and new rules to govern the international monetary system.

THE NON-SYSTEM OF FLEXIBLE RATES

Advocates of the shift from fixed to flexible exchange rates believed that this change would resolve the fundamental problem of the clash between domestic autonomy and international norms. Under the Bretton Woods system of fixed exchange rates, national economies had become closely linked, thereby constraining domestic policy options. When exchange rates remained fixed, a disequilibrium in the balance of payments necessitated domestic adjustments and required changes in national levels of economic activity or (even less likely to occur) the imposition of direct controls over the economy such as restrictions on capital flows. This system of fixed rates collapsed because the differential rates of inflation between the American and other advanced economies imposed increasingly high costs on domestic economies.

With the official shift to a regime of flexible rates following the Jamaica conference, it was assumed that national economies would be delinked from one another. It would therefore no longer be necessary for a state to regulate the domestic level of economic activity in order to maintain existing currency values; adjustment could take the form of market-induced changes in currency values. This would isolate the national economy and domestic economic management from external developments and international constraints. Of equal importance, domestic policy decisions in one economy would not impinge on other economies, so each economy would be free to carry out its macroeconomic policies and to set its own economic priorities depending upon its preferences, such as that of the presumed trade off between the rate of inflation and unemployment levels.

For this solution to the adjustment problem to work as expected, states had to be willing to leave the determination of their exchange rates up to the market. Yet, in a highly interdependent world economy, states are tempted to manipulate their exchange rates in order to improve their relative position, and the actions of one country can seriously impinge on the welfare of others. For example, a state may engage in "dirty" floating to depress its currency and thereby improve its trade competitiveness or, alternatively, may attempt to raise its currency in order to fight inflation. The system of flexible rates proved once again that international money *does* "matter."

A number of fundamental changes in the nature of the international political economy explain why expectations for the success of the flexible exchange system were not fulfilled. A system of flexible rates was generally expected to: (1) insulate an economy against supply shocks like those engineered by OPEC in 1973-1974 and 1979-1980 (Williamson, 1983, p. 209), (2) limit synchronizations and amplifications of the business cycle like those that occurred in the global inflation of 1973 and the recession of 1975 when industrial economies simultaneously pursued first expansionary and then restrictive policies (Williamson, 1983, p. 385), and (3) stabilize exchange rates (Williamson, 1983,

p. 233). Flexible exchange undoubtedly did facilitate international accommodation to the economic upheavals of the 1970s: the two energy shocks, hyperinflation, and the breakdown of Bretton Woods (Cooper, 1983, p. 36).

In the mid-1980s there had been no test of whether or not the flexible exchange system would permit desynchronization of business cycles so that alternately some economies would expand while others contracted. This was generally due to the European and Japanese fear that expansionary policies would cause renewed inflation (Williamson, 1983, pp. 385-86). The system of flexible rates failed to achieve its objective of monetary stability. Exchange rates became highly volatile following its inception, and this had harmful effects on international trade and financial markets.

The crucial assumption that, under a system of flexible rates, domestic economic management would not be constrained by international factors had become increasingly unrealistic beginning in the late 1950s with the European removal of capital controls and the formation of the so-called Eurodollar or Eurocurrency market. This change in economic reality ("revolution" might not be too strong a characterization) continued with (1) the tremendous growth of world liquidity and financial assets due largely to the chronic American payments deficit and the subsequent generation of the OPEC surplus and (2) the increasing integration of world financial markets. By the mid-1970s, due to new technologies and the deregulation of national financial institutions, the volume of the international flow of capital assets exceeded the volume of world trade many times over.[9] According to one estimate, in 1979 total exports were \$1.5 trillion compared to foreign exchange trading of \$17.5 trillion; by 1984, whereas exports had increased only to \$1.8 trillion, foreign exchange trading had ballooned to \$35 trillion (*The New York Times*, May 4, 1986, p. F10). In a world where huge amounts of money and capital overwhelmed trade flows and were free to move across national boundaries in search of security and higher interest rates, international capital movements and the overall balance of payments became an important determinant of international currency values and especially of the exchange rate of the dollar.

Economists remain divided on the issue of what determines exchange rates, especially short-run movements, in a system of floating exchange rates. Several contending theories have been put forward by Keynesians, traditional monetarists, and other schools to explain exchange-

[9] BIS (1986) analyzes the causes and nature of the revolutionary changes in international finance.

rate behavior (Williamson, 1983, pp. 206-248). In such a situation the noneconomist should be cautious in drawing conclusions on these matters.

What does appear to be substantiated, however, is that macroeconomic policies, and particularly American fiscal/monetary policies, have become an important determinant of exchange rates, most certainly for the dollar, at least in the medium term. These American policies, principally through their influence on interest rates, largely determine the international flow of capital, which in turn affects the exchange rate and currency values. When the Bretton Woods system was established and when the shift to flexible rates was made at Jamaica, little attention was given to the possibility that capital movements would significantly affect exchange rates. However, in the early 1970s and again a decade later, capital movements became a destabilizing feature of the international monetary and financial system.

As such developments indicate, national economies are indeed linked together so that flows of capital and assets in response to differential rates of interest tend to undermine domestic policy autonomy. Macroeconomic policies in one country do affect the economies of other countries. The fiscal and monetary policies of all open economies affect one another through the international capital market. If a country restricts its money supply in order to fight inflation, the consequent rise in the domestic interest rate causes an inflow of capital that then defeats the original policy objective and raises the exchange rate. The adjustment problem and exchange-rate stability are intimately related to domestic policies, and it is impossible to keep the pursuit of domestic objectives separate from the stability of the international economy and monetary values.

Because of these interrelationships, the transition from fixed to flexible rates was followed by erratic exchange-rate fluctuations, especially for the dollar. This volatility in turn caused international transmission of economic disturbances. Rather than smooth adjustment of rates, excessive swings of currencies characterized the system. Since the dollar continued to be the basis of the international monetary system and because the American economy had such a large scale, fluctuations and disturbances tended to originate in the United States. American monetary expansion in 1976-1977 caused a sharp depreciation of the dollar in 1977-1978 and an increase in world inflation. In October 1979, restrictive American monetary policy led to a sharp appreciation of the dollar, accentuated the global recession triggered by the second OPEC price rise of 1979-1980, and stimulated the spread of trade protectionism (Kenen, 1984, p. 18). In 1981, restrictive monetary policy designed

145

FIGURE 2
The World Economic Cycle under the Reagan Administration

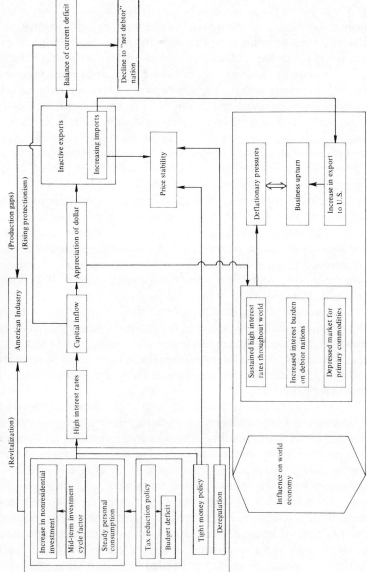

Source: *White Paper on International Trade—Japan 1985* (Tokyo: Japan External Trade Organization, 1985), p. 8.

to fight inflation dried up world liquidity, drove up the value of the dollar and global interest rates, and aggravated the world debt problem. By the mid-1980s, expansionist American economic policy caused the dollar to become greatly overvalued, with detrimental effects. Whatever the United States did, its policy had a negative impact on the rest of the world. As one European quipped, the American economy was unsafe at any speed (ibid., p. 19).

Erratic American macroeconomic policies and the equally self-centered responses of other governments undermined the stability of the international monetary system. The movement to flexible rates had encouraged a cycle of worldwide inflation and recession. The United States alternately poured too much or too little liquidity into the system, and other nations, because of their own domestic structural problems, responded in ways that aggravated the problem. In the words of Ronald McKinnon, the international monetary system became "out of control." President Ronald Reagan's economic policies and their impact on the rest of the world, as will be argued below, provided the most dramatic example of this judgment. (See Fig. 2.)

The most significant response to these developments in the area of international monetary relations was the 1978 launching of the European Monetary System and the creation of the European Currency Unit (ECU) (Kruse, 1980). Faced with an extremely weak dollar and the transmission of American inflation abroad, the West Germans and other Continental powers agreed to strengthen the alignment of their currencies, to increase coordination of their economic policies, and to lessen the probability of policy competition. As Robert Triffin has suggested, this initiative implied an increasingly decentralized and regionalized international monetary system (Triffin, 1985, p. 22).

With increased interdependence and frequent spillovers from one economy to another, national economies were in a classic Prisoner's Dilemma: although they could all gain through cooperation, a powerful incentive existed to attempt to gain at the expense of other economies. Every government was tempted to export its domestic problems of unemployment and inflation to its economic partners. Such noncooperative action creates the possibility that everyone may lose and be in a weaker position than if they had cooperated with one another. For example, under flexible rates, a government has a powerful incentive to pursue policies that cause its currency to depreciate and thereby improves its international competitive position. If every government did this, however, the results would cancel one another, because all countries would have excessively contractive policies and thus cause a drop in global output and losses for every economy (Sachs, 1983).

This dilemma and the strategic interaction of national policies are inevitable consequences of an interdependent world economy composed of nation-states pursuing independent economic policies. The situation has been accentuated by the shift to flexible rates and the decline of American economic leadership. The nature of the problem has been well expressed by Cooper:

the structure of the world of nations lies far from what would be required to meet the conditions of perfect competition. There are only about 160 members to the community of nations, many of which are large enough to influence *some* of the markets in which they operate, a few of which are large enough to influence all of the markets in which they operate. In short, the community of nations exists in the presence of extensive monopoly power—although, as with private monopoly power, it is limited by the alternative opportunities that other nations have. The attempt to exercise this limited monopoly in the pursuit of national objectives—to improve the terms of trade or to draw resources from the rest of the world—violates the conditions of "competition" and gives rise to the pervasive possibility of pushing economic policies toward global suboptimality. That in turn gives rise to possible gains from collusion, or, as it is more politely called in the context of economic policy, cooperation and coordination in order to enhance attainment of national economic objectives (Cooper, 1985, p. 1221).

In *The Economics of Interdependence* (1968), Cooper first presented the need for international cooperation to achieve optimal outcomes as follows: (1) "interdependence increases the number and magnitude of the disturbances" to a nation's balance of payments, (2) it "slows down the process by which policy authorities are able to reach domestic objectives," and (3) economic integration can cause "nations to behave with counteracting motions that leave all countries worse off than they need be" (summarized in Hamada, 1979, p. 294). Thus, the preferred solution to the Prisoner's Dilemma caused by increasing interdependence was international economic cooperation, which would keep the benefits of international economic relations without sacrificing the pursuit of legitimate domestic objectives and thereby would reconcile the clash between international norms and domestic autonomy (Cooper, 1968, p. 5).

The achievement of macroeconomic policy coordination necessitates a formal resolution of the $N-1$ problem discussed earlier (Frenkel, 1985, p. 17). Whether one is discussing a system of relatively fixed or floating rates, a particular currency or a prescribed basket of currencies must be established as the yardstick by which the value of all other currencies can be determined. The achievement of such an agreement will be exceptionally difficult because of its implications for domestic welfare and trade balances.

Under the system of fixed exchange rates, as noted above, the solution of this crucial problem and the achievement of macroeconomic policy coordination had been a rather simple matter. The United States maintained the gold parity of the dollar at $35 per ounce and other countries committed themselves to peg their own currencies to the dollar. As the United States seldom intervened in foreign exchange markets, there was little possibility that American and foreign monetary authorities would operate at cross-purposes. The dollar-exchange system worked and national policies were coordinated because of an implicit political agreement upon a set of economic policy tradeoffs; other governments subordinated their monetary and other policies to the maintenance of fixed rates and the United States reciprocated by stabilizing the domestic and international purchasing power of the dollar.

The breakdown of this cooperation resulted in the collapse of the system of fixed rates. In 1970, the Federal Reserve lowered U.S. interest rates in order to stimulate the economy and thereby help reelect Nixon. West Germany, then the second-greatest monetary power, was attempting to hold interest rates up or actually raise them in its fight against inflation. As the two financial systems were joined through monetary and financial markets, the billions of dollars created in the United States to lower interest rates there flowed into the German economy. The American "liquidity deficit" of $2 to $4 billion a year suddenly ballooned to $20 billion in 1971 and $30 billion in 1972, thereby flooding the world with inflationary dollars. The German government refusal to buy these dollars and thus support the increasingly overvalued dollar and the subsequent stampede out of the dollar led to the August 15, 1971, actions of the Nixon Administration and the subsequent denouement of the Bretton Woods system of fixed rates.

The onus for this collapse of political and economic agreement and the destruction of the Bretton Woods system falls largely upon failures of American political leadership. For both foreign policy and domestic reasons, successive American administrations pursued expansionary and inflationary monetary policies that eventually undermined the value of the dollar and destabilized the monetary system. Subsequently, other governments became less willing to subordinate their own macroeconomic policies to the objective of international economic cooperation. The result has been that national policies frequently have interacted to produce a cycle of inflation and recession. In the 1980s, economists and policy makers became greatly concerned about breaking this cycle, and some of the proposed solutions are indicative of the severity of the problem.

For purists, a return to the automatic mechanism of the gold standard provides the best solution to international monetary instability. The essence of the problem, according to this position, is the lack of social discipline in the modern welfare state. The growth of unwieldy government welfare programs, the extreme temptation to finance government through budget deficits, and the powerful inflationary pressures inherent in Keynesian policies are seen as products of the newly found capacity of governments to control the money supply. A return to the discipline of the gold standard and the elimination of "political" money would abolish the inflationary bias of modern governments. International norms would be firmly reimposed on errant politicians. However, whatever the economic merits of this solution might be, no state appears prepared to reverse the Financial Revolution by voluntarily relinquishing control over its money supply and abandoning domestic policy autonomy.

The Reagan Administration, especially during its first term, believed that the solution to the problems of the world economy was policy convergence. It believed that difficulties derived primarily from the misdirected policies and economic structures of other countries. Although the United States joined its economic partners as early as the 1982 Versailles summit in declaring that "we accept a joint responsibility to work for greater stability of the world monetary system," until September 1985 it remained largely committed to its own version of "benign neglect" announced in the spring of 1981. The responsibility for solving the problems of the international monetary order and the American trade deficit lay with other countries.

Rather than the extensive policy coordination and reduction of its budget deficit advocated by its allies and by most American economists, the principal Reagan Administration solution to world economic problems was that of the convergence of domestic policies. This meant the alignment of national economic policies to lower inflation, the use of the IMF to monitor the accomplishment of this task, and the adoption by other countries of expansionary economic policies in order to reduce the American trade deficit. According to this formulation, the American economy had been restructured to enable it again to pursue noninflationary growth policies. Moves toward the elimination of government regulation and the privatization of the public sector, the reduction of economic interventionism, and the dismantling of the welfare state under the banner of supply-side economics, the Reagan Administration argued, had weakened the sources of domestic inflation. If other economies carried out similiar policies, they would also be able to overcome their problems of high unemployment and slow growth. The strong dollar was believed to be proof of American economic strength and the correctness of the American policy. The solution, therefore, was the convergence of the policies of other governments toward those of the United States. In the mid-1980s, however, few other governments were prepared to accept either this diagnosis or the Reagan Administration economic prescriptions.

International coordination of economic policies was the third and most popular solution within the American economics community, one that would win the support of the Reagan Administration in its second term due largely to the influence of Secretary of the Treasury James Baker III. The diagnosis given by economists supporting policy coordination was that the increased interdependence among economies through the integration of financial and product markets, the intensified linkages among prices and interest rates, and the increased information flows had led to a high level of policy interdependence among the advanced economies (Cooper, 1985). These developments had locked the United States, Western Europe, and Japan into a classic game-theoretic or strategic situation in which the policy decisions of each influenced and affected the policy decisions and outcomes of the others. Each government had to take account of the actions and possible responses of others as it formulated its own economic policies, and achievement of its objectives depended upon the behavior and reactions of other economies. In such a situation, optimum outcomes and the avoidance of policy competition could be achieved only through international cooperation.

The solution proposed by a number of distinguished economists was that the United States and its principal economic partners should coordinate their macroeconomic policies and in effect formulate a macroeconomic policy for the entire world. The objective would be to achieve economic growth and full employment for every economy. Through agreement on the growth of aggregate global monetary levels, the dominant economic powers would be able to contain inflation and carry out counter-cycle economic policies. Collective leadership of the world economy would be substituted for the decline of American leadership.

THE ISSUE OF POLICY COORDINATION

Although the meanings of the term "policy coordination" range from ad hoc agreements such as the so-called G-5 agreement of September 1985 to formal and highly technical proposals, it can be understood as an attempt to recapture the spirit of cooperation that had provided the political foundation for the operation of the Bretton Woods system of fixed exchange rates and international stability from 1945 to 1971. However, a return to a dollar-based system of fixed exchange rates is assumed to be impossible for both economic and political reasons. In an era of integrated capital markets and attractive alternatives to the dollar such as the mark and the yen, the U.S. Federal Reserve by itself can no longer manage the international monetary system. Furthermore, what others had earlier perceived as American abuse of the monetary system along with the relative decline of American power appears to necessitate a cooperative solution to the problem of international monetary instability. Although the best long-range solution, in the judgment of many experts, would be a world bank, a strengthened IMF, or the establishment of a common world currency such as the SDR, the second-best solution was believed to be international policy cooperation (Cooper, 1984, pp. 2-4).

Among the several proposals for macroeconomic policy coordination, none was more ingenious or more illustrative of the problems involved than that put forth by Ronald McKinnon (1984). Whereas traditional monetarists focused on the growth of the money supply in an individual country, McKinnon's "global monetarist" view was that the integration of national economies necessitated the control of the "world money supply." The alternate contraction and expansion of this global supply, according to his analysis, was the cause of deflationary and inflationary fluctuations of the international economy. Because the economies of three countries—the United States, West Germany, and Japan—accounted for nearly two-thirds of the industrial world's output, destabilizing fluctuations in the global supply of money could be controlled if these three countries coordinated their money supply.

In essence, McKinnon proposed that the three major centers of economic power agree upon and set a target for the growth of the world's money supply. Each would direct its domestic monetary policy toward exchange-rate stabilization, expanding and contracting the money supply as necessary to maintain monetary values. Together, these three "hard currency" countries would in effect impose a rule of global monetary growth on the rest of the world, ensuring a stable and noninflationary increase in world liquidity. This cooperation among the three dominant powers would be tantamount to a return to the regime of fixed rates.

The purpose of this tripartite condominium would be to coordinate the global supply of money while preventing synchronized contraction and expansion of national monetary policies. The tendency of these economies, according to this global monetarist analysis, has been to pursue Keynesian understimulation or overstimulation of their economies and thus produce a global cycle of deflation and inflation. A leveling-out of the global money supply could be achieved if one or another of the major economies contracted its money supply in order to offset the expansionary polices of its partner(s). Through the displacement of synchronous policies by offsetting or countercyclical policies, the three major centers of economic power would be able to stabilize the value of the dollar and bring order to the system.

The actual composition of the global money supply in terms of dollars, marks, and yen would be determined through the combination of a complex econometric formula and central bank decisions rather than on the basis of particularistic national objectives. An international monetary rule would displace national discretion and determine the global supply of liquidity. Thus, technical economic criteria and objective factors rather than parochial political and national interests would determine the rate of monetary creation. In time, the experience of monetary cooperation would and should lead to "complete financial unification among the reserve currency countries" (McKinnon, 1984, p. 75). Over the long term,

the international cycle of inflation and deflation—through uncontrolled changes in world money and the dollar exchange rate—would be smoothed. The efficiency of international trade should be restored and protectionist sentiment should diminish once arbitrary changes in exchange rates are eliminated. As in an idealized gold-standard regime, domestic and international money would become virtually the same (ibid.).

The world would be returned to the liberal dream of a neutral, automatic, and depoliticized international monetary system.

An unspoken but major purpose of this scheme would be to rein in the United States, the rogue elephant of the global economy. Whether intentionally or not, its erratic macroeconomic policies have seriously disrupted the international monetary system, caused destabilizing fluctuations in the value of the dollar, and stimulated massive speculative flows of capital seeking to take advantage of interest-rate differentials or projected changes in exchange rates. Policy coordination like that proposed by McKinnon would force the United States to become once again a stabilizing influence, as it was under the system of fixed rates.

In effect, McKinnon proposed the creation of a world economic government. The United States had assumed an hegemonic role of economic governance in the 1950s and 1960s; its central bank had managed the international monetary system and its currency had become the world's principal currency. Now, in the late 1980s and beyond, a "triumvirate" (to use McKinnon's term) of the United States, Japan, and West Germany would govern the international economy. Their central banks would cooperate to manage the money supply and their stable currencies would replace the dollar as the world currency. Thus, the fading hegemony of the United States would be replaced by the leadership of the three dominant economic powers.

For this system to succeed, the three governments would be required to subordinate their domestic policies and, for the United States at least, perhaps even some of its independence in foreign policy, to agreed international economic norms. (Under such a scheme, for example, the United States would not be able to fight a major war as it did in Vietnam, with the attendant monetary consequences, unless it had the explicit support of Japan and West Germany.) Fiscal, commercial, and balance-of-payments policies as well as monetary policies would have to be coordinated. Even labor costs would have to be coordinated and kept under a tight lid to avoid inflationary wage settlements that could cause monetary values to get out of alignment. In short, the political and economic prerequisites of successful policy coordination (at least as conceived by McKinnon and other experts) would be formidable indeed.

Despite its inherent difficulties, this type of coordinated solution gained support in the 1980s, within the Reagan Administration and elsewhere. Some in Washington saw the coordination of national economic policies as a means of overcoming the domestic political stalemate with respect to the budget deficit and economic policy. If the United States could not resolve its own problems, perhaps it could get its economic partners to help. Similarly, other countries saw policy coordination in terms of relieving their own economic difficulties by getting the United States or Japan to take certain actions. It would not be too much of an exaggeration to say that the purpose of policy coordination, in the eyes of each of the leading economic powers, is to get its economic partners to do what it wants done but without doing what they want done.

THE REAGAN ADMINISTRATION AND POLICY COORDINATION

The Economic Recovery Tax Act of 1981 and the ensuing federal budget deficit of approximately 5 percent of the GNP had a profound and unanticipated impact on the world economy. What occurred, however, had been predicted in a classic article written in 1966 by Robert Mundell. As summarized by Peter Kenen, Mundell argued that:

when international capital flows are sensitive to interest rate differences and exchange rates are floating, a country that runs a large budget deficit and does not finance it by printing money will incur a large current-account deficit but will have a strong currency too. The budget deficit will push up interest rates and pull in foreign capital. When exchange rates float, however, a country with a net capital inflow has to have a matching current-account deficit, and its currency must appreciate sufficiently to generate that current-account deficit. In other words, the country must become less competitive in its own and world markets" (Kenen, 1984, pp. 18-19).

Although American consumers and exporters to the United States benefited from this expansive fiscal policy, it had major detrimental effects on the American and world economies. The need to finance the U.S. budget deficit raised global interest rates and reduced investment throughout the world. Other economies responded by restraining domestic demand in order to hold down inflationary pressures and shifted to export-led growth strategies. American absorption of huge amounts of world capital to finance its budget deficit and to compensate for the low rate of U.S. savings moderated the consequences for capital formation in the United States. The resulting overvalued dollar, however, had a devastating impact on American exports and on large sectors of American industry and therefore triggered powerful protectionist forces. In addition, high interest rates exaggerated the world debt problem. The shift to flexible rates and the integration of capital markets had greatly magnified the impact of American macroeconomic policies on the rest of the world.

Despite the impact of its macroeconomic policies on American producers and the balance of trade, throughout its first term the Reagan Administration adhered to the concept of policy convergence. The strong dollar and the flow of funds into the United States were interpreted as a sign of economic strength and the success of Reaganomics, and other sluggish economies were admonished to follow the American example. The attitude of the administration toward the complaints of other countries that the U.S. budget deficit and high dollar were distorting the international monetary and financial system was succinctly expressed in the arrogant words of Treasury Department Under Secretary Beryl Sprinkel: "Let them worry about their exchange rates and we will worry about ours." Benign neglect had become malign neglect.

During the second Reagan term this attitude of indifference began to change. The massive growth of the national debt, the huge trade deficit, and the advent of a new economic team headed by Baker led to the abandonment of the orthodoxy of supply-side economics and also, verbally at least, of the concept of policy convergence. Although the inflation rate had been lowered and economic growth had been restored during the second half of President Reagan's first term, the overvalued American dollar had become a serious problem in its own right and many believed that the correction of the exchange rate should, for the first time, become an explicit and primary objective of economic policy. The American trade imbalance was distorting the American economy, stimulating protectionist sentiments, and destabilizing international economic relations. The administration had realized that the cooperation of its economic partners was required if the situation were to be corrected.

In September 1985, the Reagan Administration launched its first serious effort to achieve macroeconomic policy coordination and secure the monetary cooperation of its economic partners. Alarmed over increasing protectionist sentiment in Congress, the Reagan Administration pressured West Germany, Japan, and other major economies to intervene in monetary markets in order to lower the value of the dollar and to stimulate their own economies, thereby eliminating the growing U.S. trade deficit. The dollar had appreciated approximately 60 percent between June 1980 and March 1985. The task of policy coordination was to bring it back down and make American goods competitive once again in world markets.

In combination with important changes in market forces such as lowered interest rates, the prospect of a declining American budget deficit, and the dramatic drop in the price of oil, this coordinated interventionism by the Group of Five (G-5) caused an estimated one-third devaluation of the dollar against the yen and the mark by March 1986 from the peak value it had reached in early 1985. The ostensible American shift from policy convergence to policy coordination had apparently worked, and the administration grew optimistic that the trade deficit would disappear.

The early success of the G-5 policy coordination led Reagan, in his State of the Union message delivered in February 1986, to make policy coordination a major objective of the United States for the first time. The stated purpose of coordinated action would be to eliminate currency fluctuations and achieve agreed-upon "target zones" for the major currencies; in effect, the administration was proposing a return toward fixed exchange rates. Thus, the G-5 agreement and the President's pronouncement revealed a significant movement away from the earlier stance of the administration on the issue of policy coordination. The United States had been stirred to decisive action by its growing realization that the huge American trade deficit was leading to trade protectionism.

The story of the impact of the Reagan budget and resulting trade deficits on the American economic position in the world and foreign economic policy is told in Figure 2 above and in Table 2. Between 1976 and 1984, the trade deficit jumped from $9.3 billion to $108.3 billion, of which a rising fraction was with Japan. Even in sectors of traditional competitive strength such as agriculture and "high-technology" products the American surplus was declining. To finance its budget deficit, the United States borrowed heavily from other countries, with the result that its net foreign claims shifted in the mid-1980s from positive to negative. Whereas its net earnings on foreign investments were over

TABLE 2. The U.S. Trade Balance *(in billions of current U.S. dollars)*

	Total			Manufactured Goods[a]		
	U.S. Exports	U.S. Imports	Net Exports	U.S. Exports	U.S. Imports	Net Exports
U.S. Multilateral Trade						
1976	114.7	124.1	−9.3	67.3	64.6	2.7
1977	120.8	151.7	−30.9	69.6	76.9	−7.3
1978	142.0	175.8	−33.8	81.9	100.1	−18.2
1979	184.5	211.8	−27.3	99.4	110.9	−11.6
1980	224.2	249.6	−25.3	123.2	122.4	0.8
1981	237.0	256.1	−28.1	133.1	139.1	−6.0
1982	211.2	247.6	−36.4	119.8	140.3	−20.6
1983	200.7	262.8	−62.1	112.7	159.3	−46.6
1984	220.3	328.6	−108.3	121.4	217.9	−96.5
U.S.-Japanese Bilateral Trade						
1976	10.0	16.9	−6.9	2.8	16.0	−13.2
1977	10.4	20.3	−9.9	2.8	19.2	−16.5
1978	12.7	26.5	−13.8	3.7	25.2	−21.6
1979	17.4	28.2	−10.8	5.2	26.8	−21.5
1980	20.8	33.0	−12.2	6.6	31.4	−24.7
1981	21.8	39.9	−18.1	7.2	38.1	−31.0
1982	20.7	37.7	−17.0	6.8	38.2	−31.3
1983	21.7	41.3	−19.6	7.5	41.5	−34.0
1984	23.3	57.3	−34.0	8.1	57.9	−49.8

[a] Manufacturers, machinery and transport equipment, and miscellaneous manufactures.

NOTE: Figures for total trade are f.o.b. Exports of manufactured goods are f.a.s., and imports are c.i.f. (Thus, imports of manufactured goods can be larger than total imports.)

SOURCE: Stephen E. Haynes, Michael M. Hutchison, and Raymond E. Mikesell, *Japanese Financial Policies and the U.S. Trade Deficit*, Essays in International Finance, no. 162, International Finance Section, Dept. of Economics, Princeton University, 1986, p. 3; Haynes et al. cite *Survey of Current Business* and *Highlights of U.S. Exports and Import Trade*, both U.S. Dept. of Commerce, various issues.

$34 billion in 1981, by 1985 the United States also was moving toward a deficit with respect to investment income. This dramatic reversal of the trade and investment positions was causing American protectionism, especially against the Japanese, to increase significantly.

By the late spring of 1986, in order to arrest this deteriorating situation, the Reagan Administration moved more forcefully toward policy coordination and adopted the concept of "automaticity." It wanted an international agreement on a set of predetermined rules and automatic procedures to force other countries into corrective actions to bring down the value of the dollar and eliminate the American trade deficit. The administration had moved decisively away from its earlier monetarist position of letting the market determine exchange rates. Intervention in exchange markets, changes in domestic economic policies, and the realignment of currencies would be based on a set of objective economic criteria such as national inflation rates, growth rates, and unemployment rates. The world would thus be returned to what the Reagan Administration regarded as a mutual compatibility of economic policies.

At the Tokyo summit meeting of Western leaders in early May 1986, the Reagan Administration tried to act on the basis of its conversion to the concept of "managed floats." Although the other summit participants agreed with the idea of increased cooperation, they refused to accept the American concept of "automaticity" and the establishment of a set of objective criteria and formal rules to govern national economic policies. They preferred a more discretionary approach to international cooperation, one that would enable them to exercise domestic economic autonomy.

America's economic partners feared that agreement on a system of managed currencies would mean a return to the problems of the 1970s, and they were strongly opposed to a close relinking of their economies with that of the United States. A commitment on their part to defend established currency values could subject them to inflationary dollar inflows, as had happened before, or the United States might force them to adopt high exchange rates that would harm their export industries. As one European official put it: "We would all be dependent on the U.S. dollar . . . and the U.S. doesn't take sufficient notice of other nations in international monetary affairs" (*The Wall Street Journal*, March 14, 1986, p. 30). They regarded the initiative of the Reagan Administration for automatic and binding rules as an attempt to reimpose American hegemony on the global economic system.

The summit agreement for "enhanced surveillance" over exchange rates and economic policies was a compromise between the American desire for inflexible rules and the desire of its partners for discretion. In order to end exchange volatility and to realign currencies within agreed-upon target zones, the Western powers committed themselves to "close and continuous" coordination of their economic policies. A system of managed currencies would be achieved through agreement on mutually beneficial economic goals. Through the creation of a new international body, the Group of Seven, composed of finance ministers and central bankers, national economic goals and target exchange rates would be supervised by taking into account such "economic fundamentals" as growth rates, inflation rates, unemployment rates, budget deficits, trade balances, monetary growth, currency values, etc. Thus, currency values would be linked to the overall economic performance of the capitalist economies. Whenever "significant deviations" from an agreed-upon national policy occurred (i.e., whenever one nation's policy caused difficulty for others), the economic officials were to "make their best efforts to reach an understanding" on what corrective action was to be taken, for example, altering interest rates, reducing budget deficits, and, if necessary, intervening in the foreign exchange market. In such cases, however, although "peer pressure" would be exerted, the decision on the specific action to be taken would rest with the delinquent country itself (*The New York Times*, May 8, 1986, p. A6).

Although at this writing it is much too early to determine the probable success of this initiative for multilateral surveillance and a coordinated management of the world economy, the obstacles to be overcome are profound. They reside in the fundamentally different economic and political agendas of the major powers, differences that were masked by the language of the agreement. The international coordination of economic policies had a significantly different meaning for each of the summit participants and it is questionable whether compromises could be found among their conflicting objectives. The lowest common denominator of the agreement was the hope that it would forestall a breakdown of the international economy and could provide a basis to get other countries to take particular desired actions.

Despite its ostensible abandonment of the concept of policy convergence, the United States continued to adhere to this idea as the solution to the difficulties of the world economy and its own economic ills. The Reagan Administration believed that the fundamental problem was the "growth gap" between the American and other economies and not the American budget deficit. From its perspective, the purpose of international coordination of economic policies was to prod the two other strong economies—Japan and West Germany—to reverse course and restimulate their economies. Through expansionary economic policies these economies would move away from their reliance on export-led growth and would increase their imports. If Japan and West Germany took appropriate actions, the administration believed, the problems of the overvalued dollar and the U.S. trade deficit would be eliminated.

Japan and West Germany, on the other hand, considered the American budget deficit and lack of economic discipline to be the fundamental problem of the world economy. American fiscal policy, in their judgment, was primarily responsible for high global interest rates, the overvalued dollar, and the consequent American trade imbalance. Therefore, they believed that the purpose of policy coordination was to encourage the United States to eliminate its huge budget deficit. This corrective action, by bringing down interest rates and the value of the dollar, would stimulate world economic growth and reduce the U.S. trade deficit. Both were resistant to the idea of stimulating their own economies and were reluctant to see a substantial appreciation of their own currencies lest it decrease their exports and trade competitiveness. They believed that the problems of the world economy would be solved only if the United States took the appropriate action.

THE PROSPECTS FOR POLICY COORDINATION

The concept of international policy coordination as the solution to the problems posed by economic interdependence in a world of autonomous states encounters a number of severe difficulties. If it is to succeed, three major obstacles must be overcome. Although it would be foolish to suggest that international policy coordination cannot be achieved in a pluralistic state system and in the absence of a hegemonic power, it would be equally foolish to ignore its inherent complexity. There are problems, not easily disentangled, regarding its theoretical foundation, economic desirability, and political feasibility.

The first problem to be solved if international policy coordination is to be successful is that of its theoretical foundation. Whether right or wrong, the Bretton Woods system of fixed exchange rates had been based on a general consensus, at least on the part of the United States and Great Britain, on the fundamental determinants of exchange rates; the system and its rationale were largely engineered by an American civil servant, Harry Dexter White, and a British economist, John Maynard Keynes (Gardner, 1980). This basic understanding or, if one prefers, "ideological hegemony" in Gramsci's terms, regarding the working of the economic system has been completely shattered by the dethroning of Keynesian economics, the increasing integration of global financial markets, and the greater interdependence of macroeconomic policies. Even the triumphant monetarists are at a loss because the deregulation of the financial system, the expansion of fiscal instruments, and the proliferation of new types of money (M1, M2, ad infinitum) have shattered the traditional concept of the money supply.[10] The postwar achievement of what was called "the neoclassical synthesis" and enshrined in Samuelson's influential text has been displaced by a cacophony of economic sects.

Without the continued dominance of the Keynesian model or any orthodoxy to take its place, rival theories contend on such subjects as the determinants of exchange rates, the fundamental issue of reconciling full employment and price stability, and other basic questions of economic theory. Should exchange rates, for example, be set by the method of purchasing-power parity, as advocated by McKinnon and others, or by the restoration of equilibrium in the American balance of payments, favored by the Reagan Administration? The divergence of views among economists and policy makers on these crucial issues makes agreement on policy matters very difficult. As Richard Cooper, William Branson, and other authorities have noted, until the analytics or theoretical framework of determining exchange rates is somehow put in place and a new theoretical consensus reestablished, it will be impossible to determine what exchange rates should be or how they can possibly be achieved (Cooper, 1985).

A second issue is that of the economic desirability of policy coordination (Branson, 1986). Due to the relationship of nominal and real exchange rates, if one cannot change nominal rates, then, the adjustment of exchange rates must come through changes in domestic policy.[11] The resulting inflation or deflation, however, might be even more harmful than letting exchange rates change. Under the type of policy coordination envisioned by the Tokyo summit, for example, the Reagan budget deficit would have played havoc with the American economy. Without the rise in the value of the dollar and the resulting inflow of capital, the United States would have suffered from either high interest rates detrimental to business or strong inflationary pressures. It must be asked, therefore, whether it is desirable to interfere in the market if this could

[10] Currency (M1) has been joined by checking accounts, credit cards, and other instruments of credit creation.

[11] The nominal exchange rate between two currencies is found by dividing one by the other. The real exchange rate is the product of the nominal rate times the relative inflation rate of the two economies. Thus, if nations are prohibited from changing the nominal exchange rate, then the coordination of real rates must come through domestic policy changes that affect relative inflation rates, and one is back to a world in which the international economy may impact negatively on domestic economies (Branson, 1986).

cause even greater economic damage than the damage caused by volatile exchange rates themselves.

A more general difficulty affecting the economic desirability of policy coordination relates to the establishment of predetermined or automatic rules like those favored by McKinnon and the Reagan Administration. Anticipating the nature of the problem is in itself a problem. McKinnon's sophisticated and complex solution, for example, deals only with instabilities and fluctuations caused mainly by financial flows among various currencies. Its technical and automatic formula is designed to prevent synchronous contraction or expansion of national economies. The Reagan Administration, on the other hand, wanted a set of rules precisely to force other economies to join it in a synchronous expansion. One set of rules to solve a particular problem may not be appropriate for other types of problems, and therefore international policy coordination at best should be ad hoc in response to a specific problem. This more flexible approach, however, encounters the question of political will.

The third and most important problem regarding the international coordination of economic policies is the conflict over policy objectives. Is there sufficient agreement among the major and expanding economic powers on economic and political objectives to enable them to subordinate short-term advantage to the benefits of long-term cooperation? With the relative decline of American economic hegemony, one must inquire whether a political base exists that can and will facilitate the pluralistic management of the international political economy.

Past experience does not permit one to be very sanguine about the political prospects for policy cooperation. No political issue has been more divisive than that of the coordinated expansion of the three major economies. Whereas the United States on several occasions has attempted to pressure the Japanese and West Germans to stimulate their economies, they have tended to resist due to such concerns as the fear of renewed inflation or the desire to reduce government spending. For example, at the London economic summit in May 1977, the United States called upon its major economic partners, particularly West Germany and Japan, to carry out a coordinated expansion in conjunction with the United States. The logic behind this so-called locomotive theory was that the American economy was no longer big enough by itself to be the engine of world economic growth. The others, due largely to their own internal domestic constraints, refused to follow the lead of the United States and to expand their economies; this contributed to deterioration in the American trade and payments position and forced an unwanted devaluation of the dollar. In 1979, a similar failure to reach agreement forced the United States to contract its economy and produced the recession that helped elect Ronald Reagan.

The G-5 Agreement well illustrates the political problems of pluralist management of the world economy. The United States, when forcing the revaluation of the yen and the mark, failed to recognize adequately the considerable diffusion of economic power that had taken place in the 1970s and early 1980s. McKinnon had postulated a monetary triumvirate composed of the United States, West Germany, and Japan that could control exchange rates and hence trade balances; yet the rise of the NICs undermined this determination of monetary and trading relations by the great powers. South Korea, Canada, and other countries were among the principal beneficiaries of the dollar devaluation because they had pegged their own currencies to the dollar. For example, the export of Korean cars soared at the expense of Japanese exporters, and the United States lost a significant portion of the gains it had anticipated from a devalued dollar. The improved competitive position of other countries in turn made them attractive hosts for American and Japanese multinations. In brief, monetary coordination will require the achievement of consensus among a growing number of competitive economies if it is to be "successful."

Throughout the Reagan Administration, the United States and its economic partners have continued to be in conflict over economic policy. In order to decrease the U.S. trade and payments deficit, the administration called upon West Europeans and especially the Japanese to expand their economies and deemphasize their strategies of export-led growth. Both refused and argued that domestic economic conditions, in particular the fear of renewed inflation and the existing public debt, made expansion impossible. They countered that the cause of the international monetary problem was the American budget deficit and that no solution was possible until this was brought under control. Domestic economic conditions and differing national priorities in the three centers of world capitalism make policy coordination or the convergence of national policies a very difficult means for managing a highly interdependent world.

One of the major political obstacles to policy coordination is the desire for a trade surplus. Although the ostensible purpose of policy coordination is to eliminate currency volatility, the real purpose in many cases is to achieve a preferred exchange rate. As Hans Schmitt has convincingly argued, a powerful mercantilistic bias exists in modern economies, due to the employment and technological benefits of an export surplus; the increased output and economies of scale provided by exports facilitate a more rapid rate of technological advance (Schmitt,

1979). In this connection, it should be noted that one of the first actions taken by both Japan and West Germany immediately following the Tokyo summit was to intervene in currency markets to dampen an appreciation of their currencies. Both the Germans and the Japanese have wanted the other to be the one to appreciate its currency and to shift to an expansionary economic policy. The G-5 action can in fact be seen as an attempt by the Americans and the Europeans to pressure the Japanese to revalue the yen, to shift from an export-led to a domestic-growth strategy, and to cut their massive trade surplus. As will be argued in subsequent chapters, pressures have greatly increased in the United States to pursue a similar mercantilistic trade policy.

The acquisition of greater influence over Japanese economic policy was a primary motive of the American initiative at the Tokyo summit and for the mechanism of policy coordination that it put in place. Through pressures on Japan to stimulate its economy and to raise the value of the yen, the United States wished to reduce its massive trade deficit with Japan and to force the Japanese to open their economy. These pressures and the substantial appreciation of the yen since September 1985 to a record high of 153 yen to the dollar have caused great resentment in Japan. Although Japan has gained some benefits, the level of unemployment has risen sharply, profit rates have been reduced, and the small businesses that benefited greatly from the high dollar have been harmed. The idea of a neutral and generally acceptable exchange rate for the dollar and other currencies is a chimera and cannot be achieved.

The United States has also become less willing to subordinate its economic policies to the concerns of its economic partners. It was reluctant to change its economic and political priorities even though, in the judgment of other countries and of most U.S. economists, American fiscal policy and the American budget deficit have been the crux of the global economic problem. Rather than altering its own policies, the United States has preferred that other economies do the adjusting.

The powerful desire of states for policy autonomy is the most fundamental problem encountered by efforts toward policy coordination. When the interests of states coincide, as they did in the coordinated reduction of interest rates achieved in March 1986, then success is assured. The proposals of the Reagan Administration and various economists for increased policy coordination, however, run into strong political resistance. Despite the ostensible reversal of its own position on policy convergence and its expressed willingness to coordinate macroeconomic policies, the United States has shown little disposition to shift permanently away from the unilateralism that caused President

Nixon to overthrow the Bretton Woods system in August 1971. Nothing in the behavior of the Reagan Administration suggests that policy coordination means anything other than getting the Europeans and the Japanese to do its bidding. By the same token, other nations do not wish to subordinate themselves once again to American domination, to tie themselves to erratic American macroeconomic policies, and to forego their mercantilistic desire for trade surpluses.

Unless the dominant powers can resolve the $N-1$ problem in some formal and systematic way, the coordination of macroeconomic policy will not be achieved. A more concerted exercise of American leadership than had been demonstrated in the 1980s will be required. The Bretton Woods system of policy coordination, it should be recalled, broke down in part because other economies had lost confidence in American leadership. The fact that the United States has infrequently considered the concerns of others in the formulation of its own policies has made the Europeans and the Japanese wary of American calls for policy coordination. To other countries, President Reagan's proposal for increased coordination has seemed less an abandonment of American unilateralism than an attempt to regain influence over their internal economic affairs and to subordinate them to American objectives.

As Jacob Frenkel has commented, "a reform of the international monetary system might be viewed as a constitutional change that occurs once in a lifetime" (Frenkel, 1985, p. 18). The history of constitution making, however, suggests that this is no easy task. A large array of economic and political factors must be correct, as they were in the founding of the Bretton Woods system. By the late 1980s, these favorable conditions had largely disappeared. There was little to suggest that economic and political conditions were conducive to the making of a new constitution for the international monetary system.

The fact of the matter is that if the economic and political prerequisites for the achievement of policy coordination were in place, coordination would not really be considered necessary. The breakdown of the Bretton Woods system was caused initially by the refusal or the inability of governments, especially the American government, to maintain monetary discipline and to subordinate what they considered to be their national interests to the rules and norms of the existing monetary regime. Would there be any need for policy coordination if the United States brought its budget deficit under control and maintained a stable set of economic policies? Other governments have been equally unwilling to forego national sovereignty in economic matters; they also have structural problems in their economies that constrain domestic economic policies. Would there be a need for policy coordination if the Europeans and the Japanese stimulated their own economies and gave up their mercantilist export policies? The problem is not policy coordination as such but autonomous state action in an increasingly interdependent world economy.

The irony of the situation in the mid-1980s has been that the requirements of the type of policy coordination considered necessary by economists have become far more stringent and demanding than those of the defunct system of fixed rates. That system broke down because domestic and (in the case of the United States) foreign policy objectives took precedence over international economic cooperation. The delinking of economies through the system of flexible rates was believed to be the solution to this clash between national priorities and international norms in the mid-1970s. Yet this system proved impossible due to the intensification of financial interdependence that actually relinked national policies. Because of their autonomous pursuit of domestic and other objectives, the advanced capitalist economies have been driven back to the need for some mechanism to govern their economic relations.

One is therefore forced to return to the fundamental issues of international political economy raised in Chapter One: Is any government willing to subordinate its national autonomy and independence in economic matters in the interest of international economic stability? Is international cooperation possible for long in a capitalist world economy? Can cooperation be achieved without an unchallenged hegemonic leader willing to subordinate its narrowly defined interests to the larger objective of maintaining a liberal international economy? The answers to these questions remain unclear.

From the very inception of the liberal international economic order in the late 1940s, divergent national interests and differing perspectives on economic policy have posed a threat to that order. America's economic partners have worried about the international instabilities generated by a United States whose concerns and traditions have been those of a closed economy rather than one concerned about the impact of its actions on the rest of the world (Elliott, 1955). The Europeans have never liked the idea of subordinating themselves to a set of universal norms. As for the Japanese, their primary concern has been the preservation of what they consider to be the unique features of their culture. Whether and how these differences can be reconciled in an increasingly interdependent world economy continues to be problematic.

American behavior in the mid-1980s suggested that the United States would not abandon important domestic economic or foreign policy objectives for what most liberal economists would identify as a larger international good. The West Europeans have exhibited a growing reluctance to lower external trade barriers and subordinate themselves to international norms. Similarly, the Japanese have demonstrated a stubborn resistance to changing their traditional ways and to carrying out the "internationalization" of domestic economic practices. Lacking the type of political will, imaginative leadership, and broad consensus on economic and political matters that led to the original creation of the Bretton Woods system, skepticism is warranted regarding the possibilities of economic policy coordination to solve the problems of the international monetary order.

The "embedded liberalism" of the Bretton Woods system worked because of responsible American leadership and the willingness of other nations to subordinate their domestic policies to international norms during the early postwar years. These political conditions made it possible to reconcile domestic policy autonomy, fixed exchange rates, and currency convertibility. In time, however, the regime of fixed rates collapsed because domestic policy freedom led to global inflation. Its successor, the regime of flexible rates, functioned poorly because of the combination of policy autonomy and the massive financial flows that followed currency convertibility. If the instabilities of the nonsystem of flexible rates continue and policy coordination proves to be impossible, the only alternative left for nations or blocs of nations that wish to protect themselves from external disturbances is the exercise of national or regional control over international capital and currency movements.

In place of the American monetary hegemony of the early postwar era and in the absence of a formal mechanism to coordinate national policies, the international monetary system has become an uneasy coexistence of the three dominant currencies—the dollar, the mark, and the yen. As will be argued in Chapter Seven, the reign of the dollar has continued since the end of the Bretton Woods system because it has had the support of first the Germans and subsequently of the Japanese. If this tacit support were to collapse, the political basis of the international monetary system would break down and the postwar trend toward increased economic interdependence would be dramatically reversed.

The fundamental problem is the clash between economic interdependence and political autonomy. The preferred solution in the postwar period has been the development of a set of monetary rules and norms that balance these two objectives. If a satisfactory balance cannot be achieved, the "solution" to the problems created by increasing interdependence will be to reduce interdependence itself and to reverse the postwar process of economic integration. Indeed, by the mid-

167

1980s, this process of disengagement in the monetary area was well advanced. Despite, or perhaps because of, the intensification of monetary and financial integration, nations have been strongly reasserting policy autonomy. The European Monetary Union (read Deutschmark system) and the increasing international role of the yen (to be discussed below) have indicated that a greater decentralization of the monetary system is taking place. The eventual outcome of this trend will depend upon the ability of the three centers of international capitalism to coordinate their macroeconomic policies, or at the least of the United States to be a source of financial and monetary stability once again.

CONCLUSION

This chapter has argued that the Financial Revolution of the nineteenth century altered the automaticity of the international monetary mechanism envisaged by Hume in his price-specie flow theory. The innovation of paper money, credit instruments, and central banking transferred to the state enormous powers over the supply of money and hence over economic affairs. As in so much of political life, this newfound state power has been a force for both good and evil. It has given the state an unprecedented capacity to intervene in and to guide the domestic economy in the interest of economic growth and full employment, but the state's control over the money supply has also encouraged policies that have caused rampant inflation and undermined the stability of the international monetary order.

Both in the nineteenth century and in the decades immediately following the Second World War, stability was preserved because the dominant economic powers—Great Britain and the United States—defended the integrity of the international monetary order. These hegemons used their influence to suppress and contain those policies of other states that were destructive of the system. As the power of each declined, the conflict over international monetary policy became increasingly acute. The British system collapsed under the pressures of the Great Depression and the conflicting monetary blocs of the 1930s. As the twentieth century draws to a close, despite American abuse of its role as international banker and guardian of the system, the dollar continues to reign. This is due to the political and security ties between the United States and the other major centers of economic power and the absence of any viable and effective alternative.

The current system has been characterized as a nonsystem. The system of fixed rates and Keynesian fine-tuning associated with the Bretton Woods system has not been replaced by a stable system and new orthodoxy; exchange rates have become highly erratic. Whereas in the past, payments imbalances tended to be distributed evenly throughout the system, the United States in the 1980s began to run a massive deficit and its policies became a threat to the stability of the system. In contrast to the relative immobility of capital in the past, capital flows have become increasingly fluid, surging from one country to another, upsetting exchange rates, and undermining domestic economic policy.

Both economic theory and the real world of economic affairs have come a long way from the automatic equilibration of Hume's price-specie flow mechanism. Keynesian economics and the theory of economic policy attempted to understand and control an economic world in which the price mechanism did not automatically produce a full employment equilibrium and where economic tradeoffs were discovered. The solution envisioned in the 1960s to domestic economic problems was that the state should follow a set of prescribed policies, one for each objective to be achieved. Thus, state action was required to make the market function properly (Odell, 1982, p. 22). This solution, however, assumed a relatively closed national economy or at least one not closely linked to the outside world. However, with the growth of economic interdependence in the 1960s, the nature of the economic problem changed. Independent states pursuing their policy objectives began to come into conflict with one another. In this Prisoner's Dilemma world of strategic interaction, each is tempted to export its economic problems to other economies; policy competition and strategic trade policy have become a reality. Economists have learned that in a highly interdependent world, the domestic economic problem probably cannot be solved unless the international economic problem is also solved. Although new economic theories and techniques may help in the search for a solution, the problem is primarily a political one.

As Robert Triffin has observed, "the thrust of history" has been in the direction of replacing commodity and national moneys with manmade and international money (Triffin, 1968). For Triffin, the logical outcome of this historical process would be a world monetary government. Perhaps such a centralization of political authority over the international money supply will yet occur. Until it does, however, the possible loss of control over the international monetary and financial system is the greatest threat to the liberal world order itself (Strange, 1985c).

In surveying the history of international money matters one is struck by a profound irony. As we have seen, the advent of political money has given the modern state unprecedented control over the economy, and this financial and political revolution made possible the contemporary liberal capitalist society. The welfare state and Keynesian management of the economy could not have occurred without the state acquiring control over the money supply. With the advent of "embedded liberalism," at least for a moment, the inherent problems of a market or capitalist economy identified by Marx appeared to have been finally resolved.

However, what may be possible and beneficial for a single state has proven to be a disaster for the international system as a whole.[12] When many states pursue independent economic policies in a highly interdependent world and do not coordinate their macroeconomic policies, these policies can and do conflict with one another so that everyone may suffer more than if they had cooperated with one another. Until policy coordination can be achieved and the international monetary system brought under international control, the prospects for the continued existence of a liberal world economic order are dim.

The fundamental problem, as Richard Cooper has pointed out, is the existence of a high degree of economic interdependence and extensive linkages among national economies without any centralized political control over the system. Whatever liberals may hope, the search for a neutral and automatic monetary mechanism that would hold the system together and prevent untoward events is a hopeless enterprise. The dreams of "leaving it up to the market" or of returning to a politically neutral gold standard cannot succeed because the nature of the monetary system has a profound impact on the interests of powerful groups and states. Affected groups and states will always try to intervene in the operation of the system to make it serve their interests. The question of whether or not there is any way in which cooperation and policy coordination among the centers of economic power can replace previous hegemonic leadership has not yet been answered.

[12] This is, of course, an excellent example of the fallacy of composition discussed earlier.

The Politics of International Trade

T RADE IS the oldest and most important economic nexus among na- tions. Indeed, trade along with war has been central to the evolu- tion of international relations. The modern interdependent world mar- ket economy makes international trade still more important, and developments in the 1980s have had a profound effect on the nature of the international political economy.

THE IMPORTANCE OF TRADE

For centuries the taxation of trade was one of the most important sources of wealth for political elites and for imperial powers. Many em- pires developed at trade crossroads and fought to control the trade routes of Asia, Africa, and the Middle East. Brooks Adams in *The Law of Civilization and Decay* (1895) considered shifts in trade routes and their control to be the key to human history.

In the late twentieth century economic growth, which permits do- mestic sources of revenue to displace tariff revenues in the financing of government, has diminished the revenue effects of trade; yet its taxa- tion remains a major source of revenue for the political elite and the official bureaucracy of many less developed countries. Because the overdeveloped bureaucracies in many societies have an inadequate do- mestic tax base and because it is much easier to place the direct taxation burden on outsiders, these countries tend to have unusually high tariff rates; this increases the cost of imported goods and thus discourages economic advance (Little, Scitovsky, and Scott, 1970).

Trade has expanded in every epoch because societies have sought goods not readily available at home, and this expansion has produced many related results: (1) technological diffusion, which contributes to the economic welfare of all peoples, (2) a demand or Keynesian effect on the economy that, through the operation of the "multiplier," stim- ulates economic growth and the overall efficiency of the economy, (3) benefits for individual firms as trade increases the size of the market, promotes economies of scale and increases the return on investment while also stimulating the overall level of economic activity in the econ- omy as a whole, (4) increased range of consumer choice, and (5) reduc- tion in the costs of inputs such as raw materials and manufactured components, which then lowers the overall cost of production. Moreover, in the late twentieth century, export-led growth has itself become a major strategy used to acquire needed imports and promote economic growth. Although these many benefits of trade are most relevant to market-type economies, they can also apply to every kind of domestic economy.

Trade has another and more controversial effect, and that is its cultural effect, its impact on the values, ideas, and behavior of a society (McNeill, 1954). Liberals have generally considered this impact to be positive, since they believe contact among societies leads to the diffusion of new ideas and technological advances and that trade stimulates social progress. Economic nationalists, on the other hand, frequently regard trade negatively, believing it to be destructive of traditional values and also corrupting in its encouragement of materialism and the pursuit of luxury goods considered harmful to individuals and society. Many critics see international trade as a form of cultural imperialism that must be strictly controlled.

The effect of trade on international politics is another subject of intense controversy. Liberals consider trade a force for peace because they believe that economic interdependence creates positive bonds among peoples and promotes a harmony of interest among societies; further, it gives states a stake in the preservation of the status quo. Economic nationalists and contemporary Marxists, on the other hand, regard trade as pernicious, since economic specialization and interdependence make states insecure, dependent, and vulnerable to external developments. Trade is therefore viewed as a source of political tensions and economic leverage and as an instrument that removes from a society the ability to govern its own affairs.

Two very different theories of international trade underlie these controversies. One is found in the liberal tradition; this is orthodox trade theory, which can be traced from Adam Smith and David Ricardo to its contemporary embodiment in the Heckscher-Ohlin-Samuelson model and other neoclassical formulations. The second theory is the nationalist tradition identified with the mercantilist writers of the early modern period, the German Historical School of the late nineteenth century, and economic nationalists of the late twentieth century. These two positions differ fundamentally on the purposes, causes, and consequences of international trade.

The Liberal Theory of International Trade

Although liberal theory has changed in form and content from the simple ideas of Adam Smith to the sophisticated mathematical formulations of the present day, it rests ultimately upon the belief that economic specialization produces gains in productive efficiency and national income. Liberal theory also believes that trade enlarges consumption possibilities. International trade thus has beneficial effects on both the demand and the supply sides of the economy.

Adam Smith argued in the *Wealth of Nations* in 1776 that the key to national wealth and power was economic growth. Economic growth, he reasoned, is primarily a function of the division of labor, which is in turn dependent upon the scale of the market. Therefore, when a mercantilist state erects barriers against the exchange of goods and the enlargement of markets, it restricts domestic welfare and economic growth. Smith asserted that trade should be free and nations should specialize in what they could do best so that they could become wealthy and powerful. The advantages of a territorial division of labor based on *absolute* advantage formed the foundation of Smith's theory of trade (Ellsworth, 1964, pp. 60-61).

In his *Principles of Political Economy and Taxation* (1817), Ricardo provided the first "scientific" demonstration that international trade is mutually beneficial. His law of *comparative* advantage or cost provided a new basis for liberal trade theory and also a cornerstone for the whole edifice of liberal economics. Although his theory has been modified to take into account many complications that he did not foresee, Ricardo's law of comparative advantage continues to be one of the fundamental principles of liberal international economics along with modernized versions of David Hume's price-specie flow theory and John Stuart Mill's law of reciprocal demand.

Building on Smith's pioneering ideas, Ricardo established the law of comparative advantage as the fundamental rationale for free trade. Smith had assumed that international trade was based on an absolute advantage, that is, on an exporter with a given amount of resources being able to produce a greater output at less cost than any competitor. Such absolute advantage had, in fact, historically been the basis of international trade, and this is still the case in many commodities (El-Agraa, 1983, ch. 6). Unfortunately, if nature had been so parsimonious that a nation possessed no absolute advantages, according to this theory its trading prospects were inauspicious, to say the least. The Industrial Revolution and the growth of industry changed this situation, and it was Ricardo's genius to recognize the profundity of the transformation.

In his law of comparative advantage he demonstrated that the flow of trade among countries is determined by the relative (not absolute) costs of the goods produced. The international division of labor is based on comparative costs, and countries will tend to specialize in those commodities whose costs are comparatively lowest. Even though a nation may have an absolute advantage over others in the production of every good, specialization in those goods with the lowest comparative costs, while leaving the production of other commodities to other countries, enables all countries to gain more from exchange. This simple notion of the universal benefits of specialization based on comparative costs remains the linchpin of liberal trade theory.

No one has stated the liberal faith in the material and civilizing benefits of unfettered commerce better than Ricardo himself:

Under a system of perfectly free commerce, each country naturally devotes its capital and labour to such employments as are most beneficial to each. This pursuit of individual advantage is admirably connected with the universal good of the whole. By stimulating industry, by rewarding ingenuity, and by using most efficaciously the peculiar powers bestowed by nature, it distributes labour most effectively and most economically: while, by increasing the general mass of productions, it diffuses general benefit, and binds together, by one common tie of interest and intercourse, the universal society of nations throughout the civilized world. It is this principle which determines that wine shall be made in France and Portugal, that corn shall be grown in America and Poland, and that hardware and other goods shall be manufactured in England" (Ricardo, 1871 [1817], pp. 75-76).

While working out and demonstrating this law, Ricardo used his famous example of Portuguese wine and English cloth. Portugal, he reasoned, could produce both wine and cloth more cheaply than England. However, since Portugal had a comparative advantage in the production of wine because its soil and climate enabled it to produce wine even more cheaply and efficiently than cotton, it would gain more by specializing in the production of wine and importing cloth from England than by producing both. England would gain by specializing in cloth and importing wine. This idea of the "gains from trade" was truly revolutionary. Paul Samuelson has called the law of comparative advantage "the most beautiful idea in economics." Ricardo conceived of international trade not as a zero-sum game, but as based on a harmony of interest founded on specialization and comparative advantage; this harmony of interest doctrine underlies the liberal view of international economic relations.

The classical theory of trade as expounded by Ricardo, John Stuart Mill, and others was based on a number of important assumptions or abstractions from reality. It omitted the cost of transportation and assumed that the factors of production were mobile domestically but immobile internationally. Comparative advantage was static, a gift of nature, and could not be transferred from one country to another. The theory was also based on the labor theory of value, that is, the belief

174

that the amount and efficiency of labor-input is the principal determinant of the cost of production. In addition, the law of comparative advantage was based on a two-country model.

Subsequent criticisms and refinements in the late nineteenth and twentieth centuries modified classical trade theory in a number of important ways (Condliffe, 1950, pp. 173-78). Neoclassical writers have added the cost of transportation, assumed greater mobility of the factors of production among countries, and stressed the importance of increasing returns to scale as an explanation of trade. Attention has also been given to the dynamic nature of comparative advantage, and the theory has been elaborated by mathematical techniques and statistical data. Factors other than labor have been added to the cost of production, leading to the concept of relative-factor endowment as an explanation of trade flows. The concept of labor itself has been modified to "human capital" and cost has been redefined as "opportunity cost." The central ideas of neoclassical economics—marginal utility theories and general equilibrium theory—were added to explain the terms of trade and other matters.

This neoclassical reformulation has become known as the Heckscher-Ohlin-Samuelson (H-O) theory or model of international trade and is the standard liberal position in the 1980s. The theory maintains that a nation's comparative advantage is determined by the relative abundance and most profitable combination of its several factors of production, such as capital, labor, resources, management, and technology. More specifically, "a country will export (import) those commodities which are intensive in the use of its abundant (scarce) factor" (El-Agraa, 1983, p. 77). Modern trade theory has thus become more fluid, dynamic, and comprehensive than the classical theory of comparative advantage.

The H-O model continues to be the most relevant theory for explaining interindustry trade, for example, the exchange of manufactured goods for commodities. It is therefore appropriate in accounting for much of North-South trade, but it is less successful with respect to trade among the industrialized countries themselves. This type of trade has necessitated a number of crucial modifications in neoclassical theory and the formulation of other explanations (Krugman, 1981a). Whereas the H-O model emphasizes factor endowments and perfect competition, newer theories such as the "technology gap" theory and the product cycle theory emphasize technology, economies of scale, and the dynamic nature of comparative advantage (Deardorff, 1984, pp. 493-99). Although no detailed treatment of these newer theories will be at-

intra-industry trade

, says something about taste

tempted here, several theoretical developments and their significance need to be discussed.

Perhaps the most important recent development in trade theory is the effort to account for the rapid expansion in the postwar era of intra-industry trade, for example, advanced countries importing some models of automobiles while exporting different models.[1] These theories, which apply primarily to North-North trade, emphasize the importance of learning curves, economies of scale, and differentiated consumer preferences. They also stress the increased importance of monopolistic or imperfect competition, the application of the theories of the firm and industrial organization to trading relations, and the increasing integration of international trade and foreign investment.

A further and closely related development is the expansion of intra-firm and interfirm trade, which is trade that takes place entirely within the confines of a single multinational corporation or among several firms cooperating through mechanisms like joint ventures or the subcontracting of component parts. The theories recognizing these developments respond to the international spread of oligopolistic corporations and the internationalization of production in recent decades. They attempt to explain the strategies of multinational corporations, such as the mix of trade and overseas production or the locus of global production.

A far more controversial recent development is the concept of strategic trade policy. The basic argument of this theory is that in a highly interdependent world economy composed of oligopolistic corporations and competitive states, it is possible, at least theoretically, for the latter to initiate policies that shift profits from foreign to national corporations. Insofar as this theory has merit, it entails a significant rapprochement between the liberal and nationalist theories of trade. The significance of this and other theories as well as the emergent trading patterns that they are attempting to explain will be discussed later in this chapter and also in Chapter Six.

The essence of these novel theories is, in the words of Paul Krugman, "that trade theory is the study of international industrial organization" (Krugman, 1981a, p. 22). Its core is the increasing importance in international trade and foreign investment of oligopolistic corporations that can take advantage of increasing returns, learning by doing, and barriers to entry against rivals. As will be noted below in the discussion of strategic trade policy, a similar development took place earlier in this century *within* national economies. The current integration of global

[1] Linder (1961) is the classic work on this subject.

markets and international production, however, is taking place in a world divided among competing nation-states. The crucial difference in this increasingly interdependent world economy is that individual corporations can gain competitive superiority over foreign firms because of the demand generated by a large domestic market, because of government subsidies, especially in research and development, and by means of protectionist policies. It is precisely this new combination of international interdependence and national firms that opens up the possibility that states may pursue strategic trade policies on behalf of their own multinational corporations.

The contrast between traditional trade theory and these newer approaches is striking. Whereas the emphasis of trade theory from Ricardo to Heckscher-Ohlin was on interindustry trade, these recent theories focus on intra-industry, intrafirm, and interfirm trade. The classical and neoclassical theories assumed that labor and capital were immobile, comparative advantage was static, and only finished products were exchanged. These newer theories, on the other hand, attempt to account for a world in which capital is highly mobile and products are exchanged at every step of the production process, from technological knowledge to intermediate goods and component parts to the final product itself. Of equal importance, in contrast to the older theories, which neglected foreign direct investment and production abroad, the newer theories regard export trade and foreign production as complementary aspects of the strategies of multinational corporations. Finally, the epitome of traditional theory was the view of the economist Frank Graham that trade is between firms regardless of their location. More recent approaches attempt to incorporate the fact that trading relations are between firms of different nationalities and take place in a world where the modern state plays a much more active role than in the past.

This industrial organization approach to international trade helps explain three basic facts of international trade in the postwar era.[2] First, it accounts for the fact that most trade has been among advanced countries with similar industrial structures. More than 60 percent of their trade is among themselves. Second, it explains why this trade has tended to be intra-industry trade, that is, exchanges of similar products, and also accounts for the overseas expansion of multinational firms in particular sectors such as automobiles, consumer durables, and machine tools. Third, it explains why intra-industry trade has moder-

[2] Krugman (1981a) presents a brief and excellent summary of these developments in trade theory.

ated the distributional and conflictual aspects of trade. In contrast to the implications of conventional trade theory, the survival of whole industrial sectors has not been threatened by the increase in intra-industry trade; instead firms have shifted to specialization in particular products, thus minimizing the effects of trade on their workers.

The industrial rise of Japan and the newly industrializing countries (NICs), however, appears to be changing this situation by displacing intra-industry trade with interindustry trade. For example, the rapid advance of Asian industry has threatened whole sectors of the American electronics industry, whereas in the past, Japanese competition damaged only consumer electronics. This shift is causing intense distributional concerns in many advanced countries and is stimulating the spread of protectionist policies.[3]

Underlying this last development is an important change in the status of the concept of comparative advantage. At least in its simpler formulations, this fundamental principle of liberal trade theory has lost some of its relevance and predictive power (Corden, 1984a). Its explanation of trade patterns, based on the intensity and abundance of the factors of production, is of declining relevance to a world of intra-industry trade and rapid technological diffusion. Comparative advantage is now regarded as dynamic and is also considered to be arbitrary and a product of corporate and state policies. As the concept of comparative advantage has lost status, the argument for free trade has necessarily lost some of its efficacy and has become less relevant. This more equivocal situation has been summarized by one authority, Harry Johnson, in the following qualified defense of free trade:

'the case for free trade, frequently asserted with considerable dogmatism in the past, appears in contemporary international trade theory as an extremely qualified proposition, dependent on the maintenance of international monetary stability, on efficient representation of alternative social opportunity costs by money costs and prices in the domestic currency, on the social acceptability of the resulting distribution of income or the adoption of a social policy with regard to income distribution, and on the possible need for international income transfers' (quoted in Cooper, 1970, pp. 438-39).

The varying patterns of trade in the contemporary world and the proliferation of theories explaining them leads to the conclusion "that no single theory is capable of explaining international trade in *all* commodities and at *all* times" (El-Agraa, 1983, p. 85). In effect, the general and unified body of trade theory has been displaced by a number of spe-

[3] See the discussion below of the Stolper-Samuelson theorem and its implications for the rise of economic protectionism.

cific explanations for different types of trading relations. Even the H-O model, which comes closest to a unified theory, is most relevant to North-South trade. Regardless of theoretical differences, however, liberal economists maintain their basic commitment to the mutual benefits of free trade, to specialization based upon comparative advantage, and to the virtues of a global territorial division of labor (Condliffe, 1950, pp. 160-61). From the classical theorists to the present, liberals subscribe to the doctrine of free trade.

Nevertheless, liberals have become more cautious about prescribing free trade as the best policy for everyone at all times; they acknowledge that under certain circumstances free trade may actually be harmful. They also recognize that large economies and monopolists can exploit their positions through the adoption of optimum tariffs (Corden, 1984a, pp. 82-86). States may also improve their terms of trade through the use of "effective tariffs," that is, the manipulation of their tariff schedules on raw materials and finished goods (Scammell, 1983, pp. 166-68). Despite these and other caveats, however, liberal theorists believe emphatically that individual and international welfare is maximized by economic specialization and free trade.[4]

It is important to stress what liberal trade theory does *not* assert. Liberals do not argue that everyone will necessarily gain from free trade, at least not in the short run and not without adapting appropriate policies. Rather it asserts that there are potential gains. World welfare would be increased and everyone would gain in the long run if they pursue a policy of specialization based on comparative advantage. Furthermore, liberal trade theory does not argue that everyone will gain equally even if they do follow the proper policies. Instead, it maintains that everyone will gain in absolute terms, although some will gain relatively more than others due to their greater efficiency and natural endowments. The argument for free trade is based not on grounds of equity and equal distribution but on increased efficiency and the maximization of world wealth. It is regarding precisely these distributive matters, however, that nationalist theory takes issue with the liberal approach.

Liberals consider free trade to be the best policy because specialization and the international division of labor increase individual productivity and hence the accumulation of both national and global wealth; in addition, it increases consumption possibilities. They believe that the

---

[4] Actually, the possibility of adopting optimal tariffs and the terms of trade appear to be of little relevance for the determination of commercial policy, but domestic concern over the unemployment level is crucial (Beenstock, 1983, p. 224).

only purpose of exports is to pay for imports. (On the many benefits of trade, see Blackhurst, Marian, and Tumlir, 1977, pp. 25-29.) If economic distortions prevent trade or mean that imports would inflict unnecessary damage on a society, the liberal's "first-best" solution is to eliminate the distortions rather than to impose restraints on trade. If this is impossible, then the next best solution is the corrective use of subsidies and taxes (Corden, 1974). After that come tariffs, because they at least preserve the price mechanism. If nontariff barriers are necessary they should be transparent and clearly acknowledged. Despite these admonitions, as this century draws to a close, nations are unfortunately failing to heed this order of preferred policy choices and the nationalist approach to trading relations has gained ground.

The Nationalist Theory of International Trade

Economic nationalists emphasize the costs of trade to particular groups and states and favor economic protectionism and state control over international trade. Their criticisms of liberal trade theory may be summarized in three broad categories: (1) the implications of free trade for economic development and the international division of labor, (2) relative rather than absolute gains (the distributive effects of trade), and (3) the effect on national autonomy and impact on domestic welfare (Blackhurst, Marion, and Tumlir, pp. 29-42).

Although the roots of economic nationalism can be found in the mercantilist writers of the seventeenth and eighteenth centuries, Alexander Hamilton's *Report on the Subject of Manufactures*, presented to the U.S. House of Representatives in 1791, contains the intellectual origins of modern economic nationalism and the classic defense of economic protectionism (Hamilton, 1928 [1791]). Hamilton modernized the eighteenth-century mercantilist thesis and developed a dynamic theory of economic development based on the superiority of manufacturing over agriculture. He set forth what we today would call an "import-substitution" strategy of economic development: "Not only the wealth, but the independence and security of a country, appear to be materially connected with the prosperity of manufactures. Every nation, with a view of these great objects, ought to endeavor to possess within itself, all the essentials of national supply. These comprise the means of subsistence, habitation, clothing, and defense" (ibid., p. 284). From Hamilton on, nationalists have argued that the location of economic activities should be a central concern of state policy.

As the economic theorist of the first colony to revolt against a European imperial system, Hamilton's ideas are worth considering in some detail. According to Hamilton and subsequent proponents of economic nationalism, governments can transform the nature of their economies and thus their position in the international economy through what are now called "industrial policies." The transfer of the factors of production from more advanced economies can be encouraged to develop particular industries. Hamilton argued, for example, that the migration, especially of skilled labor, should be encouraged to expedite industrialization. The nation should also encourage the importation of foreign capital and should establish a banking system to provide investment capital. In short, Hamilton's *Report* set forth a dynamic theory of comparative advantage based on government policies of economic development.

Like other mercantilists before him, Hamilton identified national power with the development of manufactures and regarded economics as subordinate to the fundamental task of state building. Although his ideas on protectionism were not to achieve full force in America until the victory of the rapidly industrializing North in the Civil War, they exerted a powerful influence at home and abroad. Developing nations that emphasize protectionism, industrialization, and state intervention owe more than they may appreciate to Hamilton's conception of economic development.

In the nineteenth century Hamilton's ideas had their greatest impact in Germany, where the intellectual ground had already been prepared by Johann Fichte and Georg Hegel. Friedrich List, after a number of years in the United States, carried Hamilton's views to Germany. With Wilhelm Roscher, Gustav Schmoller, and others, List helped establish the German Historical School of economic analysis, whose ideas found ready acceptance in a Germany whose traditional industries were under attack by a flood of low-cost British imports. This school's fierce and systematic attack on liberalism had a powerful influence on the development of Germany and on the world economy generally.

In his influential *National System of Political Economy* (1904 [1841]), List argued that the free trade theories of the classical British economists were the economic policy of the strong, that there was no "natural" or immutable international division of labor based on the law of comparative advantage, and that the division of labor was merely a historical situation resulting from prior uses of economic and political power. The British, List argued, had actually used the power of the state to protect their own infant industries against foreign competition while weakening their opponents by military force, and they only became champions of free trade after having achieved technological and industrial supremacy over their rivals (Condliffe, 1950, p. 71).

List believed that the British were merely seeking to advance their own national economic interests by gaining unimpeded access to foreign markets through free trade. He regarded British promotion of what is now called an "interdependent world economy" as another expression of Britain's selfish national interests and believed that a true cosmopolitan world economy as espoused by economic liberals would be possible only when other nations became equal to Great Britain in industrial power. List and other German economic nationalists advocated political unification, development of railroads to unify the economy physically, and erection of high tariff barriers to foster economic unification, protect the development of German industry, and thus create a powerful German state.

Many believed that the success of protectionism in Germany and the role of the state in German industrial development vindicated the theories of economic nationalism. As Thorstein Veblen argued in his classic study, *Imperial Germany and the Industrial Revolution* (1939), Germany was the first society to pursue a systematic industrial policy and the scientific development of its economy. The rapid advance of German wealth and military power in the latter part of the nineteenth century set an example for other societies. Whereas the economic success of Great Britain initially seemed to establish the virtues of liberalism, that of Germany legitimized the doctrine of economic nationalism as a guide to trade policy and economic development.

Proponents of economic nationalism at the end of the twentieth century again challenge the liberal assumption that comparative advantage is relatively static. They argue that the law of comparative advantage is primarily a rationalization for the existing international division of labor and advocate a trade policy that encourages the development or preservation of domestic industry. On the one hand, nationalist emphasis on industrialization has, in the less developed economies, focused on the adoption of an "import-substitution" development strategy. On the other hand, a number of advanced countries, responding to the stunning success of the Japanese economy in the 1970s and 1980s, have adopted industrial policies designed to develop specific industrial sectors. These nationalist tendencies will be evaluated below.

Whereas economic liberals emphasize the absolute gains in global wealth from a regime of free trade, economic nationalists of the nineteenth century and their twentieth-century descendants stress the international distribution of the gains from trade. Nationalists note that in a world of free trade the terms of trade tend to favor the most industrially advanced economy. The German Historical School asserted that the British pursued protectionist policies until British industry was strong enough to outcompete every other economy and that British technical superiority in manufactured products and processes enabled Great Britain to enjoy highly favorable terms of trade relative to the exporters of lower-technology products, food, and raw materials.

Economic nationalists also believe that free trade undermines national autonomy and state control over the economy by exposing the economy to the vicissitudes and instabilities of the world market and exploitation by other, more powerful economies. They argue that specialization, especially in commodity exports, reduces flexibility, increases the vulnerability of the economy to untoward events, subordinates the domestic economy to the international economy, and threatens domestic industries on which national security, established jobs, or other values are dependent. Although these arguments are frequently used to cloak the special interests of particular groups and industries, they are important in the formulation of national economic policy in all countries.

The economic nationalists of the German Historical School called attention to the ways in which the rise of a highly interdependent world economy affected national security, while nineteenth-century liberals were accurately arguing that the world had never before enjoyed a comparable era of peace and prosperity. The expansion of trade, the flow of foreign investment, and the efficiency of the international monetary system ushered in a period of economic growth that spread from England throughout the system. Perhaps never before or since has the cosmopolitan interest been so well joined to the national interest of the dominant power as under the Pax Britannica. But although all may indeed have gained, some did gain more than others, as the nationalists emphasized. The expansion of global economic interdependence created new forms of national insecurity and novel arenas of international conflict along with economic growth.

FREE TRADE VERSUS ECONOMIC PROTECTIONISM

Numerous controversies between liberal proponents of free trade and their nationalist critics have emerged with the intensification of international trade and interdependence since the 1850s. The issues are concerned with the effects of international trade on domestic welfare and industrial development, the economic and political effects of increasing interdependence, and the role of government policies and corporate power in the distribution of benefits as well as other crucial questions. Unfortunately, relatively little research has been done on many of these issues and there are serious problems in testing trade theories. As one authority put it, there is much room for disagreement over trade and its effects because most propositions have never been tested (Dixit, 1983, p. 80). Indeed, the issues may never be resolved because the assumptions and objectives of the two positions are so different.

The issue of free trade versus protectionism lies at the heart of the conflict between economic liberals and economic nationalists. This debate historically has appeared in differing forms: the "infant" industry argument for protection, the debate over the benefits and costs of international specialization, and (for lack of a better term) the "senile" or perhaps the "second infancy" industry problem (Dixit, 1986, p. 5). These three controversies are interrelated, but the following discussion will attempt to keep them separate.

Liberals believe that the historical record supports the superiority of a policy of free trade over protectionism. Great Britain, they point out, surpassed its rivals after 1848 precisely because it adopted a policy of free trade. France, an industrial leader in the eighteenth century, fell behind because it resorted to high levels of protectionism and its industry then became inefficient (Kindleberger, 1978b, ch. 3). Nationalists, on the other hand, note that Britain used force against its economic rivals and adopted free trade only after its industry had developed behind the shield of protectionism. As for Germany, it too protected its nascent industries from what has been characterized as the "imperialism of free trade," that is, the British effort to direct investment abroad away from competitive industries (Semmel, 1970).[5] The advantages of being first, nationalists argue, are so great that industrialization requires the protection of infant industry.

In principle, both liberals and nationalists accept the rationale for protecting infant industries (Corden, 1974, ch. 9). Both acknowledge that an industrial economy may have particular advantages over a non-industrialized economy that make it very difficult for the latter to establish its own industries. In the words of John Stuart Mill, "there may be no inherent advantage on one part, or disadvantage on the other, but only a present superiority of acquired skill and experience. A country which has this skill and experience yet to acquire, may in other respects be better adapted to the production than those which were earlier in the field" (Mill, 1970 [1848], pp. 283-84).

Liberals and nationalists disagree fundamentally, however, on the specific purpose of protectionism as it relates to infant industries. For liberals, protectionism is in the nature of an experiment to test whether

[5] The concept of the "imperialism of free trade," developed by Gallagher and Robinson (1953), is that free trade is but another form of economic imperialism.

a nation really does have an inherent comparative advantage in a particular industry. Mill said "it is essential that the protection should be confined to cases in which there is good ground of assurance that the industry which it fosters will after a time be able to dispense with it; nor should the domestic producers ever be allowed to expect that it will be continued to them beyond the time necessary for a fair trial of what they are capable of accomplishing" (Mill, 1970 [1848], p. 284). Liberals regard protectionism at best as a necessary but temporary expedient and as a stepping stone to a system of free trade.

Economic nationalists, on the other hand, tend to regard protectionism as an end in itself. The nationalist's foremost objectives, at least in the short run, are not free trade and wealth accumulation but state-building and industrial power. In most developing countries industrialization is the primary goal of national policy, and the fundamental purpose of a tariff is to establish particular industries frequently without regard to the economic rationale for doing so.

Economic nationalists assume the superiority of industry over both agriculture and commodity production. Industry is believed to be not only valuable in itself because it contributes a high value-added to national production, but it is alleged to have powerful secondary effects, positive externalities, and "backward linkages" or spinoffs that stimulate the entire economy and speed overall economic development (Cornwall, 1977). Its effects on the quality of the work force, business entrepreneurship, and the overall options of the society make industrialization an objective in its own right.

In response to the nationalist argument for protection, liberals argue that every economy has a comparative advantage in something and therefore should not fear free trade. Through each doing what it can do best, regardless of what that is, everyone can gain. Thus, in anticipation of the nationalist contention that the advent of intra-industrial trade and the application of industrial organization theory to trade gives aid and comfort to the nationalist defense of protectionism, Krugman has defended letting the market determine international specialization and trade patterns:

But who produces what? Can we say anything about the direction of trade? Obviously not: by ruling out comparative advantage we have made the question of who exports what indeterminate. In any case, it doesn't matter. To realize the gains from trade, all that matters is that countries specialize in producing different things. Whether Germany produces large refrigerators and France small ones, or vice versa, is not important; that they do not each produce both types is (Krugman, 1981a, p. 10).

For nationalists, however, who produces what is of the utmost importance. What concerns them is precisely the international location of those economic activities that, in their judgment, contribute most to the political position and overall developmemt of the economy. In a world in which comparative advantage is highly arbitrary and where, again to quote Krugman (1981a, p. 19), "the other interesting point is that the outcome of the process of specialization may depend on initial conditions. . . . History matters. A country, having once been established as an exporter in some industry, may maintain this position simply because of the economies of scale gained—unless comparative advantage moves far enough away." The nationalist can find in this statement ample support for the protection of infant industries.

The traditional nationalist defense of infant industry protection has been joined in recent years by the prospect of strategic trade policy, to be discussed later in this chapter. Whereas infant industry protection is largely defensive, strategic trade policy is essentially offensive. Its central message is "import protection for export promotion." Through the erection of entry barriers, the use of government subsidies, and the husbanding of domestic demand to give advantage to domestic firms, one's own corporations can acquire the economies of scale and other advantages that will enable them to dominate world markets. In the modern world of intra-industry trade, the line between defensive infant industry protection and strategic trade policy has become very thin indeed.

The outcome of the debate over the protection of industries is indeterminate. As List and more recent authors have noted, every country has protected its industries to some extent in the early stages of industrialization. Contemporary developments in trade theory have provided a new and additional rationale for this protectionism. Yet it does not follow that protectionism necessarily leads to the development of a viable industrial structure. Indeed, in many instances protectionism has demonstrably hindered the development of an efficient industrial base, for example, import-substitution strategies have proved bankrupt in many less developed economies. The success of strategic trade policy, as exemplified by the commercial difficulties of the European Airbus consortium, has yet to prove its worth. The whole issue of free trade versus protection does not lend itself to easy answers.

Considering only the issue of infant industry protection, one may conclude that trade can be both a destroyer and an engine of growth (Gould, 1972, ch. 4). The superior competitiveness of industry in advanced economies can wipe out economic sectors in less developed economies, as happened to the historic Indian handicraft textile industry. But as a rapidly industrializing India and other NICs have demonstrated, trade between advanced and less developed economies can also be an important source of economic growth for the latter. The developing country's response to the opportunities provided by the international trading system is critically important.

It is worth noting that nationalists are myopic in their evaluation of trade and protectionism when they stress the inequitable international distributive effects of free trade while overlooking the domestic distributive effects of protectionism (H. Johnson, 1967). The domestic consequence of protectionism is a redistribution of income from consumers and society as a whole to the protected producers and the state. Liberals correctly note that protectionism creates economic rents that these latter interests collect.[6] Economic nationalism thus may be viewed as sacrificing the welfare of the whole society to that of particular groups. It is an alliance of the state with producer interests and, for this reason, the primary proponents of protectionist doctrine tend to be state bureaucracies and domestic producers whose economic interests lie with the protected industrial sectors.

The more important consideration, however, is that liberals and nationalists have different objectives and judge the success of policies by different standards. Liberals judge trade and protectionism in terms of consumer welfare and the maximization of global efficiency. Nationalists stress what they consider to be producer and state interests.

Liberals and nationalists also divide on the benefits and costs of specialization. From Adam Smith on, liberals have believed that specialization and an expanding market lead to increased efficiencies in production and hence to a more rapid rate of economic growth. They also believe that the long-term benefits of specialization and free trade outweigh any associated costs, because national specialization based on comparative advantage will maximize both domestic and international economic welfare. Economic nationalists, stressing the costs of international specialization and increasing interdependence, believe those costs to range from the loss of national sovereignty to an enhanced vulnerability of national welfare to the negative impact of foreign developments.

[6] A "rent" is defined by economists as "a payment to a resource owner above the amount his resources could command in their next best alternative use. An economic rent is a receipt in excess of the opportunity cost of a resource" (Tollison, 1982, p. 577). They are "earned only by the owners of resources that cannot be augmented rapidly and at low cost to meet an increased demand for the goods they are used to produce" (Posner, 1977, p. 9). Land and skills are good examples. In the modern world a technological monopoly can produce rent or technological profits. This fact is central to the debate over what is called strategic trade policy.

In this debate over the benefits and costs of specialization, the fact that the industries most vital for national security and military power are frequently the ones most involved in international trade is significant (Condliffe, 1950, p. 799). Furthermore, import-sensitive industries frequently are major providers of domestic employment. Thus, specialization and changes in specialization raise fundamental issues of national concern.

The clash between liberals and nationalists over the benefits and costs of specialization, although partially based on differing economic and political objectives, also rests on differing assumptions regarding the nature of international economic relations. Liberals consider these relations to be essentially harmonious; nationalists believe that conflict is inevitable. As will be argued below, neither assumption is valid in itself. Rather, its validity rests on the larger configuration of global economic and political conditions at a particular time. The degree of harmony or disharmony is dependent upon the extent of complementarity of trade as well as the overall political relations among trading nations. Liberal trading practices flourish best when governed by a liberal hegemonic power or agreement among dominant liberal states.

Another controversy regarding free trade and protectionism may be labeled the "senile" or declining industry argument; this assumes that there are certain advantages to backwardness or disadvantages to being first (Rostow, 1980). As newly industrializing countries catch up with older industrial countries, the former enjoy the benefits of lower wage rates, of being able to adopt advanced and efficient technologies, and other advantages (Gerschenkron, 1962). Industry in the older industrial country therefore needs protection against the aggressive and "unfair" tactics of the newcomer. Whereas liberals reject the protection of inefficient declining industries as a wasteful diversion of scarce resources from investment in more promising growth industries, nationalists employ a variety of stratagems to defend declining industrial sectors. Arguments put forth include the need to protect industrial sectors vital to national security and emotional appeals to save jobs threatened by the unfair practices of foreign competitors. Although there may be occasions when such arguments have validity, in most cases the real purpose of protectionism is to safeguard particular threatened inefficient industries.

In the 1980s an effort has been made by certain economists, including some of a liberal persuasion, to develop a rationale for protecting senile industries that is complementary to the argument for protecting infant industries.[7] They argue that the usual disadvantages of being first

---

[7] Whitman (1981) sets forth the rationale for protecting "senile" or mature industries.

have been enhanced by the increasingly rapid rate of global changes in comparative advantage and the intensified impact of external shocks. They note that with the quadrupling of the price of energy in 1973, the existing capital stock of all advanced countries was made obsolete and consumer preferences were suddenly transformed. Further, adjustment to these rapid and massive changes has been retarded and transition costs are aggravated by low rates of economic growth, domestic economic rigidities, and market imperfections. It is argued that the transition costs of phasing out older industries in favor of newer ones have grown so much that the costs of adjusting to rapid change may exceed its benefits. Furthermore, business investment may be discouraged if overly rapid obsolescence and intense foreign competition make it impossible for a business to capture the benefits of the investment. Under these circumstances, an industry may find itself caught "in a process of change and adaptation so profound as to put it in a position akin to that of an infant industry," for example, American automobile manufacturing (Whitman, 1981, p. 22). The state, therefore, should develop an industrial policy to cushion the effects on the economy of untoward external developments.

More generally, there are those who argue that both liberalization of trade and industrial specialization have reached a point of diminishing returns, causing a shift in the benefits and costs of free trade. Although traditional trade theory maintains that the benefits of trade and specialization will always be greater than its costs, it has assumed a relatively slow rate of change in comparative advantage so that displacement of workers is gradual and associated adjustment costs are low. At the end of the twentieth century, however, the liberalization of trade, the increasing number of sellers, and the dynamic nature of comparative advantage have greatly accelerated the rate of industrial change and thus raised adjustment costs.

Some liberal economists argue that specialization based on considerations of static comparative advantage has even become extremely risky in a highly uncertain world where governments constantly intervene in the market (Brainard·and Cooper, 1968). Specialization makes the welfare of the society vulnerable to the market and to political forces beyond national control. In the past this situation was applicable only to the producers of raw materials, but now it applies increasingly to industrial producers as well. Some argue that the solution to this increased uncertainty and rapid rate of change might be is for the country to develop a "portfolio" of industries and protective tariffs that will reduce the cost and risk of specialization. A major purpose of industrial policy is to ensure that the nation does not put all of its eggs in one industrial basket and does develop an optimum level of foreign trade.

To summarize, economic nationalists criticize the liberal doctrine of free trade because the doctrine is politically naive and fails to appreciate the extent to which the terms of trade and the rules governing trade are determined by the exercise of power, because the doctrine is static and slights the problem of adjustment costs, and because it ignores the problems of uncertainty in its stress on the benefits of specialization. Despite these serious limitations, however, liberal trade theory retains its essential validity; it cannot be dismissed simply as a rationalization of the interests of the strong. Although trade does tend to benefit the strong, at least in short-run terms, all *can* gain in absolute terms and some gain both relatively and absolutely, as is seen in the present-day examples of Japan and the NICs. It is important to remember that when the world has reverted to nationalist trade policies, as it did in the 1930s, everyone has lost. The ultimate defense of free trade, as Smith pointed out, is that there are benefits for *all* from a territorially based international division of labor.

As one would expect from economic theory itself, there are both costs and benefits to free trade, and tradeoffs always exist. These must be considered by every nation as it formulates its commercial policy; no nation has yet chosen to pursue either an exclusively free trade or an exclusively nationalistic policy. A nation's mix of these two policies is a function of its domestic economy and of conditions prevailing in the world economy. The interplay of these domestic and international factors has produced swings between liberal and nationalist trade regimes over the past two hundred years. In the late twentieth century, an analysis of the postwar regime of liberalized trade reveals that the pendulum is once again swinging in the direction of economic nationalism.

Until the early 1970s, the history of the postwar trading system was one of increasing liberalization. Led by the American hegemon, the major trading nations moved in the direction of the precepts of liberal trade theory. With the relative decline of American power and the development of adverse economic conditions, this movement was reversed. By the mid-1980s, economic nationalism had become a potent force in global trading relations. To appreciate this change and its significance, one must begin with the General Agreement on Tariffs and Trade (GATT).

THE GATT SYSTEM

The General Agreement on Tariffs and Trade, established in 1948, has provided the institutional basis for trade negotiations in the postwar era. The fundamental purpose of the GATT was to achieve "freer and fairer trade" through reduction of tariffs and elimination of other trade barriers. GATT has operated on the basis of three principles: (1) non-discrimination, multilateralism, and the application of the Most-Favored Nation Principle (MFN) to all signatories, (2) expansion of trade through the reduction of trade barriers, and (3) unconditional reciprocity among all signatories. GATT's goal was to establish a world trade regime or universal rules for the conduct of commercial policy (Whitman, 1977, p. 28).

From the very beginning there were important exceptions to these principles, for example, the British Commonwealth, the permissibility of common markets or free trade area agreements, and Article XIX (safeguards provision) of the GATT; these exceptions recognized special economic relationships or encouraged countries to take the risk of moving even more toward completely free trade. Although the Eastern bloc and certain less developed countries (LDCs) never signed the GATT and did not accept GATT principles and a number of OECD countries never completely fulfilled their GATT obligations, the basic principles of the GATT provided the basis for the postwar liberalization of world trade (Whitman, 1977, pp. 33-35).

Under the formula of what was called in Chapter Four the "compromise of embedded liberalism," countries could accept the obligations of the GATT and join in tariff-reduction negotiations without jeopardizing their domestic economic objectives. The goal was nondiscrimination and multilateralism rather than the complete abandonment of national controls over trade barriers (Ruggie, 1982, p. 396). Moreover, the GATT contained ample escape provisions and protection against harmful domestic impact (Lipson, 1982, pp. 426-27). The guarantee of increased stability encouraged nations to move in the direction of trade liberalization (Ruggie, 1982, p. 399).

In the 1980s, the GATT principles of multilateralism and non-discrimination as well as the "compromise of embedded liberalism" have come under increasing attack. For many countries and powerful groups the legitimacy of the GATT and of its principles have been weakened by structural changes in the world economy. New challenges have raised the issue of whether the GATT or some functional substitute can continue to maintain the regime of liberalized trade and, if not, what form or forms of trade regime might possibly replace the postwar liberal trade order.

Challenges to the GATT

Following the Second World War, successive rounds of trade negotiations within the framework of the GATT led to an astounding decline of tariff barriers and growth in world trade. As a consequence of numerous GATT negotiations in the early postwar period (the Dillon Round in 1960-1962, and, most significant of all, the Kennedy Round in 1962-1967), the merchandise trade of industrial countries grew from 1950 through 1975 at an average rate of 8 percent a year, twice the growth rate of their gross national product (4 percent) (Cline, 1983, p. 5). The growing network of international trade began to enmesh national economies in a system of economic interdependence and lead some observers to speculate that a tightly integrated world economy was inexorably emerging. Then the balance between the forces of liberalization and economic nationalism began to shift; by the mid-1970s, economic nationalism had begun to tip the scales away from trade liberalization and the growth of trade slowed.

Trade liberalization was put on the defensive as early as the 1950s with the formation of the European Economic Community (EEC). The Dillon Round was initiated by the United States to counter the threat of the EEC's external tariff and the Common Agriculture Policy (CAP) of production subsidies. The sectoral or item-for-item approach of these negotiations, however, showed meager results. When tariff reductions in the early 1960s began to impinge on key industrial sectors and the interests of powerful groups, it became clear that a new approach to tariff reduction was required (Scammell, 1983, p. 172).

A new method of tariff negotiations was employed in the Kennedy Round, concluded in 1967; it produced an across-the-board tariff cut of 35 percent on 60,000 products, incorporated an antidumping agreement, and provided for food assistance to the less developed countries. Yet the round failed in three important respects; it did not deal with the increasing problem of nontariff barriers, the special problems of the LDCs, or the problem of agricultural trade (Scammell, 1983, p. 172). Despite these failures, the Kennedy Round was the high point of the postwar movement toward trade liberalization. One authority has compared it to the Cobden Treaty of 1860, which appeared to have brought the world to "the threshold of free trade" (ibid.). As in the late nineteenth century, however, the forces of economic nationalism continued to gain strength.

By the mid-1980s, the GATT regime and liberal world trade were very much on the defensive. In the words of the *Economic Report of the President* for 1985 by the Council of Economic Advisers, "the world is moving away from, rather than toward, comprehensive free trade. In major industrialized countries, for example, the proportion of total manufacturing subject to nontariff restrictions rose to about 30 percent in 1983, up from 20 percent just 3 years earlier" (1985, p. 114).

Although the total value of world trade continued to expand into the 1980s, the spread of protectionism increasingly affected the nature of the trading system and the international locus of industrial production.

Several fundamental developments in the 1970s accounted for the slowing of the growth of trade and the revival of economic protectionism: (1) the shift to floating exchange rates and the consequent erratic behavior of the rates, (2) the OPEC revolution in the winter of 1973-1974 and the massive increase in the price of world energy, (3) the intensification of Japanese competition, (4) the entry of the highly competitive newly industrializing countries (NICs) into world markets, (5) the relative decline of the American economy, (6) the increasing closure of the European Economic Community, and (7) the emergence of global stagflation. Together, these developments slowed and began to reverse the movement toward trade liberalization.

The 1973-1974 and 1979-1980 massive increases in the price of world energy had a significant impact on world trade. One consequence was that energy became a much larger factor in the dollar value of world trade and in part caused its continuing high value. By the same token, this change intensified the competition among energy-importing nations for export markets. The increased cost of energy also forced many economies in the developing world to go into debt to finance energy imports. The world's industrial plant, based on inexpensive energy, suddenly became largely obsolete, and this raised a massive adjustment problem. Furthermore, the price rise was inflationary, amounting to approximately 2 percent of the world gross product from the 1973-1974 price increase alone; it had a two-fold and contradictory impact on the international economy. First, it was highly inflationary because of the central role of petroleum in the modern economy as both a fuel and an industrial raw material. Second, the price increase also acted as a huge tax on the world economy, absorbing financial resources and depressing economic activities (Corden and Oppenheimer, 1974). The effect of all these developments was to reduce dramatically the rate of growth of world trade. The increase in the underlying rate of inflation, the shift to recessionary monetary policy, and the consequent global stagflation accelerated the spread of trade protectionism (Corden, 1984b, p. 5).

Another development transforming world trade in the 1970s was the intensification of Japanese and NIC competition. The rapid technological advance of Japan and the breaking of the Western monopoly of modern industry with the industrialization of South Korea, Brazil, and other NICs significantly increased the number of manufacturing exporters at the same time that the volume of world trade was declining and world markets were closing. In one industrial sector after another from textiles to steel to consumer electronics, the result was global overcapacity. For many in the advanced economies, the most disturbing development was that Japan and especially the NICs were combining state of the art productive techniques with the traditional low-wage advantage of developing countries. Due to these unprecedented circumstances, it was argued, protectionism against exports from Japan and the NICs was necessary to safeguard the living standards of the most advanced economies (Culbertson, 1985).

The relative decline in the size and competitiveness of the American economy also contributed to the slowing of world trade and the rise of protectionism. Between 1953-1954 and 1979-1980, imports as a share of GNP more than doubled, from 4.3 percent to 10.6 percent (Cline, 1983, p. 9).[8] In the 1980s, due to the macroeconomic policy of the Reagan Administration and the overvalued dollar, the American competitive position rapidly deteriorated as imports climbed from 11.4 percent to 15.3 percent of national goods production from 1980 to 1984, and thus intensified the level of competition in a remarkably short period (Destler, 1986, p. 101). By 1985, the American trade deficit was $150 billion, and $50 billion of that was with Japan. Even with respect to Western Europe, the United States had slipped from a $20 billion surplus in 1980 to a $15 billion deficit in 1984. In the first part of 1986, the United States had achieved the impossible: it had a deficit with almost every one of its trading partners. Not since 1864 had the U.S. trade balance been so negative (ibid., p. 100). America's relations with its major trading partners began to change in response to this increased openness and deteriorating trade situation. Previously the West European and Japanese economies had pursued aggressive export policies while simultaneously importing American goods to rebuild their own war-torn economies. In the 1970s and 1980s, the relatively smaller, more open, and less competitive American economy became highly sensitive to imports at the same time that other economies began to import relatively fewer American goods. As trade deficits and domestic unemployment rose, so did the protectionist pressures.

Another cause of rising protectionism has been the enlargement and increasing closure of the European Community. During much of the postwar period the development of the Common Market has contributed significantly to the overall expansion of world trade. Yet, since the mid-1970s, the Europeans have attempted to protect their traditional

[8] Symbolic of this change is that in 1983 the annual report of the Council of Economic Advisers moved the chapter on international developments from the end to the middle of the report.

industries and to safeguard employment against imports from Japan and the NICs. The tendency to turn inward has been enhanced by the enlargement of the Community, as the Mediterranean peripheral countries have been incorporated, the ties with the European Free Trade Association have grown, and a number of less developed countries have become associated with the Community through the Lomé Conventions of trade preferences. The West European market in manufacturing and temperate agricultural products (especially food grains) has grown more closed and the EEC has negotiated with outside powers more and more as a unified bloc. In short, Western Europe has increasingly operated as a regional trading system.

Thus, by the late 1970s, several broad changes had begun to erode the GATT system of trade liberalization. As tariff barriers within the GATT have fallen, nontariff barriers in most countries have risen. Barter or countertrade has grown rapidly, especially with respect to the less developed countries; the U.S. Commerce Department estimates that between 1976 and 1983, barter increased from approximately 2-3 to 25-30 percent of world trade (Goldfield, 1984, p. 19). Also, the state has become a more important actor in trading relations, from the sale of armaments to the negotiation of tied-aid packages and international cartels (Zysman and Cohen, 1982, pp. 42-46). Industrial and other domestic policies have increasingly influenced trade patterns. By one estimate, "the ratio of managed to total trade has increased sharply, from 40% in 1974 to 48% in 1980" (*The Economist*, December 25, 1982, p. 93). And if one includes intrafirm trade associated with the expanded role of the multinational corporations in world commerce, the percentage of controlled trade would be still greater.

The Multilateral Trade Negotiations (Tokyo Round), begun in 1973 and completed in 1979, constituted the first and foremost effort of the major trading nations to find new ways to deal with many of these changes in trading practices. Whatever its long-term significance for the regime of liberalized trade, the Tokyo Round transformed the basic framework for international negotiations over trading relations. The nature of its effect on the liberal trade regime, however, remains very much in dispute. One writer aptly entitled his own evaluation of the agreement "Tokyo Round: Twilight of a Liberal Era or a New Dawn?" (Corbett, 1979).[9]

The Tokyo Round, 1973-1979

The Tokyo Round made the first systematic attempt in the trade area to resolve the developing conflict between the increasing economic in-

[9] The definitive evaluation of the Tokyo Round negotiations is Winham (1986).

terdependence among national economies and the growing tendency of governments to intervene in their economies to promote economic objectives and domestic welfare (Whitman, 1977, p. 9). The round also dealt with a growing agenda of American complaints against its principal trading partners. The United States also wanted to reaffirm the commitment to a multilateral trading system, to codify international rules that limit domestic policies, and to eliminate discrimination against American exports by the Common Market and the Japanese (Krasner, 1979).

The vast array of subjects discussed in the Tokyo Round included the following:

(1) violations of the nondiscrimination or Most-Favored Nation Principle through preferential trading arrangements (e.g., the Lomé Convention between the EEC and certain LDCs) and the resultant increase in the fragmentation and regionalization of the world economy;

(2) resolution of issues related to unilateral imposition of import restrictions in cases of serious injury to domestic industry (Article XIX or "safeguard" provision of the GATT) and the increased use of "orderly marketing arrangements" or "voluntary export restraints" (Hindley, 1980);

(3) overall tariff reductions and the removal of nontariff barriers;

(4) liberalized trade in agriculture and increased access to the Common Market and Japan for American agricultural products;

(5) consideration of commodity agreements in wheat, coarse grains, dairy products, and meats;

(6) establishment of codes of conduct in a variety of areas, e.g., public procurement, export subsidies, and various types of government standards.

The primary goal of the Tokyo Round was to stabilize trading relations among the advanced OECD countries; this meant reformulating Article XIX (the safeguards provision), creating new codes for export subsidies, regulating countervailing duties and public procurement, and eliminating nontariff barriers. The concerns of the less developed countries for "special and differential" treatment embodied in their demands for a New International Economic Order (such as extension of "generalized preferences," access to developed countries for their manufactured exports, and formulation of commodity agreements) were partially recognized. During the 1970s the United States and other developed countries did adopt the Generalized System of Preferences, which lowered the duties on a number of LDC exports in manufactured products, and it was generally assumed that the less developed countries would benefit from measures that ensured a stable growth of world trade. The highest priority in the negotiations, however, was to deal with the expanding number of trade problems among the advanced countries themselves.

The Tokyo Round succeeded in several areas, including a further reduction of tariff barriers on industrial products of the major countries (OECD, 1985, p. 18). Its most important accomplishment was the establishment of a number of "codes of good behavior" regarding nontariff barriers (NTBs). These codes apply to such nontariff barriers and trade promotion policies as restrictions on government procurement, the granting of tax benefits, and the use of export credits. The purpose was to make the nontariff barriers at least visible if not to eliminate them entirely, to decrease the uncertainties generated by government intervention in the market, and thereby to stabilize the trading environment (Deardorff and Stern, 1984). In short, the codes were designed to limit a return to mercantilist trading practices and destructive policies of the 1930s.

The round also attempted to extend trade rules into new areas, such as safety and health standards and government procurement, and to clarify international norms in such areas as the use of export subsidies, antidumping regulations, and the use of countervailing tariffs.[10] In general, it sought to make more "transparent" and available to international scrutiny those nontariff barriers and other national practices associated with what is called the New Protectionism.

In a number of important areas, however, the Tokyo negotiations failed to reach agreement. These areas included a number of the special problems of the LDCs, the agricultural issue (which was of great concern to the United States), the provision for dispute settlement, issues of foreign investment related to trade, and the expanding trade in services and high technology. The growing use of nontariff barriers since the round indicates that the most serious shortcoming of the negotiations was its failure to revise the "safeguards" clause, which permits a country to restrict imports in order to protect an economic sector. This escape clause had been established to encourage the removal of trade barriers and to limit the damage to the regime of free trade if and when a nation imposed emergency protection to deal with actual or threatened serious injury to an industry by imports. Article XIX requires, however, that several preconditions be met: damage had to be demonstrated, the affected exporting countries had to be consulted and com-

[10] Despite its crucial importance in trade friction and negotiations, there appears to be no generally accepted definition of a subsidy.

pensated, and any restrictions had to conform to the GATT principle of nondiscrimination.

In the Tokyo Round the West Europeans wanted the right to apply restrictions selectively to the exports of particular countries (Japan and, to a lesser extent, the NICs), a modification that would have entailed a violation of the nondiscrimination principle. Japan and the NICs, needless to say, were intensely opposed to such a modification; the United States was generally indifferent. This fundamental controversy has not been resolved, and individual governments and the European Community have imposed "orderly marketing agreements" (OMAs) and voluntary export restraints (VERs) more frequently. The use of voluntary export restraints, a practice that is outside the GATT framework and violates the requirements of the "safeguards" principle, has had a growing impact on the character of the international trading system.[11]

In retrospect, it seems remarkable that the Tokyo Round succeeded as well as it did. The 1970s were a decade of economic upheaval. The problem of hyperinflation, the OPEC revolution, and the collapse of the Bretton Woods system strained international economic relations severely. With the spread of global stagflation after 1973, pressures for trade protectionism mounted. In these circumstances, the Tokyo Round and its many years of intense negotiations were indicative of the transformed nature of the international trading regime.

The round occurred during a global trend toward economic nationalism. Although its development of new codes helped to limit arbitrary government behavior and the proliferation of nontariff barriers, the new codes clearly acknowledge the extent of the retreat from international norms and the setbacks to previous GATT tariff reductions. Whereas the several GATT agreements of the 1950s and 1960s were negotiated multilaterally and followed the Most-Favored Nation or nondiscrimination principle, since the Tokyo Round the "rules" of international trade have more frequently been set unilaterally, negotiated bilaterally and, in some cases, have involved only the OECD countries. Particularist domestic interests in the advanced industrial countries have become increasingly important in the determination of these rules. Furthermore, the Tokyo codes apply only to signatory countries and in

---

[11] As Hindley (1980) points out, important economic and political differences exist between the invocation of Article XIX and the use of voluntary export restraints as a means of dealing with trade problems. Among other differences, the latter create rents through their allocation of market shares and the distribution of these shares are bilaterally negotiated. Yoffie (1983) is an excellent analysis of the use of VERs in the textile area by the United States against the NICs.

general have been rejected by the less developed countries. This could lead to a two-tier system of world trade composed of the OECD countries with their LDC trading partners on the one hand and all the rest of the world on the other (Curzon and Curzon Price, 1980). Despite its achievements, therefore, the overall success of the Tokyo Round was limited in important ways.

EMERGENT TRADE ISSUES

Although the Tokyo Round was by far the most complex and wide-ranging trade negotiation ever, it nevertheless left untouched many complex and difficult problems that have since become increasingly significant in international economic relations. Among the important and neglected issues were those of agriculture, the expanding global role of services, particularly finance and telecommunications, and high-technology industries (R. Baldwin, 1984b, pp. 610-612). In 1986, services accounted for approximately one quarter of the $2 trillion annual value of world trade (*The New York Times*, Sept. 21, 1986, p. 1). It is important to note also that agriculture and services were never covered by the GATT. Moreover, both services and high technology industries are closely associated with foreign direct investment by multinational corporations, which also lies outside the GATT framework. All three areas are extremely sensitive politically and, for this reason, may not fit well with the GATT principles of multilateralism and unconditional reciprocity.

Since these sectors have become more important, politically if not economically, the Tokyo Round may well have been the last trade negotiation of the old industrial era. Since the conclusion of the Tokyo Round, the far more intricate exchanges of the "information" economy and the "knowledge-intensive" industries, along with agriculture, have become the key subjects of the eighth round of trade negotiations. At the least, the changing environment and patterns of world trade suggest that future trade negotiations will have to be vastly different from those of the past.

In September 1986, at Punta Del Este, Uruguay, the members of the GATT decided after intense debate to launch an eighth round of multilateral trade negotiations to deal with these issues. The strongest proponent of what one source has called the "Uruguay Round" (*IMF Survey*, September 30, 1986, p. 299) was the United States, supported primarily by the Japanese and the economies of the Pacific Basin and opposed by certain members of the European Community and the larger LDCs. With financial and other services accounting for 70 percent of the American GNP, American agriculture in serious trouble, and rising protectionist pressures in Congress, the United States demanded that other nations open their economies to American service industries (including American multinationals), remove agricultural export subsidies, and write rules preventing the piracy of patents, trademarks, and other forms of intellectual property rights. Other countries were well aware that behind these American demands was the increasing danger of protectionist legislation from Congress. There are exceptional difficulties inherent in efforts to reach a multilateral agreement on any of these issues.

The problem of world trade in agriculture almost defies solution. Global overcapacity in agricultural production has arisen because many countries have become self-sufficient in food and the high dollar of the 1980s encouraged the opening of new sources of supply in many commodities. This massive surplus (tragically existing in a world of mass famine) necessitates a restructuring of agricultural support programs in Western Europe, the United States, and elsewhere. Yet few economic sectors enjoy greater domestic political influence than does agriculture. The universal tendency, therefore, is not only to erect import barriers, but to subsidize agricultural exports. Although Japan has set some of the highest import barriers, the subsidization of agricultural exports has been most prevalent in the European Economic Community, which is cemented by the Common Agricultural Policy. The United States, which itself began extensive export subsidies in the 1980s, and certain of the less developed countries have been the principal losers from these protectionist and export policies and the foremost advocates of a reform of agricultural trade.

The trade issues in the service and high-technology sectors have important characteristics that enhance their economic and political significance and make them especially difficult to resolve. In the first place, these industries have become the primary growth sectors for the advanced economies, particularly for the United States. At the same time, a growing number of NICs such as Brazil, India, and South Korea have targeted these sectors for development and are protecting them from foreign competition. As they rapidly become the "commanding heights" of the contemporary world economy, competition and conflict are destined to be fierce. Second, these sectors (in addition to agriculture) comprise the expanding export markets of the United States and hence are of intensifying concern to American policy makers, who consider the removal of West European, Japanese, and LDC restrictions against American service industries to be the litmus test of future trading relations. Third, the service industries (finance, communications, and information processing) permeate domestic social relations and institutions, which means there is strong resistance to outside pressures for change and the opening of national markets. For example, American demands on Japan to open its economy in these areas are resisted because they are believed to threaten Japanese cultural values and national self-sufficiency in strategic sectors.

The conflict between the advanced and developing countries over services and high-technology industries has become intense. The United States and other developed countries believe that it is impossible for the developing countries to demand greater access to Northern markets for their increasing output of manufactured goods unless they are willing to reciprocate by opening their own markets to the service and high-tech industries of the advanced countries. However, for the NICs and other LDCs free trade in services and high technology would mean unrestricted access for the multinational banks and corporations of the United States to the economies of the developing countries. This would deny them the opportunity to protect and develop their own similar industries, and the LDCs argue that they would then be forever behind and dependent upon the more advanced economies in the expanding high-technology industries.

On the other hand, the United States and, to some extent, the other advanced economies have become increasingly sensitive to high-technology issues. The increased significance of technological diffusion and the increasingly arbitrary nature of comparative advantage as well as military security concerns are causing the United States to make the protection of its high-tech industries an important priority. In addition to its own efforts to slow down the outflow of industrial know-how, the United States has placed the international protection of intellectual property rights on the agenda of trade negotiations.[12] This growing effort by the United States to safeguard the competitive position of American corporations against intellectual piracy and the overly rapid diffusion of their comparative advantage runs directly counter to the desire of other countries to climb the technological ladder.

The service sectors of finance, data processing, and the like are closely associated with the overseas operation of multinational corporations and this fact raises a difficult problem. These sectors are infrastructure industries and affect the overall control as well as international competitiveness of the economy. Because they are central to the

[12] The literature on the increasing importance of technology transfer or diffusion in economic relations is enormous. Technology has in effect become an independent factor of production. Giersch (1982) is a representative collection of different views.

way in which an economy operates and to its basic mode of production, these sectors tend to be nationalized or highly regulated. Thus, the highest trade barrier to be hurdled is the role of the state in these sectors, and therefore negotiations for increased economic liberalization in the service industries and for access by foreign multinationals have become extremely sensitive politically. Increased openness raises the issue of whether or not a greater harmonization of domestic practices and institutions is necessary. The United States believes strongly that harmonization is required to enable American corporations to operate successfully in Japan and the LDCs, but the latter denounce American pressures in this direction as a new form of imperialism and a violation of national sovereignty (Diaz-Alejandro, 1983, pp. 307-308). Despite American pressures for multilateral negotiations in these areas, it is doubtful that these issues can be treated by the multilateral and MFN approach of the GATT. It is more likely that they will be negotiated bilaterally and without reference to the principles of the GATT.

The conflict between further trade liberalization and domestic economic practices has presented itself most forcefully in the case of Japan. Although Japan has reduced most of its formal trade barriers (with some major exceptions, such as agriculture and certain high-technology industries), what foreigners characterize as the illiberal structure of the Japanese economy, the "administrative guidance" role of the bureaucracy, and the economic behavior of the Japanese themselves make the Japanese market very difficult to penetrate. A case in point is the highly restrictive and inefficient (at least as judged by Western standards) Japanese distribution system, intended in part to protect small stores and the integrity of neighborhoods. Other examples of informal Japanese barriers are also frequently cited. The existence in Japan of industrial groupings and long-standing business relationships as well as the Japanese preference to do business with one another and to "buy Japanese" constitute formidable obstacles that limit foreign entry into the market. American pressures on the Japanese to harmonize their domestic structures with those of Western countries and to open up their economy obviously contribute to economic conflict, especially when Japanese formal trade barriers, at least, are lower than American barriers.

Although deregulation and privatization have become important themes of contemporary economic discourse, state intervention to protect domestic values continues to be the universal norm. Furthermore, it is exceptionally difficult for trade liberalization to proceed when resistance to increased economic openness is located in the very nature of a society and in its national priorities. Under these circumstances, it may actually be impossible to remove barriers to trade, at least through the traditional means of multilateral negotiations. The question of whether or not a liberal trade regime can exist in a world composed largely of "illiberal" states is highly problematic.

A further obstacle to success is that the GATT is no longer the American–West European club that it was in the 1960s when even the Japanese were a minor party. It has over ninety players and it is easier than in the past for a coalition to block all actions. Agreement will be very difficult to achieve. For example, the United States has demanded that liberalization of services be the key concern of the negotiations, yet the larger NICs, such as Brazil, India, and Yugoslavia, have strong reservations about the inclusion of services in the GATT. They are concerned that the advanced countries will link the opening of the latter's markets for LDC manufactured exports to concessions regarding services and multinational corporations. The major demand of most less developed countries is that the advanced countries open their markets to the manufactured goods of the LDCs without the LDCs having to make concessions on services. The West Europeans are divided and some European countries may have little to gain from the negotiations or, from their perspective, even have much to lose. Although the Japanese favor continued reduction in trade barriers, they are reluctant to make concessions in agriculture and services. Even in the United States there are basic and traditional industries that oppose concessions in their sectors in return for foreign concessions to American service and high-technology industries. Without any outstanding leadership from the United States and in the presence of strong opposition abroad, it is difficult to be optimistic regarding the prospects for the negotiations (Aho and Aronson, 1985).

Thus, developments in the 1980s suggest that the impressive advance achieved by the postwar era of successive rounds of multilateral trade negotiations ended with the completion of the Tokyo Round. In each of the three dominant centers of the international economy—Western Europe, the United States, and Japan—as well as among the LDCs, strong resistance has developed to the further removal of what some critics regard as trade barriers through multilateral negotiations based on GATT principles. Although changes in national attitudes and defined interests do not necessarily mean the termination of efforts to eliminate tariff and nontariff restrictions, they do suggest that the nature and pace of the freeing of trade have shifted significantly; in some cases national policies entail an actual retreat from the achievements of the past several decades.

New Trading Patterns

In the 1980s, transformations in global patterns of international trade were caused by the New Protectionism, the growing effects of domestic economic concerns on trading relations, and the increasing significance of oligopolistic competition and strategic trade policy. In addition, the rapid rise of Japanese and NIC trade competitiveness and the increasingly dynamic character of comparative advantage have put severe strains on the system. These developments in turn have stimulated new theorizing regarding the determinants of global trading patterns and increased speculation on the future of the international trading regime.

The New Protectionism

Most aspects of the "old protectionism," especially the high tariffs left from the economic collapse of the 1930s, were eliminated by successive rounds of GATT negotiations. However, a proliferating array of non-tariff barriers and other devices has created a "New Protectionism," which has become a major obstacle to further liberalization of world trade. This consists of the erection of nontariff barriers, like domestic content legislation, and a host of other restrictive measures (Deardorff and Stern, 1984). These actions have frequently been accompanied by governmental attempts to expand exports and support specific industrial sectors through such policies as export subsidies, credit guarantees, and tax incentives to particular industries. In short, the New Protectionism entails expanded governmental discretionary powers that influence trade patterns and the global location of economic activities.

As Max Corden has pointed out, the New Protectionism is especially difficult to affect through traditional techniques of trade liberalization (Corden, 1984b). Assessment of the actual extent of trade protectionism is complicated by "the lack of openness or transparency." In many cases it is even difficult to distinguish between nontariff barriers and more traditional activities like customs inspection, performance requirements, and other government regulations. Another complicating factor is "the move from firm rules to administration discretion" through measures that range from government procurement policies to exchange controls. The "return to bilateralism" also aggravates the situation.

The foremost manifestation of the New Protectionism has been governmental use of voluntary export restraints and orderly market arrangements, or what the French euphemistically call "organized free trade." By one estimate, nearly one-third of the American and some European markets in manufactured goods were covered by nontariff barriers in the early 1980s (Cline, 1983, p. 16). Although the total percentage of world trade covered by voluntary export restraints remained relatively small, their impact has been magnified because they frequently cluster in several critical sectors such as textiles, electronics, leather goods, steel, and especially automobiles (Hindley, 1980, p. 316). These controlled sectors are generally characterized by global overcapacity (Strange and Tooze, 1981) and are also usually heavily unionized industries that are major sources of blue-collar employment. The comparative advantage in these labor-intensive sectors, which have previously been sources of economic growth in the advanced countries, is rapidly shifting to the newly industrializing countries, where they constitute major export opportunities (Sen, 1984, p. 191).

The industrial rise of the NICs has been most dramatic in automobiles and such associated sectors as steel and machinery. NICs first appeared in this sector, once the sine qua non of a Western advanced economy, when they began to export components through such mechanisms as foreign investment, joint ventures, and contractual arrangements. By the mid-1980s, these countries were manufacturing automobiles and, especially in the case of South Korea, were exporting to the advanced economies. In just a few short years, comparative advantage in these sectors had shifted considerably in the direction of the NICs.

The New Protectionism has also spread to the service sectors and to high-technology industries believed to be both strategic sectors and the future growth industries of the advanced countries. The Asian NICs have become major exporters of such services as construction; East Asia is also an emergent center of the electronics and information industries. Because of the economic and political importance of both the older and the more advanced sectors, the major industrial powers have engaged in heated negotiations and unilateral actions to protect or increase their relative market shares in these areas (Hindley, 1980). This trend toward sectoral protectionism has become a major feature of the evolving trade regime (Lipson, 1982, pp. 428-33). The concluding chapter, of this book will return to the question of its significance.

The first and most important effort to divide up the world market and to parcel out shares was the Long-Term Arrangement on Cotton Textiles (1962), later extended to become the Multifibres Agreement of 1973 (Blackhurst, Marian, and Tumlir, 1977). Similar cartel-like arrangements have spread to automobile, steel, and other areas. The United States and Western Europe have forced Japan and the NICs to limit their export of particular goods "voluntarily"; Japan has behaved similarly toward the Asian NICs. Further, developed countries are beginning to enact or to threaten to enact "domestic content" legislation, that is, requirements that locally produced components be incorporated in foreign goods.

Although there is general agreement that nontariff barriers are an important determinant of global trading patterns, it is difficult, if not impossible, to measure with any precision their extent or their effect. Nontariff barriers have existed for a long time, but their relative importance has increased as other tariff barriers have been lowered or eliminated. Their significance has also no doubt increased because the items they covered have shifted from light-industry to higher-technology products such as automobiles, color televisions, and computer microchips. The fact that the targeted exporter has most frequently been Japan intensifies the political impact. It is clear that, at the least, nontariff barriers and voluntary export restraints are altering the structure of world trade; the New Protectionism has affected who is trading, who is left out, and what is being traded. Yet the extent to which the New Protectionism is affecting the total volume of world trade remains unclear.

One reason that estimates differ greatly and the actual extent of nontariff barriers is difficult to gauge is that they are hidden from view by their very nature. In many cases, even the identification of a nontariff barrier is subjective; what is a nontariff barrier to one person is a legitimate activity to another. (On the difficulty of measuring nontariff barriers, see Deardorff and Stern, 1984.) Yet it is quite certain that in the 1980s a sizable and growing percentage of world trade lies outside the GATT and is governed by nontariff barriers, especially by bilaterally negotiated voluntary export restraints.

A noticeable tendency exists to discount the significance of the New Protectionism because the volume of total trade and the manufactured exports of countries most affected by the restrictions has continued to grow. Some contend quite correctly that much of the New Protectionism has been in the form of political rhetoric and has not yet been translated into economic policy (Judith Goldstein, 1985). A strong tendency exists, therefore, to dismiss the actual effects of the New Protectionism. However, as perhaps the most authoritative report on the growth of protectionism notes, mounting evidence suggests that the effects of the New Protectionism are real and a significant transformation of the trading regime is taking place (OECD, 1985, p. 19). Important trade restrictions and government interventions exist in a relatively small but growing number of sectors that account for more than a quarter of world trade in manufactured goods. These sectors include such traditionally protected sectors as textiles, steel, and footwear as well as such previously unaffected sectors as automobiles, consumer electronics, and machine tools. The mechanisms of government intervention in these areas are high tariffs, nontariff barriers, and distorting subsidization (ibid., 1985, p. 18).

Conservative estimates suggest that during the period 1980 to 1983, the share of restricted products in total manufactured imports of the United States increased from 6 to 13 percent and that for the EEC the rise was from 11 to 15 percent. For the major economies as a whole, the product groups subject to restriction jumped from 20 to 30 percent of total consumption of manufactured goods. As the OECD report states, "within the protected sectors, the scope of protection has both deepened and widened" with the "absolute number of non-tariff barriers" quadrupling between 1968 and 1983. For example, trade among the advanced countries in automobiles (excluding trade within the European Common Market) affected by discriminatory practices, increased from less than 1 percent in 1973 to nearly 50 percent in 1983! Significantly, the revival of economic growth in the early 1980s failed to reverse this protectionist trend (OECD, 1985, p. 18).

Another major aspect of the New Protectionism has been its effect on the structure of international trade and the location of world industry. The primary targets of nontariff barriers and voluntary export restraints have been Japan and the Asian NICs. Between 1980 and 1983, the share of their exports affected by discriminatory restrictions increased from 15 to over 30 percent (OECD, 1985, p. 18). According to one source, 25 to 40 percent of Japanese exports to the United States and Western Europe are subject to various kinds of export restraints (*Far Eastern Economic Review*, October 25, 1984, p. 81).

These restrictions in turn have had three somewhat contradictory effects on market structure, trade, and the international location of industry. First, they have promoted oligopolies; the cartelization of market sectors inhibits the entry of new firms (Calder, 1985). Second, the target countries have been forced to move up the technological ladder within a product line to higher value-added exports. For example, voluntary export restraints on Japanese automobiles have caused the Japanese to shift their exports in the direction of luxury models. The third effect has been the dispersion of the industry, especially through direct investment by the multinational corporations, to new locations in developing countries not yet subject to voluntary export restraints or orderly marketing agreements. For example, restrictions on the Japanese have forced production in electronics, steel, and other products to shift to the Asian NICs and, as these countries themselves have become subject to voluntary export restraints, to still other less developed countries. Ironically, the consequence of this dynamic is that voluntary export restraints have a tendency to spread to higher levels of technology and to an increasing number of exporting countries and to encourage the growth of extensive regulations to prevent transshipment, as governments and pressure groups attempt to catch up with these developments and to limit their impact. The result is an increasing global surplus capacity in a growing number of industrial sectors and a continuous encroachment of the New Protectionism into more product areas and exporting countries.

Another effect of the New Protectionism has been to alter the mechanisms of trade negotiations and to increase the overall extent of discrimination, which violates the unconditional MFN principle. As the OECD reports, a significant shift has occurred away from GATT Article XIX (applied on a nondiscriminatory basis) and toward bilateralism and discrimination (OECD, 1985, p. 18). As voluntary export restraints create lucrative economic rents to be shared by privileged foreign exporters and protected domestic industries, they have greatly intensified the politics of international trade and the issue of who benefits from these practices. The major losers, of course, have been the consumers in importing countries.

The New Protectionism has probably slowed and distorted but certainly has not prevented the global shift in the locus of industrial production and the consequent change in trading patterns (Strange, 1985c). Indeed, one of the most noteworthy features of the international political economy in the mid-1980s is the rapid rise of the NICs as producers and exporters of manufactured products (OECD, 1986). The process of rapid industrialization is generally concentrated in the smaller NICs of the Pacific Basin and in a relatively few large countries of immense potential such as India and Brazil. This historic transformation of the international division of labor parallels the changes that accompanied the prior industrialization of the United States and continental Europe.

The earlier transformation occurred in an age when the doctrine of laissez faire still had impact, at least in the declining hegemonic economy of Great Britain. At the end of this century, however, the United States and Western Europe are strongly resisting the operation of market forces. The multinational corporations and international production have also profoundly altered the international political economy. As comparative advantage has shifted to Japan and the NICs, American and other multinationals have shifted their locus of production to other countries and governments have frequently responded by encouraging this development. A complex web of economic alliances and production sharing is emerging among national governments and corporations of differing nationalities; this may mitigate some of the political conflicts generated by the New Protectionism. Finally, the continuing military supremacy of the United States and security ties among the dominant economic powers serve to moderate divisive economic conflicts. These novel and contradictory features of the international political economy make it difficult to extrapolate from past experience.

As the New Protectionism continues to spread, a number of questions should be asked regarding its effects on the economics and politics of the emergent international political economy: (1) Which firms and countries will be included in the trading regimes and the cartelized world markets? (2) Who will share the economic rents and who will be left out? (3) On what political or other basis will these determinations be made? (4) Will the powerful countries seek to reward their friends and punish their enemies in the determination of voluntary export restraints and orderly marketing agreements?[13] (5) How can tradeoffs be determined and international agreements be negotiated successfully, given the inherent difficulty of measuring the extent and welfare costs of nontariff barriers and the benefits of eliminating them? (6) Does the New Protectionism inevitably mean a collapse of the world economy similar to the 1930s or merely its transformation into an economically more stable and politically more sustainable set of global economic relations? The answers to these important questions will be revealed only in the next several decades.

The Effects of Domestic Policies

The domestic economic policies of national governments and the interactions of these policies are important determinants of the volume and direction of international trade. Paradoxically, as international economic interdependence has increased, national policies have grown in their significance for trading relations. The shift from fixed to flexible exchange rates was expected to decrease the significance of domestic policies but instead has intensified it. The effect of macroeconomic policies on international trade is complex, pervasive, and a matter of intense controversy among several competing schools of economic theory, including the Keynesians, the traditional monetarists, and the rational expectations school. It is certain, however, that both fiscal and monetary policies strongly influence the several economic variables

[13] The fact noted above that voluntary export restraints create rents and establish an export cartel raises the profoundly important political questions of who collects the rents and who benefits from being incorporated into the cartel (Hindley, 1980).

that in turn (along with commercial policy) set the world's trading patterns. The massive contraction of the American economy during the initial years of the Reagan Administration and, then, the even more massive expansionary policies beginning in late 1982 (at the same time that its major economic partners were pursuing restrictive policies) are only the latest and most dramatic examples of the roller-coaster effects of macroeconomic policies on trading relations.

The resulting massive trade and payments imbalances of the United States have given a powerful impetus to protectionist sentiments. There has been a prolonged period of cyclical global economic activity, and this boom-and-bust behavior of the world economy has accelerated the spread of protectionism through its devastating impact on specific economic sectors and its more general effect on economic expectations. Individual economies try to cushion the internal impact of external forces over which they have little control. Protectionist pressures will no doubt continue to increase unless the problems created by domestic macroeconomic policies and their interactions can be resolved through international policy coordination among the dominant economic powers.

Microeconomic policies also influence the patterns of international trade. The most important and controversial development in this area is the expanded reliance of a number of advanced economies upon industrial policy. Although industrial policy means different things to different people, "it basically involves the active participation of the state in shaping the industrial pattern of development" (R. Baldwin, 1984c, p. 26); the means employed range from financial assistance for specific industries to governmental determination of production levels.

Industrial policy, sometimes used to aid senile or dying industries, is also intended to create new industries, especially export industries in emergent high-technology sectors. Through "picking winners" and targeting particular industries for development and financial support such as export subsidies, governments are systematically attempting to develop comparative advantage and to promote international competitiveness. In almost every market economy there is an important partnership between government and corporations for the purpose of promoting exports and capturing world markets. This is quite explicit in some economies, more indirect and subtle in others. For example, in the United States (as West Europeans correctly charge) expenditures on military research and development such as those on President Reagan's Strategic Defense Initiative constitute an important subsidization of technologies with commercial significance.

Systematic intervention by a state in its economy and industrial development obviously is not new. In the late nineteenth century the Germans were the first to transform their economy and capture world markets through the adoption of such interventionist policies (Veblen, 1939). Fascist Italy in the 1930s and Soviet Russia are more recent examples. Since the Second World War, however, it is Japan that has most systematically implemented industrial policies credited with having propelled that island nation from crushing defeat to the status of the world's foremost, or at least second most, competitive economy (C. Johnson, 1982). The success of "Japan Incorporated" has spurred one country after another to adopt industrial and related policies to improve its own economic and trading position, even though the Japanese themselves are abandoning many aspects of their industrial policy and are moving toward greater liberalization of their economy.

The New Protectionism and the perceived success of Japanese industrial policy are changing the rules of the game in important ways. Whereas the primary purpose of the old protectionism was to protect threatened industries and to support an import-substitution strategy, a major purpose of the New Protectionism and industrial policy is to create comparative advantage and internationally competitive industries, especially at the "high-value added" end of the industrial spectrum, and also to promote an export-led growth strategy. More and more states seek to establish their predominance in the production and export of "product cycle" goods, that is, products characterized by the use of high technology. The growing practice of "industrial or technological preemption" by which states attempt to jump over their competitors into higher levels of industrial technology will be discussed later in this chapter.

The increased importance of technology, technological change, and technological diffusion for international competitiveness and the consequently more arbitrary nature of comparative advantage in determining trade patterns is leading to new forms of technological protectionism and government interventionism. Nations are attempting to slow down the diffusion of their own technology while also forcing other countries to share theirs. Governmental restrictiveness regarding the transfer of technology for commercial reasons is extended by the enhanced importance for national security of "dual technology," that is, technology with both military and commercial applications (Gilpin, 1982). The trading of market access for technology transfers, the role of technology sharing in intercorporate alliances, and related practices reflect this enhanced importance of industrial technology in economic relations (Nussbaum, 1983). Without question, technological issues are becoming among the most important ones in the international political economy.

The development of new modes of state interventionism such as the reliance on nationalized firms and the crucial role in most advanced countries of joint research ventures financed and organized by the government reflect a number of changes in the economic and political environment: increasing global economic interdependence and openness of economies to foreign goods, the innovation of a broad array of policy instruments through which states can intervene in and influence industrial developments, and the growing role of oligopolistic competition in the determination of trading patterns. Throughout the world awareness is growing that economic development requires the functioning of efficient export industries; governments (wisely or not) are resorting to industrial policies to achieve this goal (Strange, 1985c). As Japan is the foremost model for these efforts, its policies and an evaluation of their success will be the foci of our discussion of government interventionism.

As my colleague Avinash Dixit has pointed out, government intervention in the economy may be categorized in terms of macro, compensatory, or adjustment policies. Each has had varying degrees of success, both in Japan and in its imitators. The different rationales and relative successes of these policies need to be distinguished from one another, but frequently such distinctions are not made; indeed there is a tendency to place them all under the heading of industrial policy and consequently to give industrial policy per se credit that it does not deserve.

Macro-policies refer to the various efforts of the state on an aggregate level to facilitate the smooth operation of markets and the accumulation of the basic factors of production. They include not only what is normally called "macroeconomic" policy, that is, fiscal and monetary policies, but other general policies affecting the overall economy such as the support of education, the financing of basic research and development, and the encouragement of high rates of national savings. For example, Japan in the postwar period has maintained a level of national savings and investment twice that of the United States. Its policies have encouraged rapid productivity growth, the moderation of wage increases, the importing of foreign technology under license rather than through direct investment, and the transfer of labor from agriculture to more productive industrial sectors. Internally, the Japanese government has stimulated intense competition in crucial industrial sectors at the same time that the Ministry of International Trade and Industry (MITI) has discouraged fractious competition overseas. In short, Japan, with some major exceptions, has been more of an example of Adam Smith's ideas than those of John Maynard Keynes in its overall economic policies.

Another type of economic policy may be called compensatory. Ongoing economic activities produce winners and losers everywhere. Although no society could afford to compensate all the losers, in times of rapid change the costs may be especially painful and harmful to particular groups and therefore necessitate government assistance. For example, the government may enact programs to restrain workers whose skills have become obsolete due to shifts in national comparative advantage. Such compensation policies have become an integral feature of the modern welfare state (Kindleberger, 1978c, p. 5).

A more controversial type of state interventionism is found in so-called structural adjustment or industrial policies, which are designed to affect the ways in which the economic structure, that is, the national organization and composition of economic sectors, reacts to outside forces or tries to assume international leadership in an industry. Such policies may include the targeting of specific industrial sectors for research intervention and particular industries and technologies for commercial development. Most economists believe that such policies are probably not necessary in a market economy, with the possible exception of a few areas where market failure or a collective good may exist (e.g., pollution control, public health, or national security).

The Japanese and certain of the NICs have been exceptionally successful in their use of macropolicy. These economies have pursued remarkable growth-oriented fiscal and monetary policies, have made substantial investments in education, and have encouraged exceptionally high rates of national savings. The thrust of these policies has been to accumulate the basic factors of production and increase the overall efficiency of the economy. It is correct to conclude, therefore, that this type of "macroindustrial" policy and state intervention works. Japan and a number of other societies have also pursued compensatory policies with a considerable degree of economic success.

The record on the efficacy of structural adjustment policy (i.e., what is usually labeled industrial policy) is unclear; it is difficult, if not impossible, to reach any definitive conclusion. It is doubtful, for example, that the stunning success of Japan in one product area after another can be attributed primarily to the perspicacity of MITI and Japan's economic managers. Indeed it is not even certain that MITI and its industrial policies have outperformed the market. There is a story told that MITI initially opposed Japanese entry into the world automobile market. On the other hand, it is not sufficient to retort, as skeptics do, that Japanese bureaucrats and businessmen simply looked around the world to see what others were doing and then took advantage of Japan's undervalued yen, accumulated factors of production, and comparative advantage in the low-cost mass production of standardized products. MITI and its policies at least should be given credit for encouraging and enabling Japanese corporations to climb the technological ladder (C. Johnson, 1982).

Some attribute Japan's success largely to its macropolicies, undoubtedly the world's best example of the application of "supply-side" economics (Gibney, 1982, p. 5). Others draw attention to the high cost of those mistaken industrial policies that have caused overexpansion and surplus capacity in a number of industrial sectors, i.e., shipbuilding, steel, and textiles. Japanese policies have led to excessive concentration in particular industrial sectors and consequent generation of exports that have stirred foreign resentment. Judgment regarding the ability of the Japanese or any other state to pick "winners" and to guide the structural adjustment process appropriately should be suspended for the moment. Yet it can be said that the Japanese have succeeded remarkably in improving upon and marketing the technological innovations of other societies, as did the United States during its ascent to industrial preeminence a century ago.

The most important lesson to be drawn from the success of Japan and other rapidly rising industrial powers relates to the changing conception of comparative advantage and to its implications for national policy, trading practices, and ultimately for economic theory. These countries have unquestionably demonstrated that comparative advantage in a macro sense can be created through appropriate national policies that facilitate the accumulation of the factors of production. Economists have of course long acknowledged the dynamic nature of comparative advantage; the competitive performance of Japan and the NICs in the 1970s and 1980s, however, has given new significance to this qualification of trade theory.

Regardless of how one evaluates these developments, there is no doubt that industrial policy (whether poorly or intelligently conceived) and trade policy (whether liberal or protectionist) are becoming more tightly integrated. As economist J. David Richardson has noted, trade and industrial policies are being used in an attempt to create particular types of industrial structures (Richardson, 1984, p. 4). Nations are utilizing both import protection and export promotion to safeguard traditional high-employment industries while simultaneously securing a strong position in the high-technology industries of the future.

These new types of policies differ from earlier forms of protectionism and state interventionism in that they are usually selective and sector-specific, rather than across the board, and are intended to protect or promote particular industrial sectors (Aggarwal, 1985). Protectionism and industrial policies of all types are on the increase in the mid-1980s, and their primary objective is to protect and stimulate those economic sectors that political leaders consider most relevant to the domestic welfare and the nation's political ambitions.

Strategic Trade Policy

International trade is also being influenced by the increasing importance of strategic trade policy. This is an attempt by a state to change the international strategic environment in ways that give advantage to the home country's oligopolistic firms. Through protection, subsidization, and other policies, the state endeavors to ensure for its own firms a larger share of the market and hence of the economic rents that exist in any oligopolistic market. Because other states can also seek to influence the nature of international competition, trade policy and trading relations are characterized by strategic interaction (Buckley, 1986, p. 3).

Although the extent and significance of strategic trade policy are a matter of intense controversy, the exercise of state power in the international arena through the use of threats, promises, and other bargaining techniques in order to alter the trading regime in ways that improve the market position and increase the profits of national corporations is certainly of increasing importance. The factors behind this change are the increasingly dynamic nature of comparative advantage, the emergence of the multinational corporation, and the greatly enhanced importance of oligopolistic or imperfect competition in trading relations (Helpman and Krugman, 1985).[14]

As a number of economists have observed, the international economic environment is one characterized largely by oligopolistic competition and strategic interaction (Kierzkowski, 1984). In the perfectly competitive world of orthodox trade theory, the number of actors is too large and their individual size too small to determine economic outcomes; in such a market economic decisions are based principally on variables such as the price, quality, and characteristics of goods. A strategic environment is one composed of a relatively few large actors; in such an imperfect or oligopolistic market, powerful actors can significantly influence market outcomes. A strategic situation with a limited

---

[14] There is a growing and important debate among economists over the possibility of strategic trade policy. The issue is whether a nation can successfully adopt policies that shift profits in the direction of its own firms. Krugman (1986) contains the major views on this issue.

number of important participants requires that greater attention be given by each player to the policies and responses of other actors.

In their own policy making, governments must take cognizance of and attempt to influence the actions and probable reactions of other governments. Policy interactions become of crucial importance. Will, for example, other governments respond to a policy initiative by retaliation or by cooperation? What threats or promises can effect the likely response? Are preemptive or retaliatory actions the most effective course? The interaction of economic and political actors increasingly influences trading relations in important ways.

By mid-1985, strategic interaction and governmental bargaining had grown in significance in the international political economy due to the expanding global role of the multinational corporation and the growth of economic interdependence among national economies. The novelty of this situation was not located in oligopolistic competition as such, because it had long existed. Rather it was in the enhanced importance of nonprice factors in the competition, the emergence of powerful multinational corporations of competing nationalities, and the enhanced role of the state in attempting to assist their own corporations and affect the "rules of the game" (Grossman and Richardson, 1985, p. 6). Consequently, the orthodox liberal model of atomistic competition in which individual consumers and producers are assumed to be price-takers (i.e., the market alone sets the price) and the state is not a participant has become less relevant in a number of economic sectors. In many industrial sectors, especially in high-technology areas, international trade has become dominated by huge multinational corporations that can powerfully influence relative prices, trade patterns, and the location of economic activities.

An oligopolistic market composed of very large firms permits super-profits to exist and profit shifting to take place. Individual producers can exploit a technological or other advantage to increase their economic return. As governments recognize that the international market is really one of imperfect competition rather than the ideal competition of liberal theory, they may well reason that it is far better for their own firms, rather than other countries' enterprises, to enjoy the resulting high profits (Dixit and Grossman, 1984, p. 1). It is this real world of imperfect competition and multinational corporations that tempts governments to provide support for a country's national economic champions and to develop a strategic trade policy that shifts profits to national firms (Grossman and Richardson, 1985).

Strategic trade theory challenges traditional liberal trade theory as it asserts that an "activist trade policy" can benefit a country relatively

216

more than does a policy of free trade (Krugman, 1986, p. 12). In the first place, an activist national policy can capture the "rents" created by an oligopolistic trading situation; the state can pursue policies that give advantages of scale or similar benefits to its national firms. Second, the state has a powerful incentive to intervene in trading relations because technological innovation has become a major factor in international competitiveness, comparative advantage is largely arbitrary, and externalities or spillovers from one industry to another exist; the knowledge generated in one sector can benefit other sectors and raise the overall technological level of the economy. Thus, the state should support and protect those industrial sectors that produce rents and are considered to have strategic value for international competitiveness.

The increasing importance of strategic trade policy is a product of what was identified earlier as the industrial organization theory of international trade. In this world of imperfect competition government policies impinge significantly on the success and operations of multinational cooperations. Although states have always sought to help their own firms, new tactics have become available (Spence, 1984). One of the especially important policies is to block access to domestic markets ("industrial preemption"); this tactic gives domestic firm a strong competitive cost position. Also, subsidies are used to reduce the costs borne by the national firm; this increases the market share of a national firm and its profits. Another policy is to support research and development through joint research ventures and similar measures, which give the national firm dynamic scale advantages and generates knowledge of use to the firm and the economy (Branson and Klevorick, 1986). In these ways, the state can take strategic actions to benefit its own firms and harm those of other countries (Buckley, 1986).[15]

When the tactic of "industrial preemption" or "home market effect" is employed, the home market for a product is protected so that the growth of demand enables a domestic firm to achieve economies of scale and also efficiency by advancing along the learning curve. This tactic of "import protection for export promotion" has been practiced most systematically by Japan and some of the NICs; this sophisticated form of infant industry protection entails the denial of market access to foreign and particularly to American producers, until "a Japanese manufacturer achieves international cost and quality levels" (Rosovsky, 1985). At the point of competitive equivalence, Japanese firms begin their export drive for overseas markets and the Japanese market is

---

[15] Dixit (1986), Branson and Klevorick (1986), and Grossman and Richardson (1985) provide contrasting analyses of the effects of domestic policies on trading relations.

opened, as has occurred in automobiles, electronics, and other areas of high technology.

Although this type of practice does not determine the overall trade balance of Japan, it most certainly does affect the structures of its economy and its foreign trade. In reversing the "product cycle," that is, in preventing imports or direct investment by foreign firms, the Japanese and NIC governments enable their own corporations to reap a significant share of the benefits and "value added" of foreign innovations. "Industrial preemption" thus causes intense negative reactions in the United States and other economies.

In this evolving strategic environment, international trade and international production by multinational corporations are closely intertwined. Intrafirm trade, sub-contracting, and joint ventures have become important aspects of the international political economy. Trading patterns and the global location of industrial production have been strongly influenced by corporate strategies intended to minimize taxes, skirt trade barriers, and take advantage of global shifts in comparative advantage. For example, components made in a subsidiary or under contract in one or more countries may be sent to another country for final assembly into a finished product and then exported to yet another country where the product is ultimately marketed. By one estimate, nearly 50 percent of American imports in 1977 consisted of intrafirm transfers (Helleiner, 1981, p. 10). This integration of trade and foreign production, frequently within the confines of a single corporation, is creating a more managed and increasingly complex global economy (Deardorff, 1984, p. 501).

Liberal economic theory presupposes an ideal world in which the internationalization of industrial production and the integration of national markets would pose few problems. International trade and foreign production would just be alternate means of reaching world markets. Trading patterns and the location of production would be determined primarily by criteria of economic efficiency, and the international economy would increasingly resemble the integrated national markets that characterize advanced industrialized societies. At the international level such a competitive market would create a situation in which the rate of profit would be restricted by the interplay of market forces. Entrepreneurial profits would be quickly dispersed by the entry or the threat of entry of new producers. This is not, however, what is actually occurring in much of the real world of the 1980s.

Instead, the process of economic integration in many sectors is being carried out by national firms in an increasingly interdependent world of competing states. The oligopolistic corporations that have become more influential in the determination of trade patterns and the global location of economic activities are not truly multinational; they are not divorced from a particular nationality. Home governments not only have the incentive but also may have the power to fashion commercial and other policies designed to benefit their own multinationals at the expense of competing firms and other economies.

The factors impacting on the nature of the international economy and international trade in the late twentieth century thus are similar to those that previously transformed the structures of domestic economies. For a century or more, every advanced economy has witnessed the partial displacement of competitive markets composed of many small firms by imperfect markets in which immense concentrations of corporate power exist. With the decline of trade barriers and increasing economic interdependence, a similar phenomenon has appeared at the level of the international economy. A few large American, Japanese, and European firms as well as some NIC firms have been able to integrate production and other activities across national boundaries. The expanding role of these giant corporations in global markets has meant that the world economy has increasingly become characterized by oligopolistic competition.

In the closing decades of the century, global trading patterns, the distribution of economic benefits, and the national location of production have been affected to an indeterminate extent by strategic interactions among oligopolistic firms and national governments. The Tokyo Round and its codes of proper behavior failed to bring this emerging world of strategic interaction and intergovernmental bargaining under international control. The possibilities for nationalistic conflict over market shares and the distribution of corporate profits have been considerably enlarged by the increasing importance of oligopolistic competition, the availability to governments of a wide array of policy instruments to assist national corporations, and the weakening of international leadership.

Trade patterns and the location of industry in a number of economic sectors have been affected by the exercise of power and by international negotiation over market shares. How many cars Japan may export to the United States or how much American beef Japan will buy have become matters of high politics. Although this "politicization" of the international division of labor does not mean a complete transcendence of the market or efficiency considerations, it does mean that price competition has become a less important factor influencing the flow of trade. The New Protectionism, the industrial policies of individual states, and strategic trade policy are influencing international trading relations in important ways. The intensified interplay of market, state, and corporation will largely influence and in some cases determine the future of international trade.

The extent to which states can effectively pursue strategic trade policy and shift profits (in counterdistinction to the ability of monopolistic corporations to reap monopoly rents on their own initiative) remains a matter of debate. The issues in dispute range from the practical feasibility of shifting profits to the magnitude of possible gains. Because anyone can play the game and retaliation could trigger a trade war in which everyone is the loser, nations may be deterred from practicing strategic trade policy. On these matters, the historical evidence is too sparse to support any firm conclusions (Krugman, 1986, ch. 1).

A more relevant consideration, however, is that political leaders have begun to believe that others are employing the tactics of strategic trade policy. With numerous departures from the principles of the GATT, fear grows that others are not "playing fair." As international leadership weakens, the possibilities increase that nationalistic conflict over market shares and distribution of corporate profits may occur. Thus, although the effectiveness and long-term significance of strategic trade policy are in doubt, there is no doubt of its growing political relevance.

The renewed American emphasis in the mid-1980s on "reciprocity" in trading relations and similar shifts in American trade policy should be considered against this background. The Japanese strategy of industrial preemption and the increasingly arbitrary nature of comparative advantage have caused the United States to be more aggressive in its trade policy. A major motive behind these policy changes is to prevent foreign economies from appropriating American technologies and the monopoly rents generated by innovation; without such rents there would be little available capital or incentive to invest in scientific research and technological development. Thus, however poorly conceived the policy of reciprocity may be, it should be seen in part as a reaction to the policies of foreign governments that appear to threaten the basis of America's capacity to compete in world markets.

Changes in U.S. and other national trade policies are causing a metamorphosis of the global trading regime. The shift is clearly in the direction of negotiated market shares, bilateral bargaining, and the conditional Most-Favored Nation principle (i.e., the granting of a trade concession only if one is granted in return). These more nationalistic approaches to international trade are displacing to a considerable degree the basic GATT principles of nondiscrimination, multilateralism, and the unconditional MFN principle as the governing features of the international political economy. The advanced economies and the

NICs are fashioning a new international economic order, but it is not the one desired or envisioned by the large majority of the less developed countries.

THE RAPPROCHEMENT OF LIBERAL AND NATIONALIST THEORIES

The patterns of world trade in the 1980s have diverged significantly from the generally accepted theory of international trade based on natural endowments, perfect competition, and immobile factors of production. As Richard Cooper has noted, the gap between the theory and the reality of international economic relations has widened considerably since the Second World War (Cooper, 1970, p. 437). Economists are attempting to narrow, if not close, this widening gap between liberal trade theory and the realities of international trade. These efforts, however, are also decreasing the gap between the liberal and nationalist theories of international trade.

The changes in the importance of imperfect markets, the nature of comparative advantage, and the role of the state in trading relations have raised serious problems for traditional trade theory. Relative market shares, the terms of trade, and the composition of national imports and exports become strongly influenced by bargaining and negotiations among the relevant actors as relative efficiency, prices, and demand are not sufficient to determine outcomes. This indeterminacy will increase as the power and negotiating skills of multinational corporations and national governments grow. Trade theory then becomes tied to bargaining theory, and trade policy emerges from the development of a national industrial strategy and bargaining tactics.

The most significant theoretical development is the changing conception of comparative advantage. Both liberal trade theory and the GATT have assumed the existence of perfect markets (markets without economies of scale or other dynamic factors) in which comparative advantage arises primarily from natural endowments. However, the dynamics of factor accumulation, technological change, and the impact on international competitiveness of factor movements (through such mechanisms as foreign direct investment and technology transfer) have significantly undermined this traditional and generally static conception of comparative advantage; it is now primarily applicable to the trade of food, raw materials, and other commodities. It is also useful in the definition of certain physical limits within which comparative advantage can be developed.

One might speculate, of course, that as global levels of technological competence tend to equalize, national resource endowments could reassert themselves as the primary determinants of trading patterns. Thus, the agricultural and raw material wealth of the United States could increase in importance as America's former technological advantages diffuse to other countries. At present, however, the determinants of comparative advantage, at least among the advanced countries, are technological, organizational, and similar factors.

Whatever the long-term reality, for the moment liberal trade theory has had to take into account the increasing importance of "arbitrary comparative advantage" characterized by William Cline:

In some manufacturing products, the traditional bases for trade specialization—such as differences in relative national availabilities of labor, capital, skilled labor, and technological sophistication—may no longer dominate (as industrial and some developing countries become more similar in these attributes), while other traditional determinants of trade (such as natural resource endowment) may not be germane. In such products, the pattern of trade specialization may be arbitrary, and factors such as noncompetitive firm behavior and government intervention may determine which country prevails (Cline, 1982a, p. 9).

The transformation of trade practices and theory means that liberal and nationalist trade theories have, at least with respect to trade in a wide range of manufactured goods, converged to a considerable degree (more than liberal economists acknowledge). Through the past century, liberal trade theory has moved in the direction of nationalist contentions. In the classical Ricardian formulation, trade was based on fixed and immutable factors such as climate, natural endowments, and relative abundance of labor; international migration of the factors of production did not take place. Subsequently, the neoclassical reformulation of the Heckscher-Ohlin-Samuelson model (in agreement with Hamilton's *Report on Manufactures*) postulated trade patterns as more flexible and based on differences in *total* relative factor abundance, comparative advantage as more dynamic, and productive factors as diffusing via foreign investment and other means. In the early postwar period, product cycle, product differentiation, and other types of theory attempted to account for a world in which temporary technological advantages largely determined trade and investment patterns, comparative advantage diffused rapidly from more to less developed economies, and intra-industry trade based on differing tastes, economies of scale, and related factors characterized trade among advanced countries. More recent theorizing attempts to encompass a world in which these developments and arbitrary comparative advantage, to use Krugman's language, "lead to an essentially random division of labor among countries" (1986, p. 8). Most economic nationalists would feel quite comfortable with and justified by this analysis of the determinants of world trade.

The evolution of liberal trade theory suggests that liberal economists have begun to give more credence to the basic nationalist contention regarding the arbitrary nature of comparative advantage. They have had to come to terms with a world in which comparative advantage, international competitiveness, and the international division of labor result in large measure from corporate strategies and national policies. The contention of economists that as long as comparative advantage exists, its origin is not significant is no longer satisfactory. In a world where who produces what is a crucial concern of states and powerful groups, few are willing to leave the determination of trading patterns solely up to the market.

In the mid-1980s trade practices and liberal theory have shifted remarkably in the direction of the nationalist conception of the dynamic and arbitrary nature of comparative advantage. Liberals and nationalists continue to differ, however, regarding the extent and significance of the shift. Nationalists tend to believe that comparative advantage can be created by sector-specific industrial policies; liberals stress general macropolicies designed to foster the accumulation of the basic factors of production and to leave commercial developments up to the market and the private sector. Liberals are more apt than in the past to stress the role of state policy in the creation of comparative advantage, but they also emphasize its inherent dangers and warn against the overall efficiency losses of economic conflict. The liberal emphasis on the superiority of and welfare benefits of an international division of labor based on free trade and economic specialization remains very different from the ideas of economic nationalists.

THE PROSPECTS FOR THE LIBERAL TRADE REGIME

In the mid-1980s, opinions vary considerably on the significance of the New Protectionism and related developments for the future of the trading system. For some, the movement away from the GATT principles of multilateralism and nondiscrimination meant an irreversible trend away from trade liberalization. For others, the only way to arrest the steady deterioration of the trading system was bilateralism and greater discrimination. The differences between the two groups were less concerned with the economic costs of the movement away from GATT principles than with matters of political feasibility.

Most economists believe that the New Protectionism and related developments entail a significant loss of economic efficiency and pose a threat to the liberal trading regime. The tendency to substitute conditional MFN status for the unconditional and multilateral MFN of the GATT has slowed the postwar movement toward free trade. Many fear that the Tokyo codes, because they apply only to signatories, could lead to a multitier system of trading relations that would divide nations according to whether or not they subscribed to particular codes (Curzon and Curzon Price, 1980). Discrimination and preferential treatment based on the increased use of nontariff barriers could cause a return to the aggressive policies of the 1930s.

These practices penalize emergent efficient producers of industrial goods, retard the adjustment of advanced economies to ongoing global shifts in comparative advantage, and thereby prevent transition to a new structure of international economic relations. Such developments aggravate and prolong the economic crisis of the late twentieth century much as the old protectionism did in the 1930s. Some liberal economists believe that the regime of free trade, like a bicycle, is "dynamically unstable" and will fall down if it does not continue its forward momentum (Cline, 1983, pp. 9-10). Such a collapse of the international economic order could give rise to economic conflicts threatening to world peace.

Others are more sanguine about the prospects of an open trading regime and have a generally positive view of the New Protectionism and other changes in the trading regime. They argue that negotiated and bilateral arrangements among small groups of like-minded nations constitute the best and, in fact, the only way to expand trade in a world of increased uncertainty, greater emphasis on domestic economic security, and an unprecedented rapidity of change in comparative advantage. The mere mechanics of negotiating GATT agreements among scores of states in a fast-paced world is held to be a major impediment. Governments will no longer surrender their economic autonomy in a highly uncertain world and an interdependent international economy. As Susan Strange has written, the doctrine of free trade requires that states subordinate all other national values such as freedom, order, and justice to the goal of increased efficiency (Strange, 1985c).

Some argue that in the present era, the principles of nondiscrimination and unconditional MFN status may actually slow down trade liberalization, because they require that concessions made to one party must be given to everyone, and this encourages "free riding" (Conybeare, 1985, p. 27). Bilateralism, the use of the conditional MFN principle, and what Robert Keohane (1986) has called "specific reciprocity," on the other hand, do not suffer from this liability and do overcome the free-rider problem; the exchange of concession for concession provides incentives for cooperation and institutionalizes equal treatment. Such "cooperative protectionism," this position argues, has been trade-creating, actually constitutes a new way of making rules, and does not signify the collapse of international regimes (Keohane, 1984b, p. 38).[16]

The exchange of explicit concessions in specific sectors and the creation of a "web of contracts" approach to trade liberalization, these writers argue, enable a state to safeguard other values and protect itself against the free-rider problem. According to this formulation, only those willing to accept the obligations become participants in the system. It is believed that, as the historic barriers of time and space disappear due to advances in transportation and communication, nontariff barriers and voluntary export restraints have become necessary to cushion the disruptive effects of the expansion of world trade and of the continuing diffusion of industrial technology and comparative advantage to Japan and the NICs. Through interstate negotiations and "self-enforcing agreements" based on cooperation and mutual interests, the trading regime can be preserved in a much more nationalistic world (Yarbrough and Yarbrough, 1986). From this perspective, the New Protectionism is less a restriction on total world trade than a means of controlling the untoward effects of unregulated trade.

Whatever the ultimate outcome of the debate between the critics and the supporters of the changes in the nature of the GATT system, the New Protectionism, domestic policies, and oligopolistic competition *are* altering the nature of the international trading regime. The world is witnessing the rise of an interlocking network of bilateral and regional relationships. The principle of conditional MFN status has begun to replace the unconditional, specific reciprocity has become more important than diffuse reciprocity, and trade is increasingly taking place outside the GATT framework. In fact the legitimacy of the GATT principles themselves are being challenged. These developments suggest that new rules and norms may soon be required to govern trading relations in a much more interdependent world.

Violations of GATT principles and challenges to their legitimacy suggest that if the multilateral trade regime is to continue, increased international cooperation and a greater harmonization of domestic institutions and national policies may be required. It is possible that a new

[16] Aggarwal, Keohane, and Yoffie (1986) is a systematic discussion of cooperative protectionism.

set of internationally accepted rules will have to apply directly to the internal workings of societies rather than focusing only on the removal of formal import barriers as with the GATT. For example, the United States, by breaking up the American Telephone and Telegraph Company and deregulating its own telecommunications industry, removed a significant barrier to foreign entrance into the American market. Although American consumers may have benefited, this unilateral domestic policy decision conveyed an economic benefit to the rest of the world for which the United States was not compensated. Most other countries continued tight government control of the industry (Branson and Klevorick, 1986, pp. 246-47). This example demonstrates the incongruity of considering domestic policy decisions in isolation when trade has made them highly interdependent. Reform of the trading regime must take cognizance of this fact. International regimes to regulate imperfect competition may have to be established, and national practices such as antitrust policies and government support for research consortia must be made more uniform across national boundaries.

At the national level, a reordered trade regime might also have to determine what are and what are not legitimate governmental policies and interventions in the economy. The positive and negative effects of domestic policy changes upon other nations may have to be weighed and decisions reached regarding the need for appropriate compensation or reciprocal actions. It may be necessary to coordinate and harmonize national practices to prevent governmental intervention in the market and the establishment of policies giving unfair advantages to national firms. Since national and corporate behavior significantly influence the pattern and outcome of trading relations, rules are needed to limit harm to weaker nations and to prevent a breakdown in the trading regime through the pursuit of "beggar-my-neighbor" policies.

Most economists believe that the harmonization of domestic policies and practices is not necessary for a liberal trade regime to function effectively. In economic theory, nations are regarded as black boxes, and all that is required for mutually beneficial trade is that the exchange rates among the boxes be in equilibrium. However, the history of the European Economic Community seems to demonstrate that at some point the process of economic integration necessitates increased international cooperation and greater harmonization of national practices to prevent distortions and cheating (Robson, 1980). At the global level, if increased cooperation and greater harmonization of national practices do not occur, it is likely that international economic conflicts will intensify as each nation seeks to improve the relative position and competitive advantage of its own multinational corporations.

Even if economic institutions do not matter, as many liberal economists assert, and even if the harmonization of domestic practices is unnecessary, states and powerful groups do believe that domestic institutions and practices are important in determining trade. Whether or not the structural features of the Japanese economy actually serve as nontariff barriers to keep out foreign products, most Americans and West Europeans believe that illiberal aspects of Japanese society do constitute formidable obstacles to their exports; furthermore, Americans and West Europeans believe such "illiberal" institutions to be illegitimate.[17]

As trade negotiations have reduced the barriers among national economies and the world has become more interdependent, the issue of the legitimacy and harmonization of domestic structures has moved to the forefront of international economic and political relations, as Gary Saxonhouse points out:

The increasing appreciation of how barriers in the international movement of capital and technology, and discriminatory domestic microeconomic policies can undermine the global benefits resulting from liberal agreements on trade in goods has meant much expanded rules of the game for participants in the international economic system. If domestic policy instruments can always be good, functional substitutes for the foreign economic policy instruments which are the traditional objects of international diplomacy, it seems that liberal domestic economic policy by all rather than just some of the major participants in the international economic system, is a necessary prerequisite for the continuing legitimacy of that system. Thus, the thrust of international economic diplomacy has already moved from tariffs to quotas and from quotas to standards, subsidies and government procurement. The agenda for international economic harmony is now demanding that much of the domestic economic affairs of participants in the international system be governed by fully competitive open bidding and contractual relationships. The history of postwar international economic diplomacy has shown that implicitly, but not yet explicitly, the increasingly difficult task of maintaining the legitimacy of the international economic system requires not just nondiscriminatory treatment of foreign goods in national markets, but also a more far-reaching harmonization of microeconomic institutions (Saxonhouse, 1983, pp. 269-70).

Unless the legitimacy issue can be resolved or somehow transcended, economic nationalism and regionalism will make deeper inroads into the postwar regime of liberalized trade. This intensifying problem dem-

[17] Saxonhouse (1983, pp. 270-71) provides a list of alleged illiberal Japanese economic institutions and business practices.

onstrates that a liberal international economic order must rest on a firm political and ideological base. The United States and its conception of a liberal order have dominated the postwar era. With the relative decline of American power and the rise of economic powers that have different conceptions of legitimacy, the future of the liberal world economy has become severely threatened.

The most likely outcome of these developments is a "mixed" system of trading relations. It is improbable that the trade regime will collapse as it did in the 1930s; there is enough momentum to keep the bicycle of trade liberalization from falling over. Yet it is equally improbable that there will be a return to the liberalizing trends of the early postwar decades. Although strong elements of multilateralism based on GATT principles will continue to characterize many facets of world trade, they will be joined by bilateral, cartelized, and regional arrangements. The GATT regime, with its emphasis on universal rules, will remain at odds with the increased importance of government discretion and interventionism to promote national interests and domestic priorities.

Undoubtedly the most prominent feature of the emergent trading regime and the most significant departure from historic patterns will be the expansion of sectoral protectionism. In a substantial and growing number of services, basic industries, and high-technology areas, governments and corporations negotiate market-sharing agreements. Involving principally the advanced economies and the NICs, such horizontal accords are intended to gain market access, acquire strategic technologies, and preserve employment. Although an international trading regime based in large part on negotiated market shares and cartelization would be highly inefficient and characterized by gross inequities, powerful forces continue to push the world economy in that direction.[18]

CONCLUSION

The GATT system of trade liberalization was based on the idea of permitting the market to determine the international location of economic activities. Trade barriers have fallen and the total volume of world trade has greatly expanded on the basis of its liberal precepts. The very success of this ongoing liberalization, however, has raised a host of new and troubling issues. In many societies the domestic social costs of adjustment to changing patterns of comparative advantage are believed to

[18] Aggarwal (1985), Patrick and Rosovsky (1983), and Strange (1985c) discuss the rise of sectoral protectionism.

outweigh the advantages of further trade liberalization. The relatively perfect markets in which equilibrium solutions were possible have been displaced to an indeterminate degree by strategic bargaining among corporate entities and national authorities.

The various codes instituted by the Tokyo Round to regulate government intervention in the economy attempted to deal with the new and uncertain international economy in which strategic interaction and bargaining among states and corporations have become increasingly the norm and where industrial policy and trade policy have become merely different sides of the same coin. Although it has increased global efficiency, trade liberalization has had a severe impact on many societies and has even raised the question of whether or not it can proceed without greater harmonization of national societies. Is it possible for trade liberalization to continue in a world composed of societies with vastly different social and economic structures? In the emergent world economy the determination of trade patterns is no longer simply a matter of lowering tariff barriers or of "letting the market decide." Instead, shares of exports and imports for particular countries and corporations and the location of industrial production are determined as much by political as by economic factors.

There are thus several conflicting developments in international trade in the mid-1980s. Although the pace of trade liberalization has slackened due to both cyclical and secular factors, the dominant economic powers continue to favor the elimination of tariff and nontariff barriers. Yet the New Protectionism, economic regionalism, and illiberal domestic structures constitute trade restrictions and lead to international competition in a proliferating number of economic sectors. A highly ambiguous situation exists in which there is an ebb and flow from trade liberalization to economic protectionism across economic sectors rather than the continuously expanding trade liberalization of the 1950s and 1960s or a nationalism leading back to the chaos of the 1930s.

This mixed trade regime is the product of the interaction of two opposed tendencies. On the one hand, never before has trade been more nearly free or economic interdependence so great. Tariff barriers have declined dramatically during the postwar period, the foreign sector in most economies has expanded, and international competition has increased. Yet this greater openness has given rise to and is paralleled by powerful countertendencies: economic closure in the form of the New Protectionism, the economic nationalism embodied in industrial policy, and the temptations of strategic trade policy made possible by the enhanced importance of oligopolistic competition. The ultimate balance that will be established among these forces is as yet undefined.

Adaptation to these economic developments provides a serious challenge to the international community. Yet the United States and certain other societies are limited in their adjustments by an unquestioned commitment to the principle of free trade, even though this ideal has become unrealistic under the present circumstances. Indeed, attempts to achieve what Americans conceive as free trade by pressuring others to open their markets and to harmonize their domestic structures may even be counterproductive because, as in the case of Japan, they may create powerful negative reactions. Bilateralism and similar arrangements, although they have their own dangers, may be the only way to move even haltingly in the direction of a more open trading system.

Ironically, John Maynard Keynes, the economist whose name is most frequently associated with the postwar liberal international economic regime, may also have been more prescient than others in foreseeing the erosion of the GATT that has occurred. He wrote to a colleague in October, 1943:

> As you know, I am, I am afraid, a hopeless sceptic about this return to nineteenth century *laissez faire*, for which you and the State Department seem to have such a nostalgia.
> I believe that the future lies with—
> (i) State trading for commodities;
> (ii) International cartels for necessary manufactures; and
> (iii) Quantitative import restrictions for non-essential manufactures.
> Yet all these future instrumentalities for orderly economic life in the future you seek to outlaw (quoted in Harrod, 1951, pp. 567-68).

Whether these restrictions on international trade recommended by Keynes will prove to be stabilizing or instruments of conflict has yet to be determined.

Multinational Corporations and International Production

SINCE THE END of the Second World War no aspect of internation- al political economy has generated more controversy than the global expansion of multinational corporations.[1] Some consider these powerful corporations to be a boon to mankind, superceding the na- tion-state, diffusing technology and economic growth to developing countries, and interlocking national economies into an expanding and beneficial interdependence. Others view them as imperialistic preda- tors, exploiting all for the sake of the corporate few while creating a web of political dependence and economic underdevelopment.[2] A few experts have even predicted, in more exuberant moments, that by the end of the century several dozen immense corporations would virtually control the world economy.[3]

A simple working definition of a multinational corporation is a firm that owns and manages economic units in two or more countries. Most frequently, it entails foreign direct investment by a corporation and the ownership of economic units (services, extractive industries, or manu- facturing plants) in several countries. Such direct investment (in con- trast to portfolio investment) means the extension of managerial con- trol across national boundaries. The international operation of these corporations is consistent with liberalism but is directly counter to the doctrine of economic nationalism and to the views of countries com- mitted to socialism and state intervention in the economy.

Both hopes and fears about multinational corporations are well founded. Many multinationals are extremely powerful institutions and possess resources far in excess of most of the member-states of the United Nations. These corporations have continued to grow in impor- tance. Total worldwide foreign direct investment was about half a tril- lion dollars in 1981 (U.S. Dept. of Commerce, 1984, p. 1). The scope of operations and extent of the territory over which some multinational

---

[1] Although many types of firms operate internationally, the multinational corporation is the most important because of its effects on the integration of national economies.

[2] An excellent collection of representative pieces on the multinational corporation is Modelski (1979).

[3] Some sections of this chapter have been adapted from Gilpin (1975) and other writings.

corporations range are more expansive geographically than any empire that has ever existed. They have integrated the world economy more extensively than ever in the past, and they have taken global economic interdependence beyond the realms of trade and money into the area of industrial production. This internationalization of production impinges significantly on national economies.

Although the domination of the world economy by multinational corporations seemed assured in the 1960s, an event took place in 1973 that profoundly challenged and altered their seemingly invincible position in the world economy. The oil embargo by OPEC and the subsequent massive rise in the price of petroleum demonstrated that nation-states had not lost their capacity for counterattack. Within a relatively short period of time, the gigantic oil companies—previously the quintessential international corporations—had had many of their foreign subsidiaries nationalized and had become subservient to states earlier considered powerless and servile. World history records few equivalent redistributions of wealth and power in such a short period.

Subsequently, another significant change took place. Although some of the oldest and most successful multinational corporations are non-American, U.S. corporations had dominated the scene throughout the 1960s and into the next decade. After the mid-1970s, however, their preeminence was challenged and, in some cases, surpassed not only by European and Japanese corporations but also by the multinationals of such newly industrializing countries as Brazil, India, and South Korea (*The Economist*, July 23, 1983, pp. 55-56). Resurgence of the nation-state and the emergence of powerful non-American corporations made the picture far more complex by the mid-1980s than it had been. This shift to the "New Multinationalism" will be discussed below.

THE NATURE OF THE MULTINATIONAL

What are the distinguishing characteristics of a multinational corporation? An MNC tends to be an oligopolistic corporation in which ownership, management, production, and sales activities extend over several national jurisdictions. It is comprised of a head office in one country with a cluster of subsidiaries in other countries. The principal objective of the corporation is to secure the least costly production of goods for world markets; this goal may be achieved through acquiring the most efficient locations for production facilities or obtaining taxation concessions from host governments.

Multinational corporations have a large pool of managerial talent, financial assets, and technical resources, and they run their gigantic operations with a coordinated global strategy. The multinational attempts to expand and perpetuate its market position through vertical integration and centralization of corporate decision making. IBM, Exxon, General Motors, Mitsui, Toyota, Fiat, and Nestlé are typical examples. Until the last quarter of this century, the two most prominent types of foreign investment were manufacturing investments in developed OECD economies and extractive industry investments, especially petroleum, in the less developed world. In later decades services have also been more and more dominated by the multinationals.

Foreign direct investment is generally an integral part of the global corporate strategy for firms operating in oligopolistic markets (Caves, 1982). Whereas traditional portfolio investment is driven by differential rates of return among national economies, foreign direct investment is determined by the growth and competitive strategies of the oligopolistic corporations. Although the former has most frequently been concentrated in government loans and infrastructure types of investment, direct investment tends to be sector-specific and is usually based on the existence of some competitive advantage over local firms, advantages that the corporation wishes to exploit or preserve. As this type of investment creates economic relations of an integrative nature and involves the corporation in the internal economic affairs of a country, it has become extremely controversial.

In the 1960s, foreign direct investment experienced a metamorphosis for several reasons: the compression of time and space due to improvements in transportation and communications, government policies favorable to the multinational corporations, and the supportive international environment provided by American power and economic leadership. American corporations, wanting to maintain access to a relatively closed yet growing market, began to make massive investments in Western Europe largely as a response to the formation of the European Common Market and the subsequent erection of a common external tariff. Direct investments by American corporations searching for petroleum and other resources also expanded in the Middle East and elsewhere. Subsequently, European, Japanese, and other corporations began to emulate the Americans until by the mid-1980s corporations of many nationalities reached into all parts of the globe.[4]

As these corporations increased in importance, economists and others endeavored to explain this novel phenomenon. Initially, the two available types of explanation were those of international capital

[4] Wilkins (1986a, b) discuss the relatively unknown early history of European and Japanese multinational corporations.

movements and international trade. Capital movement explanations accounted for foreign investment simply on the basis of higher rates of return abroad, which was adequate to explain portfolio but not direct investment; traditional trade theory had little to contribute and largely ignored the subject. It became obvious that a new theory was required, and early efforts focused on the significance of trade barriers, exchange rates, and favorable public policies. They also stressed the importance of technological developments, such as the jet airplane and satellites, that reduced the costs of transportation and communication. There was also a growing emphasis on the role of oligopolistic competition.

This eclectic approach was intended to incorporate the many different motives for and types of foreign direct investment. In time, however, economists began to set forth more general explanations. An exposition of these complex and more inconclusive theories would take this book far from its central concerns, but an abbreviated consideration of this theoretical effort helps to underscore the significance of the emergence of the multinationals for the political economy of international relations.

Although a unified theory that explains all cases of foreign direct investment has yet to be developed, the principal factor explaining the multinational corporation is the increasing importance of oligopolistic competition as one of the preeminent features of the contemporary world market economy (Kierzkowski, 1984). Foreign production has become a vital component in the integrated global strategies of the multinational corporations that now dominate the international economy. Thus, the same developments that have transformed the international trading system, discussed in Chapter Five, also account for the multinational corporations. Their global dominance is due to the increased importance of economies of scale, monopoly advantage, and barriers to entry in a particular economic sector. Multinationals have been able, through their trade and foreign production strategies, to take advantage of the relatively more open world economy produced by the several rounds of trade negotiations.

Two theories stand out among those that emphasize the oligopolistic nature of these corporations. The first is "product cycle theory," developed principally by Raymond Vernon (1966) and subsequently elaborated by other economists. The second and more recent variant is the "industrial organization theory of vertical integration" (Krugman, 1981a, p. 8). The product cycle theory applies best to foreign direct investment in manufacturing, the early overseas expansion of American corporations, and to what is called "horizontally integrated" investment, that is, the establishment of plants to make the same or similar goods everywhere. The more general industrial organization theory, on the other hand, applies best to the New Multinationalism and to the increased importance of "vertically integrated" investment, that is, the production of outputs in some plants that serve as inputs for other' plants of the firm. This production of components or intermediate goods has been greatly extended through contracting and joint ventures. Although many multinationals engage in both types of foreign investment or variations of these arrangements, the distinction is important in understanding corporate behavior and its effects.[5]

Product cycle theory, though it does not capture all important aspects of trade and investment, does incorporate some of the most important elements: the development and diffusion of industrial technology as a major determinant of the evolution of the international economy, the increasing role of the multinational corporation, and its integration of international trade and production. The theory is well suited for explaining American foreign investment in the 1960s and the reason why this investment generated intense hostility not only abroad but also from American labor. According to this view, the patterns of international trade and investment in industrial goods are largely determined by the emergence, growth, and maturation of new technologies and industries. The theory maintains that every technology or product evolves through three phases in its life history: (a) the introductory or innovative phase, (b) the maturing or process-development phase, and (c) the standardized or mature phase. During each of these phases, different types of economies have a comparative advantage in the production of the product or its components. The evolution of the technology, its diffusion from economy to economy, and the corresponding shift in comparative advantage among national economies explain both the patterns of trade and the location of international production (S. Hirsch, 1967).

The first phase of the product cycle tends to be located in the most advanced industrial country or countries, such as Great Britain in the nineteenth century, the United States in the early postwar period, and Japan to an increasing extent in the late twentieth century. Oligopolistic corporations in these countries have a comparative advantage in the development of new products and industrial processes due to the large home market (demand) and to the resources devoted to innovative activities (supply). During the initial phase, the corporations of the most advanced economy or economies enjoy a monopolistic position, primarily because of their technology.

[5] See Caves (1982, ch. 1) for an analysis of this distinction.

As foreign demand for their product rises, the corporations at first export to other markets. In time, however, the growth of foreign demand, the diffusion of the technology to potential foreign competitors, and rising trade barriers make foreign production of the good both feasible and necessary. During this second or maturing phase, manufacturing processes continue to improve and the locus of production tends to shift to other advanced countries. Eventually, in the third stage of the cycle, the standardization of manufacturing processes makes it possible to shift the location of production to less developed countries, especially to the newly industrializing nations, whose comparative advantage is their lower wage rates; from these export platforms either the product itself or component parts are shipped to world markets. Such intrafirm trade has become a prominent feature of the contemporary world economy.

Although the product cycle existed in some form in both the late nineteenth and early twentieth centuries, since the end of the Second World War several important changes have taken place in its operation. The rates of technological innovation and diffusion have dramatically accelerated; modern research and development activities and communications have enhanced both the competitive importance of innovations and their more rapid diffusion to competitors throughout the global economic system. International production has become an important ingredient in corporate strategies as oligopolistic corporations increasingly try to maintain their monopolistic position and market access through foreign direct investment. Finally, the combination of highly standardized products and production techniques with the existence of relatively cheap labor has made the NICs significant sources of industrial products and components. The consequent acceleration of shifts in comparative advantage and of changes in the location of international production have made both international trade and foreign investment highly dynamic.[6]

In brief, product cycle theory helps account for a number of the important features of the contemporary world economy: the significance of the multinational corporation and oligopolistic competition, the role of the development and diffusion of industrial technology as major determinants of trade and the global location of economic activities, and the integration of trade and foreign production in corporate strategy. These developments have stimulated both home and host governments

[6] Whitman (1981, pp. 12-13) discusses the example of the changing world automobile industry.

236

to utilize industrial and other policies to make these powerful institutions serve what each perceives to be its own national interest.

The limitations of product cycle theory led to a concerted effort to develop a more general and inclusive theory of the multinational corporation and foreign direct investment. This industrial organization theory of vertical integration combines both industrial organization and international economic theory; it begins with the modern theory of the firm and transfers it to the international economy. Its central ideas, which can be noted here only briefly, help explain the New Multinationalism and the contemporary role of the multinationals.

The industrial organization approach began with the recognition that the "costs of doing business abroad" involve other costs to the firm than simply exporting from its home plants. Therefore, the firm must possess some "compensating advantage" or "firm-specific advantage," such as technical expertise, managerial skills, or economies of scale that enable it to obtain monopoly rents from its operations in other countries. "These unique assets, built essentially in the home market, were transferrable abroad at low cost, implicitly through internal markets, and provided the ability to compete successfully with host country firms" (Casson, 1983, p. 38). This basic approach, first developed by Stephen Hymer and Charles Kindleberger, has been greatly extended by drawing upon the theory of industrial organization.[7]

The expansion and success of this vertical form of multinational enterprise have involved three factors. The first has been the internalization or vertical integration of the various stages of the business, primarily to reduce transaction costs. The firms have tried to bring all facets of the productive process, such as the sources and transfer prices of raw materials and intermediate products, within the confines of the corporation and under their control. The second is the production and exploitation of technical knowledge; because of the increasing cost of research and development, the firm endeavors to appropriate the results of its R & D and to retain a monopoly as long as possible. The third is the opportunity to expand abroad made possible by improvements in communications and transportation. The same factors that led to the domination of national economies by large oligopolistic corporations are transforming the international economy. The result of this evolution has been a complex and sophisticated international corporate structure.

The strategy of the vertically integrated multinational is to place the various stages of production in different locations throughout the

---

[7] Caves (1982) and Casson (1983) are excellent discussions of this approach.

globe. A primary motivation of foreign direct investment is to take advantage of lower costs of production, local tax benefits, and, especially in the case of American firms, U.S. tariff schedules that encourage foreign production of component parts. The result of this internationalization of the production process has been the rapid expansion of intrafirm trade. A substantial fraction of global trade has become the import and export of components and intermediate goods rather than the trade of final products associated with more conventional trade theory.

In addition to the other motives analyzed above, the multinational corporation also attempts to erect barriers to entry through its foreign investments. In oligopolistic industries where economies of scale and home demand are important factors in international competitiveness, the firm invests in many economies in order to thwart the emergence of foreign rivals. In this endeavor it is frequently assisted by the industrial and trade policies of its home government. Thus, this element of the multinational's global strategy is the firm's counterpart of the tactic of "industrial preemption" discussed in Chapter Five.

As with international trade, the transfer by the multinational corporation of the domestic system of industrial organization to the international realm has had significant economic and political consequences. The fact that foreign direct investment and the internationalization of production has taken place in a politically divided international system of competitive nation-states raises major political problems. It has opened the possibility of home states utilizing and manipulating the multinationals in order to achieve foreign policy and other objectives. Important sectors of labor in the home country regard foreign direct investment as a threat to their interests. And host states fear that the penetration of their economies by the multinationals has been detrimental to their economic, political, and other interests. These topics will be discussed following a brief history of the multinationals in the early postwar international economy.

THE ERA OF AMERICAN MULTINATIONALS

For many years the term "multinational corporation" was largely a euphemism for the foreign expansion of America's giant oligopolistic corporations (Wilkins, 1974). From an accumulated direct investment of only $11.8 billion in 1950, the book value of American direct investment abroad had risen to approximately $233.4 billion by 1984 (U.S. Department of Commerce, 1984, p. 11; Council of Economic Advisers, 1986, p. 371). In 1981, American foreign direct investment was more than two-fifths of the world's total foreign direct investment (U.S. Department of Commerce, 1984, p. 1). Prior to the Second World War, Latin America absorbed most of this investment; afterwards, Canada, Western Europe, and other industrial regions received the great bulk of it. Investment in the production of raw materials and in traditional manufacturing industries was substantial, but the largest fraction of postwar investment went into advanced manufacturing industries, where it was heavily concentrated in the advanced industrial sectors (particularly automobiles, chemicals, and electronics). The other large segment of American foreign direct investment has been in petroleum (ibid., p. 12), and at one time it accounted for about 36 percent of American direct investment in the less developed countries.

By the early 1970s the United States had become more of a foreign investor than an exporter of domestically manufactured goods. International production by American multinational corporations had surpassed trade as the main component of America's international economic exchange. Foreign production by the affiliates of U.S. corporations had grown nearly four times as large as American exports. Moreover, a substantial proportion of U.S. exports of manufactured goods were really transfers from an American branch to an overseas branch of a multinational. By 1969, the American multinationals alone produced approximately $140 billion worth of goods, more than any national economy except those of the United States and the Soviet Union. Many of America's largest corporations had placed more than half of their total assets abroad, and more than half of their total earnings came from overseas. These earnings in turn became an important factor in America's overall balance-of-payments position. Although the rate of growth of foreign investment declined by the 1980s, the United States remained heavily dependent on its multinationals for access to foreign markets and for the earnings they produce. In fact, one could describe American commercial policy since the end of the war as one of following the product cycle.

By the early 1970s, the flow of MNC international investment had began to shift in important ways. The rate of foreign investment by American multinationals had peaked and had begun to taper off; European and subsequently Japanese multinationals also had begun to invest heavily and to produce abroad; and the multinationals of several NICs and even some Eastern bloc countries were investing abroad. Although Americans continued to dominate the field, European and Japanese multinationals expanded rapidly in the 1970s and especially in the 1980s, thus balancing the former U.S. predominance. These new entrants produced a mixed and complex picture of crisscrossing investments of multinational corporations in one another's home economies (Ohmae, 1985).

The pattern of overseas investment began changing because the technology gap between the United States and other economies had narrowed. With the revival of the European and Japanese economies, the product-cycle phenomenon became less relevant for American firms and more relevant for foreign ones. Subsequently, fluctuating exchange rates and currency instabilities became significant factors affecting foreign direct investment. Intensified political uncertainties led multinationals to reduce their investments in many developing countries and encouraged investment in the United States. The dramatic rise of trade barriers around the globe, however, has become the most important determinant of foreign investment in both developed and less developed economies. Corporations have learned that they must establish foreign subsidiaries in a growing number of countries or enter into joint ventures or other arrangements with local firms in order to reach protected markets. Consequently, in the final decades of the twentieth century, intense competition among the MNCs of many nationalities exists in almost all world markets.

In this new environment of economic and political insecurities, Japanese multinationals began to expand rapidly into the American and, to a lesser extent, into the European and other markets. Traditionally, Japanese corporations had invested abroad mainly to acquire raw materials or lower-cost components that were then sent home for processing and incorporation into final products for export to world markets. Whereas American direct investment, one Japanese expert argued, was "antitrade" and displaced exports from the United States, the Japanese were following a "protrade" strategy. In the words of Kiyoshi Kojima, Japanese corporations kept the "high valued-added" phase of industrial production in the Japanese economy itself (Kojima, 1978).

Although this "protrade" strategy was continued into the last quarter of the century, rising barriers to Japanese goods in the United States, in the European Common Market, and elsewhere caused Japanese corporations to invest and produce more abroad. In effect, through the imposition on the Japanese of voluntary export restraints, the threats of "local content" legislation, and the pressures for higher trade barriers, Japan's economic partners forced Japanese corporations to go multinational. In the 1980s, the appreciation of the yen accelerated this trend. The consequent "multinationalization" of Japanese industry has become one of the most remarkable features of the international political economy.

Several generalizations can be made about multinationals at the end of the century. They tend to be American and, to a lesser extent, European oligopolistic corporations; yet these giants are increasingly being joined and even, in some cases, surpassed by Japanese corporations and those of the newly industrializing countries, in particular South Korea, whose access to foreign markets is being restricted by rising trade barriers. Also, the multinationals are most frequently oligopolistic corporations and are located in economic sectors where they can take advantage of economies of scale, low transportation costs, or their superiority in research and development. They operate most effectively in the OECD countries because of the existence of relatively standardized markets and generally low barriers to trade and foreign investment; with the exception of component production, they are found less frequently in the Eastern bloc and less developed countries. Their importance is growing because of their large presence in particular sensitive and strategic high technology industries (Whitman, 1977, p. 38).

The Multinationals and Home Countries

Most writings on the highly controversial issue of the relationship of the MNCs to their home governments fall into one or another of the three basic positions on the relationship of economics and politics: the liberal (or orthodox), the Marxist (or radical), or the nationalist (or neomercantilist) position (Gilpin, 1975, ch. 6). Each provides a different interpretation of the relationship of the multinationals and their home governments. Because American corporations have been the foremost investors abroad and the United States more than other countries has followed an overseas production strategy, the emphasis in this section will be on the relationship of American multinationals and the United States. The general argument, however, applies as well to the corporations of other countries and their relationship to their governments.

Although the interests of American corporations and U.S. foreign policy objectives have collided on many occasions, a complementarity of interests has tended to exist between the corporations and the U.S. government. American corporate and political leaders have in general believed that the foreign expansion of American corporations serves important national interests of the United States. American policies have encouraged corporate expansion abroad and have tended to protect them (Sigmund, 1980). This conjuncture of interests has existed in several areas.

Until the 1970s, American multinational corporations by and large controlled the non-Communist world's access to raw materials, especially petroleum; this guaranteed security of supply and preference for American customers in times of shortages (Krasner, 1978). This control was also exercised to moderate price increases during critical periods such as the Korean and Vietnam wars and on occasion was used as a source of political leverage.[8] After the establishment of the Materials Policy Commission (Paley Commission) following the outbreak of the Korean War, the United States placed a high priority on unimpeded access to foreign sources of raw materials; such access was achieved through ownership and control of the resources abroad by American extractive multinationals. Although American corporate control of raw materials access had diminished greatly by the 1980s, an American presence in world commodity markets continues to be of high priority and, it should be noted, other major economic powers have also sought diligently to gain a position for their own multinationals in these markets.[9]

Furthermore, American political leaders have believed that the national interest has also been served by the foreign expansion of U.S. corporations in manufacturing and in services. Foreign direct investment has been considered a major instrument through which the United States could maintain its relative position in world markets, and the overseas expansion of multinational corporations has been regarded as a means to maintain America's dominant world economic position in other expanding economies, such as those of Western Europe and Japan. This expansion is believed to result in more rather than fewer exports from the United States itself. Also, foreign production in developing countries of labor-intensive goods or components enables American corporations to compete against other low-cost producers. Although this strategy means that American corporations export both capital and technology, the real locus of corporate power—finance, research and development, and managerial control—remains in the U.S. economy. Multinationals of other nationalities have also expanded production in foreign economies in order to maintain or increase their share of world markets.

American multinationals have also been viewed as serving the interests of the U.S. balance of payments. The American government did not appreciate this situation until the late 1960s, when the country's trading and balance-of-payments position first began to deteriorate

---

[8] Furthermore, prior to 1973, the United States utilized its near-monopoly position with respect to petroleum as a political weapon. The best example was the 1956 Suez Crisis. The American threat to cut off petroleum to the British and French was a significant factor in forcing them to withdraw from their invasion.

[9] Vernon (1983, chs. 2, 3) is an excellent discussion of these matters.

sharply. The multinationals were then recognized as major earners of foreign exchange (and foreign exchange was needed to purchase goods as well as to maintain America's global military-political position) and therefore as an important factor in American economic welfare and global influence. Although the repatriated earnings of American multinationals have never reached the level anticipated prior to the nationalization of many petroleum and other resource investments in the 1970s, they do constitute a substantial portion of America's overall balance-of-payments position.

The multinational corporation has also been regarded as an instrument of global economic development and as a mechanism to spread the ideology of the American free enterprise system. Beginning with the Marshall Plan, many have seen the multinational corporation as a way to strengthen foreign economies and thereby to contain Communism by demonstrating, through the export of American technology, capital, and managerial know-how, an alternative to the Communist or socialist models of economic development.

President Reagan's program for the less developed countries announced on October 15, 1981, made a strong role for the multinationals an essential element. This commitment to the multinational corporation as a vehicle for spreading the free enterprise system is reflected in the American position on almost all international economic issues, ranging from the future of the World Bank to the solution of the global debt problem. Private foreign investment has been preferred to reliance on international organizations or borrowing by foreign governments in the world's capital markets as a means of developing the LDCs and integrating them into the world market economy.

American multinational corporations have also been regarded as a tool of diplomacy, in most cases to the displeasure of their business leaders. The U.S. government has tried to manipulate or control the activities of American corporations in order to induce or coerce other governments to do its bidding. A key ingredient in Secretary of State Henry Kissinger's policy of détente with the Soviet Union, for example, was to promise the latter an increase in American trade, investment, and technology exports; Kissinger hoped to modify Soviet behavior through the creation of a web of interdependence between Russia and the outside world. President Reagan, on the other hand, attempted to use denial of American technology to the Soviet Union as a tool of political coercion and economic warfare in the case of the Soviet–Western Europe gas pipeline agreement. There are many similar instances of attempts by the United States and other governments to enlist multinationals in the conduct of foreign policy.

243

Although the important role of multinational corporations in the overall economic and political strategy of the United States is without parallel, other nations have also increasingly viewed their own multinationals as instruments of national policy. European and Japanese multinationals have been employed by their governments to make their own sources of raw materials more secure. As American petroleum MNCs' influence has weakened, for example, Japanese multinationals and those of other countries have endeavored to replace them (Vernon, 1983, ch. 5).

As other economies have matured and increased in economic power, they have in varying degrees followed the American example of relying upon their multinationals to advance their perceived national interests (Spindler, 1984). For example, as trade barriers have risen, governments have encouraged their own multinationals to invest abroad to help maintain their nation's share of world markets. Much to the distress of the Reagan Administration, the West German and other European governments regard their multinationals as a means of increasing economic ties with the Soviet bloc, in part to ensure friendly political relations.

In the United States, the close identification of corporate interest and national interest began to wane after the 1973 energy crisis. Organized labor and certain academic critics had long been concerned about the implications of foreign investment for domestic employment, the distribution of national income, and the competitive position of the American economy. Such criticism became more general at the time of the Arab-Israeli War of October 1973, when U.S. oil companies were viewed as aiding the Arab oil embargo of Western countries. Subsequently, with the relative decline of American industry and the onset of massive trade deficits, high unemployment, and chronic balance-of-payments difficulties, the belief has spread that multinationals export U.S. jobs and decrease U.S. exports. Some critics have argued that multinationals should be forced to invest in the American economy and to limit severely the transfer of American technology to competitor economies.

Although strong support for foreign direct investment continued into the 1980s, political sentiment in the United States has become more equivocal. During the initial decades of the postwar era, the economic pattern that developed between the United States and its major economic partners was one in which the United States reached world markets through foreign production while other economies exported locally produced goods to the United States. As the relative size of the American economy has declined, U.S. policy makers have attempted to reverse this relationship by increasing exports of American-made products and encouraging direct investment by foreign corporations in the American economy. The U.S. government has, however, retained its basic commitment to foreign direct investment by American corporations.

In the 1980s, the reversal of the direction of investment flows and increased foreign investment in the United States has undoubtedly been a major factor in the decline of intense hostility toward overseas investment, such as that represented in the Burke-Hartke bill of the mid-1970s (Calder, 1985, p. 603). Nevertheless, American public opinion in the 1980s has became more critical of multinational corporations and overseas investment. Despite the increased foreign investment in the United States, many Americans have become concerned that foreign direct investment by American firms has contributed to the deindustrialization of the American economy. As the American trade deficit ballooned in the 1980s, fear intensified that the American economy had become merely an assembler of components manufactured abroad by American multinationals.

Despite the volumes that have been written on this controversy, the resolution to the debate between the proponents and critics of the MNC remains inconclusive. For example, one can well ask whether a corporation would make the same investment in the American economy if it had not made a foreign investment, or would it make no investment at all? It is impossible to be certain what would occur if American firms were forbidden to invest abroad. As Raymond Vernon has put it, a judgment about whether foreign investment displaces or supplements domestic investment is based on a set of essentially unprovable assumptions (Vernon, 1971, p. 157). Nevertheless it is important to recognize that American perceptions are changing and that American policies toward the multinational have become more circumspect.

THE MULTINATIONALS AND HOST COUNTRIES

When asked by a group of students for his views on multinational corporations, an economist of liberal persuasion answered "The multinational corporation doesn't exist." He meant that every corporation responds similarly to a set of price and other signals, regardless of its nationality or multinationality. The question of the national ownership of the means of production does not enter into the liberal economist's model of economic behavior. As the same economist stated on another occasion, the function of the postman is to deliver the mail, regardless of the color of his uniform.

However, a very different view is found in those countries that are hosts to foreign international corporations. As President of France, Charles de Gaulle denounced and tried to stem the tide of American economic penetration of Western Europe in the 1960s; best-selling French author Jean-Jacques Servan-Schreiber called upon Europeans to meet the "American challenge" (Servan-Schreiber, 1968). By the 1980s, similar criticisms within the advanced countries had been muted. American corporate overseas expansion had slowed and a counterflow of European and Japanese investment in the United States had begun to produce a crisscrossing of direct investment among these advanced economies. Between 1977 and 1984 foreign direct investment in the United States grew from $34.6 billion to $159.6 billion (Council of Economic Advisers, 1986, p. 371). Indeed, concern developed over the acceleration of Japanese direct investment in the United States and in Western Europe, especially in high-technology and growth sectors.

The clash between multinationals and host countries has been most intense in the less developed economies. Individual critics and public officials have leveled vociferous charges against the policies of international corporations and their alleged negative consequences for the economic well-being and development of the host nations. This section will evaluate these criticisms.

Foreign investment by the corporations of advanced economies in the economies of less developed countries is as old as the activities of the East India Company and other companies of merchant-adventurers. In the modern world there have been three waves of such investment. In the period of the "old colonialism" of the seventeenth and eighteenth centuries, Spanish, Dutch, and English companies established mines and plantations in the New World and in parts of Asia; these activities in most cases plundered and exploited the native peoples for their mineral and other riches. During the second wave of the "new imperialism" in the late nineteenth century, Africa, Southeast Asia, and other lands were brought within the several imperial systems. Although exploitation did not cease, European investments in port facilities, railroads, and urban centers at that time did create an infrastructure that is still important to many less developed countries.

The third wave began in the 1960s, when these less developed societies launched import-substitution strategies as the most rapid route to industrialization. Through the erection of high trade barriers, various tax inducements, and other policies, they encouraged the multinationals of the United States and other developed economies to establish manufacturing subsidiaries within their borders. Corporations also set up branch plants in certain NICs to produce components and to serve as export platforms for developed economy markets. The very success of these policies, however, gave rise to new controversies over the role of manufacturing multinationals in the less developed countries and to demands for their international regulation that became key elements in the struggle of the LDCs for a New International Economic Order. With political decolonization, nationalization, and increasing local control in the latter half of the twentieth century, the significance of foreign investment in commodity production in the less developed economy has declined.

Charges against the multinationals by host governments and radical critics fall into several categories. The economic argument is that foreign direct investment distorts the economy and the nature of economic development in less developed countries. This associated or "dependent development" is alleged to have several deleterious economic consequences (Evans, 1979). The multinationals are charged with the creation of a branch-plant economy of small inefficient firms incapable of propelling overall development; local subsidiaries exist as mere appendages of the metropolitan corporation and as enclaves in the host economy rather than as engines of self-reliant growth. The corporations are also accused of introducing inappropriate types of technology that hinder indigenous technological developments and of employing capital-intensive productive techniques that thereby cause unemployment and prevent the emergence of domestic technologies. Another charge is that multinationals retain control of the most advanced technology and do not transfer it to the LDCs at reasonable prices. In addition, many assert that foreign direct investment increases the maldistribution of income in the less developed countries. And, through the repatriation of profits abroad and their superior access to local finance, multinationals drain the host country of development capital and prevent the rise of indigenous entrepreneurship (Vaitsos, 1974).

Other critics argue that foreign direct investment has had negative political consequences for the LDCs. They assert, for example, that because the corporations require a stable host government sympathetic to capitalism, dependent development encourages the emergence of authoritarian regimes in the host country and the creation of alliances between international capitalism and domestic reactionary elites. This exploitative alliance is sustained by the intervention of the corporations' home governments in the internal affairs of the less developed countries. In this fashion foreign investment tends to make the host country politically dependent upon the metropolitan country.

It is also alleged that there are negative effects of foreign direct investment on the cultural and social well-being of LDCs. The domineering presence of foreign corporations in the host society is characterized as constituting a form of cultural imperialism, or Coca-Cola-ization of the society, through which the developing country loses control over its culture and its social development. The foreign corporation is viewed as undermining the traditional values of the society and introducing through its advertising and business practices new values and tastes inappropriate to the host nation. Some view these foreign values as not only bad in themselves but as detrimental to the development of the country because they create demands for luxury and other goods that do not meet the true needs of the masses.

It must be acknowledged that there is some basis for all of these charges. Foreign direct investment by international corporations in the less developed countries *can* have and *has* had unfortunate consequences for the economic, political, and social development of the LDCs. The 1985 Bhopal disaster and the alleged negligence of Union Carbide could be cited as an example. Certainly it is not difficult to find numerous cases of corporate malfeasance, but this is not the question. Critics charge that the multinational corporations and foreign direct investment by their very nature operate *systematically* to harm the host society. They argue that the relationship between foreign corporations and host governments must necessarily be ruinous for the latter. This blanket criticism is made not only of particular individual corporations but of multinationals as an institution.

The available evidence does not support an indictment in this extreme form. On the whole, the record of the multinationals in the developing countries is a favorable one. Indeed their role—whether benevolent or malevolent—is exaggerated by proponents and opponents alike. Many examples of the perceived negative consequences of foreign investment are actually either the result of the policies of the less developed countries themselves or an integral part of the development process itself. This assessment can be supported by a brief review of some of the specific charges brought against multinational corporations by less developed countries.[10]

Although it is true that international corporations have frequently established inefficient manufacturing subsidiaries in the less developed countries, this can be and primarily has been a function of the small scale of the local market in most of these nations. As part of their strategy of import-substitution industrialization and high tariffs, the LDCs have encouraged corporations to invest in protected markets where

[10] See Dunning (1981, ch. 13) for a review of these issues.

economies of scale are difficult to achieve and costs therefore are necessarily high. This practice may or may not lead to an enclave type of manufacturing economy when component-producing subsidiaries are established. In the Asian NICs, the beneficial effects of this type of development appear to have spilled over into the rest of the economy and to have become part of a process of rapid industrialization. In Mexico and certain other countries this does not seem to have happened. Whether such a favorable development takes place or an unfavorable one occurs, however, is primarily a function of the policies pursued by host governments.

In considering the issue of the transfer of inappropriate technology, it should be noted that less developed countries want not only the most advanced technologies but also labor-intensive technology (so-called appropriate technology) in order to maximize employment. These two objectives frequently conflict, yet the newly industrializing countries to which the most advanced technologies have been transferred—such as Taiwan and Singapore—have relatively little unemployment because of their overall economic performance. Furthermore, the transfer of capital-intensive technology by the MNCs is beneficial, given the capital shortage in the less developed economies. In addition, the multinationals have little incentive to develop more appropriate technologies, which would be competitive in world markets, because their investment is in a protected market and cushioned against international competition. Actually, the technology transfer issue is primarily a matter of conflicting economic interests between corporations and host governments, that is, determination of the price at which the former will sell the technology to the latter.

When considering whether or not foreign direct investment causes the maldistribution of wealth in the host economy, one must note that economic growth itself tends to create disparities of wealth (R. Frank and Freeman, 1978). Rapid economic growth, as Simon Kuznets has argued, appears to cause a U-shaped curve of increasing and then decreasing inequality (Ruggie, 1983a, p. 5). Because manufacturing multinationals most frequently invest in rapidly growing economies, it is difficult to separate the impact of the MNCs from the effects of the growth process itself. Although the multinationals generally do pay higher wages than local firms and therefore may be inflationary, there is little evidence to support the view that the national distribution of income is causally associated with foreign direct investment (Russett, 1983). On the contrary, a number of countries with heavy foreign investment, such as Taiwan and South Korea, have a more equitable distribution of income than do those LDCs that have restricted outside investment (*Far Eastern Economic Review*, February 23, 1984, p. 63). As Atul Kohli and colleagues have shown in their researches, the primary determinants of income distribution, at least in the short term, are the policies of the governments of the less developed countries themselves (Kohli et al., 1984).

The answer to the question of whether or not foreign direct investment thwarts indigenous industrial development is dependent upon the fundamental issue posed by Vernon above: Does foreign investment displace or supplement local investment? Multinationals do practice preemptive investment, so there is a basis to believe that they could crowd out local industries. Yet multinationals also bring in new capital and productive technology and generally provide an economic stimulus to the economy. In the light of these conflicting tendencies, there can be no general or conclusive answer to this question. In the case of almost all the NICs, however, local and foreign investment appear to be complementary.

The validity of the argument that foreign direct investment has adverse political effects is equally ambiguous, especially given the fact that so many LDC governments are authoritarian. It is certainly true that international corporations desire stable governments and no doubt lend their support to conservative governments. One can cite notorious examples of political interference in the internal affairs of less developed countries by the corporations and their home governments; the role of both ITT and the CIA in the overthrow of President Salvador Allende of Chile is a case in point.[11] What the multinationals prize, however, is political stability rather than a particular form of government. Hence, throughout the less developed world, alliances of convenience exist between corporations and local governments of many different political hues. In socialist Angola, for example, a paradoxical situation exists in which Communist Cuban troops have protected the oil production facilities of the capitalist Gulf Oil Company from "freedom fighters" supported by the United States government.

The charge of cultural imperialism can also be supported in part. Certainly there are examples of international corporations having, according to most disinterested observers, a detrimental impact on a particular society through their promotion of the consumption of partic-

[11] Although the actions of ITT against Allende were primarily motivated to protect their investments, the American government itself was primarily motivated by security considerations. The primary concern of the Nixon Administration was the perceived Soviet penetration of Latin America rather than a desire to safeguard American corporate interests. By the time of Allende, the major American investments in Chile had in fact already been nationalized (Moran, 1974).

ular products. Once again, however, one must acknowledge that the very process of economic development itself is destructive of traditional values, since it necessarily involves the creation of new tastes and unaccustomed desires. That, after all, is what development is all about. Furthermore, although the corporations may foster the desire for so-called inappropriate luxury goods, the consumption patterns of the developed countries in themselves have a demonstration effect upon elites and masses everywhere in this world of rapid communication. Few LDCs, including socialist countries, have the social discipline or possess a sufficiently strong state to resist the allure of jeans, Mercedes, and transistor radios, whether or not there is any foreign direct investment.

Whatever the intrinsic merits of these criticisms of foreign direct investment, some less developed countries have gained considerably during the 1970s and the 1980s at the expense of the corporations and the corporations' home countries. The balance of power in petroleum and to a lesser extent in other extractive industries shifted decisively to the host nations in the 1970s. In the area of manufacturing and even in high technology, a number of developing countries successfully pursued policies that increased their own benefits from foreign investments. LDC imposition of performance requirements on foreign investors changed the terms of investment in favor of the host countries; these changes include greater local participation and more joint ventures, expanded technology transfers, the exporting of locally manufactured goods, increased local content in final products, and restrictions on the reparation of profits, etc. Despite the significant gains of a number of less developed countries, however, as a group they have not gained, nor have they succeeded in enacting international corporate regulations that would change the terms of investment to their advantage. Whatever the specific terms of the emergent LDC-MNC relationship, they are being set through bilateral negotiations between corporations and host governments and in accordance with the bargaining skills and relative power of the actors (Reisinger, 1981).

The combination of LDC political pressures and global changes in the economics of industrial location has meant that certain less developed countries have benefited enormously from foreign direct investment. Whether to satisfy host political demands, to gain access to expanding markets, or to create export platforms, American and other multinationals have transferred advanced technologies to India, South Korea, and other LDCs and have greatly assisted their technological development (Grieco, 1982). In many cases, individual corporations and host countries have become partners—willing or otherwise—competing with other corporations and governments for world markets.

This type of cooperation or economic alliance has become an important aspect of the global shift of comparative advantage for many products to the developing countries and also of the trading regime discussed earlier.

The corporations are neither as positive nor as negative in their impact on development as the liberals or their critics suggest. Foreign direct investment can help or hinder, but the major determinants of economic development lie within the LDCs themselves. On balance, as even certain Marxist writers have concluded, the effect of the multinationals has been generally beneficial (Warren, 1973). The real issue in the relationship between the multinationals and the LDCs is the terms of the investment. The question of how the benefits of the investment will be divided necessarily divides the corporations and the LDC governments. Whatever the legitimacy of their concerns, few countries have outlawed foreign investment in manufacturing or asked industrial firms to go home.

THE NEW MULTINATIONALISM

Observers with varying points of view have been proved wrong in their predictions for the multinational corporations. Multinationals have neither superceded the nation-state nor gone the way of the East India Company.[12] Both state and corporation have proven themselves to be remarkably resourceful and versatile in dealing with one another. The efforts of the United Nations, the OECD, and regional organizations to impose an international code of regulations on corporations have not succeeded, nor have American efforts to implement regulations restricting the behavior of host governments toward the multinationals (Krasner, 1985, ch. 7). The international investment regime is being fashioned by negotiations among individual corporations, home governments, and host governments rather than according to universal regulations or complete freedom of corporate action. The result of this interaction is a complex and contradictory pattern of relations between multinationals and governments that, barring a major catastrophe,

[12] I must confess that in my earlier writings I was much too pessimistic regarding the possibility of American multinationals adjusting to changes in the world situation. The slowing-down of American investment abroad and the increase in foreign direct investment in the United States undercut many of my earlier concerns. On the other hand, the MNCs must now function in a highly restricted political environment and the nature of the MNC operations has changed importantly with the rise of what I call the New Multinationalism.

could last indefinitely into the future, a future that will necessarily be different from the past in several critically important particulars.

First and most important, a slowdown in the rate of growth of the aggregate level of foreign direct investment appears to have taken place due to decreased rates of economic growth and increased political uncertainties around the world. Simultaneously, the competition among both developed and less developed countries for capital and technology has intensified. Developed countries, beset by high unemployment (with the major exception of Japan), compete more vigorously to attract investment. LDCs have opened their doors wider to the multinationals in the 1980s because of the effects of world recession, the experience of the global debt crisis, and the decreasing availability of other forms of capital or means of acquiring technology (*The Economist*, February 19, 1983, pp. 86-87). Although the economic improvement of many less developed countries and the increased competition among multinationals have strengthened the bargaining position of certain LDC governments, the direction of investment has tipped more toward the advanced countries. As pointed out earlier, it is significant that the United States has not only continued to be the largest home country but has also become the largest host country.

The less developed countries have become more and more differentiated in their ability to attract foreign investment. Rising political and economic uncertainty has altered the business environment and caused the multinationals to diversify their investment, especially within the developed economies (Whitman, 1981, p. 14). The Iranian revolution, the growing number of socialist governments, and the confiscation of corporate assets have made corporations wary of making large long-term commitments in the less developed world. The investment there has tended to be increasingly concentrated in the few countries, such as South Korea, Mexico, Taiwan, the Philippines, Singapore, Hong Kong, and Brazil, whose economies emphasize export-led growth, possess pools of inexpensive skilled labor, or have large and expanding internal markets. These investments have been primarily in services and manufacturing to serve foreign or local markets rather than the extractive investments of the past. Bankers' growing reluctance to make loans to over-indebted LDCs has led to greatly increased competition among these countries for direct investment. These tendencies have accentuated the pattern of uneven development among the less developed countries and have led bypassed countries to make the paradoxical charge that the refusal of the corporations to invest in them is a new form of capitalist imperialism.

Within this overall setting, certain interrelated trends can be discerned: (1) the increasing importance of "vertical," as opposed to "horizontal," foreign direct investment, (2) the expansion of intercorporate alliances across national boundaries, and (3) the increasing importance of off-shore production and sourcing of components and intermediate goods. Multinationals have been encouraged to diversify their production of components and products among the NICs as nontariff barriers have developed within the advanced countries. These developments, which became more prominent in the late 1970s, are together transforming the international trading and investment regime (Strange, 1985c).

As has already been noted, horizontal investment involves the replication abroad of some aspects of a firm's domestic operations, and vertical investment occurs when a firm invests abroad in activities that (1) provide inputs for the home production process or (2) use the output of home plants. That is, vertical foreign direct investment entails the fragmentation of the production process and the location throughout the world of various stages of component production and final assembly of components. This fragmentation is intended to achieve economies of scale, to take advantage of cost differences of different locales, and to exploit favorable government policies such as tariff codes that provide for duty-free entry of semifinished products or of goods assembled abroad from components produced domestically. The development and increased specialization of branch plants has led to the spectacular rise of intrafirm or corporate-administered trade discussed earlier. By one reckoning, this form of trade accounts for approximately 60 percent of American imports (Ruggie, 1983b, p. 475).

The shift from wholly owned subsidiaries abroad to joint ventures and other forms of intercorporate alliances has been accelerated by a number of political, economic, and technological factors: (1) access to a market frequently requires a domestic partner; (2) the rapid pace and cost of technology necessitates that even large corporations spread the risk; (3) the huge capital requirements of operating globally and in all major markets; (4) for American firms, the loss of technological leadership in many fields; and (5) for Japanese firms, to forestall protectionism. Thus, for example, General Motors is reported to have approximately thirty alliances with other corporations (*The New York Times*, August 6, 1986, p. D2).

The global rationalization of international production has accorded increasing importance to alliances between the multinationals and overseas suppliers of products and components. At the core of many if not most of these arrangements are Japanese suppliers in automobiles, electronics, and advanced technologies. Japan supplies something like

40 percent of American component parts in electronics, automobiles, and other sectors. The role of the newly industrializing countries in this internationalization of production is also rapidly expanding (Grunwald and Flamm, 1985). Through such mechanisms as joint ventures, contractual arrangements, or the establishment of wholly owned subsidiaries, American and other multinationals are transferring more advanced technology to the NICs and entering into cooperative arrangements with an expanding number of countries like Mexico, Taiwan, and South Korea.

By combining the productive technology and global marketing organizations of the corporations with the low-wage skilled labor of the NICs, both the firms and the NICs can increase their competitive strength in world markets. For example, American and Korean firms are forging ties in a typical balance-of-power fashion to counter the rising ascendancy of Japanese firms in computer chips (*The New York Times*, July 15, 1985, p. D1). The rise of the yen and the tying of the Korean currency to the dollar have encouraged this alliance. It should be particularly interesting to observe developments in mainland China, where the Communist government has created special manufacturing zones to tap the technology of the corporations and to produce exports for overseas markets.

In effect, a shortcutting of the traditional product cycle has occurred. Whereas in the past the locus of comparative advantage and the production of goods shifted from the United States to the other advanced countries and eventually to the newly industrializing countries, in the late 1980s the initial production of a good or component may take place in the NIC itself; assembly of the finished product may occur in the advanced economy. This obviously benefits the MNCs and the NICs, but it is deeply resented by large sections of labor in the United States and Western Europe.

Interfirm alliances and cooperation, arrangements that are frequently sanctioned and promoted by national governments, have also become increasingly important (Whitman, 1981, p. 24). The escalating cost of technological development, the importance of economies of scale, and the spread of the New Protectionism have made participation in the three major markets of the world—the United States, Western Europe, and Japan—a necessity for multinational corporations; this in turn has most frequently necessitated acquisition of a local partner (Ohmae, 1985). The result is that the multinationals are invading one another's home markets and new practices are evolving (*The Economist*, February 11, 1984, p. 63). The new United Motor Manufacturing Company established in 1983 by those two powerful rivals, General Motors and Toyota, to produce subcompact cars in the United States is the most noteworthy example. As *Business Week* (July 21, 1986) observed, complex corporate alliances are increasingly important.[13]

These developments foretell the end of the old multinationalism. The day is past when corporations of the United States and a few other developed countries could operate freely in and even dominate the host economies and when foreign direct investment meant the ownership and control of wholly owned subsidiaries. Instead, a great variety of negotiated arrangements have been put in place: cross-licensing of technology among corporations of different nationalities, joint ventures, orderly marketing agreements, secondary sourcing, off-shore production of components, and crosscutting equity ownership. In the developed countries the General Motors–Toyota alliance is undoubtedly a harbinger of things to come. In the developing world the corporations see the LDCs less as pliable exporters of raw materials and more as expanding local markets and industrial partners or even potential rivals. Thus, the relatively simple models of both liberal and dependency theorists are becoming outmoded in the final quarter of the century.

These developments are also changing attitudes and policies in both the less developed and developed countries. The former have become more receptive to the multinationals but are also pursuing policies to shift the terms of investment in their favor. The responses of the developed countries—which will be vital in determining the ultimate success of this new multinationalism—are more problematic. In the United States, Western Europe, and Japan, debate is just beginning between the gainers and the losers from these changes. Both states and corporations are girding for battle in a global market where national and corporate strategies as much as traditional factors of comparative advantage will greatly influence the outcome of economic competition.

Attitudes in the United States toward foreign investment, as noted earlier, began to change in the 1970s and 1980s. Although opinion has continued to favor the multinationals, questioning of foreign direct investment has increased considerably, especially in those sections of the country most concerned about the decline of traditional industries and plagued by high levels of unemployment. Responding to changing pressures, American corporations have taken modest steps to restrict foreign production and to export abroad from domestic plants. The United States has also tried to increase its share of world investment and the benefits from foreign direct investment by the firms of other countries. Through the threat of local content legislation and protec-

[13] Ohmae (1985) provides a very good review of these developments.

tionist barriers, efforts have been made to encourage Japanese and other corporations to locate future investments in the United States. In effect, the United States is moving to reverse the flow of global investment in the direction of greater investment in the United States itself.

In the early 1980s, however, the overvalued dollar, high wage rates, and the high cost of capital along with other factors accelerated the movement abroad of industrial production and the expansion of offshore procurement. The powerful tendency toward vertical foreign direct investment and increased reliance on importing components led *Business Week* to worry that the American economy was becoming merely an assembler of foreign-produced components and American firms were becoming "hollow corporations" whose primary task had become to assemble or distribute imported goods (March 11, 1985, p. 60, and March 3, 1986). For example, the "American" automobile has almost disappeared and is largely an assemblage of imported components (*The New York Times*, August 10, 1985, p. 31). Or, to take another example, $625 of the $860 manufacturing cost of that marvel of American ingenuity, the IBM PC, was incurred overseas by subsidiaries of American multinationals ($230) and by foreign firms ($395). In brief, the United States, it was feared, was being transformed from a manufacturing to mainly a distribution economy.

Many Americans became concerned over the loss of manufacturing jobs and its income distribution effects. Capital, it is pointed out, benefits from overseas investment as does foreign labor, but domestic labor loses from the outflow of capital unless it is somehow compensated (Samuelson, 1972, p. 10). The Reagan Administration, because the thrust of its policies was away from the notion that the government should aid the losers and develop adjustment policies to assist injured businesses and workers, encouraged the spread of protectionist pressures.

A longer-term worry was the so-called boomerang effect. Critics charged that in the short run increased reliance on subcontracting and imported components might make sense as a means of meeting foreign competition, but that the importation of these goods was further weakening American manufactures and accelerating the diffusion of American technology and expertise to potential foreign competitors. In the early postwar era, the American strategy of following the product cycle meant that mature goods for which the United States no longer had a comparative advantage were produced abroad; by the 1980s, American multinationals were more and more manufacturing their newest products abroad and importing them into the United States. In the long term, such a strategy of increased dependence on foreign components manufacturers would intensify competitive pressures on the American economy. In this fashion, the New Multinationalism has raised a host of opportunities and challenges that the United States must address.

The West Europeans during the 1980s have not yet come to terms with the New Multinationalism. Although significant differences exist among the Europeans, varying from Great Britain's privatization of the economy to French nationalization, some major trends are discernible. The Continental economy has been increasingly closed to imports of goods produced elsewhere, especially those from Japan and the NICs. Meanwhile, cooperative efforts by European firms with American and Japanese corporations such as joint ventures and technology licensing have been encouraged in order to close the growing technology gap between Europe and the other advanced economies. As the Common Market has increased its barriers to imports, foreign multinationals have had to invest in Europe or at least to share their technology in order to gain access to the relatively closed European market.

Government intervention in the economy through outright nationalization, government participation, and government initiation of joint development projects such as the Airbus has increased. A considerable fraction of the private sector in Western Europe has been nationalized. Seeking to emulate the Japanese "capitalist developmental state," a term coined by Chalmers Johnson (1982, p. viii), or simply to create employment, one European government after another has taken over key sectors of the corporate economy. Through rationalizing and concentrating their industries, the Europeans are attempting to create corporate "champions" that will compete with American and Japanese multinationals in European and overseas markets. These European corporations are being fashioned into instruments of an emergent industrial policy that is contributing to the growing regionalization of the world political economy.

Undoubtedly the most significant development of the early 1980s was the increasing multinationalization of the Japanese economy. Although much less advanced than the global role of American and European corporations, the expansion abroad of Japanese multinationals in the 1980s has been truly remarkable. Still quantitatively small in 1985 by American or European standards, it was of increasing significance, especially in the United States (*The New York Times*, August 9, 1986, p. 1). Although only about 7 percent of total world foreign direct investment, it was highly concentrated in basic industries and in the increasingly important high-tech and service sectors (*The Economist*, February 19, 1983, p. 87). As *Business Week* (July 14, 1986) pointed out, the Japanese were building an industrial empire inside the American economy itself.

The traditional Japanese emphasis on exporting from home plants and investing overseas primarily in extractive industries began to give way in the mid-1970s. Responding to the energy crisis and rising labor costs at home, Japanese firms initially invested in the LDCs to acquire energy-embodied semiprocessed goods and to transfer production abroad to other Asian countries in those industries in which Japan no longer had a comparative advantage; indeed, even in the mid-1980s most Japanese foreign direct investment is in Asia (Abegglen and Stalk, 1985, pp. 244-59). The goods produced abroad in these low-technology industries have been for local consumption or for export to third economies. There has been little boomerang effect, that is, little export of the goods back to Japan itself.

Subsequently, the erection of trade barriers and the appreciation of the yen in the mid-1980s caused the Japanese to accelerate foreign production in the developed country for which the product was destined. This type of foreign direct investment has become especially important for the American and, to a lesser extent, the West European market. Whereas Japanese direct investment in the United States and Canada for the period 1951-1972 totaled only $303 million, by 1984 Japanese direct investment in the United States had reached $16.5 billion; in Western Europe the amount was $1.1 billion (Fukushima, 1985, pp. 23-24). In the 1980s American and European foreign direct investment was motivated primarily by declining comparative advantage at home; Japanese foreign investment in the other advanced economies has been almost entirely intended to get around trade barriers raised against its extraordinarily efficient corporations. In effect, these Japanese companies have been forced against their own will to become multinationals (Nussbaum, 1983, p. 246).

Japanese foreign direct investment has been generally "pro-trade" and designed to complement its overall economic strategy. Through corporate and state cooperation it facilitates exports to foreign markets and ensures access to resources and particular imports. It has also been strongly motivated by the desire to avoid trade friction and to prevent the rise of protectionist barriers abroad. Japan has viewed foreign investment principally as an instrument to maintain and expand its role in the emergent world economy.

The penetration of the American and, to a lesser extent, the West European economies by Japanese multinationals is transforming the relationships of the advanced countries.[14] Through the establishment of

[14] The relationship of American and Japanese multinationals is older than is generally appreciated (Wilkins, 1982).

wholly owned subsidiaries, the purchase of participation in foreign and especially American firms, and the establishment of joint ventures in such areas as automobiles, steel, and electronics, Japanese investments have rapidly evolved from areas of simple fabrication, assembly, and the production of light components to heavy high-technology production requiring economies of scale. By the mid-1980s Japanese automobile corporations manufacturing in the United States had become, as a group, one of the four major producers of automobiles within the country. The extraordinary pace of the increase of Japanese investment in the United States, the range of products involved, and the transplantation into the American economy of Japan's unexcelled comparative advantage in new manufacturing techniques has begun to have a profound effect on the American economy and to give rise to deep anxieties. Governor Richard D. Lamm of Colorado has spoken of "economic colonialism" by the Japanese (*The New York Times*, September 16, 1985, p. D9).

At this writing the consequences of the transfer of the full spectrum of Japanese competitive dynamism into the American market are highly speculative but nonetheless significant. In the first place, trade barriers against Japanese imports have had the paradoxical effect of intensifying competition within the American economy itself as Japanese corporations have jumped the barriers and established manufacturing operations in the United States. Second, American trade barriers and the growth of Japanese-Amercian corporate cooperation may displace and have a detrimental impact on European and NIC sales in the United States, unless the latter two pursue a similar course. And, third, important groups in the United States are responding negatively to Japanese "take-overs" in the American economy, especially in the sensitive high-technology industries; they are exhibiting all the fears manifested earlier in Western Europe and the less developed countries regarding American multinationals. The outcome of these conflicting developments in the Nichibei economy will affect not only the future of the U.S. economy but also the shape of the international political economy.

Conclusion

The multinational corporation and international production reflect a world in which capital and technology have become increasingly mobile while labor has remained relatively immobile. Continuous changes in comparative advantage among national economies, advances in modern transportation and communications, and favorable government policies encourage corporations to locate their production facilities in the most advantageous locations around the globe. Some of these advantages include the existence of pools of low-cost skilled labor, proximity to markets, and tax advantages. The result of this internationalization of industrial production has been the creation of a complex web of interlocking relationships among nation-states and the world's giant corporations.

The economic and political consequences of international production and the formation of economic alliances across national boundaries have become matters of controversy and speculation. These developments raise the classic issues debated by liberals, Marxists, and nationalists over the stability of international capitalism. Do these transnational alliances represent a transcendence of the "law of uneven development," or are they merely temporary alliances that will dissolve with the continuing uneven development of national economies?[15]

In the tradition of nineteenth-century liberals who extolled trade as a force for peace, some writers believe that the sharing of production by states and corporations of different nationalities creates bonds of mutual interest that counter and moderate the historic tendency for the uneven development of national economies to give rise to economic conflict. If corporations of declining economies are able to continue as industrial producers through foreign direct investment, it is argued, they will be less apt to resist the rise of new industrial powers. Thus some predict that the multinationals and their political allies will defend the liberal world economy and resist the forces of economic nationalism (Sen, 1984, pp. 241-45).

Other observers of "the internationalization of production," following the Leninist and nationalist traditions, are more skeptical and believe that these state and corporate alliances could fragment the world economy into rival blocs and economic groupings. For example, these transnational alliances do not solve the surplus capacity problem, the question of who will produce what, or the issue of how the losers will be compensated. If these matters are not resolved, skeptics believe that the New Multinationalism could create a world in which the corporations and their allies would engage in what former West German Chancellor Helmuth Schmidt called in 1974 "the struggle for the global product." This may be an apt phrase to characterize the New Multinationalism.

Whether Kautsky's or Lenin's predictions regarding the possibilities of intracapitalist economic cooperation and conflict will eventually prove correct remains to be seen. What can be said in the mid-1980s is

[15] Keohane (1984a, pp. 43-44) analyzes this increasingly important issue.

that the stability of the world market economy depends ultimately upon the quality of leadership (hegemonic or pluralistic), a solution of the adjustment problem, and the creation of international norms that both increase global economic stability and guarantee states an adequate degree of economic autonomy. We shall return to a consideration of these issues in Chapter Ten.

At the least, the increased mobility of capital and the increasingly arbitrary nature of comparative advantage have given rise to intensified international competition for investment. Through tax policies, the erection of trade barriers, and even the creation of a skilled and disciplined labor force (e.g., Taiwan), governments attempt to attract corporate investments and influence the international location of economic activities. The multinationals of different countries compete for access to these economies, thereby giving the host states some bargaining leverage regarding the terms of the investment.

The result of these developments is a complex pattern of relationships among corporations, home governments, and host countries that has increasingly politicized foreign investment both at home and abroad. Through individual actions and in alliance with one another, each actor attempts to enhance its own position. To the extent that one government wrings concessions from corporations, it triggers counterpressures in other countries. As host governments attempt to transform the terms of investment in their favor, they create concern at home over trade imbalances, lost jobs, and "run-away" plants. Thus, groups and states attempt to manipulate corporations for their own particularistic interests.

Governments and corporations are having to come to terms with a vastly altered international environment in which the location of the world's economic activities and the terms on which foreign direct investment take place have become of vital importance. Which countries will possess which industries, and who will reap the benefits? Answers will be determined partially by the interplay of market forces as corporations seek out the least costly sites for their production, but these issues will also be determined by the power and interests of the several participants themselves as they compete for individual advantage.

The Issue of Dependency and Economic Development

T HE FUTURE of the less developed countries is one of the most pressing issues of international political economy in our era, and the resolution of this issue will profoundly affect the future of the planet. The
intense desire of the majority of the human race to escape its debilitat-
ing poverty and join the developed world is a determining feature of
international politics. Yet in the final decades of the twentieth century,
bitter controversy exists regarding the causes of and possible solutions
to this problem.

Poverty has always been the lot of most members of the human race.
However, what may be termed a revolution has taken place with regard
to the political and moral significance of this issue, and this change has
made the immense gap between the rich Northern half of the globe and
the largely impoverished Southern half a new and explosive issue. Some
of the reasons for this historic change are of particular importance in
accounting for the present international political significance of mass
impoverishment.

The condition of poverty is less tolerable than in the past due to the
existence of instant communications. The transistor radio and the tel-
evision set have made people in even the most remote parts of the globe
aware of the wealth of others and of the benefits of material progress.
Whole societies now want that to which only the rich could previously
aspire. The advanced nations have taught the rest of the world that escape from their lot is possible, and this has made the desire for economic growth, modernization, and rapid industrialization the universal ideology of political elites in all countries.

Furthermore, society no longer regards poverty as natural, the punishment of God, or one's Karma. Because people generally believe that
poverty and its consequences are created by mankind, these conditions
have become unacceptable. The progress and demonstration effect of
the developed countries and the immense distance yet to be traveled by
most other countries only reinforce awareness, so that fewer people re-
sign themselves to being poor and accept it as their fate (Hirschman,
1981, ch. 3). The revolution of rising expectations has become a universal feature of our age, and it is almost a law of human behavior that

the rise of people's expectations outpaces the capacity of society to meet them.

Another vital change is that the issue and the demand for equality have been internationalized (Carr, 1945). Until the modern era, the differences of wealth *within* societies were far greater than the differences of wealth *among* societies. In the premodern period everywhere, a small wealthy elite was superimposed on an impoverished mass, a situation still applicable in many places. Today, however, the differences of wealth within the developed countries are less important than the differences of wealth among countries; the individual living in poverty in Europe and America is far more wealthy than the overwhelming bulk of the human race living in the Third World. In the modern world, whether one is relatively rich or poor has become increasingly a function of the particular nationality into which one is born. As a consequence, the class struggle within societies (as Marxists would describe it) has become partially displaced, if not superceded, by the conflict among societies over the international distribution of material wealth.

It is striking to realize that the rich nations of the eighteenth century comprise most of the rich ones today. In fact, the gap between European and other civilizations began to open in the late Middle Ages (Jones, 1981); the Industrial Revolution widened the distance still further. Excluding the major Arab oil exporters, the only exception to this generalization is Japan, whose rise to third place in the world economy began in the last quarter of the nineteenth century. It is historically noteworthy that in the present age new economic powers are pressing to join the club of industrial nations; the rise of the newly industrializing countries is already having an important impact on the international balance of economic power and the political economy, an impact that could prove to be as significant as the emergence of Western civilization as the dominant force in international economics.

These changes in both fact and perception have made economic development and underdevelopment a central issue in international political economy. The universal concern over the distribution of wealth is truly a novel issue in world politics; scant prior interest in the subject is to be found in diplomatic histories. Though individual nations have always desired to improve their economies, the issues of economic development and the skewed international distribution of wealth were not on the agenda of international diplomacy.

In the past the dividing line between wealth and poverty was drawn between elite and mass; in the late twentieth century the line separates nations, races, and hemispheres. It sets the poor South against the affluent North and the Third World against the First World of the market economies and, to a lesser extent, the Second World of the planned economies. The fact that the global poverty line now matches political boundaries has given the distribution of wealth an international dimension and made it a major issue of world politics.

The rancorous debate over the so-called North-South issue is centered on particularly difficult but important questions. Some believe that the operation of the world market economy and the evil practices of capitalism are the primary causes of the deplorable living conditions for much of humanity. Others believe that the problem lies with more objective economic factors or with misguided policies of the poor countries themselves. Decisions on whether integration in or dissociation from the world economy is the best route to economic development are dependent on beliefs about the causes of the situation.[1]

The most prominent theories explaining development are those of economic liberalism, classical Marxism, and the underdevelopment position. Both economic liberals and classical Marxists subscribe to the dual economy theory of the world economy; they view the evolution of the world economy as diffusing the process of economic growth from advanced to traditional economies. The less developed economies are incorporated into an expanding world economy and transformed from traditional to modern economies through the flow of trade, technology, and investment. However, liberals believe this process is generally benign and harmonious; classical Marxists believe it is accompanied by conflict and exploitation. In contrast, the underdevelopment perspective, whether in its structuralist or dependency version, regards the operation of the world economy as detrimental to the interests of the less developed countries in both the short and long term.

THE LIBERAL PERSPECTIVE ON ECONOMIC DEVELOPMENT

According to the liberal perspective, the world economy is a beneficial factor in economic development; interdependence and economic linkages of advanced economies with less developed economies tend to favor the latter societies. Through trade, international aid, and foreign investment, the less developed economies acquire the export markets, capital, and technology required for economic development. This view was summed up in the title of the Pearson Report, *Partners in Development* (1969). Nevertheless, although the world economy can help or hinder development through the diffusion process, this view holds that

[1] An excellent summary of the existing evidence on these matters is Ruggie (1983a, pp. 18-23).

the most important factor affecting economic development is the efficient organization of the domestic economy itself.

Although there is a generally accepted liberal theory of international trade, money, and investment, there is no comparable theory of economic development. The principal reason for this difference is that the body of theory regarding trade, money, and so forth assumes that a market exists; economic theory is concerned with rational individuals seeking to maximize welfare under market conditions. For liberal economists, however, economic development requires the removal of political and social obstacles to the functioning and effectiveness of a market system; they are therefore primarily concerned with the determination of how this is to be accomplished. Whereas other areas of economics tend to assume a static framework of rules and institutions within which economic activity takes place, a theory of economic development must explain behavioral and institutional change (Davis and North, 1971). Although the study of economic development has failed to produce a body of developmental theory accepted by the whole fraternity of liberal economists, there is general agreement on several points.

Liberalism maintains that an interdependent world economy based on free trade, specialization, and an international division of labor facilitates domestic development. Flows of goods, capital, and technology increase optimum efficiency in resource allocation and therefore transmit growth from the developed nations to the less developed countries. Trade can serve as an "engine of growth" as the less developed economy gains capital, technology, and access to world markets.[2] This is a mutually beneficial relationship since the developed economies can obtain cheaper raw materials and outlets for their capital and manufactured goods. Because the less developed economies have smaller markets, opening trade with advanced economies is believed to benefit them relatively more than it does the developed economies. Moreover, since the factors of production flow to those areas where they produce the highest rewards, a less developed economy with a surplus of labor and a deficit of savings can obtain infusions of foreign capital that accelerate growth.

This theory of economic growth believes that many factors required for economic development are diffused from the advanced core of the world economy to the less developed economies in the periphery. The rate and direction of this spread effect are dependent upon a number of

[2] Lewis (1974, pp. 49-59) provides a good analysis of the role of exports in economic development.

factors: the international migration of economic factors (capital, labor, knowledge); the volume, terms, and composition of foreign trade; and the mechanics of the international monetary system. Although liberals recognize that economic progress is not uniform throughout the economy (domestic or international), they do believe that over the long term the operation of market forces leads toward equalization of economic levels, real wages, and factor prices among nations and regions of the globe (Rostow, 1980, p. 360).

To support this thesis regarding the growth-inducing effects of international trade, liberal economists contrast the amazing economic success of the "export-led" growth strategies of the Asian NICs with the failure of the "import substitution" strategy of most Latin American countries (Krueger, 1983, pp. 6-8).[3] Liberal economists find the basic obstacles to economic development within the less developed countries themselves (Bauer, 1976): the preponderance of subsistence agriculture, a lack of technical education, a low propensity to save, a weak financial system, and most important, inefficient government policies. They believe that once such bottlenecks are removed and a market begins to function efficiently, the economy will begin its escape from economic backwardness.

Most liberals consider that the key to economic development is the capacity of the economy to transform itself in response to changing conditions; they believe that the failure of many less developed countries to adjust to changing prices and economic opportunities is rooted in their social and political systems rather than in the operation of the international market system (Kindleberger, 1962, pp. 109-112). As Arthur Lewis has put it, any economy can develop if it has three simple ingredients: adequate rainfall, a system of secondary education, and sensible government. For the liberal, therefore, the question is not why the poor are poor but, as Adam Smith phrased it in *The Wealth of Nations*, why certain societies have overcome the obstacles to development, have transformed themselves, and through adapting to changing economic conditions have become rich. The answer given is that these successful societies have permitted the market to develop unimpeded by political interference (Lal, 1983).

Failure to develop is ascribed to domestic market imperfections, economic inefficiencies, and social rigidities. Political corruption, a parasitic social and bureaucratic structure, and the failure to make appropriate investments in education, agriculture, and other prerequisites for

---

[3] Although economic growth and foreign trade have been historically associated, the relationship between growth and trade is a complex one (Findlay, 1984).

economic development restrain these nations. Improper public policies such as high tariff barriers and overvalued currencies harmful to export interests are fostered by burdensome bureaucracies, urban bias, and economic nationalism.[4] Although the advanced economies can indeed hinder the progress of the less developed economies by such restrictive practices as protectionist policies against Third World exports and could accelerate their development through foreign aid, liberals believe that each country bears its own responsibility for achieving meaningful change.

Accelerated capital accumulation is one vital foundation for development; this requires an increase in the domestic rate of saving. Although the advanced economies can and perhaps should assist in the process of capital formation through loans, foreign investment, and international assistance, the task rests with the less developed nations themselves. An unwillingness to suppress domestic consumption and to save is frequently considered to be the most serious retardant of economic growth. As Lewis, a sympathetic student of the LDC problems, has argued, "no nation is so poor that it could not save 12 percent of its national income if it wanted to" (Lewis, 1970, p. 236), and this amount is sufficient to put it firmly on the path of economic development.

Defending this position, proponents point out that the most successful economies among the less developed countries are precisely those that have put their own houses in order and that participate most aggressively in the world economy. They are the so-called Gang of Four: Hong Kong, Singapore, South Korea, and Taiwan. Although these newly industrializing countries have received great infusions of capital and technology from the advanced countries, they have mainly helped themselves and have established flourishing export markets. The least integrated economies, such as Albania and Burma, are among the most backward. Meanwhile, in the 1980s, even Communist China has realized its need for Western assistance, and Eastern Europe, along with the Soviet Union itself, seeks Western capital and advanced technology.

Beyond the general agreement on the primacy of internal factors, liberal development theories differ profoundly among themselves on the appropriate strategy for a less developed economy. In the first place, they disagree on the role of and the extent to which the advanced countries can or should assist the less developed ones; some advocate massive assistance programs in order to break what is called "the vicious cycle of LDC poverty"; other more conservative economists regard

---

[4] Lipton (1977) discusses the problem of urban bias as an impediment to economic development.

such outside efforts as wasteful or counterproductive. They also differ among themselves about whether a series of rather definable stages exists through which a developing economy must progress, or whether there are as many routes to development as national experiences. Some may stress balanced growth as the proper means for breaking out of historic poverty; others stress unbalanced growth. They vary regarding the emphasis given to agriculture or to industrial development. They also take different positions on the issue of efficiency versus equity in the process of economic development and on the role of the state in achieving one or the other. These and similar issues that lie outside the scope of this book constitute the subject of economic development as treated by liberal economists.

In summary, in the absence of a commonly accepted body of theoretical ideas, the debate among liberal economists over economic development is focused on strategic choices and alternative routes to economic development, that is, the determination of economic policies to achieve an efficient market economy. They share the conviction that the two foremost causes of international poverty are inadequate integration of the less developed countries into the world economy and irrational state policies that impede the development of a well-functioning market. For most liberal economists, then, the poor are poor because they are inefficient.

Liberal theory, however, tends to neglect the political framework within which economic development takes place, yet the process of economic development cannot be divorced from political factors. The domestic and international configurations of power and the interests of powerful groups and states are important determinants of economic development. The liberal theory is not necessarily wrong in neglecting these elements and focusing exclusively on the market; rather this theory is incomplete. For example, economic flexibility and the capacity of the economy to respond to changing economic opportunities are highly dependent upon the social and political aspects of a society. How else can one explain the remarkable economic achievements of resource-poor Japan and the troubles of resource-rich Argentina? Or, to take another issue, it is certainly correct to focus attention upon the crucial role of increased agricultural productivity in the economic development of Western Europe and the "lands of recent settlement" such as North America, Argentina, and South Africa. However, the fact that these fertile temperate lands were acquired by Europeans through the use of military force is also important to understanding the racial dimensions of the North-South division. In short, economic factors alone will not explain success or failure in economic development.

269

As this book emphasizes, economic forces operate within a larger political context.

THE CLASSICAL MARXIST PERSPECTIVE ON ECONOMIC DEVELOPMENT

Marx and Engels were first and foremost theorists of Western economic development; the bulk of their work was devoted to the transition of European society from feudalism to capitalism to socialism and to the elaboration of the inherent laws of capitalist development. They also formulated what can be considered a theory of economic development applicable to the less developed economies. Lenin and later nineteenth-century Marxists subsequently extended these ideas when they formulated the Marxist theory of capitalist imperialism.

Marx viewed capitalism as a world-wide dynamic and expansive economic process; by the middle of the nineteenth century it had spread from its origins in Great Britain to include Western Europe. He believed that it would eventually incorporate the entire world through imperialist expansion and would bring all societies under its mode of commodity production. Indeed, Marx asserted that the historical mission of capitalism was to develop the forces of production throughout the world. When this task of transformation and capitalist accumulation was completed, capitalism would have fulfilled its assigned role in history and would give way to its successors, the socialist and communist systems.

Marx's views on the revolutionary role of capitalist or bourgeois imperialism in transforming traditional societies and integrating the whole globe into an interdependent world economy are worth quoting:

The bourgeoisie, by the rapid improvement of all instruments of production, by the immensely facilitated means of communication, draws all, even the most barbarian, nations into civilisation. The cheap prices of its commodities are the heavy artillery with which it batters down all Chinese walls, with which it forces the barbarians' intensely obstinate hatred of foreigners to capitulate. It compels all nations, on pain of extinction, to adopt the bourgeois mode of production; it compels them to introduce what it calls civilisation into their midst, i.e., to become bourgeois themselves. In one word, it creates a world after its own image (Marx and Engels, 1972 [1848], p. 339).

The evolution of Western civilization, according to Marx, passed through relatively well defined stages. The ancient economies of primitive commodity production, like that of ancient Greece, were followed by the feudalism of the Middle Ages; next came the capitalist mode of economic production, which would then be followed by socialism and communism. Class conflict between the owners of the means of production and the dispossessed provided the driving force at each stage, and the dialectics of this class conflict moved history from one stage to the next.

When Marx turned his attention outside the European continent to Asia, the Middle East, and elsewhere—as he was forced to do in response to increasing colonial clashes and political upheavals—he discovered that his theory of European development did not apply. In these immense agglomerations of humanity the precapitalist stages did not exist; there appeared to be no stages identifiable with the ancient and feudal modes of production. These civilizations, moreover, seemed to be devoid of any internal mechanism of social change. There was no class conflict that would drive them from one stage of social development to the next. They were, Marx believed, stuck historically and unable to move ahead.[5]

To account for this anomaly, Marx introduced the concept of the "Asiatic mode of production." He argued that this was characterized by (1) the unity and relative autarky of agricultural and manufacturing production at the village level and (2) the existence at the top of society of an autonomous and parasitic state separated from the rest of society (Avineri, 1969, pp. 6-13). He believed that this conservative social structure was responsible for the millennia of social and economic stagnation suffered by these non-Western societies. Finding no internal forces to move these societies forward historically, Marx believed the external force of Western imperialism was required.

Marx's complex view of imperialism as historically progressive is well expressed in the following passage: "England has to fufill a double mission in India: one destructive, the other regenerating—the annihilation of old Asiatic society, and the laying of the material foundations of Western society in Asia" (quoted in Avineri, 1969, pp. 132-33). Thus, unlike the neo-Marxist and dependency theorists of the 1970s and 1980s and their denunciations of capitalistic imperialism, Marx and Engels regarded the global extension of the market system, even through violent means, to be a step forward for humanity. Believing that the historic mission of the bourgeoisie and of imperialism was to smash the feudalistic and Asiatic mode of production that held back the modernization of what we would today call the Third World, Marx argued in "The Future Results of British Rule in India" (1853) that British imperialism was necessary for the modernization of India and that

[5] Avineri (1969) is an excellent collection of Marx's writings on this subject.

the establishment of a railroad system by the British was "the forerunner of modern industry" (quoted in ibid., p. 136).

Imperialism destabilizes the status quo through the introduction of modern technology and creates a set of opposed classes in the colonized areas, thereby implanting the mechanism that will move the society toward economic development. Once the Asiatic mode of production has been eliminated, the forces of capitalist accumulation and industrialization will be released to do their work in transforming the society and placing it on the track of historical evolution. Although imperialism was immoral, Marx believed it was also a progressive force, since without it the less developed economies of Asia and Africa would remain in their state of torpor forever.

In his attack on the evils of capitalist imperialism, Lenin carried this classical Marxist view further. He too regarded colonialism and neo-colonialism as progressive and necessary for the eventual modernization of less developed countries. Exporting capital, technology, and expertise to colonies and dependencies, he argued, would develop the colonies at the same time that it would retard development in the advanced capitalist states (Lenin, 1939 [1917], p. 65). As the latter exported capital and technology to their colonies, their home economies would become rentier economies and their industrial and technological base would stagnate, giving the less developed countries the opportunity to overtake the advanced economies.

Lenin argued that the inherent contradiction of capitalism was that it develops rather than underdevelops the world. The dominant capitalist economy plants the seeds of its own destruction as it diffuses technology and industry, thereby undermining its own position. It promotes foreign competitors with lower wages that can then outcompete the more advanced capitalist economies in world markets. Intensification of economic competition between the declining and rising capitalist powers leads to economic conflicts and imperial rivalries. He believed this to be the fate of the British-centered liberal world economy of the nineteenth century. Marxists in the late twentieth century argue that as the American economy becomes increasingly pressed by rising foreign competitors, a similar fate awaits the United States–centered liberal world economy.

In summary, orthodox Marxism from Marx to Lenin believed that capitalism develops the world but does not do so evenly, continuously, or without limit. Traditional Marxists, however, differ from liberals on the relative importance of economic and/or political factors in the evolution of the international economy. For liberals, the incorporation of periphery economies into the world economy and their subsequent modernization is a relatively frictionless economic process. For Marxists, on the other hand, this process is laden with political conflict as nations dispute their positions in the international division of labor. Indeed, Marxists believe this process will eventually reach its limit, necessitating a transition to socialism and communism. Lenin firmly believed that capitalist imperialism would give the "colored races" of the world the tools for their emancipation and that the incorporation of non-Western societies into the world economy through trade and investment would lead to their development.

THE UNDERDEVELOPMENT POSITION

Underdevelopment theories have proliferated in response to the fact that, even though the former European colonies have achieved political independence, they either have not developed or have at least remained economically subordinate to the more advanced capitalist economies.[6] Most countries in black Africa, Asia, the Middle East, and Latin America continue to be economically and technologically dependent; they continue to export commodities and raw materials in exchange for manufactured goods, and many have been penetrated by the multinational corporations of the advanced countries. Rather than progressing into higher stages of economic development, some of these countries have in fact actually increased their reliance on advanced economies for food, capital, and modern technology. Underdevelopment theory places the responsibility for this situation on the external world economy and not on the less developed countries themselves.

The essence of all underdevelopment theories is that the international capitalist economy operates *systematically* to underdevelop and distort the economies of the less developed economies. They maintain that this is an inherent feature of the normal operations of the world market economy, and that the nature of the system is detrimental to the interests of the poorer countries. The rich who control the world economy are responsible for the poverty of the Third World due to what Arghiri Emmanuel (1972) has called *unequal exchange*. For a variety of reasons the terms of trade between advanced and less developed countries are said to be biased against the latter.[7]

The initial efforts to account for the seeming lack of Third World progress were associated with the research of scholars such as Ragnar Nurkse, Gunnar Myrdal, and Hans Singer; their position became

[6] As Kuznets (1968, p. 2, note 2) points out, the concept of underdevelopment is a highly ambiguous one and has several quite distinct meanings.

[7] A strong criticism of this argument is Samuelson (1976, pp. 96-107).

273

closely identified with the work of the United Nations Economic Commission for Latin America (ECLA) under the leadership of Raúl Prebisch. Their structuralist theory of underdevelopment focused on those features of the world economy that they alleged restricted the development prospects of less developed economies and particularly on the deteriorating terms of trade for LDC commodity exports. They believed that reform of the international economy and a development strategy based on import substitution would be a solution to these problems. Therefore, the less developed economies should industrialize rapidly and produce for themselves products formerly imported from the more advanced economies.

Subsequently, in the late 1960s and 1970s, dependency theory displaced structuralism as the foremost interpretation of Third World underdevelopment. This far more radical analysis of and solution to the problems of the less developed countries was largely a response to the apparent failure of the structuralists' import-substitution strategy, the deepening economic problems of the LDCs, and the intellectual ferment caused by the Vietnam War. According to this position, the solution to the problem of economic underdevelopment could be found in socialist revolution and autonomous development rather then reform of the world market economy.

Structuralism

Structuralism argues that a liberal capitalist world economy tends to preserve or actually increase inequalities between developed and less developed economies.[8] Whereas trade was indeed an engine of growth in the nineteenth century, structuralists argue that it cannot continue to perform this role because of the combined effects of free trade and the economic, sociological, and demographic conditions (structures) prevalent among less developed economies in the twentieth century (Nurkse, 1953). These conditions include the combination of overpopulation and subsistence agriculture, rising expectations causing a low propensity to save, excessive dependence on unstable commodity exports, and political domination by feudal elites. These structures trap less developed countries in a self-perpetuating state of underdevelopment equilibrium from which they cannot escape without outside assistance (Myrdal, 1971).

Although liberal economists believe that flows of trade, investment, and technology diffuse economic development and reduce international inequalities, structuralists argue that the opposite is happening.

---

[8] A good summary of the structuralist or Prebisch thesis is Roxborough (1979, ch. 3).

International market imperfections increase inequalities among the developed and less developed countries as the developed countries tend to benefit disproportionately from international trade. Although the "late developing" countries of the nineteenth century did enjoy the so-called advantages of backwardness that enabled them to learn from the experiences of the more advanced economies, twentieth-century "late late developing" countries are said to face almost insurmountable obstacles: the widening technological gap, their long experience of marginalization, the lack of social discipline, conservative social structures, inherited population problems, and harsh climatic and geographic conditions. These economies are thus caught in a vicious cycle of poverty from which escape is nearly impossible, and free trade only makes their situation worse. As Nurkse put it, "a country is poor because it is poor" whereas "growth breeds growth" (Nurkse, 1953, p. 4).

Although the basic ideas of the structuralist position were developed simultaneously in the 1950s by several economists and by the ECLA, they did not gain international prominence until the 1964 publication of the report "Towards a New Trade Policy for Development." This report, written by Prebisch, then the newly appointed Secretary-General of the United Nations Conference on Trade and Development (UNCTAD), set forth the structuralist argument that the world economy was biased against the development efforts of the less developed countries. The report became the focal point of the 1964 UNCTAD session and, with the more radical critique based on dependency theory, laid the foundations for what in the 1970s would become the demands of the less developed countries for a New International Economic Order (NIEO).

The structuralist argument (or what became known as the Singer-Prebisch theory) is that the world economy is composed of a core or center of highly industrialized countries and a large underdeveloped periphery (Prebisch, 1959). Technical progress that leads to increasing productivity and economic development is the driving force in this system, but technical advance has different consequences for the industrialized center and the nonindustrialized periphery due to structural features of the less developed economies and to the international division of labor inherited from the past.

The heart of the argument is that the nature of technical advance, cyclical price movements, and differences in demand for industrial goods and primary products cause a secular deterioration in the terms of trade for commodity exporters, that is, deterioration of the prices the LDCs receive for their commodity exports relative to the prices of the manufactured goods they import from developed countries. In the industrial

core, technical progress is said to arise from the spontaneous operations of the economy and to diffuse throughout the whole economy so
that employment displaced by increasing efficiency can be absorbed by
investment in other expanding industrial sectors. Without large-scale
unemployment and with the pressures of powerful labor unions, there
is an increase in real wages. Further, monopolistic corporations can
maintain the price level despite productivity increases and the decreasing cost of production. The fruits of technical progress and increased
production are thus retained in the core economy and are absorbed by
a sizable fraction of the society.

In the nonindustrial periphery, however, technical progress is introduced from the outside and is restricted primarily to the production of
commodities and raw materials that are exported to the core. Inflexible
structures and immobile factors of production make adaptation to
price changes impossible. Increased productivity in the primary sector,
a shortage of capital due to a low rate of savings, and an elite consumption pattern imitative of advanced countries all combine to increase the
level of national unemployment. With surplus labor in primary occu-
pations and the absence of strong trade unions, the real wage in the periphery economy then declines, transferring the fruits of technical advance in the periphery economy to the core economies via depressed
prices for commodity exports.

Structuralists conclude from this analysis that the terms of trade between the industrial countries and the peripheral countries tend to deteriorate constantly to the advantage of the former and the disadvantage of the latter. As a consequence of this secular decline, the
peripheral economies are forced to export ever-larger quantities of
food and commodities to finance the import of manufactured goods
from the industrial countries. Structuralists have therefore been very
pessimistic that the less developed countries could reverse their situation through the expansion of their exports; they believe that even
though those nations might gain absolutely from international trade,
they would lose in relative terms.

Structuralists have advocated several policies to deal with these
problems. One policy is the creation of international organizations like
UNCTAD to promote the interests of the less developed countries, especially the exporting of manufactured goods to the developed countries, and thus to break the cycle of circular causation. Another is the
enactment of international policies and regulations, such as a commodity stabilization program that would protect the export earnings of less
developed countries. The most important course of action advocated is
rapid industrialization to overcome the periphery's declining terms of

trade and to absorb its labor surplus. The peripheral economies should pursue an "import-substitution strategy" through policies of economic protectionism, encouragement of foreign investment in manufacturing, and creation of common markets among the less developed economies themselves.

Defending these solutions to underdevelopment and their "trade pessimism," structuralists point out that during those periods when Latin America was cut off from the manufactured goods of the Northern industrial countries (as in the Great Depression and the Second World War), spurts of rapid industrialization took place. When the ties were resumed, industrialization was set back. National planning and industrialization policies, therefore, should decrease the dependence of the less developed countries on the world market and weaken the power of those conservative elites in the commodity and export sectors that have opposed the expansion of industry. As industrial economies, the LDCs would have improved terms of trade and would be on the road to economic development.

The structuralist position that the terms of trade are biased against the less developed countries is difficult to evaluate.[9] Several different conceptions or definitions of the terms of trade are employed. Using one structuralist definition or measurement rather than another can lead to diametrically opposed conclusions on the changes in the terms of trade. Regardless of the definition employed, however, the measurement of such changes over time is unreliable at best, since not only prices but also the composition of trade changes, and factors such as the rapidly declining cost of transportation must also be taken into account. Furthermore, the concept of the terms of trade and the prices by which they are measured cannot easily incorporate qualitative improvements in manufactured exports to the LDCs. Nonetheless, several general remarks concerning their terms of trade are warranted.

The most notable feature of the terms of trade among countries is that they fluctuate over both short and long periods. There is no secular trend over the long term, but rather cyclical fluctuations. For example, the terms of trade for primary products decreased in the two decades prior to 1900 and subsequently improved from 1900 to 1913 (Meier and Baldwin, 1957, p. 265). Over shorter periods, they may vary due to changes in commercial policy, exchange-rate variations and cyclical phenomena. For example, during the period 1967-1984, the terms of trade of non-oil-developing countries have fluctuated considerably. In the early 1960s the advanced countries had favorable terms of trade;

[9] Findlay (1981) is an excellent discussion of the issue.

these were dramatically reversed in the late 1960s and early 1970s, especially after the OPEC revolution. The terms of trade were excellent for commodity producers in the late 1960s and gave rise to the Club of Rome prediction that growth would stop because the world was running out of resources.[10] This extraordinary situation then dramatically reversed itself in the mid-1970s due to the global decline in growth rates, and commodity prices fell to perhaps their lowest point ever in the 1980s.

The LDCs' concern that they and their commodity exports are more at the mercy of the vicissitudes of the international business cycle than are the developed economies and their manufactured exports is certainly well founded. This situation is partially due to the failure of many less developed countries to transform their economies and shift the composition of their exports; the argument that a *systemic* bias against them exists, however, is unsubstantiated. Ironically, as will be noted below, the United States has been one of the more serious victims of the decline of commodity prices in the 1980s.

Economists have of course long recognized that a country, especially a large one, could improve its terms of trade and national welfare through the imposition of a so-called effective tariff or an optimum tariff. The manipulation of tariff schedules on different types of products (commodities, semiprocessed, and finished goods) or the exploitation of a monopoly position with respect to a particular good or market can enable an economy to improve its terms of trade, as OPEC proved in the 1970s. Large economies can manipulate their commercial and other policies in order to improve their terms of trade (Hirschman, 1945, pp. 10-11), and the less developed countries undoubtedly have suffered from tariffs that discriminate against their exports of semiprocessed products (Scammell, 1983, pp. 166-67). Nevertheless, the costs of resulting constrictions on total trade and of foreign retaliation are sufficient to make their overall effects minimal and temporary (Dixit, 1983, pp. 17, 62). An optimum tariff may or may not lead to unilateral benefits depending on the circumstances (H. Johnson, 1953-54).

To the extent that the less developed economies do suffer from unfavorable terms of trade, the most important causes are internal to their own economies rather than in the structure of the world economy. Certainly the terms of trade for any economy will decline if it fails to adjust

[10] The "limits to growth" argument was actually a revival of the classical economists' position that over the long run the terms of trade favor commodity exporters (Findlay, 1981, p. 428).

and transform its economy by shifting out of surplus products into new exports. Contrast, for example, the cases of India and Peru; the former has successfully transformed large sectors of its economy, the latter has made little effort to do so. Indeed, the success of the Asian NICs in contrast to other LDCs is due primarily to their greater flexibility. The African countries, on the other hand, have been harmed primarily because of their failure to move away from commodity exports.

As Arthur Lewis has cogently argued, the terms of trade of many LDCs are unfavorable because of their failure to develop their agriculture. The combination of rapid population growth (which creates an unlimited supply of labor) and low productivity in food grains causes export prices and real wages in the less developed countries to lag behind those of the developed economies (Lewis, 1978a). In such circumstances, even the shift from commodity to industrial exports demanded by the proponents of the New International Economic Order would do little to improve the terms of trade and to hasten overall economic development. Whatever other benefits might be produced by such a change in export strategy (such as increased urban employment or technical spinoffs), these countries would still be inefficient producers; until their basic internal problems are solved, they will continue to exchange "cheap" manufactured exports for more expensive imports from developed countries.

A solution to the problems of the LDCs, therefore, must be found primarily in domestic reforms and not through changes in the structure of the world economy. Although the developed countries can and should assist the less developed, the key to economic and industrial progress is a prior agricultural revolution, as happened in the West, in Japan, and within the Asian NICs, especially in Taiwan and South Korea. In Lewis's words, "the most important item on the agenda of development is to transform the food sector, create agricultural surpluses to feed the urban population, and thereby create the domestic basis for industry and modern services. If we can make this domestic change, we shall automatically have a new international economic order" (Lewis, 1978a, p. 75).

In the opinion of at least one authority, economists will never agree on the terms of trade issue (Condliffe, 1950, p. 201). This is partially because the terms of trade depend upon a large number of both economic and noneconomic factors, including the relative rates of economic growth of developing and developed economies, changes in supply and demand, and the bargaining power and skills of buyers and sellers. In addition, an appraisal of the issue must take still other factors into consideration. One is that, as liberals stress, the total volume of trade can be more important for the welfare and development of an economy than the terms of trade. A greater volume of exports increases foreign exchange, expands the modern sector, transfers advanced technology, increases product variety in an economy, improves domestic efficiency, and absorbs the surplus supply of labor that is largely responsible for the low real wage in almost every less developed economy. From this perspective, the major problem has been the high barriers erected by the advanced countries against the food and commodity exports of the LDCs.

Furthermore, measurement of the terms of trade cannot take into account qualitative improvements in manufactured exports, at least those improvements not registered in the prices that provide the basis for calculation of the terms of trade. For example, the prices of computers have dropped dramatically at the same time that their quality has greatly improved. Another fact that must be recognized is that several of the most prosperous countries in the world are agricultural exporters (such as Denmark, New Zealand, and Australia). The industrialization of Japan was financed by the export of silk, and even the United States is a major food exporter. The structuralist idea that the terms of trade for commodity exporters have deteriorated over the long term and that this is the reason for their economic plight is not supported by the evidence. To the contrary, most less developed countries have probably benefited disproportionately through a quantitative and qualitative improvement in their imports from developed economies (Viner, 1952).

One variation of the structuralist argument has gained some support as trade theorists have become more interested in imperfect competition based on economies of scale and on barriers to entry into the industrial sector. This position argues that "an initial discrepancy in capital-labor ratios between [North and South] . . . will cumulate over time, leading to the division of the world into a capital-rich, industrial region and capital-poor, agricultural region" (Krugman, 1981b, p. 149). The fortuitous head start of the industrialized countries in amassing capital (or "primitive accumulation") and their relatively favorable capital-labor ratio have enabled them at times to reap excessive profits or technological rents from less developed economies (Krugman, 1979).

This formulation of the thesis, however, only begs the question. It does not account for the labor surplus of the South or the backwardness of its technology. Why did the North industrialize first? All the available evidence indicates that the industrial productivity of early modern Europe was based on prior rapid improvements in agriculture.

Yet Krugman's argument contains an ominous twist for the North. The North must continue to innovate not only to maintain its relative position but even to maintain its real income in absolute terms (Krugman, 1979). Thus, although in the short run the advanced countries may collect technological rents from the South, the long-term effect of this trading relationship, as Lenin and Hobson appreciated and as the late twentieth century has witnessed, is the transfer to the South and its newly industrializing countries of the industrial technology that has given the North its competitive advantage. As this occurs, the North, with its higher wage and cost structures, must innovate new technology at a faster rate than its older technology is diffusing to its rising competitors. In effect, the North must run faster and faster in order to maintain both its relative and absolute positions.

Some conclusions about the structuralist thesis and related arguments can be drawn. First, the concept of "the terms of trade" itself is confused, difficult to measure, and highly indeterminant over the long term. Second, the terms of trade between core and peripheral economies can be of less importance than other considerations such as the overall volume of trade and the benefits of trade in modernizing the peripheral economy. Third, even if one can establish that the terms of trade between core and peripheral countries are to the disadvantage of the latter, the causes of this situation are to be found primarily within the less developed economies themselves.

Whatever the intellectual merits of the structuralist arguments, their views and economic program had fallen into disrepute by the mid-1960s. The dependence of most of the less developed countries on commodity exports continued, the LDC need for manufactured imports increased and led to severe balance-of-payments problems, and the strategy of import substitution stimulated the manufacturing multinationals of the advanced countries to expand into LDC markets, raising fears of a new form of capitalist imperialism (Roxborough, 1979, pp. 33-35). In response to these developments, a more radical interpretation of the plight of the Third World and a related plan of action appeared.

The Dependency Position

Dependency literature[11] has become a growth industry, but the most concise and frequently quoted definition of dependence is that of the Brazilian scholar, Theotonio Dos Santos:

[11] An excellent summary of the literature on dependency theory is Palma (1978). A more critical appraisal is T. Smith (1981, pp. 68-84). Caporaso (1978) contains a range of differing views on the subject.

By dependence we mean a situation in which the economy of certain countries is conditioned by the development and expansion of another economy to which the former is subjected. The relation of interdependence between two or more economies, and between these and world trade, assumes the form of dependence when some countries (the dominant ones) can expand and can be self-sustaining, while other countries (the dependent ones) can do this only as a reflection of that expansion, which can have either a positive or a negative effect on their immediate development (Dos Santos, 1970, p. 231).

The many varieties of dependency theory combine elements of traditional Marxism with economic nationalism. Dependency theorists take their analysis of capitalism, particularly the Marxist theory of capitalist imperialism, and their concern with the domestic distribution of wealth from Marxism. From the theorists of economic nationalism they take their political program of state building and intense concern over the distribution of wealth among nations. Thus, in contrast to classical Marxism, one finds that little attention is given to the international proletariat; there are no calls for the workers of the world to unite and throw off their chains.

Although different dependency theorists lean in one direction or another—toward Marxism or nationalism—they all share several assumptions and explanations regarding the causes of and the solution to the problems of less developed countries. This position is captured by Andre Gunder Frank's statement "that it is capitalism, both world and national, which produced underdevelopment in the past and which still generates underdevelopment in the present" (quoted in Brewer, 1980, p. 158). As Thomas Weisskopf has said, "the most fundamental causal proposition [associated] with the dependency literature is that dependence causes underdevelopment" (Weisskopf, 1976, p. 3). Thus, dependency theory is closely related to the concept of the Modern World System (MWS) discussed in Chapter Three.

Liberals define underdevelopment as a *condition* in which most nations find themselves because they have not kept up with the front-runners; dependency theorists see it as a *process* in which the LDCs are caught because of the inherent relationship between developed and underdeveloped nations.[12] Development and underdevelopment constitute a system that generates economic wealth for the few and poverty for the many; Frank has called this "the development of underdevelopment" (Frank, 1969). Whereas liberals stress the dual but flexible nature of domestic and international economies, that is, the contrast

---

[12] D. Baldwin (1980) is an excellent analysis of the concept of dependence and its place in the literature of international relations.

between the modern sectors integrated into the national and international economies and the backward, isolated, and inefficient sectors, dependency theorists argue that there is only one functional integrated whole in which the underdeveloped periphery is necessarily backward and underdeveloped because the periphery is systematically exploited and prevented from developing by international capitalism and its reactionary domestic allies in the Third World economies themselves.

This functional or organic relationship between the developed and underdeveloped countries is said to have been first created by colonialism. Some allege that this relation remains even after the achievement of formal political freedom, due to the operation of economic and technological forces that concentrate wealth in the metropolitan countries rather than diffusing it to the less developed nations. Liberals assert that there is a time lag but that the gap between rich and poor will eventually disappear as Western economic methods and technology diffuse throughout the world; the dependency position is that underdevelopment is caused by the functioning of the world capitalist economy.

Dependency theory arose in the mid-1960s, partially as a response to the apparent failure of the structuralist analysis and prescriptions. Dependency theorists argue that the import-substitution industrialization strategy of the structuralists failed to produce sustained economic growth in the less developed countries because the traditional social and economic conditions of the LDCs remained intact; indeed the neo-colonialist alliance of indigenous feudal elites with international capitalism had even been reinforced by the import-substitution strategy. The result has been an increased maldistribution of income, domestic demand too weak to sustain continued industrialization, and ever-greater dependence on those multinational corporations of developed economies that took advantage of the import-substitution policies. Less developed countries have lost control over their domestic economies as a consequence and have become more and more dependent on international capitalism. Therefore, the solution must be a socialist and nationalist revolution that would promote an equitable society and autonomous nation.

The major components in dependency theory include analyses of (1) the nature and dynamics of the capitalist world system, (2) the relationship or linkage between the advanced capitalist countries and the less developed countries, and (3) the internal characteristics of the dependent countries themselves. Although the theorists differ on specific points, all dependency theorists hold that these components of the theory explain the underdevelopment of the LDCs and point the way to a solution. Each aspect will be discussed below.

One central ingredient in dependency theory is the Marxist critique of capitalism set forth by Lenin and others. This theory asserts that the laws of motion of capitalism and the contradictions existing in a capitalist economy force capitalism to expand into the less developed periphery of the world economy. Because of underconsumption and the falling rate of profit at home, the capital economies must dominate and exploit the less developed countries. This leads to a hierarchical structure of domination between the industrial core and the dependent periphery of the world capitalist economy.

Dependency theory, however, differs in several important respects from the traditional Marxist analysis of capitalist imperialism. It substitutes economic for political means of subordination; whereas Lenin believed that political control was the principal feature of capitalist imperialism, dependency theory replaces formal political colonialism with economic neocolonialism and informal control. Dependency theorists also reject the classical Marxist view that imperialism develops the "colonized" economy to the point at which it can cast off its bonds; they assert that even if development does take place, an economy cannot escape its shackles as long as it is dependent. Furthermore, they consider the multinational corporation, especially in manufacturing and services, to be the principal instrument of capitalist domination and exploitation in the late twentieth century. The great corporations are said to have replaced *haut finance* and the colonial governments that dominated the less developed countries in Lenin's analysis.[13]

Advocates of dependency theory differ in their definitions of the precise mechanism that has brought about underdevelopment. The general positions regarding the relationship of the advanced capitalist to less developed economies can be placed into three categories: the exploitation theory, the doctrine of "imperial neglect," and the concept of dependent development. Although they each work quite differently, all are alleged to have a detrimental effect on the less developed countries.

The "exploitation" theory maintains that the Third World is poor because it has been systematically exploited (Amin, 1976). The underdevelopment of the Third World is functionally related to the development of the core, and the modern world system has permitted the ad-

[13] Lenin was aware of what neo-Marxists today call "dependency" relations and noted in *Imperialism* (1939 [1917], p. 85) the dependence of Argentina on Great Britain. He apparently did not believe, however, that this type of economic relationship was very important in contrast to formal political annexation. In addition, Lenin's classically Marxist view that capitalist imperialism develops the colony was amended in 1928 at the Sixth Congress of the Communist International in favor of the contemporary dependence theory formulation (Mandle, 1980, p. 736).

vanced core to drain the periphery of its economic surplus, transferring wealth from the less developed to the developed capitalist economy through the mechanisms of trade and investment. Consequently, dependence does not merely hold back the full development of the Third World; dependency actually immiserizes the less developed economies and makes them even less successful than they would have been if they had been allowed to develop independently.

The "imperial neglect" position takes a decidedly different view regarding the effect of the world economy on the less developed economies (Brown, 1970). It argues that the problem of the less developed economies and most certainly of the least developed ones is that the forces of capitalist imperialsm have deliberately bypassed them. The expansion of world capitalism through trade, investment, and European migration has created an international division of labor that favored some lands and neglected others to their detriment. Capitalist imperialism laid the foundations for industrial development through the stimulus of international trade and infrastructure investments (port facilities, railroads, and urban centers) in a privileged set of less developed countries, most notably the "lands of recent settlement." Elsewhere capitalism's penetration and impact were insufficient to destroy archaic modes of production and thereby open the way to economic progress. The lament of those bypassed is "why didn't they colonize us?" Even in the mid-1980s, the investments of multinational corporations bring industry to some countries while completely neglecting the great majority. Thus, the world capitalist economy is ultimately responsible for underdevelopment because the patterns of trade and investment it fosters have had a differential impact on the periphery.

The "dependent or associated development" school is the most recent interpretation of dependency theory (Evans, 1979). Acknowledging the rather spectacular economic success of several less developed economies such as Brazil, South Korea, and Taiwan, this position holds that dependency relations under certain conditions can lead to rapid economic growth. It argues, however, that this type of growth is not true development because it does not lead to national independence. Proponents of this view believe such growth actually has very detrimental effects on the economy of the less developed country.

Continued economic dependency is a limiting condition on economic development and is alleged to have the following evil consequences:

(1) Overdependence upon raw materials exports with fluctuating prices, which causes domestic economic instability;

285

(2) A maldistribution of national income, which creates in the elite in-appropriate tastes for foreign luxury goods and neglects the true needs of the masses, thus continuing social inequalities and rein-forcing domination by external capitalism;

(3) Manufacturing investments by MNCs and dependent industriali-zation, which have the effect of creating a branch-plant economy with high production costs, destroying local entrepreneurship and technological innovation, and bleeding the country as profits are re-patriated;

(4) Foreign firms that gain control of key industrial sectors and crowd out local firms in capital markets;

(5) Introduction of inappropriate technology, i.e., capital-intensive rather than labor-intensive;

(6) An international division of labor created between the high tech-nology of the core and the low technology of the periphery/

(7) Prevention of autonomous or self-sustaining development based on domestic technology and indigenous entrepreneurship;

(8) Distortion of the local labor market because the MNCs pay higher wages than domestic employers and therefore cause waste and in-creased unemployment;

(9) Finally, reliance on foreign capital, which generally encourages au-thoritarian-type governments that cooperate with and give foreign corporations the political stability they demand.

Dependency theorists argue that for all these reasons dependent or as-sociated development cannot lead to true development.

All dependency theorists maintain that underdevelopment is due pri-marily to external forces of the world capitalist system and is not due to the policies of the LDCs themselves. Both LDC underdevelopment and capitalist development are the product of the expansion of inter-national capitalism. This historical situation has not fundamentally changed; the international balance of economic and political power continues to be distorted in favor of the developed capitalist econo-mies. Although the dependent less developed economy may advance in absolute terms, it will always be backward in relative terms.

The third major component of dependency theory is a quasi-Marxist analysis of the dependent economy; it is this aspect of dependency the-ory that best distinguishes it from what its adherents regard as the re-formist, bourgeois position of the structuralists. Specifically, depend-ency theory asserts that the dependent country is fastened to the world economy by a transnational class linkage. An alliance of convenience and common interest exists between the centers of international capitalism and the clientele class that wields power in the dependent economy. This parasitic or feudal-capitalist alliance is composed of agrarian interests, the military, and the indigenous managers of the multinational corporations, who have a vested interest in maintaining the linkage with international capitalism and in preventing the development of an independent and powerful industrial economy through social and political reforms. Dependency theorists argue that this coopted elite resists the loss of its privileges and is kept in power by the forces of world capitalism and also that the strategy of import substitution supported by the structuralists merely increases the foreign hold over the economy.

The crux of the attack by dependency writers on established bourgeois elites in the Third World is their assertion that the cooperation of these elites with international capitalism and the integration of the society into the world economy thwarts the economic development, social welfare, and political independence of the society. These national bourgeois elites are accused of pursuing the interests of their own class rather than being *true* nationalists and defenders of the society against international capitalism.

The solution to underdevelopment advocated by dependency theorists is destruction of the linkage between international capitalism and the domestic economy through the political triumph of a revolutionary national leadership that will overthrow the clientele elite and replace it with one dedicated to autonomous development. This new elite would dedicate itself to the industrialization of the economy, the prompt eradication of feudal privileges, and the achievement of social and economic equity. Through the replacement of capitalism by socialism and the course of self-reliant development, the new elite would create a just and strong state.

The conceptions of development and underdevelopment held by dependency theorists are as much political and social concepts as they are economic; these theorists desire not merely the economic growth of the economy, but also the transformation and development of the society in a particular social and political direction. Their objective is to create an independent, equitable, and industrialized nation-state. This goal, they believe, requires a transformation of the social and political system.

Although the major themes of dependency theory have remained unchanged, some writers have introduced subtle but important modifications. Acknowledging the obvious development of a number of NICs, they have changed the emphasis of the theory from an explanation of "underdevelopment" to an explanation of "dependent development." With the obvious success of the NICs and their strategy of export-led growth, a perceptible movement can be observed back toward the original Marxist notion that integration in the world capitalist economy, despite its attendant evils, is a force *for* economic development.

Despite these changes in emphasis, dependency theory remains an ideology of state building in a highly interdependent world economy. Although it adopts a Marxist mode of analysis and socialist ideals, dependency theory has absorbed powerful elements of the statist traditions of eighteenth-century mercantilism and nineteenth-century economic nationalism. The theory maintains that an LDC, through a strategy of autonomous or self-reliant development, can become an independent nation-state.

A Critique of Dependency Theory

The crux of the dependency argument is that the world market or capitalist international economy operates systematically to thwart the development of the Third World. Therefore, evidence that individual countries have been exploited is not sufficient to support the theory. Although it is undeniable that, in particular cases, an alliance of foreign capitalists and domestic elites has contributed to an economy's underdevelopment, for example, the Philippines of Ferdinand Marcos, the charge of a systematic and functional relationship between capitalism and underdevelopment cannot be supported.

It should be noted that a single independent variable—the functioning of the international economy—is being used to explain three quite distinct types of phenomena found in the Third World: underdevelopment, marginalization, and dependent development (Russett, 1983). From a simple methodological point of view, something is wrong with any theory in which a single independent variable is used to explain three mutually exclusive outcomes. Dependency theory is replete with ad hoc hypotheses and tautological arguments intended to account for these very different phenomena.

The general argument that the LDCs as a group have remained commodity exporters, have been exploited, and have been kept undeveloped is simply not true. Although many examples of this type of dependency relationship continue to exist in the late twentieth century, the overall argument cannot be sustained. By the late 1980s, only the countries of south Saharan Africa and a few others remained impoverished commodity exporters. Although the terms of trade for commodities have shown no secular tendency to decline, the business cycle is very damaging to those less developed countries that have failed to transform their economies. On the other hand, with the important exception of Japan, the LDCs as a group have grown faster in recent years than the advanced countries (Krasner, 1985, pp. 97, 101). In brief, little evidence supports the charge that the international economy operates systematically to the disadvantage of the LDCs.

The charge of underdevelopment and dependency theorists that the world market economy has neglected and bypassed many countries in the Third World is correct. The process of global economic integration that began in the latter part of the nineteenth century and has expanded trade and investment among developed and less developed countries has been a highly uneven one. The simple fact is that both nineteenth-century imperialism and the operations of twentieth-century multinational corporations have left many of the world's traditional economies untouched because they found too little there to be "exploited." This marginalization of destitute areas (the Fourth and Fifth Worlds) such as the Sahel and other parts of Africa, however, constitutes a sin of omission rather than one of commission. The most serious threat faced by much of the Third World, in fact, is not dependence but the likelihood of continued neglect and further marginalization. What has been lacking in the postwar world, as John Ruggie (1983b) has noted, is an adequate international regime whose purpose is global economic development. But this failing is not just that of the capitalist world; it is also a failing of the socialist bloc and the wealthy oil producers. It should be noted that the West has been far more generous than the socialist bloc or OPEC producers.

The claim that the dependent or associated development exemplified by the newly industrializing countries of Brazil, South Korea, and other countries is not "true" development is, of course, largely normative (Brewer, 1980, p. 291). However, even if one accepts the position that the objective of development ought to be national independence, social welfare, and autonomous industrialization, the evidence in support of the above contention is mixed. Many present-day developed and independent countries previously followed the road of dependent development. As those Marxist writers who incorporate Marx's own views on the subject appreciate, dependent development in a growing number of less developed countries has begun a process of sustained industrialization and economic growth (Brewer, 1980, pp. 286-94). In fact, the success of the NICs may be partially attributable to the legacy of Japanese imperialism (Cumings, 1984, p. 8).

Bill Warren, writing in the tradition of Marx, Lenin, and other classical Marxists, has provided a clear assessment of what is taking place among the less developed countries: "If the extension of capitalism into

non-capitalist areas of the world created an international system of inequality and exploitation called imperialism, it simultaneously created
the conditions for the destruction of this system by the spread of capitalist social relations and productive forces throughout the non-capitalist world. Such has been our thesis, as it was the thesis of Marx,
Lenin, Luxemburg and Bukharin" (Warren, 1973, p. 41). However, it
must be added that economic development will not occur unless the society has put its own house in proper order. As liberals stress, economic
development will not take place unless the society has created efficient
economic institutions.

The available evidence suggests that neither integration into the
world economy nor economic isolation can guarantee economic development. The former can lock a country into an export specialization
that harms the overall development of its economy. High export earnings from a particular commodity and powerful export interests can
hinder diversification; export overdependence and fluctuating prices
create vulnerabilities that can damage an economy. On the other hand,
economic isolation can cause massive misallocations of resources and
inefficiencies that thwart the long-term growth of an economy. What is
important for economic development and escape from dependence is
the capacity of the economy to transform itself. This task is ultimately
the responsibility of its own economic and political leadership. As Norman Gall (1986) has cogently shown, too many of the less developed
countries have suffered the consequences of poor leadership.

An Evaluation of LDC Strategies

However elaborate and sophisticated it might appear, every theory of
poverty and of escape from it can be reduced to one or a combination
of the following formulations: (1) that the poor are poor because they
are inefficient (essentially the position of economic liberalism) and
therefore must create an efficient economy; (2) that the poor are poor
because they are powerless or exploited (the argument of most contemporary Marxists and dependency theorists) and therefore must acquire
national power; or (3) that the poor are poor because they are poor,
that is, they are caught in a vicious cycle of poverty from which they
cannot escape (the view of traditional Marxists and present-day structuralists) and therefore somehow this cycle must be broken.[14] The development strategy advocated for the less developed countries is largely
dependent on which interpretation one believes to be correct.

[14] Nurkse (1953) appears to be the first to set forth this formulation.

Evaluation of these positions is extremely difficult because the theories underlying them are imprecise and more in the nature of prescriptive than scientific statements, because the time span is insufficient to support judgment of either the success or failure of various strategies, and because these strategies have very different objectives and definitions of economic development. If taken on its own terms, each theory and strategy must be judged by a unique set of criteria. For example, although liberals have a concern with quality of life and domestic welfare, they define economic development primarily as an increase in wealth per capita regardless of how that wealth is generated or what its implications are for national autonomy; dependency theorists and structuralists, on the other hand, define economic development in terms of socialist ideals, self-sustaining industrialization, and increased power for the nation.

Since this book focuses on the international system, it is fundamentally concerned with the relevance of each theory and its strategy for the power and independence of the newly emerging nation-states. I generally accept the dependency and structuralist position that the "name of the game" is state building, as it was for Hamilton, List, and other economic nationalists. Thus it is appropriate to ask what, on the basis of the limited available evidence in the late twentieth century, has been the best strategy for a less developed economy to pursue, either singularly or in alliance with other countries, in order to become a unified and powerful nation?

The following discussion will analyze and evaluate the economic and political strategies that less developed economies have in fact pursued over the past several decades. Excluding those few countries such as Burma or Liberia that appear to have opted out of the game of national development altogether, these strategies range from the autonomous or self-reliant development advocated by dependency theorists to aggressive participation in the world economy chosen by the NICs. The following discussion of each strategy will be brief, incomplete, and tentative in the judgments rendered. After all, the historical drama of state-creation among the less developed countries is just beginning.

Autonomous or Self-Reliant Development

Both structuralists and dependency theorists have advocated a development strategy based on national self-reliance. For structuralists, this has meant an emphasis on an import-substitution strategy, rapid industrialization behind high tariff walls, and a reform of international institutions. Dependency theories go further and argue that autonomous self-reliant development requires a social transition from a feudal-capitalist society to a socialist one. Domestic equity can be achieved, they argue, only by lessening or actually breaking the links with the world capitalist economies. Have these strategies worked in actual practice?

Import-substitution industrialization began in Latin America and certain other less developed countries during the Great Depression of the 1930s and accelerated during the Second World War. As a result of depressed prices for their commodity exports and the unavailability of manufactured imports from the industrial countries, many less developed countries began to develop their own manufacturing industries. Although this strategy has led to rapid industrialization, as in the case of Brazil, in important respects its results have been disappointing. For a number of reasons, in most countries when governments encouraged the establishment of industries in which their economies had no comparative advantage, an inefficient and high-cost industrial structure was created; foreign multinationals invested in them primarily to get around trade barriers. The more successful Asian NICs, on the other hand, pursued an export strategy in cooperation with American and Japanese multinationals. In the 1980s many of those LDCs that had chosen import-substitution began to move toward export-led growth strategy because of the recognized need to earn foreign exchange and to develop efficient industries that could compete in world markets (Strange, 1985c, p. 252).

The specific reasons for the failure of an import-substitution strategy include the following: the relatively small size of national markets led to uneconomic plants, excessive protectionism weakened incentives to improve quality of production, and the need to import industrial technology and capital goods caused massive balance-of-payments and debt problems. By the mid-1980s, it had become obvious that a strategy of industrialization based on import substitution was inadequate.

The alternate route of autonomous development advocated by dependency theorists via a domestic social transformation has been chosen at one time or another by Cuba, Tanzania, and China. Self-styled socialist or communist countries, they wanted to minimize their involvement in what they regarded as the hostile imperialist world capitalist economy and to gain domestic social justice. This strategy has failed to acheive the desired social and economic success (Rydenfelt, 1985). Moreover, dependency relationships are characteristic of the socialist Soviet Union and its clients in the Third World such as Cuba, Yemen, and Vietnam. Dependency is not a unique feature of international capitalism (Clark and Bahry, 1983).

Although Cuba and China have achieved some degree of social welfare and economic equity, it is certainly not comparable to that reached by countries like Taiwan or South Korea, which have been fully integrated into world capitalism. The export-led growth of these latter two economies has certainly been more egalitarian in its effects than Brazil's strategy of import substitution, which appears to have increased the maldistribution of income. Although the evidence on these matters is inconclusive, the distribution of national income is much more a product of historical conditions and government policies than it is a consequence of an economy's position in the international capitalist order.[15]

The level of economic success reached by the strategy of autonomous development can only be described as disappointing. Cuba's economy has changed little since it broke with the West; its exports continue to be mainly sugar, tobacco, and other commodities. Its economy is highly subsidized by the Soviet Union for political reasons; in effect, Cuba exchanged one set of dependency relations for another. Tanzania's economic performance is dismal to say the least; it lags behind its neighbor, Kenya, which has chosen a more openly capitalist route to development, and it is highly dependent on South Africa. One must look to China, therefore, for an evaluation of the strategy of autonomous development.

Although China received Soviet aid in the 1950s and 1960s, under Mao Zedong the Chinese committed themselves to a course of self-reliant development. They planned to modernize their economy outside the framework of the capitalist world economy, mobilizing the capital from their own labors and creating their own technology. Chinese industrialization would be based on labor-intensive technology, homegrown for a mass market. This self-reliant strategy was accelerated by Mao with the Great Leap Forward (1958-1961). Sympathetic Western observers praised the backyard ironworks that symbolized this massive effort to modernize China, and enthusiasts proclaimed the wisdom and success of "the Chinese model of economic development" and recommended it to others who wished to escape the yoke of international capitalism.

However, the Great Leap turned into a stumble for the Chinese economy. The resulting problems were accelerated by the Sino-Soviet split and the Russian effort to sabotage the Chinese economy by removing their technicians and eliminating all aid to China. Then came the Cultural Revolution, which caused further damage to the economy and to the scientific-technical foundations of the country. For years China

---

[15] The research conducted under the direction of Henry Bienen at the Research Program on Economic Development of the Woodrow Wilson School of Princeton University and the studies of Atul Kohli et al. (1984) and Hla Myint (1985) at the World Bank find that domestic market forces and economic policies are of most importance in determining the distribution of national income.

slipped backward as it tore itself apart. The leadership that emerged after the death of Mao, finding itself alienated from both East and West, realized that China could not achieve its objectives alone and required Western assistance. In the words of Deng Xiaoping, "no country can now develop by closing its door. . . . Isolation landed China in poverty, backwardness and ignorance" (quoted in *The New York Times*, January 2, 1985, p. A1). Marx would no doubt strongly agree.

At this writing it is too soon to know what the effects of China's reentry into the world economy will be. China has opened to Western investment, but that investment, transfer of modern technology, and enlargement of trading activities are in an early stage. Nevertheless, in the mid-1980s, it is clear that the strategy of autonomous development advocated by the more extreme of the dependency theorists holds little promise for the less developed economies. If China, with its advantages of a strong state, abundant resources, and a relatively large internal market for an LDC, could not be self-reliant, what hope is there for Tanzania? Even the Soviet Union, it should be remembered, had a strong industrial base prior to the Revolution, and infusions of Western technology continued under the New Economic Policy of the 1920s. As the Yugoslav writer, Milovan Djilas, once said to me, no communist society has or can fully develop without the assistance of capitalist economies. More generally, all development is in varying degrees dependent development; no society can develop without at least acquiring the productive technology of the more advanced economies.

Economic Regionalism

A second strategy that has been employed by developing economies as well as others is economic regionalism, wherein a group of countries in a geographically restricted area tries through economic cooperation and alliance to improve its overall position relative to more advanced economies. Cooperation may take several forms; the following are the most important:

(1) Formation of a free trade area or customs union to increase the scale of the internal market and simultaneously protect domestic producers against outside competitors;
(2) Enactment of investment codes and agreements to strengthen the bargaining position of the members vis-à-vis developed economies, especially their MNCs; and
(3) Development of regional industrial policies to rationalize and concentrate local fragmented companies into regional champions (public or private) in such fields as textiles, steel, and motor vehicles.

As the strategy of import-substitution flagged, UNCTAD, led by Prebisch, began to push for a regional approach to the problem of the less
developed countries. Arguments were made that these nations should
form regional monopolies in important industrial sectors, create a regional division of labor based on specialization, and formulate rules to
guide relationships with outside multinational corporations to overcome the problem of small national markets and to improve their bargaining position with the large multinational corporations.

These efforts at regional cooperation have produced mixed results.
Attempts have taken place in both East and West Africa, in the Caribbean, Southeast Asia, Central America, and the Andean region. Although limited objectives have been achieved in monetary affairs or in
labor migration, more ambitious efforts to create a unified common
market have invariably been torn apart by regional conflicts and economic rivalries. Intraregional competition for foreign investment and
trade has frequently undermined the common front against multinational corporations. Attempts to rationalize and concentrate industries
in order to create a regional division of labor have been countered by
the desire of each country to have the regional champion be one of its
own. The very forces of economic nationalism that prompted the initial
commitment to regional cooperation have led to its destruction as each
nation has tried to advance its own national interests.

In fact, to date there have been only two relatively successful examples of economic regionalism: the European Economic Community
(EEC) or Common Market and the COMECON in Eastern Europe,
both of which have resulted in a high degree of economic integration.
Yet the unusual circumstances surrounding both endeavors and the
limited nature of their success restricts their usefulness as models for
the less developed countries. In each case, one or another of the superpowers has played a significant role in the organization's formation;
furthermore, security motives have been of paramount importance.
Even the EEC, moreover, has been unable to advance much beyond its
common external tariff and agricultural policy. Although the Soviet
Union has forced its Eastern bloc members to specialize in a "socialist
international division of labor," resistance has been strong and these
economies have sought economic openings to the West. In Europe as in
the less developed economies, economic nationalism constrains regional integration.

A second form of regionalism is embodied in the creation of special
trading relations between developed countries and particular groupings of less developed countries. The Lomé Conventions between the
European Economic Community and certain less developed countries

and President Reagan's Caribbean Basin initiative are examples of the type of regionalism that extends preferential trading and other benefits to selected countries. For example, the Lomé Conventions give sixty or so African, Caribbean, and Pacific states privileged access to the EEC for their commodity exports and certain types of manufactures. Without exception, however, these arrangements are interlaced with restrictions on both agricultural and manufactured exports from the LDCs. In particular, they restrict exports that compete against EEC products, thereby limiting this type of regionalism as a vehicle of industrialization and a means of escaping the dependency relationship.

In recent years, a third type of economic regionalism has been gaining strength. This is the "delinking of trade" between developed and less developed economies and the forging of trade links and a division of labor among all the less developed countries while acting independently of the more advanced economies (Lewis, 1980b). Although intra–Third World or South-South trade did not grow significantly in the 1970s and in the early 1980s, it promises to be more important in the future.[16] For years to come, however, the developed countries will continue to constitute the engine of the world economy and will be the major importers of all types of LDC exports (ibid.). Moreover, the delinking strategy suffers from the general weakness of economic regionalism, in which less developed countries seek advantages for themselves at the expense of others and attempt to continue beneficial trading and investment relations with more advanced economies. Individual LDCs frequently form alliances with multinationals in order to acquire capital, technology, and access to foreign markets. By giving a multinational a monopoly position in its own closed market, it hopes to draw upon the MNC's resources and enhance its economic position. Despite the rhetoric of "Third World solidarity," few less developed countries are willing to sacrifice their perceived national interests for the sake of others LDCs.

The Formation of Commodity Cartels

Another strategy advocated by certain states in the Third World is emulation of OPEC and the formation of commodity cartels that could force a dramatic improvement in the terms of trade for Third World raw material and food exports. Such cartels have been proposed in copper, bauxite, and other commodities. There was much talk along these lines in the wake of the initial OPEC success, and there were differing responses in the developed countries. Some spoke of the threat from the

---

[16] A good discussion of the delinking strategy is Stewart (1984).

Third World, forseeing a proliferation of Southern commodity cartels that could cause havoc for the North; others argued that "oil is the exception" and that no threat existed (Krasner, 1974). The available evidence suggests that the latter position has been vindicated.

The success of OPEC in quadrupling the price of petroleum was due to a peculiar set of favorable circumstances. Both demand and supply factors were ripe when the third Arab-Israeli war in 1973 caused Arabs to impose an embargo on the West and the Shah of Iran took advantage of the situation to raise the price of petroleum exports drastically. During the months just prior to the outbreak of the war, demand for petroleum and other commodities had increased greatly while accelerating inflation had reduced the real price of oil. On the supply side, there was no longer an excess capacity available that the West could tap to compensate for the Arab-induced shortfall. In fact one can argue that the energy crisis actually began earlier, when the United States began full production from its domestic oil fields, thus losing its excess capacity and relinquishing to the OPEC cartel effective control over the world petroleum market.

A cartel has a powerful tendency to undermine itself, and its maintenance requires the existence of a large producer with excess capacity that can instill discipline; such a leader can strongly influence world prices through increases or decreases in the aggregate supply. By 1973, this pivotal position had shifted from the United States and its petroleum companies to the King of Saudi Arabia. Subsequently, the Saudis dominated world energy markets for over a decade; by increasing or decreasing their production, they maintained the cartel and influenced the world price. They thus operated the cartel to their own national advantage and that of at least some other producers.

In the early 1980s, this Saudi influence over the cartel was undermined and OPEC's fortunes were dramatically reversed. The success of conservation measures, the entry of new non-OPEC producers, especially Mexico and Great Britain, and global recession greatly reduced world demand for petroleum. At the same time, total production was increased as individual producers tried to prevent a fall in their total oil revenues. The consequent decline in oil prices from a previous high in the range of $35 or more a barrel to a low of less than $12 in the summer of 1986 caused the Saudis to increase production significantly to force a collapse in the price and thereby to reestablish their influence over the cartel. Although the consequences of this "price war" were undecided at the time of this writing, projections suggested that the world demand for petroleum would again overtake supply sometime in the early 1990s.[17] If and when this occurs, Saudi Arabia will regain its domination over the cartel and will once again strongly influence the price of petroleum and world energy.

Although commodity cartels have had varying degrees of success in raising or maintaining prices, there does not appear to be any other commodity in a situation similar to that of petroleum. Substitutes for almost all other commodities are readily available, and the world demand for many commodities has declined due to dramatic reductions in the resource content of manufactured goods (Larson, Ross, and Williams, 1986). With the exception of a few metals, the United States or one of its allies can produce the commodities. But more importantly, no single producer like Saudi Arabia exists that can control the supply and hence the price. Finally, although cartels may benefit certain less developed countries (as happened with petroleum), they do so only at the expense of most other LDCs. For many reasons, cartels in scarce commodities do not appear to provide a promising method for improving the lot of the less developed countries.

The Demand for a New International Economic Order

The perceived failure of alternative strategies (import substitution, self-reliance, and economic regionalism) and the success of OPEC led to the launching of a new strategy at the Sixth Special Session of the United Nations General Assembly in 1974. At that session a group of less developed countries (the Group of 77), led by several OPEC members, adopted a Declaration and Action Programme on the Establishment of a New International Economic Order (NIEO) that included: (1) the right of the LDCs to form producer associations, (2) linkage of commodity export prices to the prices of manufactured exports from developed countries, (3) the right of LDCs to nationalize foreign enterprises and gain sovereignty over their natural resources, and (4) the formulation of rules to regulate the multinational corporations. On December 12, 1974, the General Assembly adopted these objectives in the form of the Charter of Economic Rights and Duties of States.[18]

Although this desire for an NIEO was profoundly influenced by radical and dependency critiques of world capitalism, it was generally in the spirit of structuralism, believing that the goal of industrialization

[17] Robert Williams of the Center for Energy and Environmental Studies of Princeton University has done calculations indicating that the increasing industrialization of the less developed countries and their rapidly growing requirements for petroleum will bring demand into line with available supply.

[18] Krasner (1985) provides an excellent evaluation of the LDC demands for a New International Economic Order.

and economic development could be achieved within the framework of the world economy and that it was not necessary to overthrow the capitalist system. What was required were policy and institutional reforms that would make the international economic system operate to the advantage of the less developed countries and enlarge their role in running the system. Among the most important demands for changing the terms on which the LDCs participated in the world economy were the following:

(1) Measures that would increase Third World control over their own economies, especially in natural resources,
(2) Agreements to maintain and increase their purchasing power and to improve the terms of trade for their raw material exports,
(3) Enactment of a code of conduct increasing their control over the MNCs within their own borders,
(4) Reductions in the cost of Western technology and increases in its availability,
(5) Increases in the flow and liberalization of foreign aid,
(6) Alleviation of the LDC debt problems,
(7) Preferential treatment and greater access for LDC manufactured goods in developed markets, and
(8) Greater power in decision making in the IMF, World Bank, United Nations, and other international organizations, thus making these institutions more responsive to LDC needs.

The essence of the initial proposal for a New International Economic Order and also of subsequent reformulations is that the operations of the world economy should be made subordinate to the perceived development needs of the less developed economies (Krasner, 1985). Working toward this goal, various commissions and reports have advocated changes in the rules governing international trade, the monetary system, and other matters. In particular, they have advocated changes in international organizations—the United Nations, the World Bank, and the IMF—that would give the LDCs greater influence in the management of the world economy and its regimes.

At first there was disarray, and conflicting responses emerged among the Western powers. Numerous international conferences were held to consider the Third World demands. By the mid-1980s, however, although the debate and controversy continued over this most concerted and significant attempt by the less developed countries to change the international balance of economic and political power, the NIEO challenge had been effectively defeated. The reasons for the failure to implement the NIEO include the following:

(1) Despite rhetorical and marginal differences in their positions, none of the developed economies has been willing to make any significant concessions. Resistance to the demands has been led principally by the United States, which regards the proposals either as unworkable or as contrary to its commitment to a free market economy. Although some other Western countries have been more accommodating in spirit, they have substantially supported the American stance.

(2) Contrary to their statements and the expectations they engendered, OPEC members have been unwilling to put their power and wealth at the service of other Third World states. For example, they have not used their monetary resources to finance a general commodity fund or the development efforts of more than a few countries. Instead they have used their newly gained economic power to support their own nationalistic interests and have invested most of their financial surplus in Western markets.

(3) The rise in world petroleum prices had a devastating impact on non-oil-producing countries, particularly those in the Third World. In addition to burdening them with high import bills, it triggered a global recession that reduced the rising world demand for their commodity exports. Thus, the OPEC success in raising world energy prices and causing a global recession undercut the bargaining power of the LDCs and blunted their demands for a New International Economic Order.

The history of the NIEO demonstrates the fundamental dilemma of less developed countries that, in the name of nationalism, attempt to change the operation of the world market economy and to improve their relative position. The dilemma is that the same nationalistic spirit frequently undermines their efforts to cooperate with one another and to form an economic alliance against the developed countries. Although the confrontation with the North and the ideological appeal of the NIEO provide a basis for political agreement, powerful and conflicting national interests greatly weaken Third World unity.

Although the NIEO has failed to produce the reforms desired by its proponents, this does not necessarily invalidate the LDC grievances or make certain changes in the relationship between North and South less desirable. Many of the LDC demands do have merit and could become the basis for reforms that would improve the operation of the world economy as a whole while benefiting both developed and less developed economies. For example, although the developed countries are loath to accept proposals that would raise the real price of commodities beyond their market value, it would be in their interest to stabilize the export earnings of the LDCs. One can envisage similar mutually beneficial arrangements in other areas such as debt relief and foreign aid, and it is vital that the developed economies maintain open markets for LDC manufactured exports. Under present circumstances it would be foolish to expect, however, the enactment of sweeping reforms that would change the overall position of less developed countries in the world.

THE PROCESS OF UNEVEN GROWTH

In reality economic development of the less developed world has taken place at an amazing rate over the few decades since the Second World War.[19] The process of economic growth has rapidly spread from the core to certain parts of the periphery of the world economy as it did in the nineteenth century. The core's functioning as an "engine of growth," the transfer of resources to the periphery, and the demonstration effect of success have helped development to spread throughout the former colonial world. Although they continue to lag far behind the developed countries, the LDC share of the gross world product is rapidly rising (Reynolds, 1983).

At the same time, it must be readily acknowledged that this process has been a highly uneven one that does not create a basis for optimism. The developmental effort in black Africa appears to have collapsed; those countries have actually declined economically since colonial days. In the 1980s the rapid growth of the Latin American countries has been arrested by the debt crisis and the slowdown of global growth. The process of growth has been concentrated mainly in the newly industrializing countries of East Asia and in a few of the larger developing countries.

Three prerequisites for economic development can be identified in Japan and the East Asian NICs. First, there must be a "strong" state and economic bureaucracy that can set priorities, implement a coherent economic policy, and carry out needed reforms. Public and private economic managers must work together in the formulation of a "depoliticized" industrial policy. The economic managers have the task of making trade, investment, and other commercial arrangements serve the national interest; they shape the terms under which the domestic economy interacts with the larger world economy. In addition, these

[19] Reynolds (1983) is a short and excellent survey of the experience of economic development.

societies have made substantial and continuing investments in education and human capital. They have carried out programs of land reform, income redistribution, and rural development; they have avoided an "urban bias," such as expensive food subsidies and overvalued currencies, in their policies. And, third, they have worked with and not against the market; government intervention has been based on the market mechanism. Japan and the NICs have encouraged a well-functioning market that spurs individual initiative and promotes economic efficiency. They have demonstrated that the liberals are quite correct in their emphasis on the benefits of the price mechanism in the efficient allocation of economic resources. In brief, a strong state, investment in human resources, and an efficient market are the hallmarks of the successful developing economy (Hofheinz and Calder, 1982).

What Trotsky called the "law of combined and uneven development" is operating in these NICs (see Knei-Paz, 1978, p. 89). In Russia's late industrialization (as Trotsky observed in his analysis), in Japan's rapid climb up the technological ladder, and now in a number of developing countries, one finds examples of activist states encouraging the importation of foreign technology and combining that technology with traditional social forms. These rapidly developing states have benefited from the growth of international trade and the world economy since the Second World War. The world capitalist economy has facilitated the rapid development of those LDCs that could take advantage of the global opportunities for economic growth.

As Atul Kohli has pointed out, the success of the newly industrializing countries is changing the terms of the debate over global poverty. Although structuralism and dependency theory continue to dominate the discussion in the LDCs and elsewhere, the fact that several LDCs are in fact growing rapidly and even surpassing the growth rates of developed countries is shifting the focus of attention to why they are developing and why other LDCs are not. Nor can the NICs any longer be dismissed as cases of dependent development; every developed country including the United States and Japan is an example of dependent development and Japan remains a highly dependent country on foreign markets and raw materials. Thus, the crucial question is becoming what have the NICs done correctly to grow rich rather than that of why are most LDCs still poor.

Whether or not the favorable situation for the NICs will continue is highly problematic. As John Ruggie has observed, "for future industrializers to follow the route taken by the first tier of NICs, the absorptive capacity of world markets would have to increase by an order of magnitude the realization of which is difficult to foresee." But of equal importance, he goes on to point out, "even the sustainability by the first tier of their own past trajectory depends critically on what the OECD euphemistically calls 'positive adjustment policies' " (Ruggie, 1983b, pp. 479-80). In short, the future success of the NICs and the ability of other countries to emulate their export-led growth strategy will depend upon the global rate of economic growth, the openness of the advanced economies, and the changing character of industrial technology. These environmental conditions will profoundly influence the ultimate success of the countries themselves and the applicability of their development strategy to other less developed countries.[20]

Thus, this chapter has returned to a theme that runs throughout this book: the workings of the world market economy develops the world, but does so, as Marx and Lenin first noted, unevenly. In the nineteenth century this growth process spread from Great Britain to Western Europe, Japan, and the New World. In the late twentieth century the newly industrializing countries (Taiwan, South Korea, Hong Kong, and Singapore) and certain other countries such as Brazil, India, and China are joining the ranks of industrial countries. Although their developmental strategies have ranged from export-led growth to import substitution, the operation of the world economy has been in varying degrees a positive factor in each case. However, the capacity of the state to order its priorities and its willingness to let loose market forces have been the most important factors in those countries that have successfully developed their economies.

CONCLUSION

If one defines dependence as a conditioning factor that profoundly affects the development strategies of developing economies, then the fact of dependency can hardly be denied. Every less developed economy is certainly dependent upon fluctuating world market conditions; each must import capital, technology, and industrial know-how. Export markets are difficult to penetrate, given the advantages of powerful established exporters and protected markets in the developed countries. These aspects of dependency surely exist. A continuum exists in which every country is more or less dependent upon others, and some are certainly more dependent than others. If, however, one employs this condition of dependence as an explanation of underdevelopment, the ar-

[20] Cline (1982b) employs the fallacy of composition to suggest that what was a useful strategy for the NICs might not work if a number of other LDCs resorted to export-led growth. The resulting excess capacity and flood of exports would trigger protectionist responses. In a brief rebuttal, Gustav Ranis (1985) disagreed with this assessment.

gument loses much of its force. There is a tendency, unfortunately, to confuse these two meanings of dependence and to assume that the *fact* of dependence provides the *explanation* of economic underdevelopment.

The less developed countries have a high degree of dependence and continue to be vulnerable precisely because they are underdeveloped rather than vice versa. They are the weak in a world of the strong; they are dependent because they are underdeveloped. The lack of an effective and appropriate development strategy to overcome this situation is most important in holding them back. Their foremost problem is not external dependence but internal inefficiency. Those less developed countries that have created efficient domestic economies on their own initiative are the ones that have succeeded in achieving rapid rates of economic growth. However, even these efforts may not succeed without a growing world economy open to their exports.

There is no doubt, however, that the immense gap between the developed and the less developed economies along with global market conditions have made it much more difficult to escape dependence in the late twentieth century than it was for developing economies in the nineteenth century. Nonetheless, throughout the Third World, many societies have established the political stability, social discipline, and efficient markets that are the prerequisites for economic development. Modernizing elites in the public and private sectors have learned to exploit the opportunities provided by trade, foreign investment, and technology imports to attain a rapid rate of economic and industrial growth.

The Third World no longer exists as a meaningful single entity. In its place is a highly differentiated collection of nation-states: the economically successful Asian NICs, the potentially powerful but economically troubled states of India, Brazil, China, Mexico, Indonesia, and others, the destitute states of the Sahel, East Africa, and Southern Asia. Only the rhetoric of Third World unity remains as these nations dispute with one another in a more mercantilistic world economy and, in John Ruggie's words, are being forced "to scramble for the best possible regional and bilateral deals with specific industrialized countries (Bhagwati and Ruggie, 1984, p. 42). Like any Western predatory nation, the NICs have not hesitated to pursue policies that damage the economies of other Third World countries. In Chapter Ten we will return to the implications for the less developed countries of the transformation of the international political economy.

The competitive nation-state system, with all its capacity for good and for evil, is spreading in the Third World and is transforming that world. The concept of the Third World evolved in response to the bipolar Cold War; its leaders, rejecting both the Soviet and American blocs, wished to develop themselves independently and to preserve their unity as a third force. Subsequently, various pan-movements and regional organizations have arisen or become stronger: "pan-Arab" groups, the Organization for African Unity, etc. Inspired by structuralism and dependency theory, they formulated autonomous and cooperative routes to economic development and nation building. The two ideals of political nonalignment and Third World internationalism were expected to characterize their new world order.

In the mid-1980s, the idea of the Third World as a homogeneous and united bloc of less developed societies is rapidly decaying, as differentiation occurs in the achievements and the policies of those countries. In every region, particular nation-states are emerging as centers of power: Brazil, India, Mexico, Venezuela, Nigeria, Iran, Saudi Arabia, Indonesia, Vietnam, China, and others. They pursue foreign policies designed to further their own particular goals, and differences in national interests and ambitions are producing conflicts and even intense wars among these newly emergent powers.

As the modern nation-state system reproduces itself in what was once regarded as the unified Third World, the newly developing nation-states begin to act independently. Beliefs held by structuralists and dependency theorists alike that the less developed countries could not develop within the framework of an unreformed world capitalism but would have to cooperate to emancipate themselves are contradicted by the facts of the late twentieth century. Although the process of world economic growth is highly uneven and sporadic, in a number of societies development has been remarkable. Emerging industrialized states have become active participants in the first truly global system of international relations.

The shape and continuation of this process of diffusion will be profoundly influenced by the operation of the international financial system, whose function is to allocate resources to the growth poles of world economy. This can not happen, however, unless there is a solution of the global debt crisis and a smooth transition can take place from the United States to Japan as the dominant financial power. With these considerations in mind, the next chapter turns to a discussion of international finance.

CHAPTER EIGHT

The Political Economy of International Finance

INTERNATIONAL finance is a major force in integrating the modern world economy. From the time of the Fuggers and other Renaissance bankers, private capital has nourished the international economy in the form of loans and portfolio investment (stocks and bonds). In the contemporary era, foreign direct investment by multinational corporations has augmented these traditional means of capital flow. Governments and international organizations have also become important sources of capital through the making of loans and the giving of official aid, particularly to less developed countries. Because foreign direct investment has already been discussed in Chapter Six, this chapter will focus on other forms of international finance.

From the perspective of liberal economics, the primary function of international finance is to transfer accumulated capital to the location where its marginal rate of return is highest and where it can therefore be employed most efficiently. The flow of capital internationally is a powerful driving force in the world economy, and the transfer of capital from regions with capital surplus, where the rate of return is relatively low, to potentially more productive regions is a major factor in the dynamics and expansion of the world system. Both the lenders and the recipients can benefit from a more productive use of the world's scarce supply of investable capital. This investment expands global demand and overcomes the inherent tendencies in a closed market economy toward underconsumption and surplus capital.

International finance links the international economy and also contributes to its dynamic nature. But international finance is also the weakest link in the international economy; speculative and volatile flows of capital can be a major source of global economic instability. In the words of Charles Kindleberger (1978d), the international financial system is inherently prone to "manias, panics and crashes." It is subject to periodic debt crises and destabilizing international flows of investment, speculative, and flight capital in search of higher rates of return or safe havens.

In a world divided among competitive states, however, international finance also has significant political consequences. It creates dependency relationships and is a major source of national power. Both foreign investment and official aid involve extensive penetration of an economy and, in many cases, lead to continuing external influence over domestic activities. Although trade and monetary relations may also impinge on an economy, foreign investment, aid, and loans have a greater tendency to create a superior-subordinate or dependency relationship and thus to lead to charges of imperialism. Stockholders and creditors have been known to call upon their own governments to intervene in other societies to protect their investments, and foreign investment and international finance have frequently aroused political and nationalistic passions.

Psychological and political factors inherent in international finance cause still further sensitivity. When an investment or a loan is negotiated, the immediate and obvious benefit is to the recipient or debtor economy; the creditor is thus usually in the stronger bargaining position and can exact favorable repayment and other terms. But once the investment is in place and the loan made, the recipient economy may be in the stronger position and can press for a revision of the terms of the investment or loan. The debtor may charge the creditor with exploitation and the creditor may accuse the debtor of violating good faith and contractual obligations. Both sides tend to feel aggrieved, and a politicization of what had been solely a commercial arrangement occurs.

International finance and the exercise of influence by the hegemonic power over international economic and political affairs are closely related. The hegemon is both the manager and a primary beneficiary of the financial system. It is the primary source of capital for developing economies, and its currency is the basis of global financial relations. If a financial crisis occurs, the hegemon is the only actor that can play the role of what Charles Kindleberger has called the "lender of last resort" and can take the necessary action to moderate the threat to the system.[1] In the nineteenth century this stabilizing responsibility of managing and overcoming financial crises fell to Great Britain; since the end of the Second World War the United States has managed the international financial system. As American economic hegemony declines, the question is whether Japan, as the emergent financial power, can assume this crucial role of economic leadership.

American domination of international finance since the end of the Second World War has been crucial to the simultaneous maintenance

[1] Kindleberger (1978d) discusses the need for and the functions of a "lender of last resort." Its basic task is to provide liquidity or money to insolvent businesses and thereby give them time to solve their difficulties. This responsibility of preventing financial crises is usually assumed by a country's national bank.

of its global political position and of domestic prosperity. The United States could not have fought two major conflicts in Asia, maintained a strong position in Western Europe, and sustained a major defense buildup in the 1980s without a significant lowering of the American standard of living if it had not been for its pivotal role in the international financial system. Through exploitation of its influence over global financial affairs, the United States has been able to cover the costs of its hegemonic position, preserve a false domestic prosperity, and mask the consequences of its relative political and economic decline.

THREE ERAS OF INTERNATIONAL FINANCE

The world economy has experienced three phases of international finance within the past century: from 1870 to the outbreak of the First World War in 1914, a brief flourishing after the war until the collapse of credit markets associated with the Great Depression, and the era that opened after the Second World War.

The First Era (1870-1914)

Massive capital accumulation in Great Britain and subsequently in other advanced industrial economies from 1870 resulted in the export of capital and became a major new factor in international economics and politics.[2] Although France, Germany, and even the United States had become capital exporters by the end of the century, the foremost supplier of financial capital was Great Britain. The City of London increased its foreign holdings more than five times between 1870 and 1914. By 1914, over one-quarter of British wealth was invested in foreign government securities and foreign railroads. Britain was, in fact, investing far more abroad than it was at home. Repatriated earnings from these investments more than compensated for the fact that Britain ran a chronic trade deficit during this period. Britain had become a rentier economy by the close of the century and was living off the income from its vast overseas investments.

The economic impact of these capital exports was profound. For the borrowing countries, capital imports financed the creation of an infrastructure of urban centers, port facilities, and railroads that laid the basis for economic development. As railroads were constructed, the interiors of the continents were opened and hitherto isolated areas were linked to world commerce. The primary beneficiaries of this investment

---

[2] A brief and excellent history of this period is Condliffe (1950, ch. 11). This section draws heavily on this source. A more detailed history is Kindleberger (1984).

were the "lands of recent settlement" (e.g., the United States, Canada, Australia). At the same time, many countries became highly dependent upon the export of food and raw materials and the import of capital to balance their international accounts. This made them increasingly vulnerable to the vicissitudes of the world economy and the international business cycle.

For the capital-exporting countries, especially Great Britain, the economic consequences were mixed. British investors and financiers gained a high return on their overseas investments, and the British economy as a whole benefited from imports of cheap food and raw materials. But as John Hobson and other critics charged, the massive outflow of investment capital undoubtedly contributed to the industrial and overall decline of the British economy and accelerated the eclipse of Britain by rising industrial powers (Hobson, 1965 [1902]). While Great Britain tried to remain strong in the industries of the Industrial Revolution (coal, iron, and textiles), the United States, Germany, and other economies took the lead in the emergent industries of the Second Industrial Revolution (petroleum, steel, electrical, chemical, and motor vehicles).

Throughout much of the nineteenth century Great Britain undertook the role of what was called earlier the "lender of last resort." As first noted by Walter Bagehot in *Lombard Street* (1873), his classic study of British financial institutions, a modern financial system based on credit requires the existence of an authority that can rapidly provide liquidity to overextended and threatened financial institutions in the event of a financial panic or crisis. In domestic economies, this rescue function falls upon the central bank. This role was assumed by Great Britain and the Bank of England because of their interest in the stability of the international financial system. As the hegemonic economic power, Great Britain managed the world financial system until it collapsed with the outbreak of the First World War.

The Second Era (1920-1939)

The First World War brought to a close the first era of international finance and profoundly affected the nature and structure of international finance. The intensity and duration of the war forced the major European combatants to draw down (and in some cases even liquidate) their overseas investments to pay for necessary foodstuffs and war matériel. The war effectively paved the way for the eventual political emancipation of the colonies. And as the United States emerged from the war as the foremost creditor nation, it gradually began to change its outlook on world affairs.

Even though the United States did withdraw into political isolation

309

with the 1919 Senate defeat of the League of Nations treaty, American economic involvement with the rest of the world continued to expand. The American financial community began to recognize the increased stake of the United States in the world economy. U.S. finance assumed a growing international role; it was especially important in the funding of German reparations payments to France and other countries. This American-provided liquidity was a major factor in the stimulation of economic activity in the 1920s, and its cutoff in 1929 accentuated the severity of the Great Depression, which abbreviated the second era of international finance.[3]

During this era, both the cooperation and the rivalry between London and New York as centers of international finance intensified. Financial markets tend to be highly centralized and hierarchical in structure because of the importance of economies of scale and pooled information. This creates competition among individual centers to be dominant at the apex of the system (Kindleberger, 1978b, p. 74). That foremost center lends abroad, clears payments, and handles foreign reserves; it also serves as the "lender of last resort." In short, it manages the international financial system.

The history of international finance is one of a center that has migrated from the Mediterranean to the North Atlantic (Kindleberger, 1978b, ch. 4). In the sixteenth century Amsterdam replaced Florence as the center; subsequently London replaced Amsterdam.[4] Similarly, in the 1920s, New York began to displace London. Yet the United States had neither the power nor the will to manage and stabilize the international financial system. When economic leadership collapsed in the 1930s, international finance became characterized by increasing government intervention in financial markets, by imperial rivalries, and by economic disorder (Kindleberger, 1973). The resulting Great Depression brought the second era to a close.

The Third Era (1947-1985)

The third era of international finance, which began at the end of the Second World War, has differed from the first and second eras in several important respects. Whereas capital flows had previously consisted

[3] The causes of the Great Depression were complicated and are a matter of intense controversy. They certainly cannot be reduced to one or two factors such as the role of international finance and the absence of a hegemonic power, although the latter aspect was certainly relevant for its scope and intensity. As Kenneth Oye (1983) has argued, domestic policy choices were of crucial importance.

[4] Although Amsterdam in the seventeenth century performed the role of "lender of last resort," it did not assume the other functions of the hegemon.

almost entirely of private funds, after the war official foreign aid also became an important aspect of international finance. Initially, the United States sent aid to Western Europe through the Marshall Plan, which is estimated to have amounted to 4.5 percent of the American GNP between 1949 and 1952 (*The New York Times*, April 23, 1986, p. D2). Subsequently, as they recovered from the war, other wealthy countries gave aid to less developed economies. International organizations were created to funnel capital and other assistance first to developed and then to less developed economies. Beginning in the late 1960s, immense outflows of American dollars gave rise to the Eurocurrency market, transformed the scale and nature of international finance, and eventually contributed to the global debt problem of the 1980s. By the close of the era, Japan had become the principal creditor nation and the United States had become a major recipient of capital flows. This is thus a historical period that begins with American financial hegemony and ends with America increasingly dependent on Japanese capital for its world position and domestic prosperity.

The outstanding success of the Marshall Plan, the intensification of the ideological conflict between East and West, and the increasing recognition of the plight of less developed countries led to the establishment of large unilateral official aid programs in the 1950s. The United States and other developed countries made outright grants or low-interest loans to the less developed economies. With the launching of the "Development Decade" in the 1960s, the rich committed themselves to donating 1 percent of their national incomes to the poor countries. Although very few developed countries fulfilled this commitment, the amount of this official unilateral aid became substantial.

From its very beginning, official unilateral aid has been cloaked in controversy. Various groups in developed countries have regarded it as "pouring money down a rat hole," because the less developed countries have generally lacked the social and political base that would enable them to use the aid effectively. Conservatives have objected because they believe foreign aid encourages state intervention in the economy and discourages market approaches to economic development. They prefer to rely on foreign investment by multinational corporations and outward-oriented, export-led development strategies. Marxists and nationalists object because political and economic conditions are frequently attached to such aid, and the aid gives the donors leverage over the affairs of the less developed countries. Finally, critics and officials in less developed countries denounce such official aid as a new form of capitalist imperialism.

Although humanitarian and developmental concerns do play an important role, the primary motives for official aid by individual governments have been political, military, and commercial. The donors' desire to establish spheres of political influence, to bolster military security, or to obtain economic advantage have influenced the nature and patterns of aid. For example, when American foreign economic policy shifted in 1971, there was a reduction in total foreign aid and an allocation of a larger portion of aid to political allies (Scammell, 1983, pp. 76, 183). The two largest recipients of American aid have been Egypt and Israel. In the 1980s commercial motives explain a larger portion of Japan's aid than the latter cares to admit. In essence official unilateral aid has been an instrument of foreign or commercial policy for the two largest donors.

The postwar era of international finance has also witnessed the rise of multilateral aid agencies; the World Bank, regional development banks, and the International Monetary Fund are among the most important agencies.[5] The multilateral development banks (MDBs) are the largest source of official aid to the developing countries as well as providers of development policy advice and technical assistance. Although the United States has been the largest single contributor to these banks, its share declined both absolutely and relatively in the 1980s. In the preceding decade, countries other than the United States contributed a substantial fraction of total MDB resources, and the MDBs also borrowed in the private capital markets to supplement officially donated funds. Although the primary purpose of these banks is to provide financing for specific development projects, the World Bank has expanded its general responsibilities in light of the plight of many less developed countries. Whereas the purpose of the MDBs has been to assist development, the International Monetary Fund was established to help nations with balance-of-payments difficulties. The Fund provides the liquidity required while a nation carries out the adjustments in its economy and exchange rate that will correct its payments problem. Despite these differences in purpose, however, the tasks of the World Bank and the Fund have converged in recent years due to the necessity of dealing with the global debt problem.

Multilateral aid, like unilateral official aid, has been the subject of considerable controversy. Some conservatives in the developed countries have regarded the World Bank and the IMF as purveyors of socialism and dispensers of wealth to profligate countries living beyond their means. This was certainly the view of the Reagan Administration until it realized in 1982 that it needed the IMF to save the American

[5] Krasner (1985, ch. 6) presents a concise review of these agencies.

banking system, then threatened by the world debt crisis. Radical critics, on the other hand, denounce these Western-dominated institutions as imperialist agents of international capitalism. The recipients themselves tend to regard the aid as minimal at the same time that they denounce conditionality as a violation of their national sovereignty. Regardless of its substantial achievements, multilateral aid continues to be the focus of intense controversies.

One controversial issue is conditionality, that is, the imposition by lenders on borrowers of certain conditions for receipt of assistance, such as the reduction of budget deficits and currency devaluation.[6] The developed countries regard conditionality as necessary to ensure efficiency in the use of the aid and, in some cases, to achieve political objectives such as the Carter Administration promotion of "basic human rights" or the Reagan Administration promotion of "free enterprise." The recipients, especially in the less developed countries, denounce conditionality as imperialist interference in their internal affairs, especially when they are required to take restrictive economic measures that are politically dangerous. Conditionality will remain a highly explosive issue.

Another issue relates to concessionary or "soft" loans, that is, loans made at a low or no interest rate, principally by the World Bank's International Development Association and International Financial Corporation. Even though the number of such loans to the poorest countries has increased, the less developed and certain other countries have proposed an additional vast expansion. For both ideological and budgetary reasons, the United States has generally been critical of expanding this role of the Bank. The United States has occasionally tied concessionary loans to foreign policy objectives, as in its Caribbean and Central American initiatives; certain other donor countries follow a similar but less pronounced practice. General concessionary aid will probably never become a significant feature of the world economy, and it will undoubtedly continue to be subordinate to the foreign policy objectives of donor states.

Control of the lending agencies and of their ultimate purpose provides the core of yet another significant controversy. A major issue in the 1981 UN Conference on Global Negotiations at the North-South Summit in Cancún, Mexico, was the question of control over the MDBs, the GATT, and the IMF. There was a proposal that control be placed in the UN General Assembly where the less developed countries have a majority and could change policies regarding such matters as

---

[6] See Bienen and Gersovitz (1985) for a balanced analysis of the issue.

conditionality and concessionary loans. Another proposal would have the IMF increase world liquidity through the issuance of Special Drawing Rights and distribute the funds to those nations that need it most. Not surprisingly, the United States and other developed countries have strongly resisted the transfer of these economic institutions to the jurisdiction of the General Assembly.

The basic issue in this controversy between developed and less developed countries has been that of the purpose and control of these international economic organizations. The developed countries believe that the purpose of both unilateral and multilateral official aid is to assist less developed countries to reach a point where they can participate fully in an open, market-oriented international economy and that aid policies must therefore be subordinate to the norms of the market system. Less developed countries, on the other hand, give the highest priority to economic development and political independence; from their perspective, market norms must be subordinated to the goals of national autonomy, and control over these agencies must rest with the less developed countries themselves. These issues of purpose and control lie at the heart of their demands for a New International Economic Order, discussed in the last chapter (Krasner, 1985).

The third era of international finance came to a close in 1985. In that year, the United States itself became a debtor and Japan displaced it as the world's foremost creditor nation. Although this shift in the financial position of the United States was rightly hailed as dramatic and historic, it was the culmination and inevitable outcome of excessive American policies and mismanagement of the international monetary and financial systems ever since the escalation of the war in Vietnam and the simultaneous launching of the Great Society program. At the same time that the United States had managed the financial system, it had also used the system for its own national advantage and had thereby laid the foundations for the problems of the international financial system in the 1980s. Although problems of conditionality, concessionary aid, and purpose/control over international institutions would continue, even more vexing issues appeared with the rise of the Eurodollar market, the precipitation of the international debt crisis, and the decline of international leadership.

THE EURODOLLAR MARKET

The Eurodollar market received its name from American dollars on deposit in European (principally London) banks yet remaining outside the domestic monetary system and the stringent control of national monetary authorities.[7] In the late 1960s and 1970s, other currencies joined the dollar in that market, the Eurodollar or Eurocurrency market spread to financial centers in many countries, and American banks moved abroad to participate in that market. As noted in Chapter Four, foreign exchange trading was approximately $35 trillion in 1984. Thus, the size of the market dwarfs anything previously experienced in international finance.

A major cause of the Eurodollar or Eurocurrency market was the overly expansionary American monetary policy of the late 1960s and early 1970s. Although the market's capitalization is usually attributed to the OPEC surplus generated after the quadrupling of energy prices in 1973, the primary source was actually the huge dollar "overhang." In 1975, the rest of the world's nonbank private dollar holdings was $130 billion, by 1984 had grown to $800 billion, and threatened to reach the astonishing figure of $2.1 trillion in 1990 (Marris, 1985, p. 99). The Johnson Administration, carrying out its foreign and domestic policies, and the Nixon Administration, getting reelected, had printed dollars that eventually found their way to the Eurodollar market. The willingness of America's allies to hold dollars in excess of their needs and the crucial decision of the major OPEC nations (also friends of the United States) to continue the denomination of oil in dollars meant that dollars were in the market where they could be recycled from oil consumer to oil producer and back to the market again in the form of OPEC deposits.

The conventional wisdom of the U.S. government and the economics profession is that the great bulk of the OPEC surplus was deposited in the Eurodollar Market from whence it was recycled by the large international banks to oil-deficit LDCs and that this alleged "privatization" of the international financial system made official aid unnecessary.[8] Through a complex chain of financial intermediation, the commercial banks recycled the producer surplus to the neediest consumers. Thus, following the trauma of the oil shock, the market is believed to have worked effectively to restore equilibrium to the system.

As David Spiro (1987) has shown, what really happened was very different. The market worked to some extent, but it also had the guiding hand of the American hegemon. In the first place, a substantial portion of the financial surplus, especially from Saudi Arabia, was invested in the United States and into American Treasury bills; in effect, this im-

---

[7] The assistance and doctoral dissertation of David Spiro (1987) have strongly influenced the argument of the following two sections.

[8] The McCracken Report (OECD, 1977) is an excellent example of this position.

portant friend of the United States used part of its surplus to assist the American balance of payments. Second, only a relatively small portion of the OPEC surplus and commercial bank lending was made available to the neediest less developed countries; most adjusted primarily by reducing oil imports, and insofar as they received assistance with their oil bills, a substantial portion of that aid came from the multilateral aid agencies. Commercial bank loans were given primarily to the middle-income LDCs, a number of whom were themselves oil-exporters; in fact, relatively few of the NICs and the larger LDCs received the overwhelming fraction of the loans: Algeria, Argentina, Brazil, South Korea, Mexico, Venezuela, and Nigeria. The international commercial banks, the United States (and to some extent the other advanced countries), and certain of the richer LDCs were the principal beneficiaries of the OPEC financial surplus.

This economic "alliance" led the NICs and other LDCs to launch a new strategy of "indebted industrialization" (Frieden, 1981). For reasons of their own—the recession in the advanced economies and the promise of extraordinary profits—and in the naive belief, as one prominent American banker put it, that "nations never go bankrupt," the international commercial banks assumed the responsibility of recycling the OPEC surplus and accommodating the ambitions of the borrowers. The less developed countries fortunate enough to be classified as "creditworthy" had at last found a way around the "conditionality" of multilateral aid agencies, the influence of unilateral aid givers, and the domination of the multinationals. In this fashion the advanced economies and the United States in particular gained new and expanding markets for agricultural, machine tools, and other exports at a time when other markets were in recession. During this period, as William Branson (1980) has argued, a substantial shift in American trade took place in the direction of the Pacific and the LDCs.

This symbiotic relationship among bank creditor, LDC borrower, and advanced country exporters worked effectively throughout much of the 1970s. The market was praised for its successful recycling of petrodollars. Then came the second oil crisis in 1979, the recession of the late Carter Administration, and the even deeper recession of the first years of the Reagan Administration. These disturbing events were followed by the Reagan "revolution" in economic policy. As pointed out in Figure 2 (see Chapter Four), the world economy and America's role in it was dramatically transformed.

The massive American budget deficit and accompanying restrictive monetary policy had a profound impact on LDC debtors. The United States was forced to raise interest rates to finance its unprecedented

budget deficit; this siphoned off the world's capital. In addition to raising global interest rates and service charges, American policies induced
a world recession that decreased debtor earnings on their commodity
exports. The unanticipated reversal in interest payments placed the
debtors in an impossible position; the rise of protectionism against
their manufactured goods aggravated their plight by decreasing their
export earnings. The debtors suddenly found themselves caught between increased interest payments due to the "crowding out" phenomenon caused by the American budget deficit and decreased prices for
their commodity and other exports due to the global recession. The
world debt crisis had arrived.

In brief, the combination of the massive OPEC financial surplus, the
overeagerness of the international private banks (frequently abetted by
their governments) to recycle that surplus, and the multitude of capital-
hungry economies in Eastern Europe and the Third World proved to be
a dangerous mixture. This curious alliance of capitalist bankers hoping
to profit from the accumulated OPEC surplus and the governments of
less developed and East European countries seeking unrestricted financial support for state-directed programs of rapid economic growth
brought the capitalist world to the brink of financial disaster. Although
the tale is complicated and its conclusion has not yet unfolded at this
writing, it is clear that the debt problem introduced a novel and unstable element into the postwar international financial system.

The Debt Problem in the 1980s

Although debts and defaults have been a constant feature of the international economy, the present magnitude of the world debt problem
overwhelms the imagination. The total world debt soared from approximately $100 billion in the early 1970s to nearly $900 billion dollars by the mid-1980s. In *Time* magazine's apt phrase, "never in history
have so many nations owed so much money with so little promise of
repayment" (*Time*, January 10, 1984, p. 42). The liens are held by governments, international organizations, and, most important, scores of
commercial banks in the advanced countries. The heavy debtors, most
of whom have been unable to service their debt, included approximately ten less developed economies in 1985. Brazil ($99 billion), Mex-
ico ($97 billion), and Argentina ($48 billion) were the three largest
debtors (*The Economist,* March 1, 1986, p. 69). In these conditions,
creditor countries fear that the default of a single major debtor could
trigger a financial panic that would bring down the whole edifice of international finance.

Throughout much of the 1970s international finance appeared to be operating reasonably well. Not only did levels of consumption rise in many societies, but the strategy of indebted industrialization promised to provide a new route to rapid development of the LDCs and to reintegration of Eastern bloc countries into the world economy. Commercial banks, in contrast to the IMF and World Bank, imposed few conditions on borrowers. Moreover, less developed countries expected that their dependence on the multinationals would be lessened as the banks provided the capital with which foreign technology could be purchased and import-substituting industries created. The recycling of a massive amount of money gave a Keynesian stimulus to an otherwise depressed world economy and proved a boon to exporters of consumer and capital goods in the advanced countries. LDC exports and receipts rose faster than their debts and interest payments. Optimism reigned; the market worked.

Although lending continued, optimism faded in 1979 with the second oil crisis, produced by the fall of the Shah. Yet another massive increase in the price of energy, the shift of advanced economies to constrictive economic policies that harmed LDC commodity export earnings, and heightened interest rates quickly brought many debtor nations to the brink of bankruptcy. For the largest debtors such as Argentina and Brazil, "the ratio of debt to exports increased by a striking seventy percentage points" from 130 to 200 percent and "interest payments more than doubled as a percentage of exports from 1976 to 1982—from 10 percent to over 20 percent—and reached 50 percent for Argentina and close to that for Brazil" (Hormats, 1984, p. 168).

The shift by the United States to a more restrictive monetary policy in 1979, the spread of global recession, and the energy conservation efforts of the advanced economies produced a third oil shock, a major decline in revenues for oil exporters like Algeria, Nigeria, and Mexico. These countries had gone heavily in debt to finance development projects, subsidize food imports, and expand welfare programs. With the drop in oil revenues they found themselves unable to finance their debt burden.

The global recession, the rise in real interest rates due to the drop in the rate of inflation, and the declining terms of trade for the exports of debtor economies produced the global debt problem and a severe threat to the integrity of the international financial system. The market was unable to manage the escalating crisis. In 1982, with the Mexican economy $86 billion in debt and at the verge of default, optimism gave way to deep pessimism. Drastic and immediate action was clearly required.

The unified strategy of the creditor nations took shape during the Mexican rescheduling crisis of August 1982.[9] Suddenly awakened to the severity of the external threat to the American financial system and realizing that a "market" solution would not work, the Reagan Administration took the leadership in rescuing Mexico and established the pattern that, with some modifications, subsequently has defined the approach of the creditor nations to the problem (Kahler, 1985, p. 369).

The basic creditor strategy has had three key elements: (1) a combination of banks, governments, and international organizations has acted as lender of last resort and provided liquidity to a debtor while the rescheduling of the debt has been negotiated, (2) the debtor has been required to accept a severe adjustment or austerity program, and (3) although other actors and institutions such as the Federal Reserve and the Paris Club of creditor nations have played important roles, the IMF has been given primary responsibility for enforcing adjustment based on the principle of conditionality and for certifying eligibility for financial assistance.[10] Although there have been subsequent modifications in this creditor strategy, its primary principle that the major task in resolving the problem rests with the debtors themselves has not been substantially altered.

In the negotiations between the creditor and debtor nations, the former assumed the lead in defining the nature of the debt problem and its solution. The creditor nations have largely determined the terms on which debts would be rescheduled and the policies to be implemented by the debtors. Despite the threats of some debtors and their champions to form a debtors' cartel, the creditor nations have dominated the situation. What could be a more telling example of the failure of the less developed countries to accomplish their goal of a New International Economic Order?

In effect, the IMF, with the strong support of the creditor nations, asserted international control over the commercial banks and the international financial system as it set the rescheduling terms and the conditions for both debtors and bankers. Through the use of promises and threats on such matters as future access to finance or export markets, the IMF and the creditor coalition defeated calls for a debtors' cartel and easier terms. The creditors successfully imposed their will on the debtors.

The position of the large debtors (mostly Latin American countries),

[9] Kraft (1984) is a useful source on this subject.

[10] The Paris Club is a set of procedures for negotiating debt payment deferrals and other arrangements (Rieffel, 1985, p. 3).

which became known as the "Consensus of Cartagena," was that the debt problem was really a growth problem created by the overly restrictive economic policies of the advanced countries. Their solution was a universal package settlement that avoided severe austerity programs and did not require sacrificing economic growth in the LDCs.[11] Throughout, the debtors have demanded that the responsibility for the problem and for its solution be shared by the creditor countries. They have pushed for lower interest rates, the continuing flow of foreign capital into their economies, and the tying of interest payments to export earnings and ability to pay. The united front of the creditors as well as the weaknesses and division of the debtors, however, have meant that the remedy of the former has prevailed.

The creditor strategy of "cooperation without reform" meant dealing with each debtor on a case-by-case basis rather than attemping to find a systematic overall solution (Kahler, 1985, p. 372). This essentially "divide and conquer" strategy meant that individual debtor nations would be assisted and rewarded by the banks, the IMF, and creditor governments according to their ability and willingness to demonstrate "progress" through implementation of strong austerity measures and other internal reforms. This solution implied, of course, that the major responsibility for causing the debt problem lay with the debtors and also assumed that they had the burden of solving the problem. Consequently, deep resentments have been generated in the debtor countries as living standards have declined and domestic political stability has been threatened.

The creditor approach failed to recognize either the extraordinary nature of the debt problem or its inherent political dangers. It did not take into account the fact that the debtors have, to some extent, been the victims of profound and sweeping changes in relative prices caused by the two oil shocks, the massive increase in the value of the dollar and of global interest rates, and, in the case of oil-exporting debtors, the collapse of energy prices in the mid-1980s. All of these developments have drastically altered the favorable international environment of moderate economic growth, relatively low interest rates, and good export markets that existed when much of the debt was incurred.

Developing economies have of course always borrowed from more advanced economies to finance imports and development projects. In the nineteenth century, British and European capital financed the infrastructure investments of the United States and other "lands of recent settlement"; these lands became in turn major importers of British and

---

[11] This view of the debtors is close to that of Keynes at Bretton Woods.

European manufactures. Despite occasional defaults and panics, the export earnings of productive investments made it possible for most borrowers to repay their debts. Both creditor and debtor benefited.

There is no problem with indebtedness as such, provided that the finance is used productively, the world economy is growing, and creditor economies are open to the exports of debtors. Under these circumstances debtors have no difficulties in repaying their debts. Unfortunately, these ideal conditions did not exist in the 1930s and the system collapsed. Nor, in the final quarter of the century, do conditions assure a solution of the debt problem. Instead, structural features of the international economy along with certain developments have aggravated the problem and made it more difficult to resolve. As a result, a continuing and dangerous international financial instability exists.

The crux of the problem (at least from the perspective of the creditor nations) is the heavy indebtedness of a relatively few countries that are potentially unstable, both economically and politically. The three largest Latin American debtors (Argentina, Brazil, and Mexico) in 1985 owed approximately $260 billion; 40 percent of the $400 billion Latin American debt was held by U.S. banks. Most of these debtors had severe difficulties meeting their interest payments due in large part to the combination of decreased export earnings and higher interest rates; in the mid-1980s, for example, interest payments amounted to almost 40 percent of the annual export earnings of the region (Kuczynski, 1985). In 1985 alone, Brazil and Mexico were scheduled to pay $24 million interest on their debt (*New York Times*, Oct. 3, 1985, p. D6).

Mexico has become the most desperate case. Between 1979 and 1986, its gross external indebtedness actually increased from approximately $40 billion to approximately $100 billion. Its economy was seriously damaged by high inflation and the exodus of massive amounts of capital. Struck by a severe earthquake in 1985 and by collapsing energy prices, Mexico found its financial position slipping from illiquidity toward national insolvency. Only continuous American financial and other support has maintained Mexico's economy. In effect, Mexico has become a ward of its powerful northern neighbor.

Many of the debtors, like Mexico, were harmed by problems of their own making. In some nations excessive taxation and economic mismanagement created "flight capital" in tens of billions of dollars; by some estimates, this flight capital equaled 80 to 100 percent of the loans that those nations assumed. Frequently, these impoverished countries borrowed to finance imported consumption goods and to industrialize at what later appeared to have been too rapid a rate, given the overall state of their economies; too many investment projects were poorly chosen. Most debtors had extraordinary rates of domestic inflation, and this made the economic adjustment required by their creditors and the IMF even more difficult. The increasing number of rescheduled loans, that is, loan packages that have been renegotiated, has revealed the fundamental weakness of the global financial system.

In the nineteenth century, most debt was in the form of bonds issued by hundreds of public and private entities to literally thousands of investors; governments were less involved in the market. By the 1980s, these features had changed in ways that made the financial system more susceptible to destabilization and subject to politicization. The financial markets had become more concentrated and government-regulated. Decentralized bond markets had been replaced by mammoth banking consortia that made loans to relatively few nations. The shift to bank lending has led to the pyramiding of massive and risky bank liabilities on a thin base of assets. These complex financial structures become very fragile indeed and the collapse of one poses a threat to all. Political bargaining and the exercise of power displaces competitive market solutions as the mechanism for resolving the debt problem (Fishlow, 1985).

Furthermore, the overall economic environment has changed in ways that make the resolution of debt problems significantly more difficult. Whereas the era of the gold standard had low rates of inflation and low interest rates, in the 1980s adjustment and rescheduling frequently occurred in extraordinarily inflationary situations; at one point inflation reached 800 percent in Argentina. After 1982 some governments, Mexico for instance, had to ask their people to accept austerity programs not only in order to service their international debts but also to reduce inflation.

At the same time that interest payments were rising and debtors were told to export more in order to repay their debt, advanced countries were closing their markets to LDC goods. In this way the debt problem was greatly aggravated by the macroeconomic policies of the Reagan Administration and the protectionist policies of all the advanced countries. Caught in this vicious cycle, the debtors asked how they could be expected to repay the interest or the debt itself without some relief from their creditors. Whereas previous defaults had been sporadic and non-threatening to the system, the existence of several heavily indebted economies caught between a rising interest burden and decreased income posed a general threat to the overall financial system in the 1980s.

The political context of the debt problem has made the search for compromise solutions more difficult. The domestic and international environment has shifted from the previous relatively automatic operation of the market to a more politicized environment (Kahler, 1985, pp. 365-68). Government regulation of banking and concern for the stability of the domestic financial situation within the creditor nations complicates negotiations with the debtors. With the rise of the welfare state and mass politics, governments in debtor countries risk political suicide when they attempt to meet the austerity and other demands of creditor governments and of the IMF. Domestic political stability is undermined by the increases in unemployment, cutbacks in social programs, and reduced economic growth that follow austerity programs.

With some justification, debtors protest that the banks foisted the money on them and that the governments of the creditor countries permitted this to occur. They argue that both debtors and creditors must therefore make at least equal sacrifices to solve the problem, rather than placing the whole burden upon the debtors in the form of IMF-imposed austerity programs. Debtors have called for solutions that range from reduced interest rates to tying debt repayment to export earnings. These political pressures have elevated the debt issue to the level of international politics, and debt relief has become one of the demands of the LDCs for a New International Economic Order.

Among the issues that required solutions were the following: (1) How should the costs of adjustment be distributed among sovereign debtors, international banks, and the taxpayers of advanced economies? (2) Should the debtor nations pay the full cost as creditor nations appear to believe, because it was their allegedly profligate behavior that brought on the crisis in the first place? Or (3) as many LDC economists and political leaders argue, should a large portion of the costs be borne by the banks and the developed countries whose self-serving policies caused a systemic crisis within international capitalism? Or (4) perhaps the United States, as some critics believe, should pay a disproportionate share of the costs because its fiscal policies were so vital in causing and aggravating the crisis? (5) Could the solution be found in some combination of all the above? These and other highly political issues have been deeply embedded in the economic and technical discussions about such measures as lowering interest rates, tying interest payments to export earnings, or lengthening the payback period, and in the numerous and frequently innovative proposals for solving the debt problem.

However these issues may be resolved in the future, some conclusions regarding the economic and political consequences of the debt problem can be reached. Setting aside the special circumstances of Israel and the African countries, there are in reality three separate and distinct debt problems. One is the problem of the Eastern bloc countries, another is concerned with the Asian NICs, and the third is that of the large Latin American debtors. These specific problems and the varying interests involved in each make it unlikely that a universal or multilateral solution could or would be found. Instead, the solutions (or rather what passes for solutions) have been devised through bilateral and frequently regional negotiations on a case-by-case basis.

Even though the problem of the Eastern bloc debtors has not posed a major threat to the stability of the international financial system, it has been important because it signaled the failure, at least for the moment, of the effort to reintegrate these nations into the world economy. These economies had adopted a strategy of rapid technological modernization through borrowing capital to purchase Western technology and then repaying the debt by exporting manufactured products. Unfortunately, in too many instances they used the borrowed capital and imported technology inefficiently, as, for example, in the case of Poland. The Asian NICs followed a similar strategy of indebted industrialization, but their strategy proved successful and their superior goods soon drove East European goods out of world markets (Poznanski, 1985). Although the Eastern bloc countries will continue to borrow in Western capital markets, prospects remain remote that they will soon again become major participants in the larger world financial and trading systems.

The debt problem of the Asian NICs is more manageable because of the low ratio of debt to GNP. For example, there has been little concern over the servicing and eventual repayment of South Korea's debt because the strategy of indebted industrialization has worked very well there and in other Asian NICs. Net lending to many of these countries was, in fact, resumed in the mid-1980s. Nevertheless, in the United States, the principal international supporter of these countries, strong reservations have existed about a development strategy in which state intervention in the economy plays such a prominent role; many critics have preferred a return to a greater emphasis on American and other multinationals as the vehicle of capital export. American unions and businesses ask why the United States should support the development of industries that would compete against them in their own and world markets. It therefore seems doubtful, for economic and political reasons, that international banks will endlessly continue to finance the strategy of indebted industrialization with the enthusiasm of the past.

As has already been noted, the large Latin American debtors have provided the crux of the debt problem. Together they hold a substantial portion of the total world debt; they have also been the most susceptible to default or actual debt repudiation. Latin American commitment to an import-substitution strategy and state enterprise has generally failed, and these economies have found themselves caught in the impossible situation of being capital exporters, mainly in the form of interest payments on their accumulating debts, to the advanced economies. Since these countries also have had the highest population growth in the world, any cutback in domestic investment promises economic and political disaster.

Although adjustment programs, debt rescheduling, and interest rate or other concessions to particular debtors eased the debt crisis after 1984, the long-term solution may have become even further complicated. Following the depth of the crisis in 1982, the external debt increased at the rate of 30 percent a year to $380 billion in 1984. This increase was due mainly to further borrowings needed to make the interest payments. Although these new loans were mainly from the IMF, the World Bank, and the InterAmerican Development Bank and had lower interest rates with longer maturities than previous loans, they did not address the fundamental long-term problem.

Whereas creditor nations have argued that austerity programs and a revival of world economic growth will eventually solve the problems of the Latin American debtors, the debtors have believed that the advanced capitalist countries must overcome those structural problems of the world economy that are preventing a revival of economic growth. The latter argue that debtors can do little to solve the debt problem unless economic growth revives and interest rates are moderated. Debtors who expected to escape dependency through debt-financed industrialization feel themselves being thrown back into that position while at the same time creditors assert that a major reorientation of LDC economic policy is required and that the debtor nations must move from indebted industrialization and import substitution to an outward-oriented policy, giving a greater role to the MNCs.

In the 1980s many debtors were paying a high price in costs to their economies and in the welfare of their people due to IMF-imposed austerity programs. Although debtor governments strongly resisted these austerity programs and they were not always as austere as alleged by the debtors, the programs bred anti-Americanism and threatened to destroy the unsteady progress of Latin America toward political democracy. Furthermore, they were not really effective, because the total debt was growing faster than export earnings and the ability of the debtors even to service the debt (Bogdanowicz-Bindert, 1985/86, p. 272). Obviously these threatening circumstances required a new and even more radical approach.

At the annual meeting of the IMF–World Bank in Seoul, South Korea, in October 1985, the United States responded to the slow pace of the adjustment programs and to growing concern about their political consequences and put forth what was billed as a new approach to the problem. The so-called Baker plan proposed a three-way bargain among the debtors, the creditor nations, and the large commercial banks in order to reach a solution through economic growth rather than through austerity. The debtors would take steps to open their economies to trade and foreign direct investment, reduce the role of the state in the economy through "privatization," and adopt "supply-side" market-oriented policies. The creditor nations would stimulate their economies and open them to debtor exports, enlarge the role of the World Bank in assisting the debtors, and increase debtor financing, especially for the poorest (mainly African) debtors. The commercial banks would loan billions of new monies to the debtors in order to facilitate the shift to the new policies and increase the overall rate of economic growth.

In this action the United States acknowledged for the first time that the debt crisis was a long-term economic and political problem threatening both the development of the LDCs and world economic recovery (Bogdanowicz-Bindert, 1985/86, p. 259). The plan recognized the need for the exercise of greater American leadership and the infusion of large amounts of external capital into the debtor countries to stimulate their depressed economies. The problem of how this leadership was to be exercised and this capital was to be made available when the United States itself was shifting from the status of creditor to debtor nation and the world had an acute capital shortage was left unresolved.

Of equal importance, however, was the fact that the Baker plan also revealed what the United States and other creditors were *not* prepared to do to solve the debt problem. The creditor approach to the debtors would still be on a case-by-case basis. Although the role of the World Bank would be increased, the IMF would retain its role as the central authority in supervising the policies of the debtors. The creditor governments themselves would not put substantial new amounts of their own money into this scheme. Interest payments on the debt would not be decreased across the board nor would commodity prices received by the debtors be increased. The burden of solving the problem would continue to rest squarely on the debtors and on the hope that a revival of global economic growth would somehow solve the problem. As the Cartagena group complained, the plan did not provide for increased funding and lower interest rates. Thus, the plan did not repudiate the existing strategy of the creditor nations or fundamentally change the situation.

Implementation of the Baker plan will reinforce other developments in trade and monetary relations that will make it increasingly difficult to maintain a liberal international economy. Perhaps the most important effect will be a greater regionalization of the world economy. Despite their conflicts, debtors and creditors in particular regions are drawn together by shared concerns and interests. For economic and political reasons, Western Europe has been most concerned with the Eastern European debtors, and the United States with those of Latin America. European banks have been most heavily exposed in the East; European political and security interests are most at stake in that area. American banks have been most involved in Latin America, and American political worries are strongest there. Japan has taken initiatives to assist South Korea (Strange, 1985c, pp. 250-51). The dominant economic powers are highly motivated to give assistance or trade preferences to their own major debtors. This debt-trade linkage will become an increasingly significant factor in the further regionalization of the world economy and is explored in more detail in Chapter Ten.

The debt problem of the 1980s also meant that international capital flows to many countries were not likely to return to the levels of the 1970s. By the 1980s, the flow of all forms of capital to non-OPEC developing countries had declined dramatically (*The Economist*, March 15, 1986, p. 67). The international financial market has become increasingly segmented with a "fairly clear-cut delineation between credit-worthy borrowers" and the rest, who will have great difficulty borrowing in world financial markets (Sargen, Hung, and Lipsky, 1984, p. 2). There is general recognition, for example, that most Eastern bloc countries lack the capacity to use efficiently the large volume of loans available to them in the past. In the 1980s Latin American debtors were able to borrow only in order to service prior debt. Banks became much more circumspect about making new loans and the governments of creditor countries instituted new regulations that strictly limited foreign loans. Although Asian NICs, "friends" of creditor nations, and lands rich in raw materials will undoubtedly continue to have privileged access to bank loans, a large number of the less developed countries (such as those of tropical Africa) will most certainly not. They will remain almost totally dependent on underfunded official aid. In sum, there will be a contraction in the global supply of capital, and political criteria will play a more important role in international financial decisions. It appears that the tendency toward the politicization and regionalization of the world economy will be accelerated.

It is also likely that the debt problem will continue to be a brake on the growth of international trade and will encourage the already powerful forces of protectionism to spread. Through the 1970s the recycling of Eurocurrencies gave a Keynesian impetus to the world economy, benefiting American exporters particularly. With the developed world then in the depths of recession, debt-financed purchases had a stimulating effect on the international economy. Debtor nations used petro-currencies borrowed through the Euromarket to buy American goods, the United States purchased the exports of other developed and less developed countries, and those countries in turn bought oil, thus returning funds to the Euromarket. In the 1980s the growing reluctance to loan Eurocurrency decreased this global monetary stimulus and had a depressing effect on the overall world economy.

JAPANESE SUBSIDIZATION OF AMERICAN HEGEMONY

Along with the rise of the Eurocurrency market and the onset of the global debt problem, the third extraordinary development in international finance during the postwar period has been the historic reversal of the financial positions of the United States and Japan. This financial turnabout has transformed the political and economic relations of the two dominant capitalist powers. Each for its own reasons entered into a relationship in which the Japanese became the principal underwriters of American hegemony.

By the end of the First World War, the United States had displaced Great Britain as the world's foremost creditor nation. This financial supremacy was consolidated in the interwar period, and at the end of the Second World War the United States became the hegemonic financial power. Although its financial status diminished during the 1970s, the United States retained its dominant financial position until the Reagan Administration. Then, in the 1980s, Japan supplanted the United States as the dominant creditor nation and financial power. Never before in the history of international finance has such a dramatic shift taken place in such a relatively short time.

In 1981, Japan became the world's most important capital exporter. Its huge trade surplus, which rose from about $35 billion in 1983 to over $53 billion in 1985, enabled it to rise rapidly as a financial power. In 1983, Japan's net capital outflow was only $17.7 billion; a year later it had jumped dramatically to $49.7 billion and to an astonishing $64.5 billion in 1985 (*The New York Times*, April 27, 1986, p. 16). This last figure was more than all the OPEC countries at the height of their wealth (ibid., August 31, 1986, p. F7). By 1986, Japan's net assets abroad had risen to $129.8 billion, making it the world's largest creditor nation. Great Britain's net assets abroad were $90 billion and West

Germany's, $50 billion at that time (*The Japan Economic Journal*, June 7, 1986, p. 1). In the same period, the net asset position of the United States was approaching zero.

Although it is true that total OPEC foreign investment in the mid-1980s was substantially larger, it was primarily placed in bank deposits and thus was recycled through the market by Western commercial banks. Japanese overseas investment, however, was heavily in bonds and, as one Japanese bank official put it, "we have direct control over our money" (*Globe and Mail, Report on Business Magazine*, April 1986, p. 28). The four largest banks and six of the top ten in the world are Japanese. These banks as well as other financial institutions and the Japanese government have a significant influence over the disposition of Japan's vast savings, and their power over international finance and the allocation of capital has become formidable indeed. In the mid-1980s the leaders of Japanese finance chose to place a substantial portion of their overseas investments in United States Treasury bonds.[12]

This remarkable transformation of Japan's trading and financial position had begun in the early 1970s when, responding to the OPEC price increase, Japan drastically cut its oil consumption, expanded its exports to pay for the increased cost of energy, and accelerated the speed at which it scaled the technology ladder. In addition, several important features Japan's economy contributed to its massive trade and payments surplus. They include its high savings rate (about 18 percent in the mid-1980s) in combination with reduced domestic investment, the high productivity of Japanese industry, and the shift in the mid-1970s to a policy of economic contraction and export-led growth (Yoshitomi, 1985). The unusual structure of Japanese trade—the exporting of high value-added manufactured products and the importing of unprocessed commodities—meant that Japan was ultimately the principal beneficiary of the glut and price collapse of food, oil, and other commodities that occurred in the 1980s. These developments produced a "structural" surplus in Japan's trade and payments balances.

Using Marxist language, one could say that Japan in the mid-1980s had become a mature capitalist economy afflicted by the classic problems of underconsumption and surplus capital. It could not absorb the huge quantity of goods its factories turned out, nor could it find productive uses at home for its accumulating capital surplus. The causes of

[12] Although it is certainly the case that Japanese financial institutions invested in the United States because of interest rate differentials and other market considerations, the discretionary power of the Japanese, as revealed by past experience, is not to be denied.

this underconsumption and falling rate of profit on domestic invest-ment, however, had much more to do with internal Japanese politics than with the inevitable laws of the motion of capitalism. If the interests of the ruling Liberal Democratic Party had been different, Japan could easily have used the capital to improve the quality of Japanese life. Un-willing to make the needed domestic reforms, Japanese capitalism therefore required a "colony" to rid itself of these financial surpluses. The Japanese found this "vent for surplus" in an America experiment-ing with Reaganomics; the new "Japanese Co-Prosperity Sphere" was to be located across the Pacific Ocean in Ronald Reagan's America.[13]

At the same time that Japan was becoming a creditor nation, the United States was becoming a debtor nation. In 1981, the United States had succeeded in arresting the post-Vietnam deterioration of its inter-national economic position; it had a surplus in its current account ($6.3 billion) and its repatriated net earnings on foreign investments had reached their zenith ($34 billion); this was to be, however, the last year of an American surplus in the current account (Council of Economic Advisers, 1986, p. 366). By 1985, this favorable situation had been re-versed and the United States had become a net debtor for the first time since 1914. Between 1982 and 1984, foreign lending by American banks dropped dramatically, from $111 billion to approximately $10 billion (Emminger, 1985, p. 9). In 1984, the United States borrowed approximately $100 billion (ibid., p. 7). In that same year it had an his-torically unprecedented trade deficit of $108.3 billion, of which $34 billion was with Japan! By the end of 1985, the United States had be-come the world's largest debtor and had borrowed abroad over $100 billion in that year alone, a sum larger than the total Brazilian debt. In the mid-1980s, the United States was borrowing approximately $100-120 billion net each year and foreign holdings of American government securities soared. Projections of future borrowing indicated that by the end of the decade, the American foreign debt could reach $1 trillion. The world's richest country in less than five years had reversed a cen-tury-long trend and become the world's most indebted nation (Drob-nik, 1985, p. 1).

The immediate cause of this historic shift in the financial position of the United States was located in the tax and fiscal policies of the Reagan Administration. A massive tax cut without a complementary reduction of the expenditures of the federal government had resulted in a huge and continuing budget deficit. This deficit subsequently gave a power-

[13] Calder (1985) presents an excellent summary of the developing economic ties across the Pacific.

ful fiscal or Keynesian stimulus to the American and, to a lesser extent, the world economy. Inadequate American savings, however, meant that the United States had to finance the budget deficit through borrowing heavily in world capital markets. From 1981 on, the resulting overvalued dollar and the increase in world interest rates led to the gigantic American trade deficit and greatly aggravated the global debt crisis.

What Reaganomics Phase Two (i.e., following its induced recession) actually entailed was an economic recovery financed by foreign creditors. As pointed out by E. Gerald Corrigan, President of the Federal Reserve Bank of New York, "we are vitally dependent on foreign savings flows" that directly or indirectly are "financing half or more of the budget deficit" (quoted in *The New York Times*, November 7, 1985, p. D1). The expansionary economic policies, domestic albeit reduced investment, and the unprecedented defense buildup of the Reagan Administration were possible because they were financed by other nations.

The three largest sources of this capital were the world's surplus savers: certain Arab OPEC producers (mainly Saudi Arabia), West Germany and, in particular, Japan. Whereas the Japanese gross purchases of Treasury bonds amounted to only $197 million in 1976, in April 1986 alone the figure was $138 billion (*The New York Times*, July 28, 1986, p. D6). Of the $81.8 billion that Japan invested abroad in 1985, $53.5 billion went into bonds, particularly U.S. Treasury issues (ibid., April 27, 1986, p. 16). In the mid-1980s, the Japanese were supplying a substantial fraction of the $100-120 billion borrowed annually by the United States government and were investing heavily in all types of American assets. Without this immense flow of Japanese capital into the American economy, the Reagan Administration could not have simultaneously stimulated American domestic consumption and commenced the largest military expansion in peacetime American history. If there had been no flow of foreign capital into the economy, the Administration would have either had to decrease defense expenditures sharply or permit the increase in the domestic interest rate to cut short the economic recovery.

The importance of Japanese finance to the success of President Reagan's economic and defense program may be appreciated by contrasting it with an earlier event. In October 1979, West German unwillingness to support the dollar and to import American inflation was a vital factor in causing the United States to change its domestic economic policy and to shift to a tight monetary policy. The Federal Reserve contracted the money supply and caused the recession that helped elect

Ronald Reagan. This was the first time in the postwar era that the United States made a major change in its domestic economic policy in response to foreign pressures. In the economic realm, this policy reversal was the end of American hegemony. Henceforth, the United States required the financial backing of the Japanese.[14]

By the mid-1980s, Japan had replaced West Germany as America's principal economic ally and the financial backer of the continued economic and political hegemony of the United States. Japanese investment of their savings and of the nation's huge payments surplus in the United States supported the dollar, helped finance the defense buildup, and contributed to American prosperity. More importantly it masked the relative economic decline of the United States. Japanese financial assistance enabled the American people to postpone, at least for a time, the difficult task of coming to terms with the classic problem that faces every declining power, that is, determining how to bring its power and commitments back into a state of economic and political equilibrium (Gilpin, 1981, p. 187).

Thus, by the mid-1980s, the world monetary and financial system based on the dollar had become largely underwritten by Japanese capital. The greatly overvalued dollar would have declined and perhaps collapsed in value as a consequence of the Reagan Administration's economic policies had it not been for this Japanese financial backing. The title of a monograph, *The Dollar's Borrowed Strength* (1985), by Otmar Emminger, a distinguished German central banker, portrayed the situation only too accurately.

The principal reason for this flow of Japanese capital into American Treasury bills was the sharp increase in the difference between American and Japanese real interest rates; the Japanese had opened and liberalized their capital nearly simultaneously with the American tax cuts and budget deficit (Calder, 1985, pp. 607-608). Differential interest rates, however, do not tell the whole story. The intensifying political relationship between Ronald Reagan's America and Yasuhiro Nakasone's Japan was certainly an important factor in the eagerness of the Japanese to invest in the United States. This developing global partnership was reinforced by the symbiotic interests of a United States living

[14] The specific change was a shift away from efforts to control interest rates to the setting of monetary growth targets in order to achieve tighter discipline over the money supply and inflation rate. Former Secretary of the Treasury Michael Blumenthal has suggested that the appropriate date for the change in the American economic position is a year earlier, in November 1978. The fear of a run on the dollar led to a rise in the discount rate and a slowing of the economy.

far beyond its means and a Japan in dire need of foreign markets and outlets for surplus capital.

The special American-Japanese financial relationship had been codified in the May 1984 report of the Japan-U.S. Yen-Dollar Committee on the liberalization and internationalization of the Japanese financial system (Yoshitomi, 1985, p. 18). The committee had been established at the time of President Reagan's visit to Tokyo in November 1983. Although the ostensible purpose of the committee and its recommendations was to correct the misalignment of the yen, the core and significance of the agreement was to open up Japanese financial markets and give the United States and other foreigners greater access to Japanese capital. It also increased the international role of the yen and thus accelerated Tokyo's emergence as a major financial center and the movement toward a tripartite monetary system based on the dollar, the yen, and the Deutschmark.[15]

This agreement, comparable to the Tripartite Monetary Agreement of 1936, which laid the basis for the postwar financial cooperation of the United States and Great Britain, resulted from American pressures on the Japanese to open their financial markets and make certain reforms within their economy (Fukushima, 1985, pp. 30-31). The United States appears to have had several motives in pressuring Japan to deregulate and open up its financial system: the belief that greater international use of the yen would cause the yen to appreciate and thereby decrease Japanese exports, the expectation that Japanese business would lose the competitive advantage provided by low interest rates and capital costs, and the desire to open up the vast reservoir of Japanese domestic savings to American financial institutions.[16] The Reagan Administration believed that the United States had a comparative advantage in financial services (as Japan did in manufacturing) and that American competition in financial and related services would enable the United States to reestablish the economic balance between the two countries (McRae, 1985, pp. 21-22). Thus, the agreement was a key element in the Reagan Administration policies toward Japan and for managing the American financial deficit.

The agreement was effective in stabilizing U.S.-Japanese relations as American pressures on Japan to increase its military role were muted and the Reagan Administration intensified its resistance to protectionist legislation. Japan and the United States had established a special re-

---

[15] Frankel (1984) is a good analysis of this agreement.

[16] Why important members of the Reagan Administration believed that an increased capital outflow from Japan would cause the yen to rise was a mystery to most economists.

lationship that reflected their respective strengths and political concerns. As Peter Drucker has pointed out, the American-Japanese economic relationship in the mid-1980s was extraordinary (*The Wall Street Journal*, Oct. 11, 1985, p. 28). One key element was that the United States borrowed its own currency from the Japanese as well as from others. The scale and significance of this situation were unprecedented in international finance. "For the first time a debtor nation stands to benefit both on its capital account and on its trading account from devaluing its currency" (ibid.). With the devaluation of the dollar the United States would in effect expropriate and wipe out a substantial fraction of its debt; the drop of the dollar between March 1985 and March 1986, in fact, may have reduced the debt by as much as one third. Simultaneously, the devaluation of the dollar would regain markets that the United States had lost because of the greatly overvalued dollar.

The Japanese, by loaning dollars back to the United States, were maintaining their most valuable export market and preventing domestic unemployment; over 10 percent of Japanese jobs are tied to exports. Domestic demand in Japan has been weak because of the reluctance to stimulate the economy by increasing the already huge budget deficit. Losing the American market would have severe repercussions in strategic and high-technology industries. The actual and potential losers in this curious form of mercantilism have been both American producers, who lose their markets to Japanese exporters, and frugal Japanese savers, who will receive devalued dollars.

Despite the short-term benefits of this symbiotic American-Japanese relationship, its long-term prospects are problematic. It is doubtful that the United States and the other advanced countries will be able to support the pressures placed on them by Japan's mammoth trade and capital surplus. Previously, Great Britain and the United States had graduated from debtor to creditor status through a generally low rate of capital accumulation over a period of decades (except for the impact of World War One on the American position). Moreover, as creditor economies, they were also major importers of the industrial exports of other economies. However, Japan's rapidity of change from debtor to creditor and the immense scale of Japan's capital outflow have been extraordinary, forcing equally rapid and large changes on other economies. In addition, the structure of Japanese trade as an importer of raw materials and an exporter of industrial products has placed a further burden of adjustment on the United States and Western Europe. Although successful adjustment by the other industrial economies to Japan's new international economic role will ultimately depend on a return to a high rate of world economic growth, the pace set by Japan's rapid advances in comparative advantage and the structure of its trade will continue to cause a severe strain under any circumstances.

The alarm, especially in the American Rustbelt, over Japan's increasing trading and financial strength greatly intensified in the 1980s. Americans became concerned over the fact, as one business economist quipped, "not only are our cars made in Japan, but increasingly so are our interest rates" (quoted in *The Wall Street Journal*, February 24, 1986, p. 1). Others took note of the fact that a growing segment of American securities, real estate, and other tangible assets were in Japanese or other foreign hands. In the words of U.S. Secretary of State George Shultz, "I think one could say that, if the world were content to let the Japanese provide a major share of the savings and wind up owning more and more, it's O.K. But that is not the way the United States, at least, is oriented" (quoted in *The New York Times*, February 12, 1986, p. D2). The Secretary failed to add that it was the policies of the Reagan Administration that had created this unfortunate situation.

Nevertheless, although some concern was expressed over the budget and trade deficits in the mid-1980s, the general consensus in the United States was one of optimism. The stock market was bullish and the Reagan Administration announced that the scourge of inflation had been eliminated. As for the long-term problem of the vast accumulated debt to the Japanese and other foreign creditors, optimistic sentiment was well expressed in the view of one former high official that we simply "run the clock backwards," that is, the United States would devalue the dollar and achieve a trade surplus with which to repay the debt. According to the former Chairman of the Council of Economic Advisers, Martin Feldstein (1986, p. 4), the United States would require a balance-of-trade surplus of about $100 billion per year for a number of years to retire the accumulated foreign debt.

The problems that such a turnaround in the American trading position would cause for other nations would be considerable. Such a reversal in world trade would necessitate a considerable devaluation of the dollar along with an appreciation of other currencies. Past experience has taught both the Japanese and the West Europeans to resist strongly any large appreciations of their currencies because of its consequences for domestic levels of unemployment. At the least, considerable international cooperation over macroeconomic policy will be required if a devastating mercantilistic conflict over trade is to be avoided. Prospects for such cooperation are discussed in the concluding chapter of this book.

The notion that policies can be reversed and the clock can be turned back betrays the great faith that American economists and policy makers have in the liberal conception of market equilibrium. In the abstract world of American economists, equations run both ways; they believe that by changing the sign of a variable from plus to minus or from minus to plus or the price and quantity of x or y, the direction of historical movement can be reversed. Similarly, many believe that the damage to the international economy done by the Reagan Administration budget deficit can be set right simply by changing one price, the price of the dollar.

This overly sanguine view of the predicament of the United States in the latter part of the 1980s ignores a number of structural changes, to be discussed in detail in Chapter Nine, that have taken place in the American and world economies. Suffice it to say here that the importation of huge amounts of foreign capital and the consequently overvalued dollar have had profound and long-lasting effects on the American economy. First, the competitive position of important sectors of the American economy has been permanently damaged and the structure of the entire economy has been distorted (Emminger, 1985, p. 17). Second, repayment of the immense external debt and the associated interest payments will absorb a large share of America's productive resources for many years to come; these costs will substantially lower the standard of living for a considerable period, even if defense expenditures are considerably curtailed. And, third, the newly acquired preference of Americans for foreign goods and the expansion of productive capacity abroad have decimated many industries in which the United States once had a strong comparative advantage; America will be required to develop new products and industries if it is to regain even part of its former competitive position in world markets. The task of reversing the trends toward deindustrialization will be difficult and very costly.[17]

The Nichibei Economy and Its Prospects

The Reagan fiscal deficit and the world economic cycle to which it gave rise, as shown in Figure 2, have caused a fundamental transformation of the international political economy. As the United States has descended to the status of international debtor and the high dollar has accelerated the de-industrialization of the American economy, the Japanese have used their massive balance-of-payments surplus to finance

[17] Feldstein (1986) provides a frank appraisal of the damage to capital formation and other aspects of the American economy caused by the economic policies of the Administration.

the creation of the Nichibei economy, that is, the increased integration of the American and Japanese economies. Although the Japanese economic penetration of the American economy began much earlier, the policies of the Reagan Administration have driven and hastened this structural change. The intensification of Japanese investment in the American economy, the expansion of corporate alliances among American and Japanese firms, and related developments have made the Nichibei economy the key economic relationship in the world.

The long-term consequences of the creation of the Nichibei economy and its implications for the international political economy cannot be foreseen at this juncture. Many questions can be asked, however, regarding its stability, its effect on other economies, and especially with respect to the fundamental political question of who will become more dominant over whom. As Kent Calder has effectively argued, powerful interests in the United States and Japan favor the continuation and strengthening of the partnership, but significant sources of cleavage and conflict also exist (Calder, 1985). In the 1980s, powerful groups in both countries have needed one another. How long this mutually beneficial relationship will last has yet been determined.

Although this dependence upon Japanese and other foreign financing has been vital to the American economy and the international position of the United States in the short term, in the long term continuing dependence will further weaken American power and strengthen the Japanese. The United States therefore finds itself caught in a vicious cycle. On the one hand, it requires foreign capital to finance its budget deficit. On the other hand, the availability of foreign capital causes a greatly overvalued dollar that decreases the competitiveness of the American economy and weakens its industrial base. A weakened economy in turn increases the need for foreign capital, and the drain of interest payments further undermines the competitiveness of the economy. The most serious threat in this situation is that the competitiveness and industrial base of the American economy may erode to such a point that the process of economic decline cannot be reversed.

Perhaps the dollar should not be yardstick of system.

Doubts have also arisen on the Japanese side of the American-Japanese special relationship, and many fear an American political backlash. A number of political and economic leaders have begun to ask whether it is in the long-term interest of Japan to finance American prosperity and an international hegemony whose primary concerns are different from Japan's. The view that Japan could make better use of its newly gained financial power and emergent role as a financial center was expressed in a report by the influential Nomura Research Institute. In response to the question of what the role of the Tokyo international

337

financial center should be in the future, the report saw four important objectives:

First, the Tokyo market should be the base market for yen financing and yen investment. Second, Tokyo should become a major financing place for multinational companies, governments, and supranational institutions. Third, Tokyo should be an information center for the international portfolio management. Fourth, Tokyo should be the core international financial center for the Western Pacific Region, channeling globally traded funds into regional markets. Fifth, Tokyo should be a supply source of innovative ideas in the financial sector, contributing to efficient global funds allocations" (Nomura Research Institute, 1986b, p. 179).

In brief, Japan should establish itself as the financial hegemon of the fastest-growing region in the world and not merely subsidize American hegemony.

If Japan should continue to perform as it has in the past and becomes one of the principal financial centers in the world, how would it use the power that accompanies this role? What would its relations be with the two other major financial centers in London and New York? Would Japan continue to support the dollar, or would it ally itself with Western Europe (McRae, 1985, p. 18)? In an era of global capital shortage, would the Japanese use their financial resources to acquire leadership of the debt-ridden Third World, to strengthen their ties with other advanced economies, or, as the Nomura Research Institute implies, to carve an economic sphere of influence in the Pacific? Would they finance the development of China or Soviet Siberia? Whatever decisions the Japanese make regarding the use of their growing financial power will have profound significance for the future of the international economic and political system.

In the mid-1980s, the Japanese decided to use their financial resources to support the United States. This was partially for commercial reasons, to create a market for Japanese exports, and partly due to the attractiveness of high American interest rates. But in the long run, political concerns and interests will determine the willingness of Japan to continue financial support of American hegemony and prosperity. One political and psychological problem is that such a relationship converts the American military into a mercenary force defending Japan in return for Japanese capital. Yet U.S. pressures on the Japanese to assume a greater share of the defense burden have been deeply resented by the latter.[18] Unless the larger political and security relations of the two al-

---

[18] One could in fact argue that Japanese purchase of American government securities was tantamount to burden-sharing. American complaints over the issue appear to have

lies are placed on a more firm foundation, the economic ties are not likely to continue indefinitely.

CONCLUSION

International finance has probably been the most controversial and vulnerable aspect of international political economy, from Lenin's denunciation of *haut finance* as the cause of imperialism and world war to criticisms in the 1980s by less developed countries of international banks and official aid. The crisis of the world financial system in the 1930s brought about the collapse of the world economy in the Great Depression. At the end of the twentieth century the debt problems of the LDCs again threaten the world with a financial crisis that could lead to the collapse of the world economy and the intensification of economic nationalism.

The postwar era has witnessed three historic developments in the global financial system. The first was the emergence of the Eurocurrency market, which weakened international political control over the financial system. The second was the sudden onset of the global debt crisis in the early 1980s and the effort to reassert IMF influence. And the third was the dramatic shift of the United States to the status of a debtor and the conversion of Japan into the principal financial power. This last development transformed the nature of the international financial and, it should be added, political system. These developments raise profound issues concerning the future stability and political consequences of the international financial system.

The task of managing the international financial system in general and the debt problem in particular has become much more complex than in the past (Kahler, 1985, pp. 361-62). Under the previously prevailing philosophy of laissez faire, defaults and adjustments in debts, however painful, were considered to be a natural part of the market system. Today, there are more numerous and powerful constituencies, capable of resisting adjustments, in both creditor and debtor countries. Few are disposed to leave the resolution of the problem up to the market, with the result that financial issues are quickly politicized.

As Joanne Gowa has noted, the United States has lost interest in performing its hegemonic "responsibilities" unless its own immediate vital interests are involved (Gowa, 1983). The United States has generally abandoned its role of managing the international monetary system, and

---

decreased following the May 1984 yen-dollar agreement. Whether or not an explicit connection existed, the security and financial relations of these two allies are closely tied.

the Reagan Administration has responded to the debt crisis only when the stability of the American banking system has been clearly at stake. Despite its continuing role as engine of growth for the rest of the world, the United States has become a burden on the system.

The greatest puzzle in the field of international finance involves the possible consequences for the world economy of the transformed status of the United States and the dollar in the international system. In time the effects of this change in status and a weakened dollar will surely alter America's perceptions of its interests and relations with other countries. As a debtor the United States must necessarily achieve an export surplus in order to finance and eventually repay its debts, but one must ask what it will export and to whom, especially given the mercantilistic export-led growth strategies of so many other countries. In a world composed of an increasingly closed European Community and a Japan with a very low propensity to import manufactured goods and with high barriers against many American agricultural products, it is unclear where the United States will find export markets. American trade with the LDCs, which expanded rapidly in the 1970s, slowed with the debt crisis; trade with the Soviet bloc has been restricted for political reasons. As the United States adjusts to its new role as a debtor, relations with these and other economic actors must inevitably change.

American mismanagement of its own internal affairs and of the international financial system has caused the responsibilities of the financial hegemon to fall largely upon the Japanese. Historically, the world's leading financial power has assumed two major responsibilities: to allocate capital to those regions and industries that will use it most efficiently and to be the "lender of last resort," safeguarding the system against a financial crisis. Great Britain performed this role well in the nineteenth century and, for a time, so did the United States in the twentieth. Now it is Japan's turn at financial leadership. The future of the transformed international economy will depend on whether or not Japan assumes this role and performs it skillfully.

The Transformation of the Global Political Economy

T HE ECONOMIC era from the end of the Second World War until the 1980s was one of the most remarkable in human history. Following a period of reconstruction in the 1950s, there was an unprecedented rate of economic growth during the decade of the 1960s and the early years of the 1970s. During the approximately forty-year period the world gross national product tripled. International economic interdependence in trade, monetary relations, and foreign investment advanced at an ever more rapid pace, leading to speculations and theories regarding the long-term consequences of these developments. Mankind, liberals argued, was being integrated into a global market economy in which state and national boundaries were losing economic or political significance.

By the mid-1980s, however, this liberal dream of an expanding world economy organized in terms of a self-regulating market had been shattered. In the 1970s, the novel phenomenon of "stagflation"—the combination of a low rate of economic growth, mass unemployment, and double digit inflation—had replaced rapid and stable economic growth. This was followed by the greatly reduced rate of global economic growth in the 1980s. The achievements of successive rounds of trade liberalization were being eroded by the spread of nontariff barriers and various forms of economic protectionism, the international monetary system was in a state of disarray, and the stability of the global financial structure was threatened by the mammoth debt problems of the less developed economies. International economic interdependence began a continuing retreat on many fronts.

Efforts to understand and explain this incredible reversal of global economic fortunes and its implications for the future of the international political economy have preoccupied scholars, business executives, and public officials. Despite the proliferation of contending theories and interpretations ranging the ideological spectrum from rational expectations theorists on the right to Marxists on the left, observers have in essence fallen into two major modes of analysis, the conjunctural and the structural positions. Few analysts can be placed

341

completely within one position or the other, yet two differing groups can be identified.

The conjunctural position maintains that the world economy has been buffeted by a series of exogenous shocks and by irresponsible economic management (OECD, 1977). These external and disastrous developments include the inflationary impact of the Vietnam War, the two massive increases in the cost of petroleum (1973-1974 and 1979-1980), and the American budget deficit. Although proponents of this school of thought acknowledge that economic activities are hampered by the existence of a number of secular or long-term trends such as the increasing role of the state in the economy and the decline of the growth of productivity in many economies, they argue that bad luck or policy failures have been of primary importance in accounting for the post-1973 poor performance of the world economy. With more enlightened policies, it could be set right and returned to the path of stable and non-inflationary economic growth. The process of increasing economic interdependence would then begin once again.

In opposition to this somewhat benign view, the structural position argues that a number of significant political, economic, and technological changes have altered the structure and functioning of the international economy. These developments, which range from the relative decline of the American economy to profound shifts in supply and demand conditions, are said to have brought about a fundamental transformation in the character of the world economy. As a consequence of these structural changes, it will be very difficult, if not impossible, to return to the high levels of economic growth and global interdependence of the past unless new arrangements for managing the world economy can be found.

As in most such debates, there is merit in both positions. On the one hand, it is certainly the case that a conjuncture of unfortunate events and reckless policies did send the world economy sharply off course in the 1970s, and one would be foolhardy indeed to suggest that wise policy choices could not set it on course again. On the other hand, it would be equally vain to disregard the profound structural changes that had occurred by the mid-1980s, which will make this task exceptionally difficult. To understand the significance of these developments for the international political economy, one must begin with an examination of the fundamental causes of the remarkable success of the postwar economy and how those causes have been affected by structural changes. Only in this way is it possible to gain a perspective on these matters and to appreciate how the combination of conjunctural and structural factors have produced the global economic problem.

STRUCTURAL CHANGES IN THE INTERNATIONAL POLITICAL ECONOMY

The extraordinary performance of the world economy in the postwar era may be attributed to three principal features. The first was the favorable political environment, the second was the existence of beneficial supply factors, and the third was high demand. It was, in fact, these structural factors that made economic policy so very successful. By the same token, the changes in these structural conditions beginning in the 1970s have complicated the policy task of overcoming the contemporary problems of the world political economy.

The Rise and Decline of American Hegemony

The United States emerged from the Second World War as the dominant or hegemonic economic and military power in the international system. This unchallenged American preeminence was partially due to the wartime destruction of other industrial economies. From this perspective, the commanding nature of American leadership in the early postwar period was "abnormal" and would one day decline with the recovery of other economies. This artificial situation, however, caused false and extraordinarily high economic expectations among the American people that continued into the 1980s and made adjustment to economic and political decline extremely difficult. It also encouraged the United States to assume international obligations that discouraged its allies from making appropriate contributions to the maintenance of the international economic and political order, obligations that were beyond its own capabilities over the long term.[1]

At the conclusion of the war the United States was committed for economic and political reasons to the revival of a liberal international economy. Subsequently, the political and security ties between the United States and its principal West European and Japanese allies provided the political framework within which the liberal world market economy could operate with relative ease. In the interest of alliance coherence both the United States and its allies were generally willing to subordinate their short-term and parochial interests to the good of the whole.

American leadership and the alliance framework provided a secure and stable basis for the development of global economic relations. For the first time ever, all the capitalist economies were political allies. American initiatives in the area of trade led to successive rounds of tariff liberalization. The dollar served as the basis of the international

---

[1] Oye, Lieber, and Rothchild (1983, ch. 1) is an excellent evaluation of these costs.

monetary system, while American foreign aid, direct investment, and technology facilitated the rapid development of advanced and certain less developed economies. Perhaps, however, the greatest American contribution to the revival and success of a liberal international economy was political and psychological. The United States assumed the defense burden of the industrial democracies, thus enabling the West Europeans and especially the Japanese to concentrate their energies and resources on economic development. American hegemony provided the favorable environment within which supply and demand forces created an era of unprecedented growth and an increasingly open international economy.

In contrast to the century-long Pax Britannica, the era of American hegemony lasted but a few decades. Its demise began with the shift to what would become excessive Keynesian policies and the escalation of the Vietnam War in the 1960s. By the mid-1980s, the evidence supporting the relative decline of the American economy had become overwhelming (Ilgen, 1985). In the early 1950s, the United States, with 6 percent of total world population, accounted for approximately 40 percent of the gross world product; by 1980, the American share had dropped by half to approximately 22 percent (Oye and Gilpin, 1986, p. 14). Whereas the United States in the early postwar period produced 30 percent of world manufacturing exports, by 1986 its share had dropped to a mere 13 percent. American productivity growth, which had outpaced the rest of the world for decades, declined dramatically from a growth rate of 3 percent annually in the early postwar years to an incredible low of .8 percent in the 1970s (Sawhill and Stone, 1984, p. 73). As American productivity lagged behind that of other advanced economies, particularly Japan, West Germany, and the NICs, the result was a less competitive economy and a substantial lowering of the American standard of living. In capital formation, technological leadership, and the quality of the labor force (human capital), the United States was falling behind in a growing field of industrial competitors. Even in the raw materials, which throughout its history had been a source of competitive strength, the United States was decreasingly self-sufficient (Rosenberg, 1977); only in agriculture and certain high technology industries did the United States retain its previously unsurpassed economic strengths (Maddison, 1982, p. 41). By the mid-1980s, in almost every other category of economic power the position of the United States had declined greatly.[2]

---

[2] In the mid-1980s, a number of writers denied that there was any decline of American power. Although this was true in absolute terms, in relative terms the decline was incon-

The events that first signify the transformation of the global position of the American economy took place in 1973. During this period, the United States lost control first over the world monetary system with the breakdown of Bretton Woods and the shift to flexible rates and second over the world energy market. Whereas the crucial action in the first case was West Germany's refusal to continue its support of the troubled dollar and its decision to assume greater monetary leadership in the European Community, in the second, it was OPEC's. For the first time in the postwar era, American economic well-being and macroeconomic policy were substantially undercut by actions of foreign governments.

By the 1980s, American hegemonic leadership and the favorable political environment that it had provided for the liberal world economy had greatly eroded. Although the United States continued to be the dominant economic and military power, its relative decline profoundly affected the role that it could and would play in the international economy and its relations with other economies. Critical problems of the world economy in the areas of trade, money, and debt were left unresolved. As its power declined, American policies became more self-centered and increased the conflicts between the United States and other countries.

Beginning with the Vietnam War and continuing into the Reagan Administration, the United States had become more of a "predatory hegemon," to use John Conybeare's term (1985), less willing to subordinate its own interests to those of its allies; instead, it tended more and more to exploit its hegemonic status for its own narrowly defined purposes. American economic policy, in the eyes of many foreigners, shifted from one of benign to malign neglect. America's exploitation of its dominant economic position was increasingly resented by its economic partners; yet they themselves were unable or unwilling to assume a greater share of the responsibilities of managing the system and were pursuing their own narrowly defined nationalistic goals.

The policies of the Reagan Administration accelerated the deteriorating long-term economic position of the United States. Despite the emphasis of the Reagan Administration on supply-side economics and raising the rate of national savings and domestic investment, both declined dramatically throughout that Administration, while the ratio of debt to GNP reached an unprecedented and disturbing level.[3] Between

---

testable. What these writers appeared to be saying was that American influence still continued to be too strong and, in their judgment, was detrimental to the rest of the world.

[3] Although this ratio was not as high as that in some other societies, it was of greater significance given the scale and importance of the American economy in the world.

1980 and 1985, the necessity of financing the budget deficit of $200 billion or more annually caused the American savings rate to drop from approximately 17 to 12 percent; during this same period the personal savings rate plunged to a postwar low of 4 percent and at times even lower. (In contrast, the Japanese savings rate has continued to be closer to 20 percent and, by some estimates, has been as high as 30 percent.) This $200 billion or so reduction of national savings per year was balanced by reduced domestic investment and foreign borrowing.

The budget deficit also meant a serious decline in capital accumulation (Feldstein, 1986, pp. 2-3). In absorbing more than half of all national savings, it raised interest rates and "crowded out" domestic investment; the rate of capital accumulation declined from about 17.5 percent of the GNP in 1979 to 16.2 percent in 1985. The long-term effect of this $1.6 trillion decline in private capital accumulation meant "a loss of $160 billion a year in perpetuity" (ibid., p. 3). The consequences of this decreased accumulation was lower productivity growth, accelerated deindustrialization of the American economy, and a significantly lower standard of living in the future. Through paying lower taxes in the 1980s and borrowing abroad, Americans have consumed more but will one day have to pay the bill in the form of higher taxes, renewed inflation, or, more likely, some combination of the two.

Contrary to the supply-side theory of the Reagan Administration, the American people responded to the tax cut by going more deeply into debt rather than by increasing their savings. The economic recovery was accompanied and in fact propelled by the accumulation of private, public, and foreign debt. Between 1980 and the end of 1985, total outstanding debt (public and private) nearly doubled from $4.3 to $8.2 trillion; in 1985, it increased 15 percent over 1984, whereas the GNP rose only 2.3 percent (*The New York Times*, April 30, 1986, p. D2). The situation was characterized by Leonard Silk in dramatic terms:

Total outstanding debt in the United States has more than doubled in the past seven years, increasing from $3.3 trillion at the end of 1977 to $7.1 trillion by the end of 1984. While the Federal debt was rising by $754 billion during that period, private debt was climbing by $2.3 trillion.

In just the past two years, total debt outstanding increased by nearly $1.5 trillion. In the final quarter of 1984, total debt, private and public, was climbing at an annual rate of $1 trillion for the first time in history. Last year the Federal government borrowed $198.8 billion to finance its deficit while private business and households added $535 billion to their debts" (*The New York Times*, September 4, 1985, p. D2).

During the first five years of the Reagan Administration, the national debt approached the $2.0 trillion level (*The New York Times*, September 22, 1985, p. E5). By the year 1990, it could reach approximately $2.3 trillion or 40 percent of GNP and, assuming 1986 interest rates, the interest payments will have increased by $200 billion and by 1990 would take 40 percent of all personal income taxes (Feldstein, 1986, p. 2). The United States was mortgaging its future to a degree unknown in world history. The level of private, public, and foreign debt of the American people and the costs of servicing this debt became, in the words of the President of the Federal Reserve Bank of New York, "unprecedented" and threatening to the financial stability of the United States and the rest of the world (Corrigan, 1985). As had been the case with other declining powers in the past, the United States had indulged itself in overconsumption and underinvestment for too long.

Because national savings along with raw materials, technology, and human skills constitute the productive resources of an economy, the possibilities of negative long-term consequences of this profligate behavior by the American people and their government became alarming. Americans were consuming the source of their national wealth and that of other societies as well rather than putting it into productive investments. Economists began to worry that the interest payments to foreign creditors would plunge the United States into a vicious cycle from which it could not easily escape; like many LDC debtors, it would have to go ever deeper into debt to service compounding interest payments. If this meant that interest payments to foreigners would eventually exceed American export and other earnings from abroad, then further borrowing would be necessary to finance debt servicing and it would become very difficult indeed for the United States to arrest its economic and political decline.

In the closing decades of the twentieth century the United States has found itself caught between its many commitments and decreased power, the classic position of a declining hegemon (Gilpin, 1981, p. 187). As Soviet military power expanded, the United States had assumed increased costs to maintain its hegemonic political and military position; simultaneously the rise of new industrial competitors and the loss of former economic monopolies in energy, technology, and agriculture had decreased the capacity of the United States to finance its hegemony. With a decreased rate of economic growth and a low rate of national savings, the United States was living and defending commitments far beyond its means. In order to bring its commitments and power into balance once again, the United States would one day have to cut back further on its overseas commitments, reduce the American standard of living, or decrease domestic productive investment even more than it already had. In the meantime, American hegemony was threatened by a potentially devastating fiscal crisis (Chace, 1981).

For a time, the United States was able to mask its decline and defer difficult choices by exploiting its hegemonic economic position. During the Vietnam War the Johnson Administration met the challenge by printing dollars and flooding the world with excess liquidity; the Nixon Administration did the same to stimulate the economy and thereby ensure the President's reelection. The result of these excesses was the high inflation that eventually destroyed the Bretton Woods system. In the 1980s, the Reagan Administration financed its massive military buildup and the remarkable economic recovery of the American economy mainly through foreign borrowing, especially with the financial assistance of the Japanese. Only the most ardent enthusiasts of supply-side economics believed that this debt-financed hegemony and economic prosperity could last indefinitely. The international role of the dollar enabled the United States to finance its massive trade deficit and its global position through the expediency of mortgaging its future. The day of reckoning will eventually arrive if and when America's creditors demand repayment.

The accumulated debt by the United States creates no problems provided that its creditors retain confidence in its ability and willingness to repay eventually. However, if America's foreign creditors were to become significantly less willing to finance America's budget deficit, excessive imports, and international position, then the United States would be faced with several cruel choices or combinations thereof (Drobnick, 1985). One choice would be to cause a large devaluation of the dollar in order to achieve an export surplus and repay the debt; the difficulties of this solution will be discussed below. Another approach would be to raise the interest rate to attract sufficient additional capital to finance the budget deficit; this would greatly depress domestic investment, saddle the American economy with accelerating interest charges, and make the long-term problem even worse. A third would be to impose exchange controls in order to restrict capital exports and merchandise imports; this would destroy the remaining elements of the Bretton Woods system. Yet another solution is that even more American productive assets could be sold off: American businesses, farmland and real estate, overseas holdings of American multinationals, and American technology; this "selling of America" had begun by the mid-1970s and, if it continues, will mean the loss of even more of America's wealth-creating resources. In addition, through a combination of devaluation, inflation, and debasement of the currency the United States

348

could in effect repudiate its debt; this last possibility would cause immense political damage to America's ties with its principal creditors, Japan, West Germany, and certain Arab oil exporters. Of course, there is also the option contained in the adage that if one owes a small amount, then the debtor is at the mercy of the creditor, but if one owes a great deal the threat of the debtor to repudiate the debt gives the debtor significant leverage over the creditor. In short, the elimination of the financial legacy of Reaganomics could force the United States to make some exceptionally difficult choices indeed.

The tragedy of the experiment with Reaganomics was that it failed to address and even actually aggravated the fundamental difficulties of the United States. It did not substantially reduce the demands of the government on the productive economy. Instead, between 1980 and 1985, the Reagan Administration "shifted about 1.5 percent of GNP from non-defense spending (excluding Social Security) over to defense with basically no net impact on the deficit" (Feldstein, 1986, p. 7). By retarding the task of adjustment to changed economic circumstances, it made the long-term structural problems of the United States much more difficult and left a burdensome legacy (Keohane, 1984b, p. 37).

The United States in the 1980s is exhibiting what Carlo Cipolla identified in a comparative study of imperial decline as the classic manifestations of declining economic and political power: excessive taxation, chronic inflation, and balance-of-payments difficulties (Cipolla, 1970, p. 13). Despite the cries of a few Cassandras, the false prosperity of the Reagan "economic miracle" hid from the American people the reality of their true situation and the fact that they were prospering only on other people's money. The country as a whole failed to appreciate the historic meaning of the budget deficit and its long-term implications for the society. In order to arrest its economic and political decline, the United States must solve three immense problems.

The first task of the United States, as noted earlier, is to repay the huge accumulated foreign debt, which will require a trade surplus of approximately $100 billion annually for many years to service the debt (Feldstein, 1986, p. 4). As William Branson has pointed out, for this to happen the dollar will have to drop relative to other currencies below its 1981 level, which was the last year that the United States had a surplus in its current account. There are two reasons why this is the case. The first is the fact that the United States has become a debtor and has lost its huge net earnings on foreign investment. It must have a sufficiently large trade surplus to compensate for these lost earnings as well as to service its debt. The second reason, discussed below, is the long-term detrimental effects of the high dollar (Branson, 1986). Such a drastic devaluation of the dollar will threaten a revival of serious inflation and will mean a further lowering of the U.S. standard of living; either one of these results has serious political implications. An American trade offensive would also of course raise the question of where the export markets would be found and whose exports would be displaced. It could very well trigger a severe mercantilistic conflict.

The second set of tasks for the United States is to reverse the process of deindustrialization, severe productivity decline, and rebuild its export economy.[4] Although some scaling down of America's industrial economy was inevitable with the shift toward services, the budget deficit and high interest rates depressed domestic investment; the 60 percent appreciation of the dollar during President Reagan's first term is estimated to have caused a reduction of 13 percent or 2.6 million jobs in manufacturing employment (Branson, 1986, p. 3). In addition, the high dollar shifted American consumer tastes toward imported goods; this "leakage" of domestic demand to other countries weakened domestic economic growth and caused underinvestment in American industrial plants and encouraged foreigners, especially Japan and the NICs, to produce goods in which the United States formerly had had a comparative advantage. To compensate for all this, the United States will be required to accelerate domestic investment in order to modernize its plant, reverse its productivity decline, and develop new industries for domestic and export markets.

Third, pending the achievement of a trade surplus and a more competitive economy, the United States has to withstand the growing pressures of American workers and producers for protection. Protectionism rather than adjustment as the chosen solution to America's economic difficulties would only accelerate national decline. This task has been made more difficult because the strong dollar encouraged a massive expansion abroad of industrial capacity and agricultural production, thereby aggravating the problem of global surpluses and creating foreign exporting interests that will resist a reversal of their newly gained position. All of this means that orchestrating a program of economic adjustment in the post-Reagan era will be difficult indeed.

In contrast to the opinion cited in the last chapter that through policy change the clock could be made to run backward and an equilibrium in America's trading and payments situation could be reestablished, a number of American economists began to worry in the mid-1980s whether this would really be possible. The overvalued dollar, they fear,

---

[4] My views on these matters have been strongly influenced by my colleague William Branson.

has caused such a drastic deterioration of the competitive position of large sections of American industry that there is a "hysteresis" in the capacity of the United States to respond to the damage caused by the misalignment of exchange rates for such a long period. The effects on the American economy may continue to press it down long after the dollar has been devalued and full recovery may not be possible (Baldwin and Krugman, 1986).

The drastic deterioration in the economic position of the United States inherent in this situation will force the United States to make difficult choices among the following uses of national wealth: consumption, investment, and defense. If it can no longer borrow abroad to finance hegemony or domestic welfare, it will be required to lower domestic consumption, to decrease capital formation further, and/or to reduce significantly its overseas military commitments in Western Europe, East Asia, or elsewhere. In essence, national expenditures must be reallocated in order to bring back into balance national resources and national objectives.

The relative decline of American hegemony has seriously undermined the stable political framework that sustained the expansion of a liberal world economy in the postwar era, and increasing protectionism, monetary instability, and economic crisis have developed. The possibilities for the establishment of a new political foundation and a reinvigoration of liberalism do not seem bright. The historical record suggests that the transition to a new hegemon has always been attended by what I have elsewhere called a hegemonic war (Gilpin, 1981). In the nuclear age this "solution" to the problem of declining economic leadership fortunately appears out of the question, yet there is no other obvious mechanism of change available, nor are there any obvious candidates to assume the role of economic leadership. International economic regimes seldom collapse all at once. As Charles Kindleberger has noted, in the late nineteenth and early twentieth centuries the forces of inertia maintained the economic arrangements associated with British hegemony long after that power had begun its decline. In effect there was an approximately fifty-year period from the reassertion of economic nationalism after 1870 to the final collapse of world trade and the gold standard in the First World War.

In the late 1970s and early 1980s, the United States and its major economic partners resorted to makeshift arrangements to maintain the remnants of the economic regimes put into place at the conclusion of the Second World War. The agreement on ad hoc adjustments preserved elements of the trading, monetary, and financial regimes. The danger in the 1980s and beyond has been that an economic or political crisis might shatter the increasingly fragile regimes associated with declining American hegemony. As the United States cannot and will not manage the decaying postwar regimes alone any longer, the preferred solution lies in the direction of renovated regimes and the achievement of international cooperation (Keohane, 1984a).

Whether or not such a cooperative solution will be possible depends on global economic conditions as well as on domestic American conditions. Here too structural changes have eliminated the favorable factors of the early postwar decades, weakened the forces for international cooperation, and threatened the continuation of a liberal world economy. The transformation of supply and demand conditions must be considered in order to understand these economic developments and their significance for the continuation of a liberal international economic order.

The Change in Supply Conditions

Many of the postwar favorable supply conditions had dramatically changed by the 1980s, at least as far as the advanced economies were concerned. Not only did these economies no longer possess inexpensive labor supplies, but in some cases they were forced to import "guest workers" or resort to the strategy of foreign direct investment in low-wage economies. The global shortage of capital raised real interest rates, thus depressing growth rates. On the positive side, at least for importing countries, the world in the mid-1980s had a glut of petroleum and other commodities due in part to conservation measures and reductions in the material content of manufactured goods (Larson, Ross, and Williams, 1986). This overcapacity, particularly in petroleum, however, was also a consequence of the restrictive growth policies pursued by many governments rather than being solely a reversal of the supply situation that had triggered the global recession in 1973; many governments had made tradeoffs of higher levels of unemployment and lower rates of economic growth for reductions in the rate of inflation and energy costs. As noted earlier, with the continuing industrialization of the less developed countries, the world demand for petroleum could once again exceed supply sometime in the 1990s.

The most problematic aspect of supply conditions has been the change in the technological situation. Although important new technological opportunities exist in computerization, biotechnology, and other advanced fields, it is highly doubtful that they will cause a replication of the unprecedented postwar global rate of economic growth. This unusual situation created elevated expectations of an ever-increasing standard of living and of expanding welfare programs in many economies, which have made adjustment much more difficult.

At the end of the war there existed in the laboratories of advanced economies (and for the Europeans and the Japanese, in the American economy itself), an immense backlog of exploitable technologies and hence of available investment opportunities.[5] Whereas the nineteenth century had witnessed the steady and gradual diffusion of new industrial technologies to all the major industrializing powers, the three great disasters of the twentieth century—the First World War, the Great Depression, and the Second World War—had severely retarded the diffusion of technologies from the laboratory into the market and from the United States to Western Europe and Japan. These technologies would create the leading sectors of the postwar boom: automobiles, electronics, and other consumer durables. The impetus for the unprecedented growth that began in the late 1960s came from the efforts of these economies to reach technological frontiers, some of which—such as the automobile—the United States had reached as early as the 1920s. The exploitation of novel technologies and the diffusion of American technologies to other advanced countries were major contributions to the rapid rate of economic growth in the latter 1950s and 1960s (Lewis, 1978b, p. 156). This fortuitous technological situation contributed greatly to the rapid expansion of international commerce and the reduction of economic friction.

The United States and its principal economic partners were able to develop complementary economic relations. Exploiting its technological lead, the United States pursued a foreign economic strategy based primarily on following the product cycle, first through trade and then through overseas production via foreign direct investment by its multinational corporations. The West Europeans and the Japanese, on the other hand, followed a foreign trade strategy that became an export-led growth strategy in 1973 after the first oil crisis.

The multiplication of products arising from the technological backlog and the specialization of firms meant that intra-industry trade, that is, the exchange of products within the same industrial sector, began to characterize commerce among the advanced countries. The expansion of trade involved "a simultaneous increase in both exports and imports *within* each of the major industrial sectors" (Blackhurst, Marian, and Tumlir, 1977, p. 11). There was no abandonment of entire industrial sectors, because national specialization was achieved primarily

[5] Rostow (1983) discusses the importance of the unusual technological situation following the Second World War.

through individual firms concentrating on fewer products in order to take advantage of economies of scale; as a result there were few losers demanding protection from foreign competition. This situation, which continued until the mid-1970s, eased the adjustment problem and encouraged the lowering of trade barriers (ibid.).

As inexpensive petroleum and large pools of underutilized labor disappeared, productivity and economic growth slowed in the 1970s (Bruno and Sachs, 1985). Completion of the technological catching-up process was undoubtedly also a factor in the decreased rate of productivity growth in all the advanced industrialized countries. For the United States in particular, the diffusion abroad of its technological advantages entailed a substantial decline in its economic competitiveness and the loss of monopoly rents that had sustained abnormally high rates of profits and the growth of real wages. The efforts by workers in both Western Europe and the United States to recoup the income losses caused by global increases in the price of food and energy strengthened inflationary pressures in these economies and made demand-management policies exceptionally difficult.

The reversal of American and European economic fortunes triggered powerful forces of protectionism. The closing of the technological frontier and the narrowing, if not the elimination, of the technological gap between the United States and the rest of the world raised new challenges. With the intensification of Japanese competition and the ongoing shift to the NICs of comparative advantage in the technologies that had propelled the postwar growth of the advanced economies, interindustry trade reasserted itself, thus threatening whole industrial sectors in a number of advanced countries and stimulating protectionism. These developments posed for all the advanced countries the question of where the growth industries of the future were to be found and, of equal importance, which nation or nations would take the lead in the emerging growth sectors.

The Limitations on Demand Management

The existence of strong effective demand in the postwar period had complemented the favorable political environment and the availability of abundant resources and investment opportunities. The Keynesian economic revolution and government demand-management policies later played a decisive role in stimulating economic growth. Beginning with the Kennedy Administration in the early 1960s, expansionary American government macroeconomic policies made the U.S. economy the engine of growth of the world economy. Especially after 1973,

American growth and imports facilitated the economic growth of its political and economic partners.

The "compromise of embedded liberalism" in which the advanced economies adopted Keynesian policies of demand management and instituted the welfare state was possible because international regimes in money and trade created in the early postwar period separated the domestic from the international realm of policy making. Until at least the late 1960s, individual countries were able to pursue domestic demand-management policies largely in partial isolation from one another. Governments could meet the demands of their domestic constituents and promote full employment through demand-stimulation policies and welfare programs without sacrificing their commitment to a stable international economy. Harmony between domestic economic autonomy and the norms of a liberal international economic order constituted a major factor in the stability of the international political and economic system. As one scholar observed, it was Keynes at home and Smith abroad.[6]

In the 1960s, growing economic interdependence began to test this solution to the clash between domestic autonomy and international norms (Kenen, 1985, pp. 634-36). Increasing flows of goods, money, and capital made it more and more difficult to isolate the domestic from the international sphere. The increased openness of national economies meant that macroeconomic interdependence became a more important factor and the economic policies of one nation impinged upon others. The combination of increased demands by society on the government, decreased policy autonomy of national governments, and increasing similarity of national economies was undermining the system. Nations were living in an increasingly interdependent world but continued to behave as if they were not (Cooper, 1985, pp. 1200-1213).

The success of "the compromise of embedded liberalism" was dependent upon certain peculiar economic, political, and social factors: private and public economic restraint, a high rate of productivity growth, and a favorable supply situation. Governments had to resist the temptation to manipulate macroeconomic policies for nationalistic or partisan advantage. Demands on the economy from businesses, labor unions, and special interest groups had to be restrained.

Unfortunately, as Schumpeter had feared, the control acquired by democratic governments over the domestic monetary system was not to be exercised with self-restraint. In almost every economy, especially in

---

[6] James Mayall makes this characterization of the clash between the welfare state domestically and laissez faire at the level of international relations.

Western Europe and the United States, public and private demands increased far more rapidly than the capacity of the economy to satisfy them. Social expenditures by national governments grew much more rapidly than the gross national product (*OECD Observer*, January 1984). The ratio of public debt to GNP grew at an alarming rate in almost every economy (*The Economist*, June 14, 1986, p. 67). The pursuit of aggressive Keynesian growth policies to push down the unemployment rate, the subsequent rise in real wages, and the significant expansion of social welfare programs (and defense programs in the case of the United States) and the growth of the public debt implanted a powerful inflationary bias in these economies.

The long-term consequence of these developments has been to blunt the effectiveness of demand-management policies. The expansion of national debt, high levels of taxation, and high real wages eventually placed heavy burdens on almost every economy. The powerful inflationary tendency built into the economy caused some governments to pursue restrictive growth; fearing that they might trigger new rounds of severe inflation, governments have restrained their economies. This produced the long global recession of the 1970s and 1980s. Although the easing of energy and other commodity prices in the mid-1980s relieved some of these inflationary pressures, they most certainly did not eliminate them.

To achieve long-term success through Keynesian economic policies, there are several requirements. Governments must be willing to pursue countercyclical macroeconomic policies; they must be willing not only to decrease taxes, run a budget deficit, and stimulate the economy in recessionary periods, but also to raise taxes, run a budget surplus, and offset inflationary pressures in an overly expansive economy. Nevertheless, the United States, beginning in the 1960s, ran a budget deficit for domestic political reasons through *all* phases of the business cycle (Calleo, 1982, p. 156). Governments must also be willing to alternate deficits and surpluses in their payments balances in order to stabilize the world monetary system, but this too is very difficult to achieve. For economic and security reasons, the United States has been in deficit almost every year since 1959, and economies with a surplus have been reluctant to revalue their currencies and run a deficit because of their mercantilist orientation and their intense fear of domestic unemployment. Finally, the wage rate must be able to fall as well as to rise, or at least to rise only moderately; the postwar era, however, has been characterized by almost constantly rising real wage rates as governments have tried to push down the unemployment level.

The novel factor in the postwar era, which distinguished it from the liberal era of the nineteenth century, was the continually rising real wage rate. The resulting high real wage caused a "wage-cost spiral" or cost-push inflation and meant that higher and higher levels of inflation became necessary to push down the level of national unemployment (Lewis, 1980a, pp. 430-31).[7] The advent of global inflation, discussed in Chapter Four, was in part the consequence of this pressure. In short, the political prerequisites for the pursuit of noninflationary and internationally stable Keynesian policies did not exist at either the domestic or international levels.

As the economist Kerry Schott has cogently argued, the initial and remarkable success of Keynesian policies and the welfare state in the early 1960s was due to a particular distribution of power in capitalist societies (Schott, 1984, ch. 3). This favorable situation, however, changed during the course of the postwar era with the shift of power toward the working class and the welfare state. The growth of unionization and of labor-based political parties, the dramatic increase in the public sector, and the expansion of the economic agenda of the state transformed the domestic balance of political and economic power.

The unintended result of this political shift in almost all capitalist economies was a huge rise in real wages, the growth of public expenditures, and the increased role of the state in the economy. Expansionary and inflationary policies were pursued to accelerate growth and push down unemployment. Throughout most of the period the United States' payments deficit, while facilitating the export-led policies of its allies and allowing them to pile up trade and payments surpluses, resulted in the global inflation that severely damaged the Bretton Woods system. At the domestic and the international level, the market economy planted the seeds of its own destruction through redistributing power domestically as well as internationally and thereby undermining the favorable political foundations upon which it had been based (Schott, 1984).

The redistribution of power in the direction of labor, special interests, and the state in the United States and Western Europe led to an increasingly inflexible and high-cost economy in which Keynesian instruments of economic management (fiscal and monetary policies) were decreasingly effective. Resistance of the newly powerful interests to changes in comparative advantage made adjustment policies difficult to implement and created the setting for industrial sclerosis (Olson,

---

[7] In more technical terms, the Phillips Curve, i.e., the tradeoff between inflation and unemployment, shifted to the left and the natural rate of unemployment increased. This fact has had profound implications for Keynesian policies. Calleo (1982, p. 37) presents an interesting non-technical discussion of this development.

1982). All governments tended to shift the costs of economic adjust-ment to their neighbors.

With real wages rising more rapidly than increases in labor produc-tivity, there was a reduction in the rate of profit (Blackhurst, Marian, and Tumlir, 1977, p. 45), which in turn discouraged business invest-ment. Despite Marx's prediction that the falling rate of profits in ad-vanced capitalist economies and the consequent disincentive for capi-talists to invest would be associated with the impoverishment of the working class, these developments have actually been the result of the redistribution of power and wealth in favor of the proletariat. As Paul Samuelson has argued in a rebuttal to Marx, the capitalist "in trying to save and increase his own profits ends up killing off the total of profits in favor of the workers" (quoted in Heertje, 1973, p. 48).

The "compromise of embedded liberalism," with its emphasis on Keynesian interventionism and welfare policies, was a victim of its own success. As Jacques de Larosière, the Managing Director of the IMF, observed in March 1985, global economic demand was driven power-fully in the postwar era by excessive fiscal policy. Following the break-down of the discipline of fixed exchange rates in the early 1970s, "the fiscal deficit as a percentage of gross national product (GNP) . . . roughly doubled for the world as a whole" (de Larosière, 1982, p. 1). Although supply shocks and the recession were partially responsible for the resort to deficit financing in advanced and less developed econ-omies alike, the underlying reason was a global "revolution of rising expectations." In Larosière's words,

The fundamental cause of the fiscal imbalances is to be found in the changing attitudes vis-à-vis the proper role of the government and in the response on the part of policymakers to those changing attitudes. Over recent decades the view of what governments should do has changed enormously. While the prevalent thinking of earlier and simpler times limited the role of the government to a few well-specified functions, in more recent years, that role has dramatically ex-panded to include (a) stabilizing the economy, (b) stimulating its growth, (c) redistributing incomes, (d) guaranteeing income levels and jobs, (e) preventing the demise of ailing and unprofitable enterprises (f) supplying particular com-modities and services at subsidized prices, and (g) regulating a myriad of other activities (ibid., p. 3).

The enormous rise of taxes to finance this expansion of government has had an inflationary impact and has depressed economic efficiency (de Larosière, 1982, p. 6). The effects of these developments have been "inflation, balance of payments disequilibrium, high interest rates, mis-allocation of resources, low growth rates, increasing unemployment, and, eventually, social tension" (ibid., pp. 7-8). By the 1980s the fundamental economic problem in advanced countries had shifted dramatically from the inadequate demand exemplified in the Great Depression of the 1930s to the danger that stimulation of the economy would cause inflation and high interest rates. Keynesian economics and the welfare state had ceased being the solution and had become part of the problem as inflation increasingly became a *systemic* problem afflicting almost the whole capitalistic world.

The weakening of the "compromise of embedded liberalism" could lead to what Marxists call the crisis of the legitimacy of the capitalist welfare state (O'Connor, 1973). The problem of welfare capitalism, as the Polish Marxist Michal Kalecki foresaw, was that it would be highly inflationary due to the efforts of Keynesian and welfare policies to drive down the level of unemployment (Kalecki, 1943). Such full employment policies, he argued, would result in deliberately engineered recessions designed to lower the wage rate periodically. Because of the tradeoff between employment and inflation, that is, the so-called Phillips Curve, democratic governments would be required to pursue what has subsequently been called a "political business cycle."

Such a "solution" to the inflationary bias of the mixed economy proved only partially successful. Democratic governments tolerated, at least for a while, unprecedented rates of inflation and accumulation of massive debt; when possible they passed on the costs of their policies to other societies (Ruggie, 1982, pp. 413-15). This global Keynesianism worked largely because the United States was unconcerned about its own payments and trade position. The shift of the United States from a creditor to a debtor nation, which has to service and one day repay its debt, has transformed this situation. There is a danger that nations will engage in intense mercantilistic conflict over world markets and thereby attempt to shift the problem of unemployment to other economies. International cooperation and the coordination of macroeconomic policies are essential if further "beggar-my-neighbor" policies are to be avoided. International norms are required to reconcile the potentially conflictual policies of national governments seeking to improve their export position.

The political anarchy of the international economic order clashes with the political management of the domestic economic order. How is it possible to reconcile a world composed of autonomous welfare states pursuing their individual and frequently conflicting economic interests with an interdependent world economy in which the principles of welfare capitalism do not apply? There is no international government to compensate the inevitable losers in the drive for economic progress, to manage global demand in a noninflationary manner, or to provide collective goods. For most of the postwar period the American hegemon carried out these functions of governance effectively and made the system work (Keohane, 1984a, pp. 37-38). If conflicts among the capitalist powers are to be avoided, a new political foundation for the international economic order must be established and solutions to the problems posed by welfare capitalism must be achieved.

THE TRANSITION PROBLEM

The structural changes in economic leadership, supply conditions, and demand management have created a new environment within which economic policy must operate and to which the world economy must adjust. The relative decline of the American economy has weakened the American commitment to a liberal international economic order and has created a new element of uncertainty that has changed expectations and created more caution about long-term investments and other economic activities. The intensified fear of inflation as well as the exhaustion (at least for advanced countries) of the growth industries of the postwar period have placed new constraints on the upper limits of global economic growth for the foreseeable future; exceeding these limits could trigger an increase in the price of energy or rekindle inflation (Cooper, 1982, p. 106). These constraints on global economic growth have created a potentially zero-sum game situation for the world economy; although it is possible for one or two major economies to pursue a macroeconomic policy of demand stimulation, it could be highly inflationary and self-defeating if all the major economies were to expand simultaneously (J. Williamson, 1983, p. 399).

The combination of the expectations generated by the welfare state, the push for both real wage increases and full employment, and the military buildup of the Reagan Administration meant that potential demand far exceeded the capacities of the world economy in the 1980s. The consequences have included a rise in global real interest rates, increased protectionism, and powerful inflationary pressures. Therefore the United States and its economic partners find themselves in a situation in which they have a strong incentive to cooperate and coordinate their policies in order to resolve the supply and demand problems, but they also have a strong incentive to cheat and to attempt to solve their own domestic problems at the expense of the others.

The world economy in the 1980s is in the midst of a significant transition from the norms and relationships embodied in the Bretton Woods system toward a different mode of organization and functioning of global economic relations. The process of uneven development of the world economy has undermined the political framework and economic conditions that had been conducive to a rapid rate of economic growth and an increasing openness and interdependence of the world economy over the past two or three decades.

Although these structural changes and new restraints on economic policy and growth have affected almost every economy, they are especially potent in Western Europe, where wage indexing has tended to keep the real wage at a high and inflationary level. In addition, as former French Prime Minister Raymond Barre has stressed, throughout Western Europe in the 1980s national budgets have amounted to roughly 50 percent of the GNP and the interest on the public debt is weighty; this places a powerful constraint on fiscal policy (Pierre, 1984, p. 5). Reluctance to stimulate their economies made Western Europe in the 1980s become heavily dependent upon exports to the U.S. and made European economies increasingly sensitive to imported goods.

Although the Japanese do not suffer the encumbrances of the Western Europeans, their experience with inflation, large balance-of-payments deficits, and national budget deficits in the 1970s taught them fiscal restraint. The subsequent lowering of the real wage and other adjustments again enabled them to achieve a noninflationary growth rate that was high by world standards although very low by postwar Japanese standards. They too have run a relatively deflated economy and have become highly dependent upon export-led growth, especially to the American market. This Japanese economic strategy has been complemented by the massive export of capital to the United States and to a few other countries.

Reaganomics worked very successfully during the latter half of Reagan's first term both because of factors internal to the American economy itself and because of international factors; the underlying dangers of a return to stagflation had not necessarily been eliminated. The reduction of the rate of inflation from 12.4 percent in 1980 to 3.8 percent in 1983 had been achieved at the cost of a deep recession imposed on the whole world (Drobnick, 1985, p. 9). A high rate of economic growth with a "moderate" rate of inflation was accompanied by a higher than usual rate of unemployment. Reaganomics did not escape the Phillips Curve and the inevitable tradeoff between inflation and economic slack (Sawhill and Stone, 1984). Of greater importance, however, was that Reaganomics benefited from fortuitous circumstances.

In the first place, the real wage in the United States, as in Japan and unlike Western Europe, had declined substantially by the time of the massive fiscal stimulus of the 1981 tax cut, thereby reducing its poten-

361

tial inflationary impact. Second, as has already been noted, other economies pursued restrictive policies permitting the United States to be highly expansionary; total world demand and inflationary pressures were held down (Marris, 1984, p. 22). As a consequence of the high-dollar and the recession in other economies, the United States was favored by relatively declining prices for energy, other commodities, and manufactured imports. And, third, the United States was able to finance its massive government budget and keep interest rates from rising through heavy borrowing in world financial markets; if this had not been possible, the necessary rise in the interest rate to finance the budget deficit would have stifled economic growth. In effect, what the United States and foreign exporters experienced under the banner of Reaganomics and "supply-side" economics was a debt-financed recovery driven by a powerful Keynesian fiscal stimulus.

The economic "success" of the Reagan Administration was largely dependent upon the pyramiding of massive debt and the siphoning of capital from the rest of the world. Whether through an explicit understanding or merely a tacit arrangement, the Japanese were indispensable in financing the economic boom from which they and other exporters benefited. The costs associated with the resulting high dollar and elevated world interest rates were imposed largely on non-American consumers, the LDC debtors, and large sections of American industry. In the 1980s, the revolt of these disadvantaged American producers and their demands for protectionism threatened the curious economic alliance of the Reagan Administration with Japanese creditors.

By 1986, the impetus behind the economic boom appeared to have spent itself. Despite an exceptionally favorable set of economic factors—a declining dollar and budget deficit, lowered inflation and interest rates, and reduced energy costs—the growth rate of the American economy had dropped substantially from the mid-1980s. The causes of this dramatic change have been a matter of intense debate, but they certainly include the legacy of Reaganomics itself, such as the leakage abroad of American demand and the buildup of debt of all kinds. Whatever the reasons, the process of adjustment of national economies and the transition of the world economy to a new basis will be complicated if this decline in the American and world rates of economic growth is not reversed.

Conclusion

The consequences of these structural changes in the world political economy have been profound for international economic and political relations. They certainly make the solution of the global debt problem and integration of the developing countries into the world economy exceptionally difficult. These developments raise the specter of trade wars and spreading protectionism as nations pursue highly competitive export-led growth strategies, attempt to export unemployment to other economies, and safeguard their own industries. Perhaps most serious of all are the ominous implications that these structural changes have for the relations of the United States, Western Europe, and Japan. If these major countries should fail to resolve the problems posed by these developments, the Prisoner's Dilemma of the 1980s could deteriorate into severe economic and political conflict.

The structural changes have produced what a Marxist would call "contradictions" in the international political economy that must be solved by the United States and its major economic partners if a liberal world economy is to survive. The first problem to be solved is that of political and economic leadership. If, as Robert Keohane argues, the world economy is one that can be characterized as "after hegemony," one must ask who or what would replace American leadership of the liberal economic order (Keohane, 1984a). Would it be a new hegemon, some form of pluralist management, or perhaps a collapse of the liberal world economy? The second problem is the economic adjustment required by the global redistribution of economic activities and the shift to new leading industrial sectors. Will the advanced economies now losing their comparative advantage in established industries be able to shift to new economic activities, and will the rising economic powers assume the responsibilities required of them if a liberal international economy is to function efficiently? The third problem is the resolution of the intensifying clash between domestic autonomy and international norms. Is it possible to reconcile Keynes at home and Smith abroad or will one triumph over the other?

In considering these questions of leadership, economic adjustment, and the clash of domestic autonomy with international norms, as will be done in Chapter Ten, it is vital to define what would or could be substituted for the postwar international regimes based on the liberal principles of nondiscrimination, multilateralism, and Most-Favored Nation. In the 1930s, when this issue could not be solved, the world economy collapsed. It remains to be seen whether or not the United States and its economic partners can fare better.

The Emergent International Economic Order

T HIS BOOK presumes that the creation, maintenance, and successful functioning of a liberal international economy require the exercise of political leadership. Some mechanism of governance must supply such collective goods as a stable currency and promote open markets. In international economic relations there are frequently powerful incentives to cheat at the expense of other actors, and political leadership is needed to perform a managerial or policing role.

Paradoxically, the modern welfare state and what John Ruggie so appropriately labeled "the compromise of embedded liberalism" have increased rather than minimized the need for a leader. In a world in which governments are increasingly held accountable for the economic welfare of their peoples, the temptation to pursue policies that benefit one's own citizens at the expense of other societies becomes overwhelming. The inherent tension between a global economy based on market principles and domestic economies based on state interventionism requires intensive coordination of national policies and economic practices.

For several decades, the United States performed this leadership or hegemonic responsibility. Beginning in the late 1960s, this task became more and more difficult. Eventually, structural changes in supply and demand conditions as well as decreased U.S. capacity and willingness to provide leadership caused the postwar liberal international economy to deteriorate seriously.

As Charles Kindleberger and others have noted, there is a powerful tendency for economic hegemony to undermine itself; the United States has been no exception. Since 1959 it has consumed more than it has saved or invested in its own economy. Excessive private and public consumption (including expenditures on the military and on foreign policy) have greatly weakened the American economy. Because of its privileged position in the world economy, however, the United States has been able to import far more goods and services than it has exported and has been able to finance its chronic balance-of-payments deficits by exporting dollars and borrowing from other countries.

The wild fluctuations of the American economy, the threat of spreading protectionism, and the dependence of American economic growth on imported capital indicate that U.S. economic leadership has weakened considerably in the 1980s. What can or will take the place of declining American leadership and on what basis can the world economy be maintained?

To find answers to these questions, the following pages consider the issues discussed in the conclusion of Chapter Nine. If a transition from the decaying institutions of the Bretton Woods system to some more stable international economic order is to be achieved, the problems discussed in Chapter One as the fundamental issues of the international political economy must be solved. That is (1) the difficulties of political leadership must be overcome, (2) the adjustment problem must be solved, and (3) a means must be developed for reconciling the growing conflict between international regimes and domestic autonomy.

The Problem of Political Leadership

There is, of course, no way to prove or demonstrate that political leadership is in fact *required* for the successful functioning of a liberal world economy. Most economists, especially adherents of monetarism, would certainly argue to the contrary that markets function best when left alone. In *After Hegemony*, Robert Keohane (1984a) makes a strong argument that cooperation or pluralist management can work in the absence of hegemony. The historical experience upon which one must of necessity draw to resolve this issue, unfortunately, is sparse indeed. The historical and theoretical considerations discussed in this book support the argument for hegemonic leadership.

The hegemonic leader, however, must be willing to subordinate its own short-term economic interests to its long-term interests and to the larger good of the international economy. The United States tended to do this primarily for political and security reasons during much of the Bretton Woods era. Beginning in the late 1960s, however, the United States began to use the system increasingly for its own more narrowly defined purposes. Many of the troubles of the world economy in the 1980s have been caused by this shift in American policy. In brief, although the case for hegemonic leadership is not conclusive and one should not rule out the possibility of pluralist leadership, it is not likely that a liberal world economy could survive without a liberal hegemon committed to its preservation.

With the relative decline of American hegemony, can pluralist management and policy coordination supplant the United States as the political foundation of the liberal international world economy? Pluralist management and policy coordination appear to have become necessary because uncoordinated national policies have led to economic outcomes that have not been optimal for the smooth functioning of the international economy. Since the mid-1970s, economic fluctuations and instabilities have resulted from the failure of the United States and its economic partners to coordinate their economic policies. But the argument for policy coordination or rules to govern national economic policies can also be made at a more general level.[1]

In a truly competitive market, an equilibrium solution can be found automatically because one must pay a cost for more of a good. At some point, costs and benefits equalize and an actor ceases to acquire a particular good. This equilibrating process, however, does not necessarily exist in the policy realm because an economy may be able to gain benefits without paying equivalent costs. Recent structural changes in the world economy and the increasing clash between domestic priorities and international norms have increased the incentives to gain an advantage for oneself at the expense of others. In a world of more severe restrictions on the global rate of economic growth, a profound temptation exists to export unemployment and pursue policies harmful to one's neighbors. A powerful actor may pursue a policy of considerable benefit to itself while the costs of that policy are transmitted to other economies. This has been the case on several occasions with respect to American monetary policy and Japanese trade policy. More likely, however, the effort of a state to cheat and to improve its own relative position will lead to a suboptimum result for everyone because of policy retaliation by other states (e.g., trade protectionism).

The Need for Pluralist Leadership

The changing nature of the international economy has resulted in a need for pluralist leadership and policy coordination. Structural changes have transformed the role of the market and of economic policy. Initially, economists believed the world economy to be an arena of perfect competition governed by automatic equilibrating processes such as Hume's price-specie flow mechanism. Subsequently, with the breakdown of automaticity due to such changes as the resistance of wages to any downward movement and the rise of the welfare state, the theory of economic policy was developed and applied to what were assumed to be isolated economies; the theory maintained that by following prescribed policy rules governments could make markets work and achieve both domestic equilibrium and international harmony

---

[1] Although economists debate the relative merits of rules versus coordination, both require a high degree of political agreement among the major economic powers.

(H. Johnson, 1972, p. 409). The theory, however, applied to a single economy. With increasing interdependence among national economies and the shift to a more strategic environment, the actions of one government necessarily impinge upon the welfare of other societies and therefore increase the need for international cooperation.

Policy competition among national governments is an ever-present possibility in a highly interdependent world economy composed of independent states. The success of one government in achieving its policy objectives may and frequently does negatively affect the policy objectives of other governments. The determination of which policies will succeed is dependent in part on the structure of the economy and the wisdom of the policies themselves, but it is also determined by the relative power and political skills of the states (Bergsten, Keohane, and Nye, 1975, p. 23). Both economic and political factors determine economic outcomes and the nature of international economic relations.

Macroeconomic policy is the most important arena within which policy competition can occur and policy coordination must take place. In the past, economists focused simply on conflicts over trade policy; they found the solution to conflict in the doctrine of free trade (Bergsten, Keohane, and Nye, 1975, p. 24). With intensified interdependence, macroeconomic policies, because of their effect on exchange rates and other fundamental economic variables, have become of increasing significance. As has already been noted, the shift from fixed to flexible exchange rates and the integration of international financial markets have profoundly affected the operation of the world economy and its impact on domestic economic policy making. Massive financial flows due to differential interest rates, speculative behavior, and political insecurities have reduced domestic monetary autonomy, caused fluctuating exchange rates, and significantly altered the competitiveness of national economies.

As of the mid-1980s, the international regimes of finance, money, and trade have become highly intertwined and can no longer be considered in isolation. National macroeconomic policies and their interactions have a far greater impact on trade balances than do trade policies. The ironic consequence of this situation, however, is that as international finance has more tightly integrated national markets, states have responded by increasing the level of trade protectionism.

The intense and dangerous trade dispute between Japan and the United States in the 1980s has been caused primarily by differences in macroeconomic policy. Other factors such as Japanese protectionism and the illiberal nature of the Japanese economy have obviously been important. But as one authoritative study has demonstrated, most of the U.S. trade deficits of $150 billion and more in the 1980s were due to the greatly overvalued American dollar, caused by the budget deficit and the highly expansionary macroeconomic policies of the Reagan Administration, especially at a time when Japan and other countries were pursuing restrictive policies (Bergsten and Cline, 1985). The result of this extraordinary mismatch of macroeconomic policies was the greatest trade and balance-of-payments deficits in world history.

The task of policy coordination, like that of hegemonic leadership, is to supply the leadership and collective goods required for the efficient operation of any economy, whether it be a national or international one. In the international realm, these responsibilities include the stabilization of monetary and trading relations, the redistribution of income through foreign aid and related programs, and the regulation of abuses (Whitman, 1944). Throughout most of the postwar era the Bretton Woods institutions, backed by the power of the United States, carried out these governance functions. Both the will and capacity of the United States to supply these collective goods have declined. Policy coordination is required to avoid competition in trade, industrial, and macroeconomic policies among the dominant economic powers.

At the same time that policy coordination has become more necessary, it has become infinitely more complex and difficult because of the diffusion of power internationally, the rise of a strategic environment, and the enhanced importance of domestic priorities. The links among policy areas such as trade, money, and fiscal policy have become more intimate, necessitating greater coordination across and not just within economic regimes (R. Baldwin, 1984a, p. 35). Undoubtedly theoretical and policy innovations are required if coordination is ever to be achieved (Cooper, 1985).

As Richard Cooper wrote in his seminal work *The Economics of Interdependence* (1968), the increasing integration of the world economy raises the following problems: the insufficiency of policy instruments, possible inconsistencies in policy targets, and the dynamic inefficiencies caused when policy instruments with strong international spillovers are adjusted by national policy makers in an uncoordinated way (see J. Williamson, 1983, p. 381). Since Cooper wrote his book, problems have intensified due to increased interdependence in trade, finance, and other areas. The autonomy and effectiveness of domestic policy have declined as a result of a large number of important changes such as the global integration of financial markets, the concentration of economic power in actors able to force up costs and wages, and the internationalization of business (Padoa-Schioppa, 1983). In those areas where national jurisdictions are no longer able to exercise control, policy coordination among governments has also become increasingly necessary. The solution of the technical problems of policy coordination both horizontally across international regimes and vertically between domestic and international levels of policy will be a major challenge to economic science, to say the very least (Cooper, 1985).

The fundamental problem of policy coordination and pluralist management, however, is not its inherent desirability or its technical feasibility, but the political problem of the absence of common purposes. Policy coordination requires the willingness of national governments to subordinate their independence in economic matters to some larger decision-making entity. The history of economic summitry since 1975 indicates that few, if any, of the major economic powers have been willing to accept the type of policy coordination recommended (Putnam and Bayne, 1984). Nor is there much evidence that the principal economic leaders are willing to accept the reform of existing economic regimes advocated by numerous writers as solutions to the problems of the international monetary and trading systems. An examination of the policies and changing attitudes of the three centers of global economic power suggests little inclination to accept the responsibilities of economic leadership.[2]

The *United States* in the 1980s has remained especially reluctant to subordinate its economic polices to international supervision. Despite its increased dependence on the international economy, America continues to behave as if it were either a closed economy or the leader whom everyone else should automatically follow. Too little effort has been exerted to weigh the effects of U.S. decisions on others or to consult with others on major policy initiatives. The foremost example has been, of course, the fiscal policy of the Reagan Administration, with its devastating impact on global interest rates and the world debt problem.

For West Europeans and Japanese, policy coordination has meant disciplining the macroeconomic policies of the Americans. The Reagan Administration, however, has interpreted it to mean that the West Europeans and the Japanese should reform their economies and take ac-

---

[2] As stated earlier, the content and determinants of trade and other types of commercial policy are not a primary concern of this book. The focus has been restricted to what were identified in Chapter One as the central issues of international political economy. Although the structure and functioning of the international political economy are obviously important determinants of the commercial policies of particular nations, as in the case of foreign and many other types of state policies, an explanation of trade, foreign investment, and similar economic policies would require a consideration of domestic factors and circumstances in each nation. The relevant literature includes analyses of the politics and the political economy of trade, of which Aggarwal, Keohane, and Yoffie (1986), Destler (1986), and R. Baldwin (1985) are excellent examples.

tions to close the "growth gap." They should stimulate their economies and should emulate the reforms carried out in the United States under the banner of supply-side economics and thereby remove their domestic impediments to economic growth (Nau, 1985).

By the mid-1980s Americans in general had become disenchanted with what they regarded as the unfair policies and practices of their economic partners and they were less and less willing to exercise economic leadership. Yet the postwar commitment of the United States to trade liberalization remained official policy. As it did in the Tokyo Round, the United States pushed for the continued reduction of trade barriers and the eradication of "unfair" trading practices. The United States particularly desired major changes in agricultural trade, especially the opening of the Japanese market, and the elimination of EEC export subsidies. The United States also pushed for the reform of foreign industrial policies (subsidies of various types, government purchasing policies, and the like), and the liberalization of services (banking, telecommunications, etc.). Although there were serious lapses, such as the cartelization of the semiconductor market and the decision to abrogate the Generalized System of Preferences for the LDCs, both of which took place in 1986, the official position of the Reagan Administration was to resist protectionism and to pursue the GATT goal of a multilateral trading regime based on nondiscrimination and universal rules governing commercial relations.

Ironically, the political support for this free-trade position was being undermined by the domestic economic effects of the Administration's macroeconomic policy and its weakening of domestic welfare programs. The overvalued dollar resulting from the budget deficit encouraged a flood of imports and forced American industry to produce abroad more and more of their components and products destined for both American and foreign markets. The once great American automobile no longer existed, but instead became more of a melange of imported component parts. The deindustrialization of significant sectors of the American economy and rising unemployment fed forces favoring economic protectionism. American agriculture, which has long been a bulwark of free trade, was devastated by high interest rates and the overvalued dollar; American farmers were in a debt crisis at the same time that they were losing traditional overseas markets. Either the Administration domestic policies had to reverse course or it would one day have to concede to the rising protectionist pressures.

American political leaders and public commentators appeared not to understand sufficiently the relationship between American macroeconomic policy and the trade deficit. Some argued that improper Japanese behavior or European commercial policies were the principal determinants of the American trade deficit. Too few recognized that the American budget deficit was primarily responsible. The following is a concise statement of this crucial relationship:

Macroeconomics impinges on the trade deficit through two laws of economic arithmetic. First, our net national dissaving—that is, the shortfall of savings in relation to the demand for them at home—must be financed by funds generated at home or abroad. Second, our account deficit equals the net capital inflow from abroad. This simply says that if the money foreigners get by selling us goods and services is not being spent to buy goods and services from us, then it must be spent in buying our assets [real estate, securities, and Treasury bonds].

If, at the prevailing exchange rates and interest rates, people's willingness to buy and sell, borrow and lend, is not compatible with these two equations, then the prices will change until the balances are restored.

The U.S. has a large national dissaving because the public-sector dissaving (the Federal budget deficit) exceeds the net saving of the private sector. This raises our interest rates until enough foreign funds flow in to close the gap. That, in turn, raises the value of the dollar and increases our trade deficit by an equal amount (Avinash Dixit in *The New York Times*, July 15, 1985, p. A18).

In more formal terms, the relationship between the budget deficit and the trade deficit can be expressed in the following simple Keynesian identity:

$$(G-T) \quad + \quad (I-S) \quad = \quad (M-X) \quad = \quad NFB$$

Budget Deficit	Investment minus Savings	Trade Deficit	Net Foreign Borrowing

(G = Government Spending; T = Taxes; I = Gross Private Domestic Investment; S = Private Savings; M = Imports; X = Exports.)

Regardless of the fact that the trade deficit was largely of its own making, the Reagan Administration began a policy of forcing other countries, especially Japan, to solve the administration's problems for it and to: (1) open up their markets, (2) set up production plants in the United States, and (3) stimulate their own economies. This strategy, however, came into direct conflict with the West European and Japanese emphasis on export-led growth and their fear of renewed inflation. Thus, the American policies ran directly counter to important concerns of U.S. allies.

Although agreeing on the desirability of a liberal and open international economy, by the mid-1980s a broad spectrum of U.S. opinion believed that America's economic partners, the Japanese especially, were not "playing fair" in their use of import barriers and export subsidies (R. Baldwin, 1984a). Previously, European and Japanese discrimination against American goods had been tolerated as essential to the revival of these economies and consolidation of alliance relations; however, demands for "reciprocity" began to increase in the 1980s, suggesting a much more aggressive posture toward other countries.

The United States, many Americans began to argue, should not only retaliate with countervailing duties and similar measures against objectionable foreign practices, but it should base continuation of its open economy upon the *effective* response of foreign governments to U.S. demands for greater liberalization. Believing that American trade imbalances are *prima facie* evidence of unfair trade, these Americans want the principle of reciprocity to be applied to the actual results of foreign actions and not merely to the removal of formal external barriers. The increase in economic interdependence in combination with the relative decline of the U.S. economy was causing a basic shift in the nation's foreign economic policy. In an attempt to forestall protectionist legislation from the Congress, new trade policies have invoked the previously abandoned concept of specific reciprocity.

If fully implemented, this important reinterpretation of the concept of reciprocity would entail a return to what Conybeare has called the predatory American commercial polices of the 1930s (Conybeare, 1985, p. 408). According to the 1934 Reciprocal Trade Agreement Act, the United States would use its economic leverage to gain advantage in bilateral economic arrangements (ibid., p. 378). Rather than following the GATT unconditional reciprocity and the Most-Favored Nation principle, the United States would pursue a policy of conditional reciprocity in which specific concessions are exchanged among two or more states but are not extended to other countries. The relative power of the actors would be crucial in such negotiations.

This movement among powerful American groups away from multilateralism and toward what has been called "minilateralism" meant that the United States would no longer subordinate its economic interests to its long-term political and security interests. Specifically, minilateralism would involve certain changes in the objectives of U.S. policy: (1) that other countries follow the American practice of dismantling the welfare state, eliminating government interventionism, and thereby leading to a greater harmonization among trading partners of domestic institutions and practices; (2) that American firms should have the same access to foreign markets as foreign firms have in the American market; and (3) that to achieve these objectives the United States should employ economic and other forms of leverage in bilateral negotiations on a sector-by-sector basis.

Another major factor in American trade policy has been the steady deterioration of the postwar free trade alliance, as organized labor, import-sensitive industries, and large portions of the eastern and midwestern sections of the country have turned toward protectionism. These New Protectionists and advocates of industrial policy have urged the United States to retaliate in kind against foreign import restrictions, export subsidies, and industrial "targeting" as well as other "unfair" practices. These sentiments were greatly exacerbated by the recession of the late 1970s and subsequent noncompetitiveness of the American products in the 1980s due to the high value of the dollar. Furthermore, the ongoing technological revolution and the new significance of so-called dual technologies (computers, telecommunications, and information processing), which have military applications as well as commercial importance, have led to demands for protection of these emergent industries. The rallying cry of these New Protectionists has been "*fair* trade" rather than *free* trade.

Although a national consensus supporting multilateralism and free trade continued into the mid-1980s, it was seriously eroded and circumscribed by political, economic, and security concerns. More important, despite American rhetoric supporting free trade and fulminations against European and Japanese protectionism, American restrictions in many sectors on foreign imports have actually been equal to or greater than those of its trading partners, for example, import quotas on textiles, automobiles, and other goods. In one industrial sector after another the United States has slipped away from its postwar commitment to free trade. American trade policy has shifted to support those domestic commercial and economic interests that have been injured by free trade and away from its role as the cement of its global security relations (R. Baldwin, 1984a, p. 1).

In *Western Europe* an even more significant departure from the commitment to trade liberalization had taken place by the mid-1980s (Hine, 1985). Unlike the United States, however, Europe has never been really committed to the virtues of laissez faire; West Europeans have always favored administrative discretion and the preferential approach to trading relations rather than the universal rules and global approach to trade liberalization favored by Americans (Whitman, 1977, p. 29). In the 1980s, new intense concerns have been added to this traditionally equivocal view toward free trade.

Increasing numbers of Europeans feel they must choose between liberal internationalism and the domestic welfare gains of the postwar period (Keohane, 1984b, pp. 34-35). They believe that the opening of their economies threatens the social and political peace that the postwar welfare state achieved. The social and political costs of adjusting to the accelerating rate of change in comparative advantage, especially the cost of mass unemployment, outweigh the economic benefits. Japan and the NICs, many believe, have set a competitive pace well beyond the rate of social and economic adjustment that the Europeans are willing to make (Hager, 1982). Protectionism is therefore considered necessary, and West European intellectuals have formulated quite remarkable economic theories and doctrines to legitimate and cover their retreat from trade liberalization (Kahler, 1985).[3]

The dual challenge of the United States and Japan in high-technology industries and of the low-wage NICs in traditional industries poses a threat to the economic position of the Europeans and to their social welfare gains. The combination of high real wages, inflexible economic structures, and extensive government interventionism make it exceptionally difficult for the West Europeans to adjust to shifts in comparative advantage (Patterson, 1983). Domestic unemployment has been at an unprecedented postwar level and productivity and economic growth have seriously declined.[4] Moreover, with the loss of many overseas markets due to the rise of Japanese and NIC competition, West Europeans have pulled back into themselves. The industries that had propelled Europe's postwar growth have matured and decreased in importance as sources of economic growth, and since 1973 the West European economies have experienced a severe deindustrialization (Linder, 1986, p. 108).

Having pioneered in the first and second phases of the Industrial Revolution, Europeans became poignantly aware of the fact that the global locus of technological innovation now lay outside Europe. In these circumstances extensive trade liberalization was increasingly regarded as incompatible with the preservation of the welfare state, the survival of European industry, and the EEC itself; American pressures to change the Common Agriculture Policy, for example, have been regarded as a threat to one of the central pillars of the Community. Therefore, a powerful tendency to retreat behind the protective walls of the European Common Market and, in some cases, national trade barriers has developed in response to what the Europeans call "the new international division of labor." The overall percentage of EEC trade that is controlled is higher than in American or Japanese trade. The consequent diversion of Japanese and NIC exports to the United States

[3] Strange (1985c) is representative of a substantial body of European opinion.

[4] Lindbeck (1985) provides a very good analysis of Western Europe's economic problems.

has greatly increased pressures in that market and stimulated American protectionism still further against the Japanese.

The changing nature of West European integration and of its place in the world has encouraged the European tendency to turn inward. In the last quarter of the twentieth century the original tight economic integration of six members of the Community ("little Europe") is shifting to a relatively loose federation of twelve states ("greater Europe"), as the southern tier is admitted. In addition, the growing economic ties between the EEC and the European Free Trade Association, the expansion of commerce with COMECON, and the Lomé Conventions have shaped a new economic bloc of considerable scale centered on the Community. Despite serious problems of integration, the members of the EEC were taking an increasingly larger share of one another's exports (*The Economist*, June 28, 1986, p. 50).

As one of France's most distinguished economists has stated, because of Western Europe's severe economic problems "internationally planned and orderly introduction of some import restrictions in selected countries that have structural deficits in their foreign trade has been proposed" (Malinvaud, 1984). Whereas the Americans had begun to speak of "fair trade" in response to the Japanese and NIC trading challenge, the West Europeans had begun to think in terms of "planned trade." For them, international policy coordination has meant the displacement of liberalism by cartelization of world markets and market-sharing agreements negotiated by the three major centers of economic power.

The expansion of "organized trade" and sectoral protectionism in Western Europe means that American, Japanese, and other firms must gain access to this relatively closed market through such mechanisms as foreign investment, joint ventures, and the licensing of technology. The West Europeans have attempted to protect their home markets and industries against foreign competitors through the device of sectoral protectionism, while (like the LDCs) also forcing those competitors to share their technology and investment capital. This European strategy to overcome its economic problems and technological backwardness will no doubt continue to politicize its economic relations.

A closed and more autarkic Europe has profound implications for the future of the world economy. The relative openness and dynamism of the European Common Market have been among the most important factors in the growth of world trade in the postwar era. Western Europe, as an importer of manufactured goods, has been a major contributor to the export-led growth strategies of the NICs and their increasing participation in the international economy. As Europe closes and its propensity to import manufactured goods declines, not only will the NICs and other countries be harmed but a much greater regionalization of the international political economy will be encouraged. In the mid-1980s, one looks in vain to Western Europe for greater international economic leadership (Lewis 1981, p. 24).

The *Japanese* have been equally poor candidates to assume economic leadership. The nature of their economy has made it difficult if not impossible for them to carry out hegemonic responsibilities. Their trade structure—the importation of raw materials and the exportation of manufactured goods—has made it unlikely that they would provide a large market for the exports of the industrializing countries as Britain and America have done. Unless Japan is able to shift significantly away from its economic strategy of moderating domestic demand in favor of export-led growth, it can hardly displace the United States as the world's "engine of economic growth." And, as many Japanese themselves appreciate, Japan could not really exercise a global leadership role without military power (Fukushima, 1985). Moreover, as an influential report on Japan in the year 2000 put it, the Japanese people and Japan's domestic systems—political, cultural, social, and educational—are not yet adequately prepared for the tasks of international leadership (*Japan Times*, 1983). Until the time is ripe, Japan has seen its role as one of supporting rather than supplanting American hegemony.

Throughout most of the postwar era Japan's economic strategy of following the product cycle and moving up the value-added curve worked remarkably well. A complementary relationship existed between its trade strategy and the foreign investment strategy of the United States. In the 1980s the closing of the technological gap between it and the United States, in conjunction with the other structural changes discussed earlier, began to alter this favorable situation and increasingly brought Japan into conflict with the other advanced economies (Calder, 1985, p. 609). With intensified Japanese competition in ever higher levels of technology, Americans and Europeans became more and more concerned over what they perceived to be Japanese industrial "targeting," the "dumping" of goods abroad, and the "pirating" of American innovations. Many Americans and West Europeans saw the Japanese as aggressively challenging the Western powers for the dominant position in the new era of the international political economy.

The economic challenge of "Japan Inc." began to raise disturbing questions about "the Japanese problem." Few Westerners or other

376

peoples were willing to tolerate what the Japanese themselves had begun to regard as the natural state of affairs—their immense trade and balance-of-payments surplus. Japan was in fact exporting more and importing less in relative terms. Moreover, despite Japanese rhetoric in praise of mutilateralism and the Pacific community, Japan only slowly opened its market to the manufactured exports of its Asian neighbors. It encouraged them to follow its own strategy of early industrialization and exporting to the United States. Along with the closure of Western Europe, Japan's export and import policies have intensified the pressures on the American market and stimulated further protectionist responses.

Many foreign observers believed, as former Chairman of the Council of Economic Advisers Martin Feldstein stated, that at least one element of the problem was Japan's high savings rate and its unwillingness to shift from an export-led growth policy to one based on domestic demand (Feldstein, 1985). A recessionary economic policy and domestic underconsumption have forced Japanese goods onto the world market (and particularly the American market) and prevented the Japanese economy from contributing to the economic growth of other economies. This "growth gap" has been a major cause of the trade imbalance and of the economic friction between Japan and other countries.

The Japanese, on the other hand, believe that they have been blamed for their frugality and efficiency. With a rapidly expanding older population, they must save and repress present consumption. They have viewed foreign complaints and pressures for greater liberalization, expansionary economic policies, and harmonization of domestic economic structures as directed at cherished Japanese values and motivated by the fact that Japan, playing by the rules of the liberal international system of the West, has been winning the global economic competition.

Japanese strength arises from its high degree of domestic consensus. Through what Saburo Okita has called "companyism," that is, the mutual loyalty of labor and management, Japan has found a more effective way to reconcile the domestic demand for equity and security with the international need for efficiency and competitiveness than has the West. The Japanese capacity to moderate inflation and the flexibility of their economy have enabled them to set the pace for the rest of the world.

The economic differences between Japan and its economic partners are not merely economic disputes; they result from a cultural clash of societies with different national priorities, social values, and domestic structures. Others complain that the Japanese live in "rabbit hutches"

377

and refuse to spend their savings on improving their lives. Japanese refer to Europe as a "museum" and America as a "farm." There is a constant danger that the economic conflict between Japan and its trading partners, especially the United States, could deteriorate into political conflict.

Moreover, the Japanese economic miracle contains serious limitations and potential vulnerabilities that make it difficult for Japan to exercise greater economic leadership. Japan has in fact many characteristics of a mature economy. Wages are high relative to those of rising competitors among the NICs and an aging population is an increasing drain on its resources. It is overly dependent upon export-led growth, the American market, and a relatively narrow range of export sectors such as electronics and motor vehicles. The appreciation of the yen is causing unemployment and the growing importance of capital exports will require major changes in the Japanese economy. Yet powerful interests in agriculture and other sectors resist adjustment in the economy and greater openness. Taxation, fiscal, and other policies have limited the capacity of the Japanese government to adjust its economic strategy from export-led growth to domestic stimulation and importation of foreign goods. A major restructuring of the Japanese economy would be required if Japan were to play a greater leadership role in the world economy and lessen economic friction with other countries (Calder, 1985).

As the Report of the Advisory Group on Economic Structural Adjustment for International Harmony (an interesting title indeed) recommended to Prime Minister Nakasone in the fall of 1986, Japan must shift to a policy of domestic-led growth and increased imports in order to reduce frictions with other countries. The so-called Maekawa Report pointed out that this in turn would require basic transformations in Japanese trade and industrial structure. The task of reorienting the Japanese economy and eliminating its massive structural trade and payments surplus is a formidable one, will take a long time to show results, and requires greater patience with Japanese economic behavior on the part of Japan's trading partners than has thus far been the case.

The Prospects for Policy Coordination

By the mid-1980s the economic and political differences among the three major centers of economic power have made it highly unlikely that pluralist management and policy coordination could save the liberal world economy of the past. Each center is exploiting the system for its own parochial ends and none is interested in subordinating its national objectives to the larger goals associated with policy coordination. Although the United States occasionally has exercised its leadership, as in the August 1982 response to the debt crisis and the relatively effective September 1985 attempt to bring down the value of the dollar, it has abandoned its former hegemonic responsibilities except when its interests are immediately involved. Neither the West Europeans nor the Japanese have been in a position to take up the slack nor have they been interested in doing so.

Despite the appeals for pluralist management, the role of the United States in the management of the international economy and the success of policy coordination has remained crucial. Although Robert Keohane's (1984a) characterization of the 1980s as "after hegemony" may be appropriate, American economic power and bargaining leverage have continued to be substantial. The United States remains the largest single economy and one of the two most dynamic economies in the world. It has not been, as declining Great Britain had been in the 1930s, beset by powerful and frequently hostile rivals on all sides. To the contrary, as long as its allies are dependent upon it for their security, they have little choice but to follow American leadership, however faltering it might be.

With Western Europe divided and Japan not yet ready for economic leadership, no alternative exists in the mid-1980s to the central role accorded to the United States. Though greatly weakened, the political framework of the system based on American hegemony has stood largely intact. The dollar (albeit supported by foreign financing) has remained the basis of the international monetary system. The American market continues to be the largest and the one to which all other nations seek access. Even though the technological lead of the United States has vanished in some areas, it is still substantial. Its major trading partners are allies or dependent upon the United States for their military security. Whatever scheme eventually replaces the receding American hegemony, the United States must still have a prominent voice in its determination.

National policy decisions that enable the operation of the market to adjust economic relations are difficult to reach in the best of circumstances. In such a period of transition as the last decades of the twentieth century, great power and strong motivation are both required to overcome resistant structures and to bring about adjustment to emergent economic realities. In the transition to the Bretton Woods system, the United States played such a role. Whether or not the United States has the strength and incentive to overcome the structural differences and conflicting interests that are eroding the liberal system at the end of the century remains to be seen.

The British led the world economy under the banner of laissez faire; this proved unsatisfactory with the increased demands of society on the state after the First World War. American hegemony has been based on the reconciliation of Keynesian economics and international norms. This "compromise of embedded liberalism" broke down with the advent of global inflation and it was replaced by the ad hoc and temporary arrangements associated with economic summitry.

Unless economists can solve the intellectual and policy problem of reconciling full employment and economic growth with low inflation in a highly interdependent world economy, any nation or group attempting to achieve policy coordination will find it a very difficult task.[5] As Richard Cooper put the problem, the clash between the integrating forces of the world economy and the centrifugal forces of the sovereign state has become one of the central issues of contemporary international relations. It raises the political problem of who will cooperate with whom and for what purpose. If this problem cannot be resolved either through some form of unified leadership or the cooperation of the dominant economic powers, then politics will eventually triumph over economics and the consequence will be at least a delinking of national economies and at worst a disintegration of the liberal world economy (Cooper, 1985, p. 1220-21).

In the early postwar period, political leadership was based on American and British cooperation; this "special relationship" had begun in the interwar years and been solidified by the wartime experience. Together, the Anglo-Saxon powers framed the Bretton Woods system and reestablished the liberal international economy. In 1967, the weakening of the British economy forced them to devalue their currency and pull away from the Americans. West Germany replaced Great Britain as the foremost economic partner and supporter of the United States. Throughout the Vietnam War and into the 1970s, the Germans supported American hegemony by holding dollars and buying American government securities. The inflationary cost to the Germans of this new special relationship caused it to weaken in 1973 and eventually to fracture in 1979. The Germans were in turn replaced by the Japanese, who subsequently provided the financial underwriting of American hegemony.

The American-Japanese special relationship, identified earlier as the Nichibei economy, is a very tenuous one. It is driven by the U.S. need to import massive amounts of Japanese capital to finance the U.S. budget deficit and the Japanese use of the American market as a source

[5] See Cooper (1985, pp. 1213-14) on the theoretical problems to be solved.

of extraordinarily high profits, a solution to the potentially serious problem of high unemployment in key domestic industries, and an alternative to far-reaching reforms of an economy overly dependent upon export-led growth.

Disturbingly the expanding integration of the two economies in trade, finance, and production, as Kent Calder has pointed out, has initiated a "vicious cycle of budget deficits, negative capital flows, and trade imbalances that is deindustrializing America . . ." (Calder, 1985, p. 621). Unless corrective actions are taken, this fragile structure will undermine itself in time and will become increasingly threatened by trade protectionism, by American-Japanese economic and political tensions, and, most of all, by the fundamental weakness of a world monetary system based on a Japanese-backed dollar. This is an up-dated version of the Triffin dilemma, in which an inevitable conflict exists between continuing Japanese provision of American liquidity and the confidence of the market in the dollar, and therefore suggests that the Japanese-financed American hegemony may also one day collapse along with the possibilities of a stable international political order.

The American-Japanese economic alliance specifically and the problem of pluralist leadership generally raise once again the problem first posed by the debate between Lenin and Kautsky: Is it possible for capitalist powers to resolve the problem of uneven development and to avoid conflict? Although their security ties in the contemporary era encourage economic cooperation, conflict is surely not out of the question as a consequence of the rise and decline of national economies. I would only amend the Marxist formulation by arguing that the source of the problem is more to be found in rival political ambitions and conflicting state interests than in the inevitable laws of motion of capitalism. As the process of economic development redistributes power and thereby undermines the political foundations of a liberal world economy, the task of the dominant economic powers is to adjust to this transformation of power relations and to find a new base for international cooperation (Keohane, 1984b, p. 36-37). The capacity of the United States and its economic partners to solve the adjustment problem is crucial to the future of the international economic system.

THE ADJUSTMENT PROBLEM

A fundamental purpose of policy coordination is, or at least should be, to facilitate the continual adjustment of national economies to changes in comparative advantage and, more generally, to other developments associated with the emerging global international economy. This task in the last part of the twentieth century entails the creation and renegotiation of regimes in the areas of trade, money, energy, debt, investment, and, if the LDCs have their way, development. These reformed, and yet to be determined, regimes must take account, among other things, of profound shifts in the global location of economic activities and new constraints on economic policies. The fashioning of novel regimes, whether based on set rules or policy coordination, to govern international economic relations lies at the heart of what is called the adjustment process.

The adjustment problem arises from the massive price changes and structural changes that have transformed the world economy. In the 1970s, economic adjustment was made necessary by the increased cost of energy and the abandonment of fixed exchange rates. In the 1980s, the major task of adjustment resulted from the huge appreciation and subsequent devaluation of the dollar, the continuing shift in the global pattern of comparative advantage, and the rapid rise of new industrial powers (Blackhurst, Marian, and Tumlin, 1977, pp. 1-2). Each of these developments has significantly affected the world economy.

Results of efforts to make such adjustments have not been particularly satisfactory.[6] The Japanese and the West Germans made a concerted effort to reduce their dependence on petroleum (Ikenberry, 1986); the United States, on the other hand, did much less to reduce its immense consumption of imported oil (valued at about $55 billion in 1985). As has already been seen, adjustment to the profound changes that have taken place in the international monetary and financial systems has been resisted; ad hoc arrangements have been preferred. With the exception of Japan, West Germany, and some smaller industrial countries such as Austria, Sweden, and Switzerland, most economies have failed to meet the challenge posed by global shifts in comparative advantage (Katzenstein, 1985). The foremost response to the rise of new industrial powers thus far has been trade protectionism.

The problem of adjustment to the profound shifts taking place in comparative advantage and in the global relocation of economic activities is a complex one. Whereas the purpose of protectionism is to delay responses to such changes, the purpose of adjustment is to transform a society's economic base from industries in which it no longer has a competitive advantage to ones in which it does. This task, however, must come to terms with recent major changes in the nature of the international political economy.

[6] As Katzenstein (1984 and 1985) demonstrates the smaller Western European economies have been among the most successful countries in adjusting to economic change.

The first of these changes is the development of the "growth gap" between the United States and the other two centers of the world economy (Marris, 1985). In the mid-1980s the United States could not continue to be the primary engine of growth for the rest of the world; during the second Reagan Administration growth slowed considerably. As a debtor nation America will have to achieve a trade-and-payments surplus once again in order to repay its creditors. Since adjustment will be greatly facilitated if the global rate of economic growth were higher, it has been important that both West Germany and Japan should pursue much more expansionary policies.

Both West Germany and Japan, however, have been reluctant to assume this responsibility. For Germany, stimulation of the domestic economy poses the threat of renewed inflation due to high wage rates, tax policies, and other factors. As the world's rapidly rising creditor, Japan might be expected to assume the economic tasks abandoned by the United States and to import more of the goods of other countries. However, the structure of Japanese trade and of the Japanese economy make it highly unlikely that Japan would be willing to accept this traditional role as the creditor and economic leader. The solution of the growth gap has required that both West Germany and Japan remove domestic impediments to higher rates of economic growth.

The second significant development is the ongoing and rapid shift in the locus of world industry and economic activities. The uneven growth of national economies has caused the center of the world economy to shift from the Atlantic toward the Pacific Basin. With the meteoric rise of Japan and the Asian NICs, the United States and Europe (both East and West) have suffered a relative decline. In addition, the continuing industrialization of Brazil, China, and other large developing countries has begun to alter the international division of labor. The result of this process has been a massive excess of global manufacturing that has greatly magnified the adjustment problem.

Third, as in earlier transitions from one economic epoch to another, the leading sectors of the past half century, that is, automobiles, consumer durables, and so forth, are no longer the major sources of growth and employment, at least in the advanced economies. These industries are slowly being displaced by services, biotechnology, and information industries. These expanding growth industries are increasingly important. As one writer aptly put it, the transition was from "energy-intensive" to "knowledge-intensive" industries (Sayle, 1985, p. 40).

If adjustment is to take place smoothly and the world economy is not to degenerate into economic conflict, then new regimes are required to replace the outmoded Bretton Woods system (Young, 1982). The

383

GATT, the IMF, and the principles embodied in these institutions were based on the assumption that the market would determine who produced what and where; adjustment to the forces of economic change would follow the logic of the market. This assumption provided the legitimating principle for the rules of nondiscrimination, National Treatment, etc., embodied in the GATT. As has been argued, reliance on the market has become increasingly irrelevant in a world of government intervention, arbitrary comparative advantage, and strategic interaction. If the semblance of a liberal economic order is to survive these changes and mercantilistic conflict is to be avoided, new regimes with new legitimating principles are required.

In 1986 a number of steps have already been taken to fashion new regimes consistent with changing economic realities. The several codes that emerged from the Tokyo Round of trade negotiations are positive efforts toward building a new foundation for a continuing liberal world economic order. The spread of nontariff barriers and the cartelization of one economic sector after another from textiles to petroleum to steel are less praiseworthy examples of newly formed international regimes. Proposals abound in the 1980s for regimes to deal with international investment, the debt problem, technology transfer, monetary affairs, and a host of other subjects.

These emergent regimes and additional proposals provide a step in the right direction. A regime does shape expectations, facilitate cooperation, and stabilize relations. However, as the less developed countries have stressed in their demands for an NIEO, the most important issue may be the determination of whose interests may benefit from the regime. Many critics of the United States regard the American emphasis on new regimes to replace America's fading hegemony as a search for a new basis for American domination over the world economy. To what extent do international regimes represent some collective good or are they merely a cloak for particularistic interests?

The simple point that regimes represent constellations of interests has frequently been lost in the discussion about pluralist management and the survival of a liberal order (Strange, 1982). As Kautsky would no doubt observe, it is not enough to demonstrate that international regimes can continue to govern international economic relations; a regime could be the embodiment of what he called "ultra-imperialism." What one wants to know is not simply whether a regime exists, but rather the distributive and other effects of a particular regime on the welfare and power of nations and domestic groups. What to one person is a stabilizing regime (Aggarwal, 1985) is to another something else entirely (Strange, 1982).

Since the international economic order in the mid-1980s is in transition from one set of international regimes to another, the content of these regimes must be determined largely through negotiations and bargaining among the great economic powers. An analysis of the possible outcome of such negotiations must be based on a consideration of the difficulties and challenges that those dominant economies must overcome, particularly in the realm of international trade. What are the prospects for a renovated trade regime?

Liberal economists consider the adjustment problem essentially to be one of letting the market determine trade flows and the global location of economic activities. As comparative advantage in the basic industries of textiles, steel, and automobiles shifts to Japan and subsequently to the NICs, the United States and Western Europe should not resist this development by protecting their declining industries; instead they should shift to emergent industrial sectors where their comparative advantage lies, for example, high-technology industries and services. In addition, they should implement the Tokyo codes and avoid the temptation of state interventionism and engagement in strategic trade policy. There are, however, serious obstacles of both a political and economic nature that make this liberal solution to the transition and adjustment problem exceedingly difficult.

In the first place, the United States and Western Europe must adjust to a dramatic decline in economic welfare. Over much of the postwar era both business and labor in these economies have enjoyed a near monopoly in basic industries, beneficial terms of trade with respect to food and energy, and an unprecedented rate of productivity and economic growth. Profits and real wages have become relatively high compared with the traditional norm. After the war the United States had a false boom in labor-intensive goods that raised the real wage relative to the subsequent growth of productivity (Branson, 1980, p. 59). The breaking of the United States monopoly by Japan and the NICs and the shift to them of comparative advantage in basic labor-intensive industries, the productivity decline in the advanced countries, and other new constraints on economic growth have imposed a dilemma on most of the advanced economies: either profits and real wages must fall considerably, or else the level of unemployment must remain abnormally high (J. Williamson, 1983, p. 396). Or, to put it in more technical terms, the natural rate of unemployment for these advanced economies has risen. In short, the extraordinarily high growth rate of profits and wages during the period prior to 1973 created economic expectations much above what the post-1973 economy could possibly deliver and built into these economies a powerful inflationary bias (Bruno and Sachs,

1985). The response in those industrial sectors most affected by this relative and absolute decline in economic welfare has been not to adjust but to attempt to shut out the challenge of foreign competition and to blame the "unfair" practices of other governments.

Agriculture presents the politically most difficult problem of economic adjustment. The Green Revolution and other advances in agricultural production have caused a global food surplus. In addition, the overvalued dollar has encouraged expansion of production and the rise of new exporters; even the United States has greatly increased its import of those foods in which it has traditionally had a comparative advantage. The instabilities of world financial markets have further aggravated the agricultural problem. The consequence of these developments has been massive surpluses and intense conflict over export markets. The adjustment of world markets to these structural changes in agriculture will pose major economic difficulties.

The nature of the economic challenge from Japan and the NICs has constituted another problem. The growth of world trade among the advanced economies during the early postwar era was based largely on intra-industry trade, rapid product innovation, and the possession of certain monopolies. This type of trade tended to be balanced among advanced economies and to benefit alike all the factors of production; it thus countered the operation of the Stolper-Samuelson theorem, which maintains that trade harms the scarce factor of production, such as labor (Helpman, 1984, p. 362). The rapid growth of Japan and especially of the NICs as exporters of manufactured goods changed this situation, so that trade indeed harmed American labor and also the import-sensitive industries in the United States and Western Europe.

The continuing displacement of intra-industry trade by interindustry trade in the 1980s has meant that many industrial sectors in advanced countries are being wiped out and the relevance of the Stolper-Samuelson theorem to the welfare of labor has greatly increased (Keohane, 1984b, p. 34). For example, because Japanese exports are largely manufactured goods sent to other developed economies and because these exports are based on cost-cutting process innovations whereas its imports are mainly food and raw materials, Japan's economic rise poses a serious threat to labor and businesses in a number of industrial sectors in other countries.

The NICs also pose a novel challenge to all the advanced economies, including Japan, because of their ability to combine inexpensive labor, state-of-the-art technology, and an exchange-rate strategy that makes their manufactured exports very competitive in the American and other markets. By tying their currencies to the dollar as it has dropped and the yen has appreciated, their competitive position has greatly improved and much of the advantage to the United States of a devalued dollar has been lost. Nothing illustrates this version of the $N - 1$ problem better than the dramatic rise of South Korea as an exporter of electronics and automobiles (*The New York Times*, August 31, 1986, p. 1). These competitive factors and anti-Japanese voluntary export restraints are causing American and Japanese automotive companies to shift a substantial fraction of their production to the NICs. In 1986, roughly one-half of the American trade deficit was with countries whose currencies had not strengthened against the dollar (*The Economist*, August 2, 1986, p. 55).

Another obstacle to the solution of the adjustment problem is found in the rapid pace set by the Japanese due to the structure of their trade, the remarkable flexibility of their economy, and their continual movement up the technological ladder. The extraordinary combination of high-quality labor and poor resource endowment account for Japan's emphasis on achieving a dynamic comparative advantage in high technology products (Saxonhouse, 1983, p. 273). In the words of Gary Saxonhouse, "to the extent that the large, natural resource-poor Japanese economy continues to grow more rapidly than its trading partners, it is almost inevitable that this will involve the transformation of its export structure. This in turn will impose structural adjustment on Japanese trading partners and competitors" (ibid., p. 279). Because Japan's exports consist of high-value goods and its imports consist mainly of unprocessed raw materials that create relatively fewer jobs abroad, it imposes on other countries a major adjustment problem and causes deep resentments. Although the appreciation of the yen in the mid-1980s has blunted the Japanese export drive, the drop in oil and other commodity prices continues to be a major factor in the bulging Japanese trade surplus.

The superior capacity of the Japanese for structural adaptation, their strategy of "preemptive" investment, and the rapid movement of their industry into higher technologies greatly complicates the adjustment problem. Although the American trade deficit with Europe and Canada is worse, "the Japan problem" has become especially acute for the United States. Unlike West Germany, an even more important exporter, Japan has no large neighbors with which to trade and its exports have been concentrated in a few areas such as automobiles and electronics. Its exports, therefore, have had a devastating impact on certain sensitive sectors. In addition, the United States and Japan have begun to compete in many of the same high-technology areas. The integration of a dynamic Japan into a world economy experiencing a slowdown in economic growth has caused vexing problems for other countries.

The social and economic structures of the advanced countries have demonstrated considerable rigidity in their ability to adjust to these developments. Powerful resistance has arisen to the potential effects on wages, welfare programs, and economic structures. Although this resistance has been especially important in Western Europe and the United States, it has even appeared in Japan in response to NIC exports. Rather than adjustment, the response too frequently has been New Protectionism and industrial policy. Whereas economists think in terms of aggregate solutions and global equilibrium, governments and special interests think in terms of specific sectors and are therefore primarily concerned about who produces what products.

In a truly multilateral trading system these tensions would in time be worked out, but with the shift toward bilateralism and the increased pressure for immediate solutions, the adjustment process works too slowly through the market mechanism. Whereas in the early postwar years the rapid growth of the world economy facilitated economic adjustment, the post-1973 decline in the global rate of economic growth has inhibited it.

The liberal world economy has begun to spiral downward; in a static growth situation the gain of one group or economy is another's loss. Failure to adjust and move to higher levels of economic efficiency further weakens economic growth and makes the adjustment process still more difficult. If this vicious cycle is not arrested, international economic relations could become a zero-sum game and intense economic conflict become inevitable.

In summary, the concentration of economic and political power in corporations, unions, and states that can resist adjustment, along with the decrease in global economic growth, have greatly limited the effectiveness of the adjustment process. Although the situation in the mid-1980s has not deteriorated to the level of the 1930s, when rigid economic structures and the failure to adjust caused the Great Depression, the resistance to the equilibrating play of market forces is sufficiently great to prevent a smooth transition to new global economic relations. The shift to the new centers of economic growth and new leading sectors is being powerfully resisted. Corporations and unions that had benefited from monopoly positions are seeking protection against foreign competition, and states struggle to maintain their relative position in the international division of labor. Although observers have generally believed the historical conflict between the norms of a liberal international economy and the desire for domestic economic autonomy had been resolved, that conflict has arisen again.

International Norms versus Domestic Autonomy

After decades of unprecedented success, the postwar "compromise of embedded liberalism" deteriorated and the clash between domestic autonomy and international norms reasserted itself in the major economies of the international system. The increasing interdependence of national economies in trade, finance, and macroeconomic policy conflicted more and more with domestic economic and social priorities. As this occurred, the fundamental question initially posed by late nineteenth-century Marxists and subsequently by Keynes regarding the ultimate compatibility of domestic welfare capitalism with a liberal international economic order once again came to the fore. In the 1930s Keynes, believing that they were *not* compatible, chose domestic autonomy. The Keynes who helped put together the Bretton Woods system was more optimistic, and for a while he seemed to have been justified. By the 1980s, however, the Keynes of the 1930s, who believed that "goods [should] be homespun," might have felt vindicated.

The growth in global interdependence increased the relevance of domestic social structures and economic policies to the successful operation of the international economy. In a world where tax policies, social preferences, and government regulations significantly affect trading patterns and other international economic relations, the clash between domestic autonomy and international norms has become of central importance. As "embedded liberalism" seems less relevant, other possible solutions are: increased policy coordination and international cooperation, harmonization of domestic structures, and, in the event the first two options fail, a move toward greater autonomy and the delinking of national economies.

Although the resolution of this issue will be known only with the passage of time, the shifting attitudes and policies of the major centers of economic power—the United States, Western Europe, and Japan—toward international regimes suggests that domestic priorities are triumphing over international norms. In Western Europe and the United States, new constellations of interests and concerns have been leading to a greater stress on domestic economic interests and a deemphasis on international norms and policy coordination. Meanwhile, the new demands placed on Japan by its economic partners have begun to raise new anxieties in the Japanese people. Because of Japan's emerging key role in the world economy, "the Japan problem" and the challenge that it poses for international regimes are particularly important.

In response to complaints from its trading partners and its own economic success, Japan by the mid-1980s had begun to change its highly protectionist policies and, in fact, had become the foremost advocate of free trade. As their strength increased the Japanese were beginning to open their traditionally closed markets and relaxing the control of the state bureaucracy over the economy. By the mid-1980s the Japanese had become, at least in their *formal* trade barriers with respect to manufacturers, the least protectionist of the advanced capitalist countries.

Even so, the liberalization measures that had been carried out by the Japanese were clearly not enough for their partners. The United States, Western Europe, and even Asian countries intensified their pressures on Japan for still more liberalization, the exercise of greater economic leadership, and the harmonization of Japanese institutions and practices with those of its major trading partners. These external pressures for liberalization raised particularly acute problems for Japanese society and its leaders.

Different interpretations of the meaning of the term "liberalization" are central to the debate between Japan and its critics. "Liberalization" has traditionally meant implementation of the basic principles and objectives of the GATT, that is, simply the removal of formal, external trade restrictions and, under certain circumstances, giving foreign firms "National Treatment"—treating them as if they were national firms and hence in a nondiscriminatory manner. For other countries, however, this interpretation is not sufficient in the case of Japan, due to the nature of the Japanese economy, and foreign demands for liberalization have challenged inherent and crucial features of Japanese culture, social relations, and political structure.

The Japanese economy is highly regulated, compartmentalized, and segmented in myriad ways. The existence of long-established informal relationships and institutional structures effectively restricts entry into many industrial and service sectors not only by foreign firms but also by Japanese firms. For example, as noted above, although it began to change in the 1970s and 1980s, the financial sector has been highly fragmented, with Japanese financial institutions confined to relatively narrow segments of the market; they have operated under tight government control by the Ministry of Finance, which tenaciously resists entry by either foreign or other Japanese firms. As has frequently been observed, the Japanese pattern in many economic sectors has been to discriminate against any "outside" firm, whether it is a foreign or even a Japanese business.

Moreover, in almost all economic sectors the reluctance of Japanese to "buy foreign," the interlocking networks of Japanese firms, and the crucial importance of personal relationships as well as the existence of numerous other informal barriers have constituted formidable obstacles to foreign penetration of the Japanese economy. (Some of Japan's more severe critics appear to believe that the Japanese language itself constitutes a nontariff barrier.) The distribution system is among the most important restrictions on entry to the market. Many believe that if the Japanese would only behave like Americans or Europeans, the economic conflicts would go away.

Westerners and Japanese also appear to have quite different conceptions of free trade. Whereas the West thinks in terms of "fairness" and full participation in the Japanese economy, Japan thinks in terms of "openness," preserving traditional structures, and not becoming overly dependant on imports. The Japanese firmly believe that they are playing by the rules; their foreign critics believe just as firmly to the contrary. Because of these cultural barriers, Americans and others regard the GATT principle of National Treatment to be an insufficient guarantor of greater access to Japanese markets. Instead, critics argue that a major overhaul of Japanese business practices and economic institutions is necesssary. What is required, they argue, is a greater harmonization of Japanese institutions and behavior with those of other countries. In effect Japan must not only remove its formal and external barriers to trade, but it must become a liberal society in the Western sense of free markets open to all. The demands of the United States on the Japanese for greater reciprocity have reflected this attitude.

Although these pressures undoubtedly have contained a large element of resentment over Japan's economic success, they also arise from genuine concerns about whether or not the Japanese have indeed been "playing fair." As Gary Saxonhouse has commented, "a good share of the expanded agenda of international economic diplomacy, and, in particular, a good share of the interest in the harmonization of domestic economic practices in the name of transparency has been motivated by a desire to ensure that the very successful, but traditionally illiberal Japanese economy is competing fairly with its trading partners" (Saxonhouse, n.d., p. 29). In international economic matters as in other spheres, justice must not only *be* done but be *seen* to be done. With increasing economic interdependence, questions of the legitimacy of national structures and practices have gained in importance. Microeconomic policy coordination as well as macroeconomic policy coordination appear to be necessary.[7]

Western liberal societies find Japanese economic success particularly threatening because it is the first non-Western and nonliberal society to outcompete them. Whereas Western economies are based on belief in the superior efficiency of the free market and individualism, the market

---

[7] Stephen Krasner has noted that the intensification of global economic interdependence has increased the importance of the perceived legitimacy of domestic practices.

and the individual in Japan are not relatively autonomous but are deeply embedded in a powerful nonliberal culture and social system (Calleo and Rowland, 1973, p. 205).

The American perception of this statism and the troubling implications of its spread to the other countries for the continuation of a liberal international economy has been expressed in Raymond Vernon's telling observation that

> the concept of free access of every country to every market and the gradual reduction of trade barriers and the openness of capital markets, served us well, given our internal political and economic structure, and given our position in the world from 1945 on. All my preferences, all my values argue for retaining this system, for as long as one can. But one observes the way in which Japan has organized itself . . . with a certain unity of purpose, which can easily be exaggerated, but nonetheless at the same time should not be overlooked. One looks at the way in which state enterprises are being used somewhat—*somewhat* . . . by the other advanced industrial countries and now by the developing countries in very considerable degree. Observing these various forms of interference with the operation of market mechanisms, I find myself reluctantly pushed back constantly to the question whether we have to opt for a set of institutional relationships and principles that reflect a second best world from our point of view. We have to somehow organize ourselves . . . (Vernon quoted in Cumings, 1984, pp. 39-40).

Unless greater harmonization of attitudes, institutions, and policies between Japan and its economic partners is possible, economic relations will surely become more difficult.[8]

Critics have argued that Japan must assume responsibility in trade, finance, and other areas commensurate with its new economic power; Japan cannot continue to respond merely by adjusting its policies to outside pressures. Although this sentiment has been vociferously expressed in the United States and, to a lesser extent, in Western Europe, it has appeared in Asian countries as well. As was noted earlier, the Japanese response to the demands of ASEAN countries and Asian NICs for greater access to the Japanese economy has been that these countries should copy its own early industrialization and should export labor-intensive goods to the United States rather than export to Japan. For those Asian neighbors with huge trade deficits with Japan, this refusal to open the Japanese market and to exercise greater leadership has been a source of great resentment.

These outside pressures for harmonization, reciprocity, and leader-

---

[8] Calleo and Rowland (1973, ch. 8), Hager (1982), and Hindley (1982-83) present an array of views on the issue of domestic harmonization of economic structures.

ship have raised the stakes in economic struggles between Japan and its trading partners. The clash with the United States became especially acute by the mid-1980s. Whereas the West Europeans have tended to respond to "the Japanese problem" by shutting out the latter's goods, American pressures to open up and transform Japanese society itself have elevated the economic disputes to the political level so that even the political ties between the two nations are threatened.

These American pressures have placed Japan in a serious dilemma. On the one hand, meeting these demands would require that the Japanese change many of their cherished social values and traditional ways, traditions regarded by many Japanese as crucial to domestic social harmony and political stability. Liberalization would threaten high unemployment in many sectors and necessitate major structural changes in the economy. As one Japanese business executive vehemently stated, "foreign requests concerning Japan's nontariff barriers [to imports] are tantamount to raising objections to Japan's social structure." He went on to assert that "there is little possibility that those requests will be met" (quoted in Sayle, 1985, p. 39).

Can a liberal international economy long survive if it is not composed primarily of liberal societies as defined in the West, that is, societies with an emphasis on the price system, markets open to all, and limited interventionism on the part of the state? Liberal economists conceive of societies as black boxes connected by exchange rates; as long as exchange rates are correct, what goes on inside the black box is regarded as not very important. With the increasing integration of national economies, however, what states do inside the black box to affect economic relations has become much more important. Although in the 1980s this issue is most immediately relevant to Japan and the clash between its Confucian social order and the American Lockean order, the issue also applies to the NICs, to the socialist Eastern bloc economies, and to the growth of nationalized industries in Western Europe and throughout the world. The advent of industrial policy, new modes of state interventionism, and the existence of domestic institutions that act in themselves as nontariff barriers have become formidable challenges to the liberal international economic order.[9]

In a highly interdependent world composed of powerful illiberal economies, the GATT principles of nondiscrimination, National Treatment, and Most-Favored Nation may no longer be appropriate. If a greater harmonization among national economic practices and domes-

[9] Jacob Viner (1951), in his discussion of the rise of state trading, was one of the first to address this increasingly important issue.

domestic structures must change

tic societies does not occur, liberal societies may be forced in their own defense to adopt industrial and other countervailing practices. The question of whether statist societies should become more liberal, liberal societies should become more statist, or, as most economists aver, domestic structures do not really matter has become central to an evaluation of the problem posed by the inherent conflict between domestic autonomy and international norms.

A Mixed System: Mercantilistic Competition, Economic Regionalism, and Sectoral Protectionism

In the mid-1980s, the liberal international economy established at the end of the Second World War has been significantly transformed. The trend toward liberalization of trade has been reversed and the Bretton Woods principles of multilateralism and unconditional Most-Favored Nation status are being displaced by bilateralism and discrimination. With the collapse of the system of fixed exchange rates, conflicting interests gave rise to intense clashes over exchange values and other monetary issues among the advanced economies. The displacement of the United States by Japan as the dominant financial power and the global debt problem have raised troubling questions about the leadership and stability of the world financial system.

Although few doubt the reality of these changes, opinion differs greatly over their significance. Some believe that these developments reflect "norm-governed change" and the continuity of common purposes among the dominant economic powers (Ruggie, 1984, pp. 412-13). Less sanguine observers, including myself, believe these changes are responses to hegemonic decline and are caused by diverging national interests among the advanced countries. As a consequence of profound structural changes in the international distribution of power, in supply conditions, and in the effectiveness of demand management, the liberal international economic order is rapidly receding.

Certain significant trends or developments can be observed. Growing mercantilistic competition threatens to increase economic nationalism; thus far the vestiges of American leadership, the forces of historical inertia, and the common interest in avoiding conflict have moderated the consequences of this situation. There is also a tendency toward regionalization of the world economy; the closure of Western Europe, the economic consolidation of North America, and the rise of the Pacific Basin point in that direction. Furthermore, sectoral protectionism has gained strength; the conflicting desires of nations both to protect particular sectors and to acquire foreign markets in these same industries strongly encourage this New Protectionism. Although the relative importance of each cannot be determined, a mixed system of nationalism, regionalism, and sectoral protectionism is replacing the Bretton Woods system of multilateral liberalization.

Intensified Mercantilistic Competition

The first factor suggesting an intensification of mercantilistic competition is the increasing role of the state and of economic power in international economic relations. States (especially large states) have begun to use political and economic leverage extensively to increase their relative gains from international economic activities. The clash between economic interdependence and domestic autonomy is more frequently resolved in favor of autonomy than interdependence, even though nations want the benefits of interdependence at the same time that they seek to limit its effects on national autonomy. They want the collective goods of liberalized trade and a stabilized monetary order without sacrificing their capacity to manage their own economy as they see fit. The result has been an expanding competition among states to maximize their own benefits from and to minimize the costs of global interdependence.

The second factor promoting mercantilistic conflict is the growing struggle for world markets. Due to such factors as domestic limits on economic growth in the form of high wages and inflationary pressures, the global debt problem, and the continuing need of most countries to import energy, almost every nation pursues export-led growth and aggressive export-expansion policies. These pressures on export markets will intensify due to the reversal of the American financial position and the fact that for the first time in the postwar era the United States must achieve an export surplus to repay its massive debt. This classical mercantilistic conflict over market shares is reflected in clashes over trade and macroeconomic and other policies.

Third, the challenge and example of Japan and the NICs also stimulate mercantilism. The structure of Japanese trade and the unprecedented rate of change of Japan's comparative advantage increase pressures on other economies. As Japan and the NICs move rapidly up the technological ladder, they impose heavy adjustment costs on other economies, thereby stimulating strong resistance and demands for protectionism. Japanese success reflects an adroit interventionist and mercantilist state that has been able to manage social consensus, establish economic objectives, and increase the overall competitiveness of the economy. This success encourages other states to emulate the Japanese and develop interventionist policies of their own.

The mercantilism generated by these developments promises to be different in purpose and method from its eighteenth- and nineteenth-century predecessors. During the first mercantilist era, the objective was to acquire specie for military purposes, and the means employed was an export surplus. The purpose of nineteenth-century mercantilism was to speed industrialization through protectionism and other policies. In the closing decades of the present century, the goal is at least survival in world markets and, optimally, the achievement of economic supremacy. Pursuing this goal, the Japanese and their imitators have implemented what Ronald Dore has called a strategy of competitive development.[10]

The success and example of Japan and the NICs thus carry one step further to its logical conclusion, the transformation in the relationship of state and market that Schumpeter predicted would result from the First World War; through its control over economic levers, the modern state attempts to direct and shape the economy to achieve its primary objective whether it be the prosecution of war, the promotion of domestic welfare, or, as in the case of Japan, the industrial and technological superiority of the society. As a result of this change in the relationship of state and economy a new form of mercantilistic competition, what the German economist Herbert Giersch has called "policy competition," has become important (Giersch, 1984, p. 106).

At the end of the twentieth century, there is a powerful incentive for governments to manipulate economic policies in order to advance their economic, political, and related interests. The Japanese tactic of "preemptive investment," the American retreat to earlier ideas of "conditional reciprocity," and the temptation of all nations to move toward strategic trade policy are examples of such competitive policies. Developments in the 1980s such as the rise of the New Protectionism, the spread of industrial policies, and governmental support of their own multinationals illustrate this predilection of individual states to adopt policies that benefit themselves at the expense of other economies.

How will mercantilism as a new form of inter-state competition affect international economic and political relations? Will nations compete, for example, on an individual basis, or will what Giersch (1984, p. 106) has called "policy cartels" arise? If nations coordinate their economic policies and form economic alliances, who will participate and to what end? The rise of economic regionalism resulting from the ero-

[10] This term was used by Ronald Dore in a lecture given on February 5, 1986, at Princeton University.

sion of a liberal international economic order may provide some answers to these questions.

Loose Regional Blocs

The difficulties of pluralist leadership, the resistance of many advanced economies to economic adjustment, and domestic priorities threaten further dissolution of the unity of the liberal international economic order. Loose regional blocs are likely to result. In the 1980s, the world economy is coalescing along three axes. Debt, monetary, and trade matters as well as changing security concerns will surely pull the regions of the world economy further apart but should not cause a complete break.

The European Economic Community constitutes one focus for regionalization of the world economy. A Europe-centered system would include the enlarged Community, peripheral European states, and many of the former European colonies. It would no doubt form close ties to the Eastern bloc and certain of the Middle East oil exporters. As has been noted earlier, this region could be relatively self-sufficient except for energy and certain commodities; by the early 1980s, it had already achieved a high degree of monetary unity and policy coordination. In a world of increasing uncertainty and politicized economic relations, a more closely integrated Western Europe would be able to confront the United States, Japan, and the emergent centers of economic power more effectively.

The United States has begun to draw its northern and southern neighbors into closer interdependence, as both the Canadian and Mexican economies have become increasingly integrated with that of the United States. Although not much attention is given to the fact, Canada is the largest trading partner of the United States, and these ties are increasing with Canada's dramatic loss of its European markets in the postwar period. The United States is the largest importer of Mexican oil, and American multinationals have made the area along the southern Rio Grande one of the principal locales of "off-shore" production. A growing percentage of Mexico's exports are sent north of the border. The Caribbean Basin Initiative has also bound that region, including parts of Central and northern South America, more closely to the United States. It should be noted that, in addition, the United States has established loose economic arrangements with its political and security dependencies: Israel, South Korea, Taiwan, and, for the moment, Saudi Arabia. Shifts in trading patterns, foreign investment, and financial flows also have reinforced the regionalizing tendencies, and the debt problem has further strengthened the polarizing forces. For economic and security reasons the United States is giving increased and special attention to its own hemisphere and to a larger economic orbit that is yet to be defined.

The third and most amorphous emerging region is that of the Pacific Basin or the Asian Pacific. Centered principally upon Japan and its East Asian trading partners, this region includes ASEAN (Indonesia, the Philippines, Malaysia, Singapore, and Thailand), Australia, Canada, New Zealand, the Asian NICs (South Korea, Hong Kong, Taiwan, and, again, Singapore), and parts of Latin America. The United States, especially the West Coast, has also become a major participant in this economic region. American trade with the nations of the Pacific overtook U.S. Atlantic trade in the mid-1970s and subsequently has expanded much more rapidly than U.S. trade with the rest of the world.

The Pacific Basin in the 1980s became the fastest growing and foremost trading region of the world (Linder, 1986, ch. 1). Between 1960 and 1982, the ratio of its exports to world exports doubled; this expansion was even more remarkable in manufactured goods (ibid., p. 14). The region is the most nearly self-sufficient one of the three in commodities, manufactures, and investable capital. But the most notable development of all was that trade *within* the region grew even faster than trade with the rest of the world. This regionalization was a function of domestic economic growth, complementarities of the economies, and the relative openness of the economies (Krause, 1984, pp. 5-7). Moreover, this intraregional trade was shifting from a series of bilateral relationships to a more truly multilateral trading network (Patrick, 1983, p. 1).

The size and dynamism of the Pacific region are indicative of its increased importance in shaping the future of the international political economy (Hofheinz and Calder, 1982). The ratio of Pacific gross product to Atlantic gross product increased from about 40 percent in 1960 to about 60 percent in 1982. The region's share of global gross product rose in this same period from 16 to almost 25 percent and its ratio to the U.S. GNP shot up from 18 to more than 50 percent (Linder, 1986, p. 10). In the 1980s Northeast Asia (Japan, Taiwan, and South Korea) became the electronics capital of the world; partially reflecting this development, a substantial portion of both American and Japanese foreign direct investment was in that region. As a distinguished European economist said, "the center of gravity of the world economy is indeed shifting from the Atlantic Basin to the Pacific Basin" (ibid.). As with prior major shifts in the locus of global economic activities, the political consequences of this development will be profound.

The shape and internal relationships of the region, however, remain unclear, and several important questions have yet to be answered. The first and most critical is whether its two economic giants—the United States and Japan—can continue to be close partners or will become antagonistic rivals. The second is how the tension between the complementarity and the competitiveness of the East Asian economies will be resolved; although the complementary factor endowments of Japan, the Asian NICs, and ASEAN could lead to a relatively self-sufficient division of labor in the region, these economies are also increasingly competitive with one another in commodities and manufactured goods in the American and other markets. The third question is whether Japan will exercise economic leadership through such measures as opening its markets to the manufactured goods of its neighbors or exporting its huge capital surplus to China and other regional economies. The answers to these and similar questions will significantly affect the place of this region in the larger world economy.

The developing pattern of trading and investment relations is creating a regional division of labor with Japan and the United States as the two anchors. Japan is the foremost exporter of consumer goods and importer of raw materials, and the American market is a vital element tying the region together; American exports of capital and high technology goods to the developing countries of the Pacific Basin and Latin America are also becoming increasingly important. Between 1980 and 1985, LDC exports to the United States increased from 40 to 60 percent of total U.S. imports, and in 1985, the LDCs took one-third of American exports (*The New York Times*, October 4, 1985, p. D1). Also, American exports to the Pacific region nearly doubled between 1960 and 1983 from about 13 percent to about 25 percent of total exports (Linder, 1986, p. 78).

The Pacific region has a number of potential problems that could thwart its development. The first is the tendency toward bipolarization between the industrialized economies of northeast Asia and the commodity-exporters of ASEAN countries; the former is pulling ahead of the latter in exports and growth (Nomura Research Institute, 1986a, p. 19). The second is the overdependence of the Asian members of the region on the American market as their engine of economic growth; they do not yet constitute a self-sustaining bloc and the decline of the American rate of growth, as occurred in 1986, has a depressing effect on the region. And, third, the political stability of East Asia since the end of the Vietnam War may not last; many domestic regimes are unstable and the Pacific is increasingly a focus of superpower confrontation. Thus, although the Pacific Basin holds great promise, its serious difficulties must not be overlooked.

The boundaries of these three partially coalesced regions are unclear and porous; the membership of the regions overlap. The trading, financial, and other commercial relations among the regions and especially among the major powers remain strong, yet the lines of demarcation among the regions are discernible and becoming more pronounced with the spread of protectionism and other changes in the world economy. In the mid-1980s the pattern of international trade is strongly characterized by regional constellations.

This tendency toward greater regionalization means that large segments of the human race will undoubtedly be excluded from the world economy. The Soviet Union lies outside these regions, and a number of the Eastern European countries, with the failure of the debt-financed industrialization strategy of the 1970s and under the pressure of the Soviet Union, will be only partially integrated. The Southern Cone (Argentina, Chile, Peru, etc.) and other Latin American countries that had become integrated into the world economy in the nineteenth century appear to be falling out of the system (Gall, 1986). Much of black Africa has become marginalized and is sinking into economic and political despair. Where China, India, and Brazil, nations with immense potential, will eventually fit is not yet determined. There is a great danger that a more regionalized world economy will be composed of a few islands of relative prosperity in a turbulent sea of global poverty and alienated societies.

A greater regionalization of the world economy also poses a threat to the economic health of the dominant economic powers themselves. As this book has argued, if a market or capitalist system is to grow and be prosperous, it must be outwardly expansive. In a closed system, the operation of what the Marxists call the "laws of motion of capitalism" threaten in time to lead to economic and technological stagnation. Considered from this perspective, the growth potential of the emergent high technology industries of the future can probably be fully achieved only in a truly global economy. The cost of their development and the scale of these technologies necessitate the generation of a level of demand that is possible only in an integrated world market (Murakami and Yamamura, 1984).

This clash between the static gains from trade that would be possible in a regionalized world economy and the dynamic gains from technological advance in a larger international economy has been well described by William Cline:

There is another, potentially dangerous, implication of the line of analysis developed in this appendix [i.e., the shift to arbitrary comparative advantage and intra-industry trade]. To the extent that a wide group of countries has endowments of resources, factors, and technology that are broadly indistinguishable, the traditional grounds for welfare benefits from trade are eroded. After all, gains from trade accrue to both parties because of the difference between their respective relative costs of the products. With similar factor endowments, resources, and technology, these differences are not likely to be great, and neither would the losses from reduction of trade. This consideration would suggest that the welfare costs of limiting trade of this sort would not be high. But this inference is dangerous not only because it issues an open invitation to protectionist interests but also because it may overlook important economic welfare effects associated with economies of scale and competitive pressure for technological change even if the static welfare costs associated with comparative costs are limited (Cline, 1982a, p. 40).

Sectoral Protectionism

The dynamic advantages to be gained from economies of scale, corporate alliances across national boundaries, and the sharing of technology suggested in the 1980s that sectoral protectionism, that is, international cartelization, particularly in high-technology and service industries, will also be a distinctive feature of the emergent international economy (Patrick and Rosovsky, 1983, p. iv). In place of multilateral tariff reductions, governments will increasingly negotiate bilateral arrangements regarding market shares in specific economic sectors, arrangements that reflect the shift away from multilateralism and unconditional reciprocity to bilateralism and conditional reciprocity.

Sectoral protectionism, cartelization, or what Vinod Aggarwal (1985) has called "liberal protectionism" is, of course, nothing new. Nations have long protected particular economic sectors such as European and Japanese agriculture. The new element is the increasing importance, as signified by the rise of the New Protectionism, of negotiating market shares on a sector-by-sector basis. In contrast, the various rounds of the GATT succeeded by negotiating tradeoffs across industrial sectors based on considerations of revealed comparative advantage; for example, concessions by a country in one sector might be matched by another country in another sector. The purpose of sectoral protectionism, on the other hand, is to divide up or cartelize individual sectors among various producers.

American and Japanese trade negotiations have become the foremost expression of this move toward sectoral protectionism. In the so-called MOSS (Market-Oriented, Sector-Selective) discussions, which have taken place over several years in Tokyo and Washington, the United States tried to decrease Japanese regulatory, tariff, and other import barriers in the sectors of telecommunications, medical equipment and pharmaceuticals, electronics, and forest products. The decision of Japan and the United States in 1986 to cartelize the semiconductor industry was the most significant outcome of these discussions; it was the first extension of the New Protectionismism from traditional industries like steel and automobiles to high-technology products. Whatever the merits of this particular action, because of the economic importance and political sensitivity of these service and high technology sectors, any other approach than that of the MOSS discussions would undoubtedly be exceptionally difficult.

An important cause of the increasing importance of sectoral protectionism has been that the new technologies associated with the contemporary technological revolution such as the laser, the computer, and bioengineering can never achieve their potential in a fragmented world economy of restricted demand. Just as the technologies of the Second Industrial Revolution (steel, electricity, the automobile, other consumer durables, etc.) could only be fully developed in the continental mass market of the United States, the exploitation of the technologies of the Third Industrial Revolution will also require the existence of a huge global market. A regionalized world economy composed of relatively impervious national and regional markets could thwart this possibility.

The nature of the contemporary technological revolution also suggests that sectoral protectionism will be prevalent. The role of basic science has become increasingly important to the generation and the diffusion of these technologies, and these new technologies are frequently neither sector-specific nor merely a new product; instead they constitute novel processes, are ubiquitous in their effects, and cut across the economy, affecting traditional as well as modern industries. The computer, for example, is transforming all aspects of economic life from agriculture to manufacturing to office management.

These newer technologies are also very costly to develop, involve large economies of scale, and will require mass markets to amortize development costs. This means that there is unlikely to be any clear technological leader as in the past; instead there will be many centers of innovation and the technology will diffuse rapidly. The importance of these techologies to the wealth, power, and autonomy of national societies means that every state will want to maintain a presence in the technology.[11]

The rise of sectoral protectionism is associated with the New Multi-

---

[11] Maddison (1982) and The Economist (August 23, 1986) present interesting speculations on technological relations among the leading economic powers.

nationalism already discussed in Chapter Six, that is, the tendency of multinational corporations to invade one another's home market. A major reason for this cross or reciprocal foreign direct investment has been set forth by Kenichi Ohmae: "In such high-tech industries as computers, consumer electronics, and communications, the rapid pace of product innovation and development no longer allows firms the luxury of testing the home market before probing abroad. Moreover, because consumer preferences vary subtly by culture and are in constant flux, companies must intimately understand local tastes—and react instantly to changing market trends and prices" (Ohmae, 1985). He also points out that direct investment will continue to be necessary because insiders have greater immunity from protectionism; further, unless a corporation operates in all three of the regional centers of the world economy, it will not be able to "achieve the economies of scale world-class automated plants demand in order to pay for themselves." The New Protectionism, the rise of joint ventures across national boundaries, and the like are reflections of the movement toward sectoral protectionism.

Under these conditions, sectoral protectionism has become attractive to governments. It enables them to keep foreign markets open while they retain some control over their own internal markets and establish a national presence in the sector. Intra-industry rather than interindustry trade will thus be encouraged. They thereby gain some of the benefits of economic interdependence without the attendant costs of a fully liberalized trading regime.

Although sectoral protectionism departs from the liberal emphasis on economic efficiency and nondiscrimination, it appears to be the only way to satisfy both the need for economies of scale and the desire of governments to possess what they consider to be high-employment and strategic industries. Those economies with bargaining leverage, that is, with large internal markets, capital availability, or technological monopolies, would be the major winners through sectoral protectionism.

In the mid-1980s, it is not possible to determine the nature and extent of the industries that will propel economic growth in the advanced economies in the forthcoming era or to project which country or countries will be the winners or the losers. Will there be, as in the past, a clear technological leader such as Great Britain or the United States or, as has been suggested, will this leadership role be shared by two or more economies (Maddison, 1982)? Whatever the answer to this question, sectoral protectionism, along with mercantilism and regionalism, is a crucial feature of the transformed international economic order. In a substantial number of economic sectors, world markets are characterized in the mid-1980s by voluntary export restraints, orderly marketing agreements, and reciprocal foreign direct investment. Bilateralism and conditional reciprocity are increasingly important determinants of economic relations.

An international economy based on sectoral protectionism might help resolve the inherent tension between a liberal world economy and a decentralized state system (Buzan, 1983, p. 145). Through encouraging international joint ventures, establishing linkages among multinationals of different nationalities, and creating crosscutting interests among the three major centers of economic power, sectoral protectionism promises to counter the inherent tendencies in a regionalized system toward destabilizing conflict.

In the emergent configuration of the world economy, what portion of international economic transactions will be governed by mercantilistic competition, by economic regionalism, or by sectoral protectionism? At the moment it is too early to determine which tendency will predominate. What can be said is that unless these three elements can be successfully balanced, the danger of severe mercantilistic conflict and destabilizing economic nationalism will surely increase.

I have written elsewhere that one should make a distinction between benign and malevolent mercantilism (Gilpin, 1975, pp. 234-35). Benign mercantilism entails a degree of protectionism that safeguards the values and interests of a society; it enables a society to retain domestic autonomy and possess valued industries in a world characterized by the internationalization of production, global integration of financial markets, and the diminution of national control. Malevolent mercantilism, on the other hand, refers to the economic clashes of nations characteristic of the eighteenth century and the interwar period of the 1930s; its purpose is to triumph over other states. The first is defensive; the second is the conduct of interstate warfare by economic means. Thus, as John Ruggie has observed, the difference between the two forms of mercantilism is one of social purpose. The former serves domestic economic and social objectives such as employment, the control of macroeconomic policy, and the preservation of key industries; the latter's objective is the accumulation of national power and domination of other states (Ruggie, 1982, p. 382).

Although there can be no guarantee that a world economy based on benign mercantilism would not degenerate into the malevolent form, in the words of Barry Buzan, "a benign mercantilist system would have a better chance of containing peacefully states with different organizing ideologies. Liberal systems force a polarization between capitalist and centrally-planned states, and malign mercantilism encourages a general alienation of each from all. Benign mercantilism perhaps offers a middle way in which divergent actors can relate to each other on more equal terms over the whole system" (Buzan, 1983, p. 141). In an era of spreading economic nationalism, one could hardly hope for more than this benign mercantilist solution to the problem posed by the decline of economic leadership.[12]

However, the dangers inherent in the tendencies toward mercantilistic competition, economic regionalism, and sectoral protectionism should not be minimized. Liberalism and the principles embodied in it depoliticize international economic relations and can protect the weak against the strong. The Most-Favored Nation principle, nondiscrimination, and unconditional reciprocity provide as close to an objective basis of judging the legitimacy of economic behavior as may be possible; they place a constraint on arbitrary actions. In a world of policy competition, regional alliances, and bilateralism, what will be the norms guiding and limiting more managed economic relations? For example, will there be increasing demands that certain economies become more like those of other nations, similar to the American demands on the Japanese for reciprocity and greater harmonization of domestic structures?

The attempts of the United States to open foreign markets, privatize other economies, and preserve a liberal economic order, all in the name of liberal principles and domestic harmonization, could prove to be counterproductive. The exertion of political pressures on the Japanese to harmonize domestic structures with those of the West and the aggressive demand for reciprocity could inhibit the search for solutions more in keeping with the new economic and political realities. It would be far better for the United States to follow the European emphasis on sectoral protectionism than to attempt to force open the Japanese economy. As two leading American experts on the Japanese economy, Hugh Patrick and Henry Rosovsky, have pointed out, sectoral protectionism has always been something with which the Japanese could more easily learn to live (Patrick and Rosovsky, 1983, p. iv). If governments fail to heed this advice, then the present global movement toward benign mercantilism could degenerate into malevolent mercantilism. Uncompromising economic nationalism might become the new international norm, replacing state efforts to work out their economic differences with due regard to both market efficiency and national concerns.

---

[12] There is a very thin line indeed between what some refer to as "liberal protectionism," "specific reciprocity," and similar formulations and what Buzan (1983) and I call "benign mercantilism" as the characterization of the changing world economy.

Over the past three centuries the modern world has witnessed a parallel evolution of the scale of technology and the scope of the international market. At the same time that the cost of technology and the need for economies of scale have increased, national and international markets have adjusted and have enlarged, thereby increasing the level of global demand. But as Eugene Staley observed during the global economic and political collapse of the 1930s, markets and politics need not ultimately adjust to technology. Many times in the past, technology and economics have ultimately adjusted to politics: "In the 'Dark Ages' following the collapse of the Roman Empire, technology adjusted itself to politics. The magnificent Roman roads fell into disrepair, the baths and aqueducts and amphitheatres and villas into ruins. Society lapsed back to localism in production and distribution, forgot much of the learning and the technology and the governmental systems of earlier days" (Staley, 1939, p. 52). The transition to the growth technologies of the contemporary industrial revolution will not be achieved without the establishment of a more stable political framework for economic activities.

CONCLUSION

The transition to a new international economic order from the declining era of American hegemony is and will continue to be difficult. Among the many factors that make a return to the halcyon days of the first decades of the postwar era virtually impossible is the decline of clearly defined political leadership. Conflicting economic and political objectives make the achievement of international cooperation and pluralist leadership of the world economy unlikely. National economies are inclined to resist adjustment to changes in comparative advantage and in the global distribution of economic activities. There is little likelihood of a return to high rates of economic growth unless market forces are permitted to relocate economic activities on the basis of shifts in competitive advantage. Furthermore, the tendency of states to place domestic priorities above international norms has serious implications for the continuation of a highly interdependent international economy. A return to the path of economic liberalization is impossible unless governments are willing to subordinate short-term parochial interests to the larger goal of a stable international economy and to carry out extensive harmonization of domestic institutions and business practices.

The diffusion of economic power and the reemergence of economic nationalism necessitate a very different international economic order from that of the Bretton Woods system. The reassertion of the state in economic affairs means a slowing, if not a reversal, of the postwar primacy of the market as the means of organizing global economic relations. Although it is impossible to predict the nature of state and market interaction in the new environment, certain developments seem likely. There has been and will be growing politicization of the international economic order and an increase in policy competition. Government intervention in the areas of trade, money, and production has grown immensely despite the revival of neoconservatism and a rediscovery of the market in many countries. Deregulation at home appears to be accompanied frequently by increased protection of domestic markets and policy initiatives designed to promote nationalistic goals. It is significant that at the same time the Reagan Administration was deregulating the American economy, it was also raising protectionist barriers more rapidly than any other postwar American administration and fashioning policy instruments to gain greater leverage over other economies (*The Economist*, March 2, 1985, p. 80).

There is also an increasing regionalization of the world economy as global economic activities cluster around the several poles of the world economy. The increased closure of the European Common Market, the continued separation of the Soviet bloc from the world economy, and the perceptible shift of the United States toward the Pacific Basin as well as the increasing importance of Japan and the newly industrializing countries are all elements in this retreat from the postwar ideal of a multilateral liberal system. The debt problem, the disorders of the international monetary system, and the cartelization of a substantial fraction of world trade are pushing the world more and more in this direction. Although it is highly unlikely that increased fragmentation will lead to a collapse of the global system as serious as that of the 1930s, regionalism will surely become a more prominent feature of international economic and political relations.

A system of sectoral protectionism or, perhaps, sectoral regimes is emerging (Aggarwal, 1985). In many economic sectors national shares of international markets and the international location of economic activities will be as much a function of bilateral negotiations among governments and economic actors as of the operation of the "laws" of comparative advantage. The New Protectionism, the emergence of industrial and strategic trade policies, and the increasing role of imperfect competition are forces moving the world economy toward sectoral protectionism. Cartelization, voluntary export restraints, and similar mechanisms to divide markets or encourage domestic production by foreign firms are becoming an integral, albeit a regrettable, feature of the international political economy. It is possible that a world economy

407

composed of a more protectionist United States, an increasingly autarkic Western Europe, and a Japan determined to preserve its traditional culture can be held together only through such devices. In a world of "arbitrary" comparative advantage, states will wish to ensure a strong national presence in emergent high-technology industries and the growth sectors of the future. Thus, although the relative balance of political and market determinants of economic activities will differ from one economic sector to another and from time to time, market shares and the global location of economic activities will be strongly influenced by bargaining among nation-states and multinational corporations.

It is paradoxical that governments have responded to the growth of global economic interdependence by enhancing their authority over economic activities. Both global market forces and state interventionism have become more important determinants of international economic relations than in the recent past. In this new environment, bilateralism or minilateralism has largely displaced the multilateralism of the GATT and political considerations have become increasingly important in the determination of economic relations and economic policy.

The new international economic order of the mid-1980s raises profound issues of economic equity for the conscience of mankind. Many societies will suffer from the closure of world markets and will require massive economic assistance if they are to have any chance to escape from their poverty. The liberal world economy based on nondiscrimination and multilateralism had defects; however, it did at least provide economic opportunities that will shrink in a more nationalistic world economy.

The mixed system of multilateral, regional, and protectionist arrangements may or may not prove stable over the long run. Yet this politicized economic world need not mean a return either to the malevolent mercantilism and economic warfare of the 1930s or to the expanding and relatively benevolent interdependence of the 1960s. The postwar age of multilateral liberalization is over and the world's best hope for economic stability is some form of benign mercantilism. The continuing residue of American power and leadership, the security ties of the major economic actors, and the promise of high technology as a source of economic growth provide support for moderate optimism. Nevertheless, at this juncture in the transition from one economic order to another, the only certainty is that a new international political economy is emerging. It is not clear who will gain, who will lose, or what the consequences will be for global prosperity and world peace.

Reference List

Abegglen, James C., and George Stalk, Jr. 1985. *Kaisha—The Japanese Corporation*. New York: Basic Books.

Adams, Brooks. 1895. *The Law of Civilization and Decay; An Essay on History*. New York: Macmillan.

Aggarwal, Vinod K. 1985. *Liberal Protectionism: The International Politics of Organized Textile Trade*. Berkeley: University of California Press.

Aggarwal, Vinod K., Robert O. Keohane, and David B. Yoffie. 1986. "The Dynamics of Cooperative Protectionism." Division of Research, Harvard Business School. Unpublished.

Aho, C. Michael, and Jonathan David Aronson. 1985. *Trade Talks: America Better Listen!* New York: Council on Foreign Relations.

Akamatsu, Kaname. 1961. "A Theory of Unbalanced Growth in the World Economy." *Weltwirtschaftliches Archiv* 86:196-215.

Amin, Samir. 1976. *Unequal Development: An Essay on the Social Formations of Peripheral Capitalism*. New York: Monthly Review Press.

Anell, Lars. 1981. *Recession, The Western Economies and the Changing World Order*. London: Frances Pinter.

Angell, Norman. 1911. *The Great Illusion; A Study of the Relation of Military Power in Nations to their Economic and Social Advantage*. 3d ed., rev. and enl. New York: Putnam.

Appleby, Joyce Oldham. 1978. *Economic Thought and Ideology in Seventeenth-Century England*. Princeton: Princeton University Press.

Avery, William P., and David P. Rapkin, eds. 1982. *America in a Changing World Political Economy*. New York: Longman.

Avineri, Shlomo, ed. 1969. *Karl Marx on Colonialism and Modernization*. Garden City, N.Y.: Anchor Books.

Baechler, Jean. 1971. *Les Origines du capitalisme*. Paris: Editions Gallimard. (*The Origins of Capitalism*. Trans. Barry Cooper. Oxford: Basil Blackwell, 1975.)

Bagehot, Walter. 1873. *Lombard Street: A Description of the Money Market*. New York: Scribner.

Baldwin, David A. 1971. "Money and Power." *The Journal of Politics* 33:578-614.

————. 1979. "Power Analysis and World Politics: New Trends versus Old Tendencies." *World Politics* 31:161-94.

————. 1980. "Interdependence and Power: A Conceptual Analysis." *International Organization* 34:471-506.

————. 1985. *Economic Statecraft*. Princeton: Princeton University Press.

Baldwin, Richard, and Paul R. Krugman. 1986. "Persistent Trade Effects of Large Exchange Rate Shocks." Unpublished.

Baldwin, Robert E., ed. 1984a. *Recent Issues and Initiatives in U.S. Trade Policy*. Cambridge, Mass.: NBER Conference Report.

Baldwin, Robert E. 1984b. "Trade Policies in Developed Countries." In Jones and Kenen, 1984, Vol. 1, Chapter 12.

———. 1984c. "Trade Policies under the Reagan Administration." In Baldwin, 1984a, Chapter 2.

———. 1985. *The Political Economy of U.S. Import Policy*. Cambridge: MIT Press.

Baran, Paul A. 1967. *The Political Economy of Growth*. New York: Monthly Review Press.

Bauer, Peter T. 1976. *Dissent on Development*. Rev. ed. Cambridge: Harvard University Press.

Baumol, William J. 1965. *Welfare Economics and the Theory of the State*. 2d ed. Cambridge: Harvard University Press.

Becker, Gary S. 1976. *The Economic Approach to Human Behavior*. Chicago: University of Chicago Press.

Beenstock, Michael. 1983. *The World Economy in Transition*. London: George Allen and Unwin.

Bergsten, C. Fred, and William R. Cline. 1985. *The United States–Japan Economic Problem*. Policy Analysis in International Economics, No. 13. Washington: Institute for International Economics.

Bergsten, C. Fred, Robert O. Keohane, and Joseph S. Nye, Jr. 1975. "International Economics and International Politics: A Framework for Analysis." In Bergsten and Krause, 1975, pp. 3-36.

Bergsten, C. Fred, and Lawrence B. Krause, eds. 1975. "World Politics and International Economics." *International Organization* 29:3-352.

Bhagwati, Jagdish N., and John Gerard Ruggie, eds. 1984. *Power, Passions, and Purpose: Prospects for North-South Negotiations*. Cambridge: MIT Press.

Bienen, Henry S., and Mark Gersovitz. 1985. "Economic Stabilization, Conditionality, and Political Stability." *International Organization* 39:729-54.

BIS (Bank for International Settlements). 1986. *Recent Innovations in International Banking*. Basel.

Blackhurst, Richard, Nicolas Marian, and Jan Tumlir. 1977. *Trade Liberalization, Protectionism and Interdependence*. Geneva: GATT Studies in International Trade, No. 5.

Blau, Peter M. 1964. *Exchange and Power in Social Life*. New York: John Wiley.

Blaug, Mark. 1978. *Economic Theory in Retrospect*. 3d ed. New York: Cambridge University Press.

Block, Fred L. 1977. *The Origins of International Economic Disorder: A Study of United States International Monetary Policy from World War II to the Present*. Berkeley: University of California Press.

Bogdanowicz-Bindert, Christine A. 1985/86. "World Debt: The U.S. Reconsiders." *Foreign Affairs* 64:259-73.

Bonn, M. J. 1939. *Wealth, Welfare or War: The Changing Role of Economics in National Policy.* International Institute of Intellectual Co-operation. Paris: League of Nations.

Brainard, William C., and Richard N. Cooper. 1968. "Uncertainty and Diversification in International Trade." *Studies in Agricultural Economics, Trade, and Development* 8:257-85.

Branson, William H. 1980. "Trends in United States International Trade and Investment since World War II." In Feldstein, ed., *American Economy in Transition*, 1980, pp. 183-257.

———. 1986. "The Limits of Monetary Coordination as Exchange-Rate Policy." April 3-4. Unpublished.

Branson, William H., and Alvin K. Klevorick. 1986. "Strategic Behavior and Trade Policy." In Krugman, 1986, Chapter 10.

Braudel, Fernand. 1979. *The Perspective of the World—Civilization and Capitalism, 15th-18th Century.* Vol. 3. New York: Harper and Row.

Bressand, Albert. 1983. "Mastering the 'World Economy.'" *Foreign Affairs* 61:745-72.

Brewer, Anthony. 1980. *Marxist Theories of Imperialism: A Critical Survey.* London: Routledge and Kegan Paul.

Brown, Michael Barratt. 1970. *After Imperialism.* New York: Humanities Press.

Bruno, Michael, and Jeffrey S. Sachs. 1985. *Economics of Worldwide Stagflation.* Cambridge: Harvard University Press.

Buckley, Thomas. 1986. "Strategic Trade Policy: Economic Theory and the Mercantilist Challenge." Unpublished.

Buzan, Barry. 1983. *People, States, and Fear: The National Security Problem in International Relations.* Chapel Hill: University of North Carolina Press.

Calder, Kent E. 1985. "The Emerging Politics of the Trans-Pacific Economy." *World Policy Journal* 2:593-623.

Calleo, David P. 1976. "The Decline and Rebuilding of an International Economic System: Some General Considerations." In David P. Calleo, ed., *Money and the Coming World Order.* New York: New York University Press.

———. 1982. *The Imperious Economy.* Cambridge: Harvard University Press.

Calleo, David P., and Benjamin M. Rowland. 1973. *America and the World Political Economy: Atlantic Dreams and National Realities.* Bloomington: Indiana University Press.

Cameron, David R. 1978. "The Expansion of the Public Economy: A Comparative Analysis." *American Political Science Review* 72:1243-1261.

Cameron, R. 1982. "Technology, Institutions and Long-Term Economic Change." In Charles P. Kindleberger and Guido di Tella, eds. *Economics in the Long View.* Vol. 1, *Models and Methodology*, Chapter 3. New York: New York University Press.

Caporaso, James A., ed. 1978. "Dependence and Dependency in the Global System." *International Organization* 32:1-300.

Carnoy, Martin. 1984. *The State and Political Theory*. Princeton: Princeton University Press.

Carr, Edward Hallett. 1945. *Nationalism and After*. London: Macmillan.

———. 1951 [1939]. *The Twenty Years' Crisis, 1919-1939*. 2d ed. London: Macmillan.

Casson, Mark, ed. 1983. *The Growth of International Business*. London: George Allen and Unwin.

Caves, Richard E. 1982. *Multinational Enterprise and Economic Analysis*. New York: Cambridge University Press.

Chace, James. 1981. *Solvency: The Price of Survival*. New York: Random House.

Choucri, Nazli. 1980. "International Political Economy: A Theoretical Perspective." In Holsti et al., 1980, Chapter 5.

Cipolla, Carlo M. 1956. *Money, Prices, and Civilization in the Mediterranean World, Fifth to Seventeenth Century*. Princeton: Published for the University of Cincinnati Press by Princeton University Press.

———, ed. 1970. *The Economic Decline of Empires*. London: Methuen.

Clark, Cal, and Donna Bahry. 1983. "Dependent Development: A Socialist Variant." *International Studies Quarterly* 27:271-93.

Clark, George Norman. 1958. *War and Society in the Seventeenth Century*. Cambridge: Cambridge University Press.

Cline, William R. 1982a. *"Reciprocity": A New Approach to World Trade Policy?* Policy Analyses in International Economics, No. 2. Washington: Institute for International Economics.

———. 1982b. "Can the East Asian Model of Development Be Generalized?" *World Development* 10:81-90.

———, ed. 1983. *Trade Policy in the 1980s*. Washington: Institute for International Economics.

Cohen, Benjamin J. 1973. *The Question of Imperialism: The Political Economy of Dominance and Dependence*. New York: Basic Books.

———. 1977. *Organizing the World's Money: The Political Economy of International Monetary Relations*. New York: Basic Books.

Condliffe, J. B. 1950. *The Commerce of Nations*. New York: W. W. Norton.

Conybeare, John A. C. 1984. "Public Goods, Prisoners' Dilemmas and the International Political Economy." *International Studies Quarterly* 28:5-22.

———. 1985. "Trade Wars: The Theory and Practice of International Commercial Rivalry." Unpublished.

Cooper, Richard. 1968. *The Economics of Interdependence: Economic Policy in the Atlantic Community*. New York: McGraw-Hill.

———. 1970. "International Economics in the *International Encyclopedia of the Social Sciences*: A Review Article." *Journal of Economic Literature* 8:435-39.

———. 1975. "Prolegomena to the Choice of an International Monetary System." In Bergsten and Krause, 1975, pp. 63-97.

———. 1982. "Global Economic Policy in a World of Energy Shortage." In Joseph A. Pechman and N. J. Simler, eds., *Economics in the Public Service.* New York: W. W. Norton.

———. 1983. "Managing Risks to the International Economic System." In Herring, 1983, Chapter 1.

———. 1984. "Is There a Need for Reform?" In Federal Reserve Bank of Boston, *The International Monetary System: Forty Years after Bretton Woods.* Proceedings of a Conference Held at Bretton Woods, New Hampshire, May.

———. 1985. "Economic Interdependence and Coordination of Economic Policies." In Jones and Kenen, Vol. 2, Chapter 23.

Corbett, Hugh. 1979. "Tokyo Round: Twilight of a Liberal Era or a New Dawn." *National Westminister Bank Quarterly Review* (February):19-29.

Corden, W. M. 1974. *Trade Policy and Economic Welfare.* Oxford: Clarendon Press.

———. 1984a. "The Normative Theory of International Trade." In Jones and Kenen, 1984, Vol. 1, Chapter 2.

———. 1984b. *The Revival of Protectionism.* Occasional Papers, No. 14. New York: Group of Thirty.

Corden, W. M., and Peter Oppenheimer. 1974. "Basic Implications of the Rise in Oil Prices." Staff Paper No. 6. London: Trade Policy Research Centre.

Cornwall, John. 1977. *Modern Capitalism: Its Growth and Transformation.* New York: St. Martin's Press.

Corrigan, E. Gerald. 1985. "Public and Private Debt Accumulation: A Perspective." Federal Reserve Bank of New York, *Quarterly Review* 10:1-5.

Council of Economic Advisers. 1985. *Economic Report of the President.* Washington: U. S. Government Printing Office.

———. 1986. *Economic Report of the President.* Washington: U.S. Government Printing Office.

Cowhey, Peter F., and Edward Long. 1983. "Testing Theories of Regime Change: Hegemonic Decline or Surplus Capacity?" *International Organization* 37:157-88.

Cox, Robert W. 1979. "Ideologies and the New International Economic Order: Reflections on Some Recent Literature." *International Organization* 33:257-302.

———. 1981. "Social Forces, States, and World Orders: Beyond International Relations Theory." *Millennium, Journal of International Studies* 10:126-55.

Craig, Gordon A. 1982. *The Germans.* New York: G. P. Putnam's Sons.

Culbertson, John M. 1985. *The Dangers of "Free Trade."* Madison: 21st Century Press.

Cumings, Bruce. 1984. "The Origins and Development of the Northeast Asian Political Economy: Industrial Sectors, Product Cycles, and Political Consequences." *International Organization* 38:1-40.

Curzon, Gerard. 1965. *Multilateral Commercial Diplomacy: The General*

Agreement on Tariffs and Trade and Its Impact on National Commercial Policies and Techniques. London: Michael Joseph.

Curzon, Gerard, and Victoria Curzon Price. 1980. "The Multi-Tier GATT System." In Hieronymi, 1980, Chapter 8.

Dahrendorf, Ralf. 1959. *Class and Class Conflict in Industrial Society.* Stanford: Stanford University Press.

———. 1979. *Life Chances.* Chicago: University of Chicago Press.

Davis, Lance E., and Douglass C. North (with the assistance of Calla Smorodin). 1971. *Institutional Change and American Economic Growth.* Cambridge: Cambridge University Press.

Deane, Phyllis. 1978. *The Evolution of Economic Ideas.* New York: Cambridge University Press.

Deardorff, Alan V. 1984. "Testing Trade Theories and Predicting Trade Flows." In Jones and Kenen, 1984, Vol. 1, Chapter 10.

Deardorff, Alan V., and Robert M. Stern. 1984. "Methods of Measurement of Nontariff Barriers." Seminar Discussion Paper, No. 136, Research Seminar in International Economics, Department of Economics, University of Michigan.

Delamaide, Darrell. 1984. *Debt Shock: The Full Story of the World Credit Crisis.* Garden City, N.Y.: Doubleday.

de Larosière, Jacques. 1982. *Restoring Fiscal Discipline—A Vital Element for Economic Recovery.* International Monetary Fund. March 16.

Destler, I. M. 1986. "Protecting Congress or Protecting Trade?" *Foreign Policy,* no. 62:96-107.

Diaz-Alejandro, Carlo F. 1983. "Comments." In Cline, 1983, pp. 305-309.

Dickson, Peter G. M. 1967. *The Financial Revolution in England; A Study in the Development of Public Credit, 1688-1756.* London: Macmillan.

Dillard, Dudley. 1967. *Economic Development of the North Atlantic Community: Historical Introduction to Modern Economics.* Englewood Cliffs, N.J.: Prentice-Hall.

di Tella, Guido. 1982. "The Economics of the Frontier." In Kindleberger and di Tella, 1982, Chapter 13.

Dixit, Avinash K. 1983. "Tax Policy in Open Economies." Discussion Papers in Economics, No. 51. Woodrow Wilson School, Princeton University.

———. 1985. "How Should the U.S. Respond to Other Countries' Trade Policies?" Unpublished.

———. 1986. "Trade Policy: An Agenda for Research." In Krugman, 1986, Chapter 12.

Dixit, Avinash K., and Gene M. Grossman. 1984. "Targeted Export Promotion with Several Oligopolistic Industries." Discussion Papers in Economics, No. 71, Woodrow Wilson School, Princeton University.

Dixit, Avinash K., and Albert S. Kyle. 1985. "The Use of Protection and Subsidies for Entry Promotion and Deterrence." *American Economic Review* 75:139-52.

Dos Santos, Theotonio. 1970. "The Structure of Dependence." *American Economic Review* 60:231-36.

Doyle, Michael W. 1983. "Kant, Liberal Legacies, and Foreign Affairs," Parts 1 and 2. *Philosophy and Public Affairs* 12:205-235 and 323-53.

Drobnick, Richard. 1985. *Debt Problems, Trade Offensives and Protectionism: The Uncharted International Economic Environment of the 1980s.* Trend Analysis Program. The American Council of Life Insurance.

Drucker, Peter F. 1983. "Schumpeter and Keynes." *Forbes*, May 23, pp. 124-28.

———. 1985. "American-Japanese Realities." *Wall Street Journal*, October 11.

Dunning, John H. 1981. *International Production and the Multinational Enterprise.* London: George Allen and Unwin.

El-Agraa, Ali M. 1983. *The Theory of International Trade.* London: Croom Helm.

Elliott, William Y. 1955. *The Political Economy of American Foreign Policy.* New York: Henry Holt.

Ellsworth, P. T. 1964. *The International Economy.* New York: Macmillan.

Emmanuel, Arghiri. 1972. *Unequal Exchange: A Study of the Imperialism of Trade.* New York: Monthly Review Press.

Emminger, Otmar. 1985. *The Dollar's Borrowed Strength.* Occasional Papers, No. 19. New York: The Group of Thirty.

Evans, Peter. 1979. *Dependent Development: The Alliance of Multinational, State, and Local Capital in Brazil.* Princeton: Princeton University Press.

Feis, Herbert. 1964 [1930]. *Europe, The World's Banker, 1870-1914.* New Haven: Yale University Press.

Feldstein, Martin, ed. 1980. *The American Economy in Transition.* Chicago: University of Chicago Press.

Feldstein, Martin. 1985. "American Economic Policy and the World Economy." *Foreign Affairs* 63:995-1008.

———. 1986. "The Future of Economic Policy." The Janeway Lectures, Princeton University. Unpublished.

Findlay, Ronald. 1981. "The Fundamental Determinants of the Terms of Trade." In Grassman and Lundberg, 1981, Chapter 12.

———. 1984. "Growth and Development in Trade Models." In Jones and Kenen, 1984, Vol. 1, Chapter 4.

Fisher, Allan G. B. 1935. *The Clash of Progress and Security.* London: Macmillan.

Fishlow, Albert. 1985. "Lessons from the Past: Capital Markets during the 19th Century and the Interwar Period" *International Organization* 39:383-439.

Frank, Andre Gunder. 1969. *Capitalism and Underdevelopment in Latin America: Historical Studies of Chile and Brazil.* Rev. ed. New York: Monthly Review Press.

Frank, Andre Gunder. 1970. *Latin America: Underdevelopment or Revolution*. New York: Monthly Review Press.

Frank, Robert H., and Richard T. Freeman. 1978. *The Distributional Consequences of Direct Foreign Investment*. New York: Academic Press.

Frankel, Jeffrey A. 1984. *The Yen/Dollar Agreement: Liberalizing Japanese Capital Markets*. Washington: Institute for International Economics.

Frenkel, Jacob. 1985. "Comment on William Branson, 'Causes of Appreciation and Volatility of the Dollar.' " Working Paper, No. 1777. Cambridge, Mass.: National Bureau of Economic Research.

Frey, Bruno. 1984a. "The Public Choice View of International Political Economy." *International Organization* 38:199-223.

———. 1984b. *International Political Economics*. New York: Basil Blackwell.

Frieden, Jeffrey. 1981. "Third World Indebted Industrialization: International Finance and State Capitalism in Mexico, Brazil, Algeria, and South Korea." *International Organization* 35:407-431.

Friedmann, John. 1966. *Regional Development Policy; A Case Study of Venezuela*. Cambridge: MIT Press.

———. 1972. "A General Theory of Polarized Development." In Niles M. Hansen, ed., *Growth Centers in Regional Economic Development*. New York: Free Press.

Frohlich, Norman, Joe A. Oppenheimer, and Oran R. Young. 1971. *Political Leadership and Collective Goods*. Princeton: Princeton University Press.

Fukushima, Kiyohiko. 1985. "Japan's Real Trade Policy." *Foreign Policy*, no. 59:22-39.

Gaddis, John Lewis. 1982. *Strategies of Containment: A Critical Appraisal of Postwar American National Security Policy*. New York: Oxford University Press.

Gall, Norman. 1986. "The Four Horsemen Ride Again." *Forbes* 138 (July 28):95-99.

Gallagher, John, and Ronald Robinson. 1953. "The Imperialism of Free Trade." *Economic History Review*, 2d ser., 6:1-15.

Gardner, Richard N. 1980. *Sterling-Dollar Diplomacy in Current Perspective: The Origins and Prospects of Our International Economic Order*. New York: Columbia University Press.

Gerth, H. H., and C. Wright Mills, trans. and eds. 1946. *From Max Weber: Essays in Sociology*. New York: Columbia University Press.

Gerschenkron, Alexander. 1962. *Economic Backwardness in Historical Perspective, A Book of Essays*. Cambridge: Belknap Press of Harvard University Press.

Gibney, Frank. 1982. *Miracle by Design: The Real Reasons Behind Japan's Economic Success*. New York: Times Books.

Giddens, Anthony. 1985. *A Contemporary Critique of Historical Materialism*. Vol. 2, *The Nation-State and Violence*. Berkeley: University of California Press.

Giersch, Herbert, ed. 1982. *Emerging Technologies: Consequences for Eco-*

nomic Growth, Structural Change, and Employment. Symposium 1981. Tübingen: J.C.B. Mohr (Paul Siebeck).

Giersch, Herbert. 1984. "The Age of Schumpeter. *American Economic Review* 74 (May):103-109.

Gilpin, Robert. 1972. "The Politics of Transnational Economic Relations." In Keohane and Nye, 1972, pp. 48-69.

———. 1975. *U.S. Power and the Multinational Corporation: The Political Economy of Foreign Direct Investment.* New York: Basic Books.

———. 1977. "Economic Interdependence and National Security in Historical Perspective." In Klaus Knorr and Frank N. Trager, eds., *Economic Issues and National Security.* Lawrence: The Regents Press of Kansas.

———. 1981. *War and Change in World Politics.* New York: Cambridge University Press.

———. 1982. "Trade, Investment, and Technology Policy." In Giersch, 1982.

———. 1984. "Structural Constraints on Economic Leverage: Market-Type Systems." In Gordon H. McCormick and Richard E. Bissell, eds., *Strategic Dimensions of Economic Behavior,* Chapter Six. New York: Praeger.

———. 1986. "The Theory of Hegemonic War." Unpublished.

Goldfield, David. 1984. "Countertrade." *International Perspective* (March/April):19-22.

Goldstein, Joshua S. 1985. "Kondratieff Waves as War Cycles." *International Studies Quarterly* 29:411-44.

Goldstein, Judith. 1985. "The Evolution and Devolution of American Trade Policy." Paper presented at the 1985 Meeting of the American Political Science Association.

———. 1986. "The Political Economy of Trade: Institutions of Protection." *American Political Science Review* 80:161-84.

Goldthorpe, John H. 1978. "The Current Inflation: Towards a Sociological Account." In Fred Hirsch and John H. Goldthorpe, eds., *The Political Economy of Inflation.* Cambridge: Harvard University Press.

———, ed. 1984. *Order and Conflict in Contemporary Capitalism: Studies in the Political Economy of Western European Nations.* Oxford: Clarendon Press.

Gould, J. D. 1972. *Economic Growth in History: Survey and Analysis.* London: Methuen.

Gourevitch, Peter Alexis. 1977. "International Trade, Domestic Coalitions and Liberty: Comparative Responses to the Crisis of 1873-1896." *Journal of Interdisciplinary History* 8:281-313.

Gowa, Joanne. 1983. *Closing the Gold Window: Domestic Politics and the End of Bretton Woods.* Ithaca: Cornell University Press.

Grassman, Sven, and Erik Lundberg, eds. 1981. *The World Economic Order—Past and Prospects.* London: Macmillan.

Grieco, Joseph M. 1982. "Between Dependency and Autonomy: India's Experience with the International Computer Industry." *International Organization* 36:609-632.

Grossman, Gene M., and David J. Richardson. 1985. *Strategic Trade Policy: A Survey of Issues and Early Analysis*. Special Papers in International Economics, No. 15. International Finance Section, Department of Economics, Princeton University.

Grunwald, Joseph, and Kenneth Flamm. 1985. *The Global Factory: Foreign Assembly in International Trade*. Washington: The Brookings Institution.

Haas, Ernst B. 1980. "Why Collaborate? Issue-Linkage and International Regimes." *World Politics* 32:357-405.

Hager, Wolfgang. 1982. "Protectionism and Autonomy: How to Preserve Free Trade in Europe." *International Affairs* 58:413-28.

Hallwood, Paul, and Stuart W. Sinclair. 1981. *Oil, Debt and Development: OPEC in the Third World*. London: George Allen and Unwin.

Hamada, Koichi. 1979. "Macroeconomic Strategy and Coordination under Alternate Exchange Rates." In Rudiger Dornbusch and Jacob A. Frenkel, eds., *International Economic Policy: Theory and Evidence*, Chapter 9. Baltimore: The Johns Hopkins University Press.

Hamilton, Alexander. 1928 [1791]. "Report on the Subject of Manufactures." In Arthur Harrison Cole, ed., *Industrial and Commercial Correspondence of Alexander Hamilton, Anticipating his Report on Manufacturing*. Chicago: A. W. Shaw Co.

Hansen, Alvin. 1964. *Business Cycles and National Income*. Expanded ed. New York: W. W. Norton.

Harrod, Roy F. 1951. *The Life of John Maynard Keynes*. London: Macmillan.

Hartwell, R. M. 1982. "Progress and Dissimilarity in Historical Perspective." In Kindleberger and di Tella, 1982, Vol. 1, Chapter 6.

Hauser, Henri. 1937. *Économie et diplomatie: Les conditions nouvelles de la politique étrangère*. Paris: Librairie du Recueil Sirey.

Hawtrey, Ralph G. 1952. *Economic Aspects of Sovereignty*. London: Longmans.

Haynes, Stephen E., Michael M. Hutchison, and Raymond F. Mikesell. 1986. *Japanese Financial Policies and the U.S. Trade Deficit*. Essays in International Finance, No. 162. International Finance Section, Department of Economics, Princeton University.

Heckscher, Eli F. 1935. *Mercantilism*. 2 vols. Mendel Shapiro, trans. London: G. Allen and Unwin.

Heertje, Arnold. 1973. *Economics and Technical Change*. New York: John Wiley and Sons.

Hegel, Georg W. F. 1945 [1821]. *Hegel's Philosophy of Right*. Trans. with notes by T. M. Knox. London: Oxford University Press.

Heilbroner, Robert L. 1980. *Marxism: For and Against*. New York: W. W. Norton.

———. 1985. *The Nature and Logic of Capitalism*. New York: W. W. Norton.

Helleiner, Gerald K. 1981. *Intra-firm Trade and the Developing Countries*. New York: St. Martin's Press.

Helpman, Elhanan. 1984. "Increasing Returns, Imperfect Markets, and Trade Theory." In Jones and Kenen, 1984, Chapter 7.

Helpman, Elhanan, and Paul R. Krugman. 1985. *Market Structure and Foreign Trade Increasing Returns, Imperfect Competition, and the International Economy.* Cambridge: MIT Press.

Herring, Richard J., ed. 1983. *Managing International Risk.* New York: Cambridge University Press.

Hewlett, Sylvia Ann, Henry Kaufman, and Peter B. Kenen. 1984. *The Global Repercussions of U.S. Monetary and Fiscal Policy.* New York: Ballinger.

Hicks, John. 1969. *A Theory of Economic History.* Oxford: Oxford University Press.

Hieronymi, Otto, ed. 1980. *The New Economic Nationalism.* New York: Praeger.

Hindley, Brian J. 1980. "Voluntary Export Restraints and the GATT's Main Escape Clause." *The World Economy* 3:313-41.

———. 1982-83. "Protectionism and Autonomy: A Comment on Hager." *International Affairs* 59:77-86.

Hine, R. C. 1985. *The Political Economy of European Trade: An Introduction to the Trade Policies of the EEC.* New York: St. Martin's Press.

Hirsch, Fred, and John H. Goldthorpe, eds. 1978. *The Political Economy of Inflation.* Cambridge: Harvard University Press.

Hirsch, Seev. 1967. *Location of Industry and International Competitiveness.* Oxford: Clarendon Press.

Hirschman, Albert O. 1945. *National Power and the Structure of Foreign Trade.* Berkeley: University of California Press.

———. 1952. "Effects of Industrialization on the Markets of Industrial Countries." In Bert F. Hoselitz, ed., *The Progress of Underdeveloped Areas,* pp. 270-83. Chicago: University of Chicago Press.

———. 1958. *The Strategy of Economic Development.* New Haven: Yale University Press.

———. 1981. *Essays in Trespassing: Economics to Politics and Beyond.* New York: Cambridge University Press.

Hobson, John. 1965 [1902]. *Imperialism: A Study.* Ann Arbor: University of Michigan Press.

Hofheinz, Roy, Jr., and Kent E. Calder. 1982. *The Eastasia Edge.* New York: Basic Books.

Holsti, Ole R., Randolph M. Siverson, and Alexander L. George, eds. 1980. *Change in the International System.* Boulder, Colo.: Westview Press.

Hormats, Robert D. 1984. "New Factors in the World Economy in the Wake of the Debt Crisis." In Hewlett et al., 1984, Chapter 12.

Hufbauer, Gary Clyde, and Jeffrey J. Schott. 1985. *Economic Sanctions Reconsidered: History and Current Policy.* Washington: Institute for International Economics.

Hymer, Stephen. 1960. *The International Operations of National Firms: A Study of Foreign Direct Investment.* Ph.D. dissertation, Department of Economics, Massachusetts Institute of Technology, 1960. Published in 1976 by MIT Press.

Ikenberry, G. John. 1986a. "The State and Strategies of International Adjustment." *World Politics* 39:53-77.

————. 1986b. "The Irony of State Strength: Comparative Responses to the Oil Shocks in the 1970s." *International Organization* 40:105-137.

Ilgen, Thomas. 1985. *Autonomy and Interdependence: U.S.-Western European Monetary and Trade Relations, 1958-1984*. Totowa, N.J.: Rowman and Allanheld.

Japan Times. 1983. *Japan in the Year 2000*. Tokyo.

Jervis, Robert. 1982. "Security Regimes."*International Organization* 36:357-78.

JETRO (Japan External Trade Organization). 1985. *White Paper on International Trade: Japan 1985*. Tokyo.

Johnson, Chalmers. 1982. *MITI and the Japanese Miracle: The Growth of Industrial Policy, 1925-1975*. Stanford: Stanford University Press.

Johnson, Harry G. 1953-54. "Optimum Tariffs and Retaliation." *Review of Economic Studies* 21 (2):142-53.

————. 1965a. "An Economic Theory of Protectionism, Tariff Bargaining, and the Formation of Customs Unions." *Journal of Political Economy* 73:256-81.

————. 1965b. *The World Economy at the Crossroads: A Survey of Current Problems of Money, Trade, and Economic Development*. New York: Oxford University Press.

————, ed. 1967. *Economic Nationalism in Old and New States*. Chicago: University of Chicago Press.

————. 1968. *Comparative Cost and Commercial Policy Theory for a Developing World Economy*. The Wicksell Lectures. Stockholm: Almqvist and Wiksell.

————. 1972. "Political Economy Aspects of International Monetary Reform." *Journal of International Economics* 2:401-423.

————. 1975. *On Economics and Society*. Chicago: University of Chicago Press.

————. 1976. *Trade Negotiations and the New International Monetary System*. Graduate Institute of International Studies, Geneva, and the Trade Policy Research Centre, London. Leiden: A. W. Sijthoff.

Jones, E. L. 1981. *The European Miracle: Environments, Economies, and Geopolitics in the History of Europe and Asia*. New York: Cambridge University Press.

Jones, R. J. Barry, ed. 1985. *Perspectives on Political Economy*. London: Frances Pinter.

Jones, Ronald W., and Peter B. Kenen, eds. 1984 (vol. 1) and 1985 (vol. 2). *Handbook of International Economics* 2 vols. Amsterdam: North-Holland.

Kahler, Miles. 1985. "Politics and International Debt: Explaining the Debt Crisis." *International Organization* 39:357-82.

Kalecki, Michal. 1943. "Political Aspects of Full Employment." *Political Quarterly* 14:322-31.

Katzenstein, Peter J. 1976. "International Relations and Domestic Structures: Foreign Economic Policies of Advanced Industrial States." *International Organization* 30:1-45.

———. 1984. *Corporatism and Change: Austria, Switzerland and the Politics of Industry*. Ithaca: Cornell University Press.

———. 1985. *Small States in World Markets: Industrial Policy in Europe*. Ithaca: Cornell University Press.

Kenen, Peter B. 1976. "An Overall View." In Fabio Basagni, ed., *International Monetary Relations after Jamaica*, pp. 7-14. (The Atlantic Papers; 4/1976.) Paris: The Atlantic Institute for International Affairs.

———. 1984. "Beyond Recovery: Challenges to U.S. Economic Policy in the 1980s." In Hewlett et al., 1984,

———. 1985. "Macroeconomic Theory and Policy: How the Closed Economy Was Opened." In Jones and Kenen, 1985, Chapter 13.

Keohane, Robert O. 1980. "The Theory of Hegemonic Stability and Changes in International Economic Regimes, 1967-1977." In Holsti et al., 1980, Chapter 6.

———. 1982a. "The Demand For International Regimes." *International Organization* 36:325-55.

———. 1982b. "Hegemonic Leadership and U.S. Foreign Economic Policy in the 'Long Decade' of the 1950s." In Avery and Rapkin, 1982, Chapter 3.

———. 1984a. *After Hegemony: Cooperation and Discord in the World Political Economy*. Princeton: Princeton University Press.

———. 1984b. "The World Political Economy and the Crisis of Embedded Liberalism." In Goldthorpe, 1984, Chapter 1.

———. 1985. "The International Politics of Inflation." In Lindberg and Maier, 1985, Chapter 4.

———. 1986. "Reciprocity in International Relations." *International Organization* 40:1-27.

Keohane, Robert O., and Joseph S. Nye, Jr., eds. 1972. *Transnational Relations and World Politics*. Cambridge: Harvard University Press.

Keohane, Robert O., and Joseph S. Nye, Jr. 1977. *Power and Interdependence: World Politics in Transition*. Boston: Little, Brown.

Keynes, John Maynard. 1919. *The Economic Consequences of the Peace*. London: Macmillan.

———. 1925. *The Economic Consequences of Mr. Churchill*. London: L & D Wolff.

———. 1933. "National Self-sufficiency." *Yale Review* 22:755-69.

Kierzkowski, Henry K. ed. 1984. *Monopolistic Competition and International Trade*. Oxford: Clarendon Press.

Kindleberger, Charles P. 1962. *Foreign Trade and the National Economy*. New Haven: Yale University Press.

Kindleberger, Charles P. 1970. *Power and Money: The Economics of International Politics and the Politics of International Economics*. New York: Basic Books.

———. 1973. *The World in Depression, 1929-1939*. Berkeley: University of California Press.

———. 1977. *America in the World Economy*. Headline Series, No. 237. New York: Foreign Policy Association.

———. 1978a. "The Aging Economy." Lecture given at the Institut für Weltwirtschaft, Kiel, July 5; published in *Weltwirtschaftliches Archiv* 114:407-421.

———. 1978b. *Economic Response: Comparative Studies in Trade, Finance, and Growth*. Cambridge: Harvard University Press.

———. 1978c. *Government and International Trade*. Essays in International Finance, No. 129. International Finance Section, Department of Economics, Princeton University.

———. 1978d. *Manias, Panics, and Crashes: A History of Financial Crises*. New York: Basic Books.

———. 1981. "Dominance and Leadership in the International Economy: Exploitation, Public Goods, and Free Rides." *International Studies Quarterly* 25:242-54.

———. 1983. "On the Rise and Decline of Nations." *International Studies Quarterly* 27:5-10.

———. 1984. *A Financial History of Western Europe*. London: George Allen and Unwin.

———. 1986. "International Public Goods without International Government." *American Economic Review* 76:1-13.

Kindleberger, Charles P., and Guido di Tella, eds. 1982. *Economics in the Long View*. Vol. 1, *Models and Methodology*. New York: New York University Press.

Knei-Paz, Baruch. 1978. *The Social and Political Thought of Leon Trotsky*. Oxford: Clarendon Press.

Knorr, Klaus. 1944. *British Colonial Theories, 1570-1850*. Toronto: University of Toronto Press.

Knorr, Klaus. 1973. *Power and Wealth: The Political Economy of International Power*. New York: Basic Books.

Kohli, Atul, Michael F. Altfeld, Saideh Lotfian, and Russell Mardon. 1984. "Inequality in the Third World. An Assessment of Competing Explanations." *Comparative Political Studies* 17:283-318.

Kojima, Kiyoshi. 1978. *Direct Foreign Investment: A Japanese Model of Multinational Business Operations*. London: Croom Helm.

Kraft, Joseph. 1984. *The Mexican Rescue*. New York: Group of Thirty.

Krasner, Stephen D. 1974. "Oil Is the Exception." *Foreign Policy*, no. 14:68-84.

———. 1976. "State Power and the Structure of International Trade." *World Politics* 28:317-47.

———. 1978. *Defending the National Interest: Raw Materials Investments and U.S. Foreign Policy*. Princeton: Princeton University Press.

———. 1979. "The Tokyo Round-Particularistic Interests and Prospects for Stability in the Global Trading System." *International Studies Quarterly* 23:491-531.

———. 1982a. "Structural Causes and Regime Consequences: Regimes as Intervening Variables." *International Organization* 36:185-205.

———. 1982b. "Regimes and the Limits of Realism: Regimes as Autonomous Variables." *International Organization* 36:497-510.

———, ed. 1982c. "International Regimes." Special issue of *International Organization* 36:185-510.

———, ed. 1983. *International Regimes*. Ithaca: Cornell University Press.

———. 1985. *Structural Conflict: The Third World against Global Liberalism*. Berkeley: University of California Press.

Krause, Lawrence B. 1984. "The Structure of Trade in Manufactured Goods in the East and Southeast Asia Region." Unpublished.

Krauss, Melvyn B. 1978. *The New Protectionism: The Welfare State and International Trade*. New York: New York University Press.

Krueger, Anne O. 1983. "The Effects of Trade Strategies on Growth." *Finance and Development* 20:6-8.

Krugman, Paul R. 1979. "A Model of Innovation, Technology Transfer, and the World Distribution of Income." *Journal of Political Economy* 87:253-66.

———. 1981a. "Economies of Scale, Imperfect Competition, and Trade: An Exposition." Unpublished.

———. 1981b. "Trade, Accumulation, and Uneven Development." *Journal of Development Economics* 8:149-61.

———, ed. 1986. *Strategic Trade Policy and the New International Economics*. Cambridge: MIT Press.

Kruse, D. C. 1980. *Monetary Integration in Western Europe: EMU, EMS, and Beyond*. London: Butterworths.

Kuczynski, Pedro-Pablo. 1985. "At the Latin Debt Hospital." *New York Times*, December 16, p. A23.

Kuhn, Thomas S. 1962. *The Structure of Scientific Revolutions*. Chicago: University of Chicago Press.

Kurth, James R. 1979. "The Political Consequences of the Product Cycle: Industrial History and Political Outcomes." *International Organization* 33:1-34.

Kuznets, Simon. 1930. *Secular Movements in Production and Prices: Their Nature and Their Bearing upon Cyclical Fluctuations*. Boston: Houghton Mifflin.

———. 1953. *Economic Change: Selected Essays in Business Cycles, National Income, and Economic Growth*. New York: W. W. Norton.

———. 1966. *Modern Economic Growth: Rate, Structure, and Spread*. New Haven: Yale University Press.

Kuznets, Simon. 1968. *Toward a Theory of Economic Growth.* New York: W. W. Norton.

Lake, David A. 1983. "International Economic Structures and American Foreign Economic Policy, 1887-1934." *World Politics* 35:517-43.

———. 1984. "Beneath the Commerce of Nations: A Theory of International Economic Structures." *International Studies Quarterly* 28:143-70

Lal, Deepak. 1983. *The Poverty of 'Development Economics.'* London: Institute of Economic Affairs.

Langhammer, Rolf J., and Ulrich Heimenz. 1985. "Declining Competitiveness of EC Suppliers in ASEAN Markets: Singular Case or Symptom?" *Journal of Common Market Studies* 24:105-119.

Larson, Eric D., Marc H. Ross, and Robert H. Williams. 1986. "Beyond the Era of Materials." *Scientific American* 254:34-41.

League of Nations. 1945. *Industrialization and Foreign Trade.* Geneva: Economic, Financial and Transit Department, League of Nations.

Lenin, V. I. 1939 [1917]. *Imperialism: The Highest Stage of Capitalism.* New York: International Publishers.

Levitt, Theodore. 1983. *The Marketing Imagination.* New York: Free Press.

Levy, Jack S. 1985. "Theories of General War." *World Politics* 37:344-74.

Lewis, W. Arthur. 1957. "International Competition in Manufactures." *American Economic Review* 47:578-87.

———. 1970. *Theory of Economic Growth.* New York: Harper and Row.

———. 1974. *Dynamic Factors in Economic Growth.* Bombay: Orient Longman.

———. 1978a. *The Evolution of the International Economic Order.* Princeton: Princeton University Press.

———. 1978b. *Growth and Fluctuations, 1870-1913.* London: George Allen and Unwin.

———. 1980a. "Rising Prices: 1899-1913 and 1950-1979." *The Scandinavian Journal of Economics* 82:425-36.

———. 1980b. "The Slowing Down of the Engine of Growth." *American Economic Review* 70:555-64.

———. 1981. "The Rate of Growth of World Trade, 1830-1973." In Grassman and Lundberg, 1981, Chapter 1.

———. 1984. *The Rate of Growth of the World Economy.* Taipei: The Institute of Economics, Academia Sinica.

Lindbeck, Assar. 1985. "What Is Wrong with the West European Economies?" *The World Economy* 8:153-68.

Lindberg, Leon N., and Charles S. Maier, eds. 1985. *The Politics of Inflation and Economic Stagnation: Theoretical Approaches and International Case Studies.* Washington: The Brookings Institution.

Lindblom, Charles E. 1977. *Politics and Markets: The World's Political-Economic Systems.* New York: Basic Books.

Linder, Staffan Burenstam. 1961. *An Essay on Trade and Transformation.* New York: Wiley.

————. 1986. *The Pacific Century: Economic and Political Consequences of Asian-Pacific Dynamism*. Stanford: Stanford University Press.

Lipson, Charles. 1982. "The Transformation of Trade: The Sources and Effects of Regime Change." *International Organization* 36:417-55.

————. 1985. *Standing Guard: Protecting Foreign Capital in the Nineteenth and Twentieth Centuries*. Berkeley: University of California Press.

Lipton, Michael. 1977. *Why Poor People Stay Poor: Urban Bias in World Development*. Cambridge: Harvard University Press.

List, Friedrich. 1904 (1841). *The National System of Political Economy*. Trans. Sampson S. Lloyd. New York: Longmans, Green.

Little, Ian M. D. 1982. *Economic Development: Theory, Policy and International Relations*. New York: Basic Books.

Little, Ian, Tibor Scitovsky, and Maurice Scott. 1970. *Industry and Trade in Some Developing Countries: A Comparative Study*. Oxford: Oxford University Press.

McKeown, Timothy J. 1983. "Hegemonic Stability Theory and 19th-Century Tariff Levels in Europe." *International Organization* 37:73-91.

————. 1986. "Theories of Commercial Policy." *International Organization* 40:43-64.

Mackinder, Halford J. 1962 [1904]. "The Geographical Pivot of History." In *Democratic Ideals and Reality*. New York: W. W. Norton.

McKinnon, Ronald I. 1984. *An International Standard for Monetary Stabilization*. Policy Analyses in International Economics, No. 8. Washington: Institute for International Economics.

McNeill, William H. 1954. *Past and Future*. Chicago: University of Chicago Press.

————. 1982. *The Pursuit of Power: Technology, Armed Force, and Society since A.D. 1000*. Chicago: University of Chicago Press.

McRae, Hamish. 1985. *Japan's Role in the Emerging Global Securities Market*. Occasional Papers, No. 17. New York: The Group of Thirty.

Maddison, Angus. 1982. *Phases of Capitalist Development*. New York: Oxford University Press.

Makler, Harry, Alberto Martinelli, and Neil Smelser, eds. 1982. *The New International Economy*. Sage Studies in International Sociology, No. 26. Beverly Hills, Calif: Sage Publications.

Malinvaud, Edmond. 1984. *Mass Unemployment*. Oxford: Basil Blackwell.

Mandle, Jay R. 1980. "Marxism and the Delayed Onset of Economic Development: A Reinterpretation." *Journal of Economic Issues* 14:735-49.

Marris, Stephen. 1984. *Managing the World Economy: Will We Ever Learn?* Essays in International Finance, No. 155. International Finance Section, Department of Economics, Princeton University.

————. 1985. *Deficits and the Dollar: The World Economy at Risk*. Policy Analyses in International Finance, No. 14. Washington: Institute for International Economics.

Marx, Karl. 1977 [1859]. *Karl Marx: Selected Writings*, pp. 388-91. Ed. David McLellan. Oxford: Oxford University Press.

Marx, Karl, and Friedrich Engels. 1947 [1846] *The German Ideology*. Ed. R. Pascal. New York: International Publishers.

———. 1972 [1848]. "The Communist Manifesto." In Robert C. Tucker, ed., *The Marx-Engels Reader*. New York: W. W. Norton.

Meier, Gerald M., and Robert E. Baldwin. 1957. *Economic Development: Theory, History, Policy*. New York: John Wiley and Sons.

Meigs, A. James. 1972. *Money Matters: Economics, Markets, Politics*. New York: Harper and Row.

Michalet, Charles-Albert. 1982. "From International Trade to World Economy: A New Paradigm." In Makler et al., 1982, Chapter 2.

Mill, John Stuart. 1970 [1848]. *Principles of Political Economy*. Baltimore: Penguin Books.

Modelski, George. 1978. "The Long Cycle of Global Politics and the Nation-State." *Comparative Studies in Society and History* 20:214-38.

———, ed. 1979. *Transnational Corporations and World Order*. San Francisco: W. H. Freeman.

Moran, Theodore H. 1974. *Multinational Corporations and the Politics of Dependence: Copper in Chile*. Princeton: Princeton University Press.

Murakami, Yasusuke, and Kozo Yamamura. 1984. "Technology in Transition; Two Perspectives on Industrial Policy." Unpublished.

Myint, Hla. 1985. "Growth Policies and Income Distribution." Development Policy Issues Series. Washington: The World Bank.

Myrdal, Gunnar. 1971. *Economic Theory and Underdeveloped Regions*. New York: Harper and Row.

Nau, Henry R. 1985. "The State of the Debate: Reaganomics. Or the Solution?" *Foreign Policy*, 59:144-53.

Nelson, Richard R., and Sidney G. Winter. 1982. *An Evolutionary Theory of Economic Change*. Cambridge: Belknap Press of Harvard University Press.

Nomura Research Institute. 1986a. *Quarterly Economic Review*. August.

———. 1986b. *The World Economy and Financial Markets in 1995: Japan's Role and Challenges*. Tokyo.

North, Douglass C. 1981. *Structure and Change in Economic History*. New York: W. W. Norton.

North, Douglass C., and Robert Paul Thomas. 1973. *The Rise of the Western World: A New Economic History*. Cambridge: Cambridge University Press.

Northrop, F.S.C. 1947. *The Logic of the Sciences and the Humanities*. New York: Macmillan.

Nurkse, Ragnar. 1953. *Problems of Capital Formation in Underdeveloped Countries*. New York: Blackwell.

Nussbaum, Bruce. 1983. *The World after Oil: The Shifting Axis of Power and Wealth*. New York: Simon and Schuster.

O'Connor, James. 1973. *The Fiscal Crisis of the State*. New York: St. Martin's Press.

Odell, John S. 1982. *U.S. International Monetary Policy: Markets, Power, and Ideas as Sources of Change.* Princeton: Princeton University Press.

OECD (Organization of Economic Cooperation and Development). 1977. *Towards Full Employment and Price Stability.* [McCracken Report.] Paris.

————. 1979. *The Impact of the Newly Industrializing Countries on Production and Trade in Manufactures.* Report by the Secretary-General. Paris.

————. 1984. "Social Expenditure: Erosion or Evolution?" *The OECD Observer*, no. 126:3-6.

————. 1985. "Costs and Benefits of Protection." *The OECD Observer*, no. 134:18-23.

————. 1986. "Change and Continuity in OECD Trade in Manufactures with Developing Countries." *The OECD Observer*, no. 139:3-9.

Ohmae, Kenichi. 1985. *Triad Power: The Coming Shape of Global Competition.* New York: Free Press.

Okimoto, Daniel I. 1984. "Between MITI and the Market: Japanese Industrial Policy for High Technology." Unpublished.

Olson, Mancur, Jr. 1963. "Rapid Growth as a Destabilizing Force." *Journal of Economic History* 23:529-52.

————. 1965. *The Logic of Collective Action: Public Goods and the Theory of Groups.* Cambridge: Harvard University Press.

————. 1982. *The Rise and Decline of Nations—Economic Growth, Stagflation, and Social Rigidities.* New Haven: Yale University Press.

Olson, Mancur, and Richard J. Zeckhauser. 1966. "An Economic Theory of Alliances." *Review of Economics and Statistics* 48:266-279.

Osborne, Michael West, and Nicolas Fourt. 1983. *Pacific Basin Economic Corporation.* Paris: Development Centre Studies, OECD.

Oye, Kenneth A. 1983. "Bargaining, Belief Systems, and Breakdown: International Political Economy, 1919-1936." Ph.D. dissertation, Department of Government, Harvard University.

Oye, Kenneth A., and Robert Gilpin. 1986. "Western Bloc Cohesion—The American System and Its Challenges." Unpublished.

Oye, Kenneth A., Robert J. Lieber, and Donald Rothchild, eds. 1983. *Eagle Defiant: United States Foreign Policy in the 1980s.* Boston: Little, Brown.

Padoa-Schioppa, Tommaso. 1983. "Perspective: The Crisis of Exogeneity, or Our Reduced Ability to Deal with Risk." In Herring, 1983, pp. 59-74.

Palma, Gabriel. 1978. "Dependency: A Formal Theory of Underdevelopment or a Methodology for the Analysis of Concrete Situations of Underdevelopment?" *World Development* 6:881-924.

Patrick, Hugh. 1983. "The Asian Developing Market Economies—How They Have Affected and Been Affected by the United States–Japan Economic Relationship." Unpublished.

Patrick, Hugh, and Henry Rosovsky. 1983. "The End of Eras? Japan and the Western World in the 1970-1980s." Unpublished.

Patterson, Gardner. 1983. "The European Community as a Threat to the System." In Cline, 1983, Chapter 7.

Pearson, L. B. et al. 1969. *Partners in Development: Report of the Commission on International Development.* New York: Praeger.

Perroux, François. 1969. *L'économie du XXᵉ siècle.* 3d ed. Augmented. Paris: Presses Universitaires de France.

Pierre, Andrew, ed. 1984. *Unemployment and Growth in the Western Economies.* New York: Council on Foreign Relations.

Polanyi, Karl. 1957. *The Great Transformation: The Political and Economic Origins of Our Time.* Boston: Beacon Press.

Posner, Richard. 1977. *Economic Analysis of Law.* 2d. ed. Boston: Little, Brown.

Poznanski, Kazimierz Z. 1985. "Competition between Eastern Europe and Developing Countries in the Western Market for Manufactured Goods." In *Compendium of Papers, Eastern European Assessment*: Vol. 2, *Foreign Trade and International Finance*, pp. 62-92. Washington: U.S. Congress, Joint Economic Committee.

Prebisch, Raúl. 1959. "Commercial Policy in the Underdeveloped Countries." *American Economic Review* 49 (May):251-73

Preeg, Ernest H. 1970. *Traders and Diplomats: An Analysis of the Kennedy Round of Negotiations under the General Agreement on Tariffs and Trade.* Washington: The Brookings Institution.

———. 1974. *Economic Blocs and U.S. Foreign Policy.* Report 134. Washington: National Planning Association.

Puchala, Donald J. 1975. "Domestic Politics and Regional Harmonization in the European Communities." *World Politics* 27: 496-520.

Putnam, Robert D., and Nicholas Bayne. 1984. *Hanging Together: The Seven-Power Summits.* Cambridge: Harvard University Press.

Radford, R. A. 1945. "The Economic Organization of a P.o.W. Camp." *Economica* 12:189-201.

Ranis, Gustav. 1985. "Can the East Asian Model of Development Be Generalized? A Comment." *World Development* 13:543-45.

Rawls, John. 1971. *A Theory of Justice.* Cambridge: Harvard University Press.

Reich, Robert B. 1983. "Beyond Free Trade," *Foreign Affairs* 16:773-804.

Reisinger, William M. 1981. "The MNC–Developing State Bargaining Process: A Review." *Michigan Journal of Political Science* 1:75-83.

Reynolds, Lloyd G. 1983. "The Spread of Economic Growth to the Third World, 1850-1950," *Journal of Economic Literature* 21:941-980.

Ricardo, David. 1871 [1817]. *Principles of Political Economy and Taxation.* In *The Works of David Ricardo.* London: John Murray.

Richardson, J. David. 1984. "Currents and Cross-Currents in the Flow of U.S. Trade Policy." In Baldwin, 1984a, Chapter 1.

Rieffel, Alexis. 1985. *The Role of the Paris Club in Managing Debt Problems.* Essays in International Finance, No. 161. International Finance Section, Department of Economics, Princeton University.

Roberts, Michael. 1956. *The Military Revolution, 1560-1660.* Belfast: Boyd.

Robson, Peter. 1980. *The Economics of International Integration*. London: George Allen and Unwin.

Rogowski, Ronald. 1978. "Rationalist Theories of Politics: A Midterm Report." *World Politics* 30:296-323.

Rolfe, Sidney E., and James L. Burtle. 1973. *The Great Wheel: The World Monetary System*. New York: McGraw-Hill.

Rosecrance, Richard. 1986. *The Rise of the Trading State: Commerce and Conquest in the Modern World*. New York: Basic Books.

Rosecrance, Richard, and Arthur Stein. 1973. "Interdependence: Myth or Reality?" *World Politics* 26:1-27.

Rosenberg, Nathan. 1977. "Reflections upon the Role of Technology in the Socio-Economic Context." Unpublished.

Rosenberg, Nathan, and Claudio R. Frischtak. 1983. "Long Waves and Economic Growth: A Critical Appraisal." *American Economic Review* (May) 73:146-51.

Rosovsky, Henry. 1985. "Trade, Japan and the Year 2000." *New York Times*, September 6.

Rostow, W. W. 1971. *Politics and the Stages of Growth*. New York: Cambridge University Press.

——. 1975. *How It All Began: Origins of the Modern Economy*. New York: McGraw-Hill.

——. 1978. *The World Economy: History and Prospect*. Austin: University of Texas Press.

——. 1980. *Why the Poor Get Richer and the Rich Slow Down: Essays in the Marshallian Long Period*. Austin: University of Texas Press.

——. 1983. *The Barbaric Counter-Revolution: Cause and Cure*. Austin: University of Texas Press.

Rousseas, Stephen. 1979. *Capitalism and Catastrophe: A Critical Appraisal of the Limits to Capitalism*. New York: Cambridge University Press.

Rowland, Benjamin M. 1975. "Preparing the American Ascendency: The Transfer of Economic Power from Britain to the United States, 1933-1944." In Benjamin M. Rowland, ed., *Balance of Power or Hegemony: The Interwar Monetary System*, Chapter 5. New York: New York University Press.

Roxborough, Ian. 1979. *Theories of Underdevelopment*. London: Macmillan.

Ruggie, John Gerard. 1982. "International Regimes, Transactions, and Change: Embedded Liberalism in the Postwar Economic Order." *International Organization* 36:379-415

——. 1983a. "Introduction: International Interdependence and National Welfare." In Ruggie, 1983c, pp. 1-39.

——. 1983b. "Political Structure and Change in the International Economic Order: The North-South Dimension." In Ruggie, 1983c, Chapter 9.

——, ed. 1983c. *The Antinomies of Interdependence: National Welfare and the International Division of Labor*. New York: Columbia University Press.

——. 1984. "Another Round, Another Requiem? Prospects for the Global Negotiations." In Bhagwati and Ruggie, 1984, Chapter 3.

Russett, Bruce. 1983. "International Interactions and Processes: The Internal vs. External Debate Revisited." In Ada W. Finifter, ed., *Political Science— The State of the Discipline*, Chapter 17. Washington: The Political Science Association.

———. 1985. "The Mysterious Case of Vanishing Hegemony; or Is Mark Twain Really Dead?" *International Organization* 39:207-231.

Rydenfelt, Sven. 1985. *A Pattern for Failure: Socialist Economies in Crisis*. San Diego: Harcourt Brace Jovanovich.

Sachs, Jeffrey. 1983. "International Policy Coordination in a Dynamic Macro-economic Model." National Bureau of Economic Research.

Saint Phalle, Thibaut de. 1981. *Trade, Inflation and the Dollar*. New York: Oxford University Press.

Samuelson, Paul A. 1972. "International Trade for a Rich Country." Business and Financial Conditions. *The Morgan Guaranty Survey* (July). New York: Morgan Guaranty Trust Company.

———. 1976. "Illogic of Neo-Marxist Doctrine of Unequal Exchange." In David A. Belsley, Edward J. Kane, Paul A. Samuelson, and Robert M. Solow, eds., *Inflation, Trade and Taxes: Essays in Honor of Alice Bourneuf*, pp. 96-107. Columbus: Ohio State University Press.

———. 1980. *Economics*. 11th ed. With the Assistance in Statistical Updating of William Samuelson. New York: McGraw-Hill.

Sargen, Nicholas, Tran Q. Hung, and John Lipsky. 1984. *The Securitization of International Finance*. New York: Salomon Brothers.

Sawhill, Isabel V., and Charles F. Stone. 1984. "The Economy." In John L. Palmer and Isabel V. Sawhill, eds., *The Reagan Record: An Assessment of America's Changing Domestic Priorities*, Chapter 3. Cambridge, Mass.: Ballinger.

Saxonhouse, Gary R. N.d. "Comparative Advantage and Structural Adaptation." Department of Economics, University of Michigan. Unpublished.

———. 1982. "Cyclical and Macrostructural Issues in U.S.-Japan Economic Relations." In Daniel I. Okimoto, ed., *Japan's Economy: Coping with Change in the International Environment*, pp. 123-48. Boulder: Westview Press.

———. 1983. "The Micro-and Macroeconomics of Foreign Sales to Japan." In Cline, 1983, Chap. 9.

Sayle, Murray. 1985. "Victory for Japan." *New York Review of Books* 32:33-40.

Scammell, W. M. 1983. *The International Economy since 1945*. 2d ed. London: Macmillan.

Schattschneider, E. E. 1935. *Politics, Pressures and the Tariff*. New York: Prentice.

Schmitt, Hans O. 1979. "Mercantilism: A Modern Argument." *The Manchester School of Economic and Social Studies* 47:93-111.

Schott, Kerry. 1984. *Policy, Power and Order: The Persistence of Economic Problems in Capitalist States*. New Haven: Yale University Press.

Schumpeter, Joseph A. 1950. *Capitalism, Socialism and Democracy.* 3d ed. New York: Harper and Row.

———. 1951. *Imperialism and Social Classes.* New York: Meridian.

———. 1961. *The Theory of Economic Development: An Inquiry into Profits, Capital, Credit, Interest, and the Business Cycle.* Trans. Redvers Opie. New York: Oxford University Press.

Semmel, Bernard. 1970. *The Rise of Free Trade Imperialism: Classical Political Economy, the Empire of Free Trade, and Imperialism, 1750-1850.* Cambridge: Cambridge University Press.

Sen, Gautam. 1984. *The Military Origins of Industrialization and International Trade Rivalry.* New York: St. Martin's Press.

Servan-Schreiber, Jean-Jacques. 1968. *The American Challenge.* Trans. Ronald Steel. New York: Atheneum.

Shonfield, Andrew, ed. 1976a. *International Economic Relations of the Western World, 1959-1971.* Assisted by Hermia Oliver. Vol. 1, *Politics and Trade.* London: Oxford University Press.

———. 1976b. *International Economic Relations of the Western World, 1959-1971.* Assisted by Hermia Oliver. Vol. 2: *International Monetary Relations.* London: Oxford University Press.

Sigmund, Paul E. 1980. *Multinationals in Latin America: The Politics of Nationalization.* Madison: University of Wisconsin Press.

Skocpol, Theda. 1977. "Wallerstein's World Capitalist System: A Theoretical and Historical Critique." *American Journal of Sociology* 82:1075-90.

Smith, Adam. 1937 [1776]. *An Inquiry into the Nature and Causes of the Wealth of Nations.* New York: Modern Library.

Smith, Tony. 1981. *The Pattern of Imperialism: The United States, Great Britain, and The Late-Industrializing World since 1815.* New York: Cambridge University Press.

Snidal, Duncan. 1985. "The Limits of Hegemonic Stability Theory." *International Organization* 39:579-614.

Sowell, Thomas. 1972. *Say's Law: An Historical Analysis.* Princeton: Princeton University Press.

Spence, A. Michael. 1984. "Industrial Organization and Competitive Advantage in Multinational Industry." *American Economic Review* 74 (May):356-60.

Spindler, J. Andrew. 1984. *The Politics of International Credit: Finance and Foreign Policy in Germany and Japan.* Washington: The Brookings Institution.

Spiro, David E. 1987. "Policy Coordination in the International Political Economy: The Politics of Recycling Petrodollars." Ph.D. dissertation, Department of Politics, Princeton University.

Staley, Eugene. 1935. *War and the Private Investor.* Garden City, N.Y.: Doubleday, Doran.

———. 1939. *World Economy in Transition: Technology vs. Politics, Laissez*

431

Faire vs. Planning, Power vs. Welfare. New York: Council on Foreign Relations.

―――. 1944. *World Economic Development.* Montreal: International Labour Office.

Stein, Arthur A. 1984. "The Hegemon's Dilemma: Great Britain, the United States, and the International Economic Order." *International Organization* 38:355-86.

Stewart, Frances. 1984. "Recent Theories of International Trade: Some Implications for the South." In Kierzkowski, 1984, Chapter 6.

Strange, Susan. 1970. "International Economics and International Relations: A Case of Mutual Neglect." *International Affairs* 46:304-315.

―――. 1971. *Sterling and British Policy: A Political Study of an International Currency in Decline.* London: Oxford University Press.

―――. 1976. "The Study of Transnational Relations." *International Affairs* 52:333-45.

―――. 1979. "The Management of Surplus Capacity: Or How Does Theory Stand Up to Protectionism 1970s Style?" *International Organization* 33:303-335.

―――. 1982. "Cave! Hic Dragones: A Critique of Regime Analysis." *International Organization* 36:479-96.

―――. 1984a. "The Global Political Economy, 1959-1984." *International Journal* 34:267-83.

―――, ed. 1984b. *Paths to International Political Economy.* London: George Allen and Unwin.

―――. 1985a. "International Political Economy: The Story So Far and the Way Ahead." In W. Ladd Hollist and F. LaMond Tullis, eds., *An International Political Economy.* International Political Economy Yearbook, Vol. 1, Chapter 1. Boulder: Westview Press.

―――. 1985b. "Structures, Values and Risk In the Study of the International Political Economy." In R. J. Barry Jones, ed., *Perspectives on Political Economy,* Chapter 8. London: Frances Pinter.

―――. 1985c. "Protectionism and World Politics." *International Organization* 39:233-59.

Strange, Susan, and Roger Tooze, eds. 1981. *The International Politics of Surplus Capacity: Competition for Market Shares in the World Recession.* London: George Allen and Unwin.

Sunkel, Osvaldo. 1972. "Big Business and Dependencia: A Latin American View." *Foreign Affairs* 50:517-31.

Tollison, Robert D. 1982. "Rent-Seeking: A Survey." *Kyklos* 35:575-602.

Tooze, Roger. 1984. "Perspectives and Theory: A Consumers' Guide." In Strange, 1984b, Chapter 1.

Torrens, Robert. 1821. *An Essay on the Production of Wealth.* London: Longman, Hurst, Rees, Orme, and Brown.

Triffin, Robert. 1960. *Gold and the Dollar Crisis: The Future of Convertibility.* New Haven: Yale University Press.

———. 1964. *The Evolution of the International Monetary System: Historical Reappraisal and Future Perspectives*. Princeton Studies in International Finance, No. 12. International Finance Section, Department of Economics, Princeton University.

———. 1968. "The Thrust of History in International Monetary Reform." *Foreign Affairs* 47:477-92.

———. 1978-79. "The International Role and Fate of the Dollar." *Foreign Affairs* 57:269-86.

———. 1985. "The International Accounts of the United States and Their Impact upon the Rest of the World." Banca Nazionale Del Lavoro, *Quarterly Review* 152:15-30.

Tufte, Edward R. 1978. *Political Control of the Economy*. Princeton: Princeton University Press.

United States Department of Commerce. 1984. *International Direct Investment: Global Trends and the U.S. Role*. Washington: U.S. Government Printing Office.

Vaitsos, Constantine. 1974. *Intercountry Income Distribution and Transnational Enterprises*. Oxford: Clarendon Press.

van Duijn, J. J. 1983. *The Long Wave in Economic Life*. London: George Allen and Unwin.

Veblen, Thorstein. 1939. *Imperial Germany and the Industrial Revolution*. New York: Viking Press.

Vernon, Raymond. 1966. "International Investment and International Trade in the Product Cycle." *Quarterly Journal of Economics* 80:190-207.

———. 1971. *Sovereignty at Bay*. New York: Basic Books.

———. 1983. *Two Hungry Giants: The United States and Japan in the Quest for Oil and Ores*. Cambridge: Harvard University Press.

Viner, Jacob. 1948. "Power vs. Plenty as Objectives of Foreign Policy in the Seventeenth and Eighteenth Centuries." *World Politics* 1:1-29.

———. 1951. "International Relations Between State-Controlled National Economies." In Jacob Viner, *International Economics: Studies by Jacob Viner*. Glencoe, Ill.: Free Press.

———. 1952. *International Trade and Economic Development*. Glencoe, Ill.: Free Press.

———. 1958. *The Long View and the Short: Studies in Economic Theory and Policy*. New York: Free Press.

Wallerstein, Immanuel. 1974a. *The Modern World-System: Capitalist Agriculture and the Origins of the European World-Economy in the Sixteenth Century*. New York: Academic Press.

———. 1974b. "The Rise and Future Demise of the World Capitalist System: Concepts for Comparative Analysis." *Comparative Studies in Society and History* 16:387-415.

Waltz, Kenneth N. 1979. *Theory of International Politics*. Reading, Mass.: Addison-Wesley.

Warren, Bill. 1973. "Imperialism and Capitalist Industrialization." *New Left Review* 81:3-44.

Weber, Max. 1978. *Economy and Society: An Outline of Interpretive Sociology.* 2 vols. Ed. Guenther Roth and Claus Wittich. Berkeley: University of California.

Weisskopf, Thomas E. 1976. "Dependence as an Explanation of Underdevelopment: A Critique." Center for Research on Economic Development, University of Michigan. Unpublished.

Whitman, Marina v. N. 1977. *Sustaining the International Economic System: Issues for U.S. Policy.* Essays in International Finance, No. 121, International Finance Section, Department of Economics, Princeton University.

———. 1981. *International Trade and Investment: Two Perspectives.* Essays in International Finance, No. 143. International Finance Section. Department of Economics. Princeton University.

Wiles, P.J.D. 1968. *Communist International System.* Oxford: Basil Blackwell.

Wilkins, Mira. 1974. *The Maturing of Multinational Enterprise: American Business Abroad from 1914 to 1970.* Cambridge: Harvard University Press.

———. 1982. "American-Japanese Direct Foreign Investment Relationships, 1930-1951." *Business History Review* 56:497-518.

———. 1986a. "The History of European Multinationals—A New Look." Unpublished.

———. 1986b. "Japanese Multinational Enterprise before 1914." Unpublished.

Williamson, John. 1983. *The Open Economy and the World Economy: A Textbook in International Economics.* New York: Basic Books.

Williamson, Oliver E. 1975. *Markets and Hierarchies; Analysis and Antitrust Implications: A Study in the Economics of Internal Organization.* New York: Free Press.

Winham, Gilbert R. 1986. *International Trade and the Toyko Round Negotiations.* Princeton: Princeton University Press.

Yarbrough, Beth V., and Robert M. Yarbrough. 1986. "Reciprocity, Bilateralism, and Economic 'Hostages': Self-Enforcing Agreements in International Trade." *International Studies Quarterly* 30:7-21.

Yoffie, David B. 1983. *Power and Protectionism: Strategies of the Newly Industrializing Countries.* New York: Columbia University Press.

Yoshitomi, Masaru. 1985. *Japan as Capital Exporter and the World Economy.* Occasional Papers, No. 18. New York: Group of Thirty.

Young, Oran R. 1982. "Regime Dynamics: The Rise and Fall of International Regimes." *International Organizations* 36:277-97.

Zolberg, Aristide R. 1981. "Origins of the Modern World System: A Missing Link." *World Politics* 33:253-81.

Zysman, John. 1983. *Government, Markets, and Growth: Financial Systems and the Politics of Industrial Change.* Ithaca: Cornell University Press.

Zysman, John, and Stephen S. Cohen. 1982. *The Mercantilist Challenge to the*

Liberal International Trade Order. A study prepared for the Joint Economic Committee, Congress of the United States, 97th Congress, 2d Session.

Zysman, John, and Laura Tyson. 1983. *American Industry in International Competition: Government Policies and Corporate Strategies*. Ithaca: Cornell University Press.

Index

ad hoc hypothesis, definition of, 42
adjustment, problem of, 77n, 114-16,
213, 350, 354, 358, 381-88; balance of
payments, 118
"advantages of backwardness," 291-94
"advantages of being first," 184
Africa, 273, 279, 295, 301, 304, 400
After Hegemony (1984), 365
agriculture, problems of, 386; and economic development, 49; as trade issue,
200
Aho, C. Michael, 203
Albania, 268
Allende, Salvador, 250
alliances, economic, 254. *See also* New
Multinationalism
American balance of payments, 357. *See
also* American economy; American
trade deficit
American-British relations, 380
American budget deficit, effects of, 155,
164, 346, 349. *See also* Reaganomics
American economy: as engine of world
growth, 354-55, 383; deindustrialization, 245, 257-58, 346, 350, 370, 381;
problems of, 345-52, 356-57. *See also*
American hegemony
American-European relations, 6, 196
American hegemony, xii, 73, 129-30,
166, 343-45; and monetary system,
134-43; decline of, 63, 137, 154, 167,
194, 332, 337, 339, 345-52, 365, 379,
384; financing of, 136, 328-36, 348,
381; problems of, 134-36, 149, 347,
351. *See also* hegemony
American-Japanese relations, 6, 328-40,
338n, 348, 371, 380. *See also* Nichibei
economy
American leadership, *see* American hegemony
American macroeconomic policy, 332.
See also American budget deficit; *specific American administrations*
American power, decline of, *see* American
hegemony
American trade deficit, 156-57, 194, 368;
causes of, 370-71

American–West German relations, 149,
164, 380
Angola, 250
Arab-Israeli War (October 1973), 244
Argentina, 269, 284n, 318, 400
Aronson, Jonathan David, 203
ASEAN, 392, 398
Asia, 5, 273, 295, 301, 304. *See also*
ASEAN; NICs; Pacific Basin; *specific
countries*
"Asiatic mode of production," 271
Australia, 27, 398
"autonomous development," strategy of,
291-94

Baechler, Jean, 46, 83n
Bagehot, Walter, 309
Bahry, Donna, 292
Baker, James III, 151, 155. *See also* Baker
plan
Baker plan (on debt problem), 325-26
Baldwin, David A., 9, 76n, 282n
Baldwin, Richard, 351
Baldwin, Robert E., 112n, 199, 277, 368,
369, 372, 373
Bank for International Settlements (BIS),
135, 144n
Baran, Paul A., 67n, 70
Barre, Raymond, 361
barter trade, 195
Bauer, Peter T., 267
Baumol, William J., 29
Bayne, Nicholas, 369
Becker, Gary S., 8, 29
Beenstock, Michael, 111, 113n, 179n
"benign neglect," policy of, 137
Bergsten, C. Fred, 367-68
Bernstein, Eduard, 35
Beveridge Plan, 131
Bhagwati, Jagdish N., 304
Bhopal disaster, 248
Bienen, Henry S., 293n, 313n
Bight, John, 56
bilateralism, shift to, 220-29, 394. *See
also* trade policy
BIS (Bank for International Settlements),
135, 144n

437

Library of Congress Cataloging-in-Publication Data

Gilpin, Robert.
The political economy of international relations.

Bibliography: p.
Includes index.
1. International economic relations. 2. Commercial policy.
3. International finance. I. Title.

HF1411.G55 1987   337   86-25562
ISBN 0-691-07732-0 (alk. paper)   ISBN 0-691-02262-3 (pbk.)

Robert Gilpin is Dwight D. Eisenhower Professor of International Affairs at
Princeton University. He is the author of *U.S. Power and the Multinational Corporation* (Basic Books), *War and Change in World Politics* (Cambridge), *American Scientists and Nuclear Weapons Policy* (Princeton), and *France in the Age of
the Scientific State* (Princeton).